CLOSER TO DIRT THAN GOLD

Discovering Life's Treasures in a California Desert

Paul Elden Huff

Closer To Dirt Than Gold Copyright
© 2025 by Paul Elden Huff.

All rights reserved. No part of this publication may be reproduced, distributed, or transmitted in any form or by any means, including photocopying, recording, or other electronic or mechanical methods, without the written consent of the publisher. The only exceptions are for brief quotations included in critical reviews and other noncommercial uses permitted by copyright law.

MILTON & HUGO L.L.C.
4407 Park Ave., Suite 5
Union City, NJ 07087, USA

Website: *www. miltonandhugo.com*
Hotline: *1- 888-778-0033*
Email: *info@miltonandhugo.com*

Ordering Information:
Quantity sales. Special discounts are granted to corporations, associations, and other organizations. For more information on these discounts, please reach out to the publisher using the contact information provided above.

Library of Congress Control Number:		2024907465
ISBN-13:	979-8-89285-069-8	[Paperback Edition]
	979-8-89285-070-4	[Digital Edition]

Rev. date: 03/03/2025

CONTENTS

Foreword vii
Dick and Lizzy 1
Hemet California 4
School Daze 15
The Wallers 29
Man Tan 35
Central Avenue House 39
Pilot Extraordinaire 45
My Horse Tony 48
War Games 54
Chicken Business 65
The Summer of 1947 73
The Wallers' Foster Home 78
Barbara Webb 87
Snow in Hemet 95
A New Foster Home 99
Life at the Carters' 108
Life on an Egg Ranch 117
Hot Rod 120
Train Wreck 123
Hitting a Moving Target 126
Hambone's Little Roadster 129
Driving a Combine 133
Misdeeds 137
Orville Runs Away 144
No More Foster Homes 155
Waddell Ranch Company 161
Good Show 170
Photo Gallery 177
Race Day 197
Pear Pickers 202

Quartzsite 207
.50 Caliber Machine Gun Shells 213
Prospectors 225
Cadiz Dry Lake...251
Orville Runs Away Again 272
Stranded 280
Blair's Homestead Cibola 288
Our Own Haystack..295
The 1928 Chevy Truck 300
Burning the River Bottom..317
Branded 337
Killing My Second Buck Deer 342
Bucked Off 349
Supercharging Our Chevy..361
We Finally Made the Big Time.....................................367
Finally, a Ford V8 374
Orville's 1955 Ford 382
Leaving Blythe and Dad Behind 384

FOREWORD

This is the story of three brothers and their four sisters. How their lives were growing up in a little town in California in the 1940s. It's about the games they played and troubles they got into as they attended school and church. It's about being poor and the boys leaving school to go to work as they tried to make a better life for themselves. It's about living in foster homes, then going to live with their father, who was much too old and cranky to be taking in his boys to raise at the age of sixty-five. It's about lessons taught to the boys that could have been done more wisely. The foul language was how their dad talked as he taught them more wrong than right. It's all true, and as best I can remember it today. Times were tough for the Huff kids, but for me looking back on it, I feel blessed to have lived it.

DICK AND LIZZY

My dad was twenty-three years older than my mother when they wed, and my dad told me how he met my mother. Dad said he was driving from California going to Indiana to see relatives. The road he was driving went through Texas, and at the town where Dad stopped at for the night, there was a carnival going on. Dad said he met my mother that night at the carnival, and he liked her. My mother was just seventeen and had a new baby, named Ernestene, but she had just been made a widow when her husband's car rolled over, breaking his neck and killing him. My dad told my mother he was passing through going to Kansas, but when he came back in a few weeks, he would like to stop by and see her.

So, true to his word, Dad found her three weeks later, and they were married, and my mother came back to California with my dad. My mother had only been married six or seven months when her husband died, and he never saw his daughter, Ernestene who was born several months later. So Ernestene is named after her real father. But Dick Huff was the only father she ever knew. My dad brought them out to California, to a town named Blythe, on the Colorado River border with Arizona.

They left Blythe to go to Fresno, California, to work in the fruit in the summer of 1928. My mother told me they were on old Highway 99 in Visalia, California, when they got into town at night. My dad's car was low on gas, and they were also low on money. They had been married in April 1928, and now they were headed up around Fresno looking for work in the fruit orchards and canneries where work was plentiful in the early summer for migrant fruit workers.

Dad had befriended a passenger in the car named John. It was late in the day when Dad told John we needed to get some gas if we could find a filling station or a tractor parked in a field somewhere. Long after dark, they passed a filling station that was closed for the night. Dad stopped the car and killed the motor. He and John pushed the car backward into the station and stopped it at the gas pump.

John took a hacksaw from the toolbox and quietly began sawing the lock off the gas pump. When John finished, Dad worked the manual pump lever to fill the gas pump with ten gallons of gas, which was the maximum it could hold. Dad had no sooner started the gas flowing by gravity from the reservoir of the pump than a dim light came on in a room on the second floor of the gas station. Dad continued to let the gas run as long as he possibly could before he dropped the hose nozzle to the ground and jumped into the driver's seat and started the motor as John jumped astraddle of the hood and said, "Give 'er hell, Dick."

They turned back south on Highway 99 toward the grapevine pass. The gas station owner came out the door and started shooting at them with a pistol.

POW, POW, POW.

The station owner emptied his pistol at the fleeing car, which was a touring car and didn't have a top. My mother was scared to death as she sat in the middle next to my dad, holding Ernestene. John was able to slide back on the fender and the running board and joined them inside the car. Dad was driving with the lights out and going like hell back the way they had come on the narrow highway.

Dad said he drove down the highway about three miles, then turned into a cow pasture with his headlights turned on briefly. He drove slowly to the back of the pasture, so as not to raise any dust that would be visible from the road, and stopped under some trees and turned the lights off again. They had sat there for about ten or fifteen minutes when they saw a police car with a red spotlight go racing past on the highway.

Dad told John and my mother, "Let's just set tight for the night, and we'll leave out early in the morning before daylight." They had an old mattress rolled up and laid crossways behind the seat of the car, but they just continued to sit in the seat as the night was very warm, and that way, they could leave at a moment's notice.

Early the next morning, they were on their way, going past the gas station once again. Dad asked John if he wanted to stop and finish filling up.

John said, "Hell, no, Dick, let's get the hell on up the road."

Later that day, they found work at the cannery in Kingsburg just below Fresno. When they unrolled the mattress that night to make camp, they found three bullets in the mattress right behind where my mother was sitting.

I think my mother was starting to have doubts about this man she had married.

HEMET CALIFORNIA

I was born on January 5, 1936, and my mother named me Paul Elden. My brother Desmond Orville, who is eighteen months younger, was born in 1937. *Orville* was the name we called my younger brother, but my parents wanted him to have the same initials as our dad. Dad's given name was *Dick Owen Huff*, thus *Desmond Orville Huff*. My younger sister Alice Marie was born in 1939. My younger brother Everett Levi was born in 1941, just a few months before the Japanese bombed Pearl Harbor and our entry into WWII.

We lived in a rented house at 123 North Ramona Street. Our dad rented the house for seventeen dollars a month. We moved here from the house that Orville and I were born in at 136 South Buena Vista Street. I was five years old, and I went to nursery school across from our house. I had three older sisters—Ernestene, Loreda, and Betty.

Orville and I liked to watch our dad work on one of his violins in his shop on the south end of our garage behind our house. He had a quart can that he would put pieces of glue into with water, which he would then heat on the stove in the kitchen to turn it into liquid. Then we would watch him brush the glue on the pieces of wood and clamp them together to make the back of the violin. My dad was building a couple of violins at the same time. He was working on the back of one of the violins; he was putting on the finishing touches. I watched as he would rub oil into the wood and set it in the sun to soak up the oil. It was to be a three quarter size violin for my sister Betty, she later took violin lessons in school and the music teacher said the violin had a very good sound. My daughter Karen Keil has the violin today. Looking through the F holes, you can see where dad wrote, "Dick Huff Hemet, California 1941."

The other violin was a full-sized violin, and I remember my dad playing the fiddle as he called it until I was drafted into the army in 1959. He knew many songs, and he would rosin up his bow and play the fiddle in the evening for us, and to entertain himself. Sometimes Dad would hand the bow to me, and I would drag it across the strings, making a screeching noise. What great fun it was for a little boy to make music this way, but I doubt it would be music to my ears today.

On the north end of the garage was a rectangular hole in the cement floor, a pit that Dad can drive over to work on his car from underneath. I've watched him change the oil on the car and also lube it with grease from his grease gun that he pumped with a handle. He warned me not to play here as I could get hurt if I was to fall into the hole.

One day my sister Loreda told us, "The doctor is bringing a new baby today, so when he gets here, we will be going next door to Mrs. Todd's." Our mother had seven children, all at home. But I remember only one. I remember the doctor arriving with a black bag at our front door: My sister Loreda said the doctor had the baby in the black bag. I remember going over to Mrs. Todd's, and I remember coming back home later. It must have been true about the baby being in the black bag because there was the baby in bed with mom.

We traipsed in to see this new arrival. Mom was holding him to her breast to nurse, but I don't remember anything more about my brother Everett until he was about two years old.

On Sunday, our family attends church at the first Baptist Church of Hemet, but writing this book now, I can remember my dad attending the church service only once. I must have been very small, but I remember my dad in a black suit and a red tie, and I'm sitting next to him in the pew. I've learned songs in Sunday school. This is my first memory of one of those songs:

The B- I- B- L- E, yes, that's the book for me,
I stand alone on the word of God, and the B- I- B- L- E.

One of my first teachers in Sunday school was Mrs. Waller. I still can see her face with glasses. She also had an artificial leg, and I think that is why her memory is so vivid in my mind. Mrs. Ellis was another teacher in Sunday school when I was in beginners. Mrs. Ellis had a daughter, Linda Ellis, who I went through grammar school with. Then there was the piano player, Mrs. Ocie Klump whose daughter Hazel was another classmate in school at Hemet, which I attended until the eighth grade. Another song we learned in Sunday school was,

Jesus loves me this I know,
For the Bible tells me so.
Little ones to him belong;
They are weak but he is strong.
Yes, Jesus loves me,
Yes, Jesus loves me,
Yes, Jesus loves me,
The Bible tells me so.

Isn't it great I can still sing it after all these years? Most of the first songs I learned were hymns. I liked Sunday school, and singing songs of faith was one of my favorite things to do.

The Todds lived next door to us on Ramona Street. Elvin Todd, their oldest son, would come home from school and catch me playing outside and would put his hands out wide and run at me screaming his head off, scaring me to death. I would run into the house crying my eyes out. That's when I found out there was evil in the world, and he lived next door to us on Ramona Street.

Belda Todd, Elvin's mother, had two daughters Alene and Mary and a baby named, Billy. Billy Todd and my brother Orville later were in the same grade, but they didn't get along and would fight sometimes at the drop of a hat, at the grammar school or on the way home.

One day, when I was five or six, my dad had taken us somewhere in his 1933 Buick, and on our way home, we stopped at a market in town on Florida Avenue. I remember pleading and begging for an ice cream cone. Finally, he bought my sister Betty and me an ice cream cone. But he wouldn't let me get back in the car with it. He told me he didn't want the ice cream on his car seats, and I had to walk home. He told my sister Betty, who was six years older, she had to walk home with me because I was too small to walk home alone.

Betty got really mad. She wouldn't let me live it down to this day. I just figured the distance in my head, and it was four city blocks. I think I'll call and tell her that when I finish this chapter. It was one half block from the store to Harvard Ave., then it was one full block to Gibble Hardware at State Street, then across the railroad tracks, and past the house that had a dog in the front yard. You would be walking along, daydreaming, almost in another world, when out of a clear blue sky, this stupid German shepherd would run at the fence, which had vines growing on it, so you didn't see him coming. This dog would be in attack mode barking as loud as he could. It would make a little boy's heart stop. Then on to Alessandro Street, one more block to Ramona Street, turn right not even a half block to our house. Betty makes it sound like it was five miles.

Well, I just finished talking to Betty, and she explained it to me. She asked me if I remembered that it was hot, and that because it was hot was the reason I wanted the ice cream. So she explained that we were both barefoot and the sidewalk and the street were so hot we had to run from shade to shade to keep from burning our feet on the hot pavement.

That hot pavement burned like the blue blazes, and it was hard to find a clump of grass or a shady spot to stop and let our feet cool off.

She said that the four blocks wasn't far on a mild day. But if you're running across a hot stove, even five feet is a long way. I stand corrected, Betty, and I'm sorry. This is another of Betty's gripes about me when I was small. I saw a preview for *Mr. Bug Goes to Town*," and I cried and cried, wanting to go see it. Betty didn't want to go see it at all. I can't remember if my dad made her take me or if she decided to make a little boy's day by taking me to see a full-length black-and-white cartoon.

As we went into the lobby of Martin's Hemet Theatre, we saw Egyptian statues on both sides of the lobby. There was a white drinking fountain on the tile wall on the left; I could barely reach the drinking fountain without someone holding me up. I always heard the warning, "And don't put your mouth on it either!"

We sat down, and the movie started. I think I lasted about halfway through when I thought, *This is stupid.* I was afraid Betty would be mad if I wanted to leave, so I told her I was going to get a drink. After I'd had something to drink, I walked out the door and went home. Betty was mad, and to this day, she still raves about how she had to take me to see that stupid movie. At least I had the good sense to get up and leave. Betty stayed to see the whole thing.

Betty was a good sister. We played jacks, hopscotch, jump rope, and "Annie over." She would be out in the back of the house and holler, "Annie, Annie, over!" I would be out in the front of the house, and I would say, "Over!" She would throw a ball to different places on the roof so I wouldn't know where it was coming over, because I was supposed to catch the ball as it came down the roof on my side.

If I caught the ball, we would change sides. If I didn't catch the ball, I would pick it up and holler, "Annie, Annie, over!" I would hear Betty behind the house holler, "Over!" And I would throw the ball up to the roof of the house, trying to make it go over the ridge. Sometimes I didn't throw the ball hard enough, and it would come rolling back to me, and I would catch it and throw it again.

One time I missed the ball, but I hollered "Caught it" anyway.

I bent over to pick it up, and there was Betty, standing at the corner of the house. She had thrown the ball and then ran around the side of the house to see if I would cheat.

I did lie to her, because I didn't catch the ball. She cheated too because she didn't trust me enough to take my word for it. I told her, "Well, if you're going to cheat, I'm not going to play anymore!" I wish Betty and I could play "Annie over" one more time, as it was fun, but she turned out to be a cheater, so alas, we stopped playing the game. Just kidding. I was the cheater.

In April, Hemet would hold the Ramona Pageant—the story about Ramona and Alessandro. It was held at the Ramona Bowl, an outdoor theatre southeast of town. I remember Victor Jory, the movie actor playing the part of Alessandro. Once or twice I saw him around town, but I was too young to go see the play. The actors rode real horses in a setting on the hillside. They fired blanks in real Winchester rifles. There was an old hacienda or mission with Mexican peons working and doing chores on the hillside. At the end of the pageant, high school students, who hid behind rocks for the whole time dressed as Indians, stood up. It was very spectacular.

The town was all decked out with banners strung across Florida Avenue and signs on light poles for three or four blocks announcing the Ramona Pageant. They also had Whiskerino Days in the town on weekends. If a man was caught in town without a mustache or beard, he was locked up for maybe a half hour in a cage. The cage was like an old-time jail cell. You could stay in for the half hour or pay a dollar, (which went to charity), to get out. Most of the men in town had a beard or a mustache during this time to stay out of jail. Some store owners wore festive costumes to promote the festival. The rest of the week, the town returned to normal.

My dad had about six beehives on the southwest corner of the property at 123 North Ramona. I remember him prying the lids off, with a smoker in his hand that would calm them down. He would take trays of honey out and slice the honeycomb off into a big pan in the kitchen. By keeping the honey warm, it would separate from the wax, and he would pour it off through a strainer. Then he would fill quart canning jars with the honey. My sisters Rita and Betty would go door to door selling the honey for fifty cents a quart jar and twenty-five cents a pint.

Betty said Rita would tell her, "Okay, now you ask at this house, and I'll ask at the next house." She said that when the person came to the door, Rita would just stand there not saying anything. So Betty would have to speak up and ask if they wanted to buy their honey. Rita just didn't have the nerve to ask the people to buy their honey. I'm timid like that too, and I would rather give it away than ask someone to buy it.

One day Orville was playing by the bees and got stung. He had an allergic reaction to the bee sting; he turned red as though he had the hives. My dad grabbed him and took him into the house; he was crying pretty loud. Dad started the water running in the bathtub, then got a box of baking soda from the kitchen and dumped it into the bathtub. He stripped Orville's clothes off and plopped him into the tub. Orville's face was swollen from the bee sting, and his eyes were little slits.

After about an hour, Dad took him out as the swelling was going down. I don't think anybody even considered taking him to a doctor. Back then, everyone just did what they knew best. It worked. Orville is still alive and mean as ever. (Just joking, Orville.)

There was a tree nearby with a limb that extended out over the beehives. My dad had found four baby owls somewhere and brought them home. He had them sitting on this limb of the tree. He would feed them a little hamburger. He would also kill rabbits and feed them the meat. At first the baby owls didn't even have feathers, just a hairy fuzz that eventually turned to feathers. I remember they grew big and flew around the yard; sometimes they would be gone all day. Then in the evening, they would come back to roost on the tree. I can't recall the day they left; we didn't watch them as closely when they came back only in the evening. One day Dad said, "I guess the owls have left. I don't see them in the tree anymore."

Our house had a front porch, my sisters would play paper dolls by standing them in an open window with a screen on it. I would go past the window as they were on their knees making their paper dolls walk across the windowsill. They would talk about going shopping with the dolls or going to buy a new outfit, and they would change the dolls' outfits to go shopping. I would hit the screen with the back of my hand and knock down all the stupid paper dolls. They would scream and come tearing out of the house after me as I ran for my life. I could outrun Betty, but Loreda, with her long legs, would catch me. I can't remember what they did to me, but I'll bet it fit the crime.

Dad had an antenna, which was a copper wire running up the side of the house from a window and then onto a high pole and out to another pole out by the bees. The antenna went under the window and was connected to his radio. The radio sat on a table; and a wire went from the radio ground wire to a glass-cased battery (that was the grounding of the radio). We would listen to, *The Whistler, The Shadow, Inner Sanctum Mystery, Fibber McGee and Molly, Lum and Abner,* Tom Mix, and my favorite, Hop Harrigan. Hop Harrigan's copilot was Tank Tanker. Hop would say, "C X4 calling control tower, C X4 calling control tower. This is Hop Harrigan, coming in."

It was about flying airplanes, and the sponsor was Pep cereal. Pep had airplanes on the carton that a child could punch out and assemble. It didn't fly, but you could hang it from a string in our room. I was always pestering my mother to buy PEP, so I could have the latest model of plane. Pep wasn't a good-tasting cereal, and when we poured milk into it, it would just turn to mush. It didn't snap, crackle, or pop.

After a while, Mom refused to buy it because nobody ate the cereal. We had five or six cellophane bags of cereal in the cupboard with no box because I had taken the box so I could punch out the model planes. I liked Grape-Nuts, and still do to this day, but there were no planes on Grape-Nuts.

Another radio program we liked was *Jack Armstrong, the All American Boy*. But on Saturday morning, we all gathered around our radio for *Let's Pretend*. They were fairytales. Stories about Jack and the Beanstalk, Rumpelstiltskin, and Heidi.

I remember coming home from church one Sunday, and for some reason that escapes me now, I changed from my Sunday clothes into my pajamas. Then someone wanted us to pose for a picture outside, next to the house. I still have the picture: I'm in pajamas looking kind of silly.

Anyway, to get back to the story of the high antenna, birds, which my dad called bee martins, would perch on the wire and dive off and swoop down and catch the bees and eat them. My dad would sit in the doorway, where he made the violins, and shoot them with our Red Ryder BB gun to keep them from eating the bees.

In the living room, there was a light that hung down with a globe and chain with a thimble-looking thing you pulled to turn on the light. My dad would put a wooden match down the barrel of our BB gun and cock it. Then we took turns shooting at the chain. Sometimes the pellets would hit the wall and strike the match, and it would fall to the floor, burning. Then we would run and step on it to put it out. Mom put a stop to it when we hit the globe and broke it. Women like to throw a monkey wrench into the machinery.

Then there was the time my dad bought me a bow and arrows. He handed it to me and said, "Now, son, don't shoot anybody with it!"

"Okay, Dad," I said while unwrapping it. Oh boy, I couldn't wait to show it to Orville. I walked out the front door, across the porch, then down three steps and around the corner of the house.

There was Orville with his back to me going toward the bees. I notched an arrow and let it fly, true and straight. I missed my brother by a mile, but my dad had followed me out of the house. He saw the whole thing; I didn't even get a chance to lie.

"Give me that, son of a bitch," he said, and I got whacked on the behind with the bow.

I was crying, and saying, "I only wanted to show him my bow and arrow."

I followed my dad back into the house, and he put the bow and arrows up on the top of the china hutch. He knew I couldn't reach them up there. I think it must have been a month before I got them back. But one day, Dad set up a cardboard target and said, "Shoot at that." Then he sat down in his rocking chair to watch me, almost as though I couldn't be trusted. Gee!

One day my mother was doing our wash and had her wringer-type washing machine set up under the pepper tree at the side of the house. My younger sister Alice was standing on a wooden chair, watching Mom run the clothes through the wringer.

My mother went into the house to get more clothes to wash. Either she left the wringer running or Alice turned it on and stuck her hand into the wringer trying to push clothes through it, wringing the clothes out to dry like she saw our mother do.

The wringer took her arm into the wringer clear up to her shoulder, and then started slipping on the armpit. Mom heard her screaming and ran out to the machine. The release lever had come off the top of the wringer. A man from the auto shop that joined our house on the south had heard my sister screaming and was there almost as soon as our mother. The man saw the problem, picked up the release lever, and put it back on the washing machine and released her arm from the wringer.

But the damage was already done. She has worn a big scar under her arm all her life. Poor little thing, and that was Mom's little Lally baby too, as my mother affectionately called her.

I don't personally remember this, but I've been told about this all my life.

Mrs. Gray, who I called Mama Gray, came home one day with a dozen turkey eggs and set the sack of eggs on the kitchen counter. A siren blasted as a fire truck came screaming past the house, and everyone ran outside to see what was happening. They told me there was a fire in a vacant lot the next street over behind our house. Mrs. Gray, my mother, and my sisters all walked to the back of our yard to watch the firemen put out the fire with their big hoses.

They returned fifteen minutes later to find me on the floor with the sack of turkey eggs, and all the eggs were broke, and I was sitting on the floor squishing them through my fingers. Mrs. Gray said she could have killed me right there and then. She had planned on making a big angel food cake with the eggs. Even her daughter Ethel Bean would retell the story over and over into my fifties whenever I happened to visit her. Today my sister Rita keeps the story alive by bringing it up now and then.

My dad always worked out of town, because there wasn't much work in Hemet, unless you owned a business or were a rancher or a farmer. So my dad came home only on weekends and not every weekend. I remember one night someone knocked on our front door that had a glass window in it. Through the glass, I saw a man with a mustache and watched as my mother opened the door and started to hug the man.

It was my dad, but I didn't recognize him with the mustache. He came into the house and began pulling silver dollars out of his pockets and throwing them down on the floor. He had seventy-five dollars in all. My brothers and sisters started playing with the silver dollars, stacking them up and rolling them to each other like wheels. Dad said he had been paid in silver dollars because he was working in Las Vegas.

Later that night, after we went to sleep, Dad picked up the coins. We never saw the silver dollars again. Dad had gathered them up, and the next day, we all went to town and bought groceries. What fun it was having Dad back home again, and I always walked on his left side with my right hand in his hand. I loved my dad. For five dollars, we had a big box of groceries that Dad carried on his shoulder. All of us little kids also carried sacks, and Mom carried a couple of sacks with eggs and bread, all of this for five dollars.

Sometimes Dad would come home on Friday evening, and if we knew he was coming, we would be out on the street watching out for him to come around the corner. When we saw his big 1933 Buick, we would run down the street, and he would stop so we could climb on the running board and ride back to the house with him, where he would swing the car wide to the left into the other lane, then make a sharp right into our driveway.

The driveway was only two strips of cement, about a foot wide, with grass growing in between them. Then Dad would get out of the car and give us all a big hug, and we would hug him back. Of course, he always had a bag of candy because he had a sweet tooth too. He liked gumdrops, especially licorice. He also liked peppermint sticks and chocolate drops too; he called the peppermint sticks barber poles.

Once, when Dad was home for the weekend, he bought a watermelon and carried it into the kitchen. As he placed it on the table, he said in a loud voice, "Me want some waddymelon."

My brother Orville, who was four years old and was playing on the floor, jumped up and came running over to the table, saying in an excited voice, "Me too, me too, me too." After that, whenever dad said, "Me want a waddymelon," he would say in an excited voice, mimicking Orville, "Me too, me too, me too." Then he would have a big silly grin on his face when recalling Orville's excitement that day long ago. My dad always said this until the day he died in 1959 at the age of seventy-one.

I remember the ladies from the First Baptist Church coming over to the house one day with a big box of clothes. They left it for us to sort through to see if there were any clothes we might be able to wear. I remember my sisters taking dresses from the box and holding them up to their neck with one hand and then smoothing the dress down their body with the other while looking down at the length to see if it would fit them.

All I remember getting from the box was a beautiful silk scarf. It caught my eye right away because it looked similar to one Roy Rogers or Gene Autry wore in their cowboy movies, which I dearly loved. It was a white scarf with a very beautiful sea-foam green and lavender floral design. I quickly grabbed it from the box and tied it in a knot around my neck, with the two ends hanging down past my shoulders on my right side. I went to look in the mirror, and sure enough, it looked just like the ones Roy Rogers wore. Since no one objected, the scarf was mine, and I couldn't have been any happier.

Now if I just had a cowboy hat, I would look just like Roy Rogers. All my sisters were interested in were those stupid dresses. It seemed as though they could have brought some Levi's for Orville and me. "We didn't wear dresses, we wore pants."

SCHOOL DAZE

When I was five years old, I had to go to nursery school, which was just across the street from our house. When we arrived each morning, as they called us inside, a teacher would be standing at the top of the steps, passing each child a small cup of orange juice with cod liver oil in it. Aaah, I hated it. We would go in and color or water paint. I think at about 10:00 a.m., we got to go outside to play. There was a metal shed with sliding doors, and inside were pedal cars, tricycles, and a little pedal tractor. We didn't have such things at home.

All I had at home was my cap gun that Dad gave me. It wasn't even a cap gun; you couldn't shoot real caps in it. It was a real gun. My dad gave me a cheap owl-head pistol that was broken. Shoot, boys didn't need any stinking caps; they could make a gunshot sound with their mouths. Well anyway I thought so. I was a master at this in the early years, pow-pow-pow, "I got you Orville, you're dead!"

A lot of times, Orville didn't play fair. I would shoot him, and he would just keep running.

He would go around a corner of the house and point his stick gun at me. He'd go around a corner of the house and point his stick gun at me, "*pow-pow-pow*, you're dead, Paul."

"No sir, I shot you and you just kept running, you were supposed to fall down until I safetyed you."

"Okay," Orville dropped to the ground. He's lying there with his cheek on his arm, looking at me.

"Are you going to safety me, he asked?"

"No, not until you close your eyes."

"Okay," he says as he closes his eyes! So I safety him so he can get up and get back into the game.

Meanwhile, back at the nursery school. It was lunch, we had a half sandwich, then we had to lie down on a cot and take a nap. I wasn't sleepy; I'm still driving around in one of those pedal cars, in my head. There's about fifteen or twenty kids lying on cots and I see Mrs. McBirney coming up the row.

As she gets to my cot, she said, "Shut your eyes."

"Okay," I responded. I don't need a nap, I'm thinking I want to go play.

"Okay children, wake up." I throw the blanket back, stretch, and wipe the sleepy out of my eyes. I look around the room, wow, I had gone to sleep after all.

We get up and go over to our tables, where we color and paint again.

Sometimes we finger paint, what great fun too. Just get some paint on your paper, squish it through your fingers and start to make art. I like to squeeze it out of the bottom of my fist because it leaves a dollop of paint on the paper. Then with your index finger, (I didn't know it was an index finger at the time), I put it next to the dollop and make a line. Then after going all the way around the dollop of paint I had a flower, "pretty!" After our painting lesson we wash our hands and they let us ride the petal cars again.

Then the teachers tell us to return the petal cars to the shed because it's time to go home. We all go back inside to get our coats and I'm putting mine on as I walk down the steps and say goodbye to Mrs. McBirney.

I head out the west side gate; I just live straight across the street from the nursery school. The school was between Ramona and Alessandro Street and was the first grammar school in Hemet. But they needed more space, so they built a new one between Kimball and Acacia Street and Thompson Street south of town.

I went to nursery school for nine months, then for some reason I didn't go to kindergarten the next year. My next memory of school was out in front of the grammar school on Kimball Street. My mother is leaving me on my first day of school, and I'm bawling my eyes out. I'm hanging on her arm, because I don't want to be left there. "I don't want to go to school," I tell her. I'm scared to death. "I don't know all these kids; I don't know anybody, Bawaa." I mean, this is traumatic for a little boy.

My mother leaves me standing there, screaming bloody murder. I can't remember, but somebody must have taken me in and put me in class. It was all the way to the backside of the school and down a long hallway.

Mrs. Olverson was my first grade teacher. I remember we made candles, she gave us a string about a foot long, and she had some hot wax that we dipped it into. Then pull it out and let it cool for a minute, then dip it again as the wax built up on the string. You had to wait longer for the wax to cool. It seems like the dipping process took about three days to make a full size candle. The bigger the candle got, the longer it took to cool each time. The children walked in a big circle so the wax would cool before dipping it again. When the candle was finished, we took them home as a present for our mother.

We also learned how to make lye soap. She had ashes that we poured water through to make the lye. Then we dumped that into lard or grease that was rendered out of fat. We mixed it all up real good and poured it into a mold. When it hardened or jelled you had lye soap. I took mine home to my mother to wash clothes in her "EASY" washing machine. As she made a big fuss over slicing the soap up and putting it in her wash water so I could see she was using the homemade soap I'd made in school. I was so proud I'd made something mom could use and she acted like it was better than Rinso White, or Duz soap from the market.

We were taught to read in our first reader, Fun with Dick and Jane. She would call on different kids to stand up and read a sentence or two. This must have been at least half way through the school year. I couldn't read very well. I'd slouch down in my seat, hoping she wouldn't call on me. Some of the kids could read really well. Now, I wonder why my sisters, who were way older, didn't try to teach us to read at home. That would have been a big help. I'm in first grade and the only books I've mastered is a coloring book, and looking at the pretty pictures in our bible.

The only other thing I remember about first grade was my dad coming to pick me up in his big Buick. He handed me a white package and said take this venison to your teacher. I ran down the long hall to the very back of the school. Mrs. Olverson was straightening up. I handed her the package and said, "My daddy said to give you this." She said, "Why thank you Paul and thank your father too."

"Okay, I will." When I got back to the car, my dad said, "Did you give it to her?"

"Yeah, she said thank you." My dad drove us home as I sat proudly beside him in the big Buick.

The next thing I remember is, I'm in the second grade. I have a new teacher, Miss Wilson. Boy is she pretty! Thinking back, she must have been twenty-five or twenty-six. I mean she was beautiful, I am eight years old and in class, I'm mesmerized by her. I want to sneak up behind her and kiss her on the cheek, then run like crazy but alas, I'm a coward.

I see kids I was in class with last year that were further up the hall than my room, which is where higher grades are. I find out that I was held back and I'm taking first grade over again. Mom said the teacher flunked me because I was immature, shoot, I don't even know what it means, how could I be immature? At least in the second, first grade I wasn't afraid of school the first day, like I was last year. I guess I matured a little bit.

I remember being out back of school and I'd hear this really good sounding car coming along, at the back of the school on Acacia. I look over towards the sound, and this pea green 41 Chevy Coupe is streaking along the street. As it gets close to the corner, the driver down shifts to second gear, and the sound from the exhaust is neat as the mufflers make a rumbling sound.

I watch the car, as it turns left down along the side street of the school, as it goes by me, I see it's Miss Wilson. My eyes light up, she is so pretty. I loved to be early for school just so I could see her arrive. She parked by the kindergarten classrooms, and then walked in the front of the school. I couldn't keep my eyes off of Mrs. Wilson, and I hated to graduate from the second first grade.

I was in Mrs. Berry's room for my third year of school, but I'm only in the second grade. I can't remember anything about the second grade except my dad told me one evening that, "Your mother said you can stay out of class tomorrow, I want you to come deer hunting with me." Then Dad said, "You think you can miss a day of school?" Could I miss a day of school? I could barely sleep that night as I lay there thinking I was going hunting with my dad. So early the next morning I felt Dad's hand on my shoulder as he shook me to wake me up. We were up before daylight and dad stuck a cap on my head and a warm coat on me. He had some fried egg sandwiches he had made the night before, and when he started the car he handed me one. "Better eat this son, we might not get back until afternoon."

When we reached the meadow up near Idyllwild, we pulled up to a gate and Dad stopped the car and said, "We'll wait a little until it gets light." He reached in his pocket and pulled out a box of Ludens cough drops. He put one in his mouth and then he handed me one. I remember my dad always carrying those Ludens cough drops, as they were his favorite kind. "Suck on one once in a while son, and it keeps your throat from getting dry." I liked them because they were sweet like candy. He also pulled a package of wafers from our sack of sandwiches, and broke off two and handed them to me. They were like the stuff ice cream cones were made of, but they had a layer of filling inside of them. Even to this day I have never liked them but at least they were sweet, so how could I turn them down.

Kit Kat is about the same thing today and once in a while they make Kit Kat dipped in dark chocolate that I like. We got out of the car as it was getting light enough to see, and dad pulled his 30-30 Winchester from the blanket he had wrapped it in. He opened a box of shells and shook some into his hand and started pushing them into the guns magazine. He worked the lever and loaded a bullet into the chamber of the gun. He put the box with the remaining shells in it into his coat pocket as he said, "Let's go son."

Dad unlatched the chain on the gate so we could pass through, then closed the gate and latched it. The meadow was easy to walk in but when we came to the hill, it was harder for me to keep up. Before we walked into the brush Dad said, "Where is the car son?" I looked down the meadow we had walked up and said, "It's right there Dad, can't you see it?"

"Yes, I can see it son, but I want you to know which way the car is before we go out of sight of it. I'm going to ask you again so you keep thinking which way the car is every time we make a turn."

Every time we stopped to rest, it was the same question, "Which way is the car?" My dad never wanted me to quit thinking about the direction of our car as we hiked into the woods. I would always point to where I thought the car was, and if he figured I was wrong, he'd say, "No, son it's over here," as he pointed to where he figured it was. We came over a ridge on the hill we were climbing and we walked out to where we could see the hill side and we sat down in the warm sun that was shining bright and clear.

"Hey, you want another of these wafer bars or a cough drop?" Dad whispered.

I whispered to him I wanted another cough drop. He handed me one and told me to sit there and keep still. "I want to watch this hillside for a while, and you keep watch too, son. If you see a deer don't say anything, just poke me and point to where you see it."

"Okay Dad, I'll watch." Dad told me he had seen many deer tracks coming into here this morning. He said, "We'll sit here a while and see if any deer come past us."

I guess we had sat there about an hour and I was fidgeting around, when Dad whispered, "For Christ's sake son, can't you set still."

"Okay Dad, I whispered, I'll be still." Dad whispered, "Well, you better be, or I won't bring you with me next time." I thought I'd show him I'd sit really still, because I wanted to come hunting with him again. It's hard to sit still when you're cold, but I knew better than to complain.

I guess we sat there for another fifteen or twenty minutes, when two bucks walked out below us on an old mountain road. They started to paw the ground and then to fight one another. You could hear their horns crash together as they fought and dust rose up around them. At first, they were hard for me to see because of the high weeds that were as brown as the bucks were. Dad had his rifle to his shoulder when "BAM," the gun exploded making my ears ring. One buck was on the ground, and I saw the other deer jump over the side of the road and disappear in the brush. The deer on the ground was thrashing around still kicking up dust. We started down the hill and had to go down into a ravine, and when we came out on the other side, the buck was gone.

"God dam it," Dad said, "I should have put another bullet in it while it was thrashing around, but I thought he was hit hard."

We got to the spot where the deer had been kicking around, and dad was looking for any sign of blood to indicate the buck had been hit. Dad couldn't find any blood anywhere, he said, "I'll bet the bullet hit his horn and only stunned the animal." We looked for the better part of an hour trying to find which direction the buck might have gone just in case he had been wounded, but we couldn't find anything. Dad told me, "If he was hit anywhere but the horns he would have never gotten up."

It was probably past noon by now, so Dad said, "Let's head back to the car, Son you lead the way." He wanted to see it I had paid attention, and could go in the direction of the car. I did pretty good for a while when Dad said, "No son, look down at your feet, see our tracks going left here down the hill." I looked down and there in the dirt were our tracks where we had come up the hill that morning. Dad said, "Son you get lost, you can always find your tracks then backtrack yourself back to the car. "Okay, Dad," I said.

I was tired when we finally got back to the car, and after a drink from our canteen I lay down in the back seat and slept all the way home. Dad carried me into the house when we got home because I was still asleep. We didn't get a deer, but I had a great time hunting with my dad, and the Ludens cough drops weren't bad either.

A few days later when I got home from school, my dad was butchering a deer on the kitchen counter. "Son, I was at the police station this morning when you were going to school getting my deer tags validated."

"I shot him just outside town as the sun was coming up."

"Maybe next year, I can get one when you are with me, sound good to you?" I told him, "Oh Dad, I hope so."

"Well, if you're a good boy I'll take you with me again," Dad told me. "Your mother is going to fix us some of this venison for supper."

Mrs. Bounds is my teacher in the third grade. I think she is kind of pretty but not like Evelyn Wilson. I knew there could never be another Evelyn Wilson.

Mrs. Bounds is a good teacher. One day, she tells us, "I don't have enough of these books so some of you children will have to sit together."

She passes out the books and I don't have one. "If you didn't receive a book, move across the aisle and share that students book." I slide in beside Georgia Powell. She opens the book and lets me hold one side while she holds the other. She smells good; I can't remember ever being this close to a girl before that wasn't my sister, and they were icky.

My hand brushes her hand as we hold the book together. My hand tingles as it touches her hand. I feel flushed and I turn to apologize for bumping her hand. Her eyes are so blue, like the clear depth on a blue marble in my pocket. She has on this medium blue sweater made of angora or cashmere or something. I can't even think, I feel like I'm intoxicated, I don't even know what intoxicated means. My head is swimming as I try to read the words but I feel a little dizzy.

We are both trying to read the book and we have our heads together. I brush her cheek with my cheek, WOW! Meteorites, skyrockets, the Fourth of July fireworks. I feel so flushed and hot, I can't even think. We're reading from, Hiawatha. I shot an arrow into the air, it came down I know not where. I know where it is! It's stuck in my heart; cupid let me have it good.

It was all over to soon, I had to return to my seat. I couldn't keep my eyes off her. She glanced over at me and smiled, darn she was beautiful, and she's my age. Not like my teacher Miss Wilson. I was in love for the first time, and with Georgia Powell. I don't know how I finished the school year, but Georgia Powell was a ball of fluff, I was smitten. Sometimes, I would ask her something just for a reason to talk to her.

I don't remember Georgia acting like it was anything special for her, like it was for me. She'd smile sweetly once in a while, as I looked into her deep blue eyes but nothing heart-stopping. I guess I'd been spurned by my first time fling with a member of the opposite sex. Or maybe she was more in control of her emotions than I was, she was probably smitten too but more in control, and just wasn't showing it, but she sure was cute.

The fourth grade was a really good year. My teacher, Mrs. Simpson had built a cement blockhouse across the street west of the school. I only lived two blocks away on Central. I passed the house quite often, in fact every time I went to town. I had never seen round corners on a cement block house before, I was fascinated by those round corners, and they came out so perfect at each corner.

Mrs. Simpson would read us a story from a book, once or twice a week. The name of it was "He Went With Marco Polo," about some boy who was in the group that traveled with Marco Polo. His name was Antonio, and when they returned from their travels, they looked to be poor beggars, but they had jewels sewn into the lining of their robes.

Eugene Boyd, Duane Unland, and myself, sat at the back of the class and drew fighter planes of World War 2. We'd draw the planes strafing (shooting), Jap machine gun nests. We'd draw ovals all stacked together like sand bags for the Jap's machine gun emplacements. Eugene taught me how to draw a fighter wing from a side profile. I was doing it wrong. When he would finish a new drawing, he would slip it to me to look at, Duane would pass his to us also.

At recess, we would be playing in the school- yard, and I'd hear the motors of airplanes flying overhead as the pilots from Ryan Field learned to fly in formation. The trainer planes were blue bodies with yellow wings. I remember a white circle with a red star on the side of the planes, and I hoped to someday be a pilot myself. That's all I remember about the fourth grade sixty years later, except I looked forward to the story of Marco Polo. On weekends, the little town of Hemet would be full of cadets from Ryan Field west of town. My sisters would often talk about a cute cadet they had seen. I don't remember playing marbles in the fourth grade. I think we were getting too big by then. We sure did play marbles in the 2nd and 3rd grades. I believe Eugene Boyd was the best shooter I ever saw when it came to marbles. He was so precise and meticulous. He was a sharp dresser also, and his hair was always combed perfect. He was the Cincinnati kid of marbles. He cleaned me out a few times.

My mother said I couldn't play marbles for keeps, she claimed it was gambling and frowned on by the church. Just try to get someone to play marbles with you, if they can't keep what they win by knocking the marbles out of the circle. I'd have both front pockets stuffed with marbles, after school I'd have to leave them in my desk, since I had three times as many as mom had bought for me. I don't have any proof, but she was the type to call the police on me and have me hauled off to jail. Maybe not though, she loved to beat me. Then she would only have Orville and Everett left to beat.

My sisters were too big to whip, all except Alice, she was Mom's favorite, Mom called her, little Lally Baby. Alice couldn't say, Alice, she called herself Yahyee.

I got scarlet fever this year, and we were quarantined for two weeks. My older sister, Loreda went to stay with her girl friend, Jeanette Reeves. Otherwise, she would have been quarantined also, and wouldn't have been able to attend high school, which was critical for her to graduate. That's all I remember of the fourth grade, after all the years have passed.

There's not much I recall about the fifth grade. I had Mrs. Trapp, for a teacher but for music we went to Miss Poor's room. Miss Poor was an American Indian. I remember her bringing an Indian Chief into class one day in full Indian dress with head bonnet and buckskins. He wore buckskin moccasins, and when he left she said, "Did you notice how silently he walked?"

One day, I remember standing by her piano singing with the class. At the end of our class she said, "Paul will you stay for a minute?" Criminy, what did I do now? If I just looked cross-eyed at someone, I would have to stand in the hall. I was notorious for standing in the hall. Kids would go by with a lavatory pass and stop to ask what I did. Usually, I'd get fifteen minutes of standing in the hall. Then the teacher would come and ask if I thought I could settle down now? "Yes," I'd say.

Miss Poor said, "Paul I'm putting a show on in the auditorium, would you sing a song in it?" I don't know, I'm kind of timid I thought, but I had stood up in church to speak a piece, as they called it more than once. *John 3:16 For God so loved the world, that he gave his only begotten son, that whosoever believeth in him should not perish but have everlasting life.* "Sure, I guess I can do it," I said. "What's the song!"

"I've written the lyrics down on this paper." The lyrics were;

> *I'm an ol' cowhand*
> *From the Rio Grande.*
> *And I learned to ride,*
> *Before I learned to stand.*
> *I'm a cowboy,*

Who never saw a cow,
Never roped a steer,
'Cause I don't know how
And I sure ain't fixin'
To start in now.
Yippee yi ow kiyaa,
Yippee yi ow kiyaa.
I'm an old cowhand
From the Rio Grande.

And I learned to ride,
Before I learned to stand.
I know all the trails
In the Lone Star State,
Because I travel them all
In a Ford V8.
Yippee yi ow kiyaa.
I know all the songs
That the cowboys know,
Because I learned them all
On the radio.
Yippee yi ow kiyaa.

I sang them around the house until I learned them. I must have learned them pretty good too, because I still remember them. Sue Clark and Sonny Reeves were to sing "Indian Love Call."

When I'm calling you o-o-o-o-o-o,
Will you answer to o-o-o-o-o-o.
That means I offer my love to you, to be your own.
If you refuse me I will be blue, and waiting all alone.
But if when you hear, my love call ringing clear,
And I hear your answering, echo so dear.
Then I will know, our love will come true,
You'll belong to me, I'll belong to you.

I learned the Sonny "Chuck" Reeves part in hopes of getting to sing to Sue Clark, who was a cutie. But, alas, it was never to be, because Sonny didn't chicken out and sang quite well.

My mother bought me a three-dollar cowboy hat and a plum-colored western shirt to wear when I sang my song. I still can't believe I did it because I was so timid.

Miss Poor played the piano, while I sang to her, not wanting to see the people in the audience. Jeanette Reeves, was my sister Rita's friend, and sister to Chuck Reeves, who was singing the other song.

Mrs. Reeves told Rita, "Paul sang real well."

What else could she say? After all, I wasn't Mario Lanza.

The sixth grade was a good year. I was in Mrs. Almquist's class. I liked the girl in the desk in front of me—Erlene Owen. Her dad had a milk route and delivered milk to homes around Hemet. She had two older sisters, Jean and Irene. Irene was in a class with my sister Betty, who was six years ahead of me. But for the entire sixth grade, I liked Erlene. She wore red sweaters and red plaid skirts a lot (some people look really good in certain colors). Georgia Powell's was blue. She was my first heart-stopping love affair. I just never got around to telling her how I felt until now.

Now here is Erlene, cute as can be, always happy and laughing. A girl named Nancy Osborne sat behind me; Erlene was in the front. I was in the second seat, and Nancy was in the third seat. On Erlene's right was Pauline Alexander; then Sue Clark was in the next seat. They gave themselves nicknames: Erlene was Inky, Pauline was Pinky, and Sue was Susie. I don't remember Nancy being part of their group.

Sometimes we would sing a song that was popular, like,

I'm looking over a four-leaf clover,
That I overlooked before.
First is the sunshine,
The second is rain.
Third are the roses,
That bloom in the lane.
No need explaining,
The one remaining.

It's somebody I adore.
I'm looking over a four-leaf clover,
That I overlooked before.

I still love that song, and it's still fun to sing, even now.

I remember Erlene wore sweaters a lot. I would pull fuzz from her sweater and hold the fuzz in my hand close to her ear and blow. The fuzz would go sailing past her head. She would turn around and ask me, "What are you doing?"

"I just wanted to see if you were awake!"

"Well, stop it, kiddo!"

I now know I just wanted attention. I really liked her, but, alas, she only had eyes for Sonny Reeves.

Sue Clark would say, "Inky, there goes Sonny," as he was going down the hall and passing our door. Erlene would run to the door and look out, watching Sonny walk up the hall to his class. Then come back and say, "He's so cute."

I thought, *I'm cute too, just not as tall as Sonny.*

I didn't say anything. Let her eat her heart out for Sonny. She'll be sorry someday!

I sat and stared out the window a lot. I just couldn't get into learning; I wanted to be outside. Erlene, Nancy, and I were on the row of desks next to the windows. I had my elbow on my desk and my head in my hand, and I was daydreaming, looking out through the windows. I imagined being out hunting with my dad or playing war or cowboys with my brothers, or maybe with Charlie and David Gray.

I was just not into learning anything that day. I could be riding a horse out on the open range, just like in the song I had to sing last year. Why did school have to take so long? I would be an old man before I was out of sixth grade. Besides, I loved the outdoors and I didn't want to be here in this class. I didn't need to learn anything.

Behind me, Nancy said something. I turned in my seat and said, "What?"

She said, "If you look like your dad, your dad sure must be good-looking."

Everyone who heard her, laughed.

"You think Paul's good-looking?"

"I didn't say Paul is good-looking! I said his dad must be good-looking."

"Well, it's the same thing," they said.

"No, it's not." And she stopped talking about it.

They were still laughing. "She thinks Paul's good-looking. How ridiculous!"

Nancy put her head down and went back to writing something. The kids around us were still making jokes, so I just went back to staring out the window.

I could be riding horses. I loved horses. I dreamed of being a cowboy; I even wore cowboy boots to school. I got laughed at a lot.

Erlene asked me once, "You think you're a cowboy?"

I didn't answer. They wouldn't understand.

THE WALLERS

Our parents divorced in about 1947. In the fall of 1947, my mother said, "The courts are taking you four youngest children away from me. Your dad won't hold a steady job and support us, so to get state aid because I can't make enough money on my own, I have to give up custody of you younger children."

She was making only twenty-seven dollars a week as a short-order cook and dishwasher at the Riverside Grill in Riverside, California.

"You are being made wards of the court."

I hadn't a clue what a ward of the court was. I knew it didn't sound good, because we were going to a foster home (*What's a foster home?* I thought) in Hemet, where us four youngest children were born. We were to be staying with the Wallers. I was eleven, and I knew the Wallers from the First Baptist Church we attended the church when we were children. The first pastor I remember was Henry C. Poole, who he left. Then there was Mr. Workman, then Mr. Rizor. The preacher who baptized me was Mr. Pankratz. I went to school with his daughter, Bonny Lou Pankratz. I was in trouble a lot at church.

When we were small boys, Mom would lay a blanket on the church pew, and Orville and I would fall asleep on it during the church service. I was on the cradle roll, and I still have a diploma for graduating to beginners.

I remember getting into trouble, somewhere along the way, getting into trouble for something—I can't remember what. I can remember the preacher saying to the congregation, "We're going to pause right here for a moment while Mrs. Huff takes Paul outside and disciplines him."

My mother grabbed me by the arm and dragged me out of the church. Out on the church steps, I got what for, but good. I was crying and screaming bloody murder.

"Shut your crying so we can go back in. Shut up, or I will give it to you double!"

Everyone had a look of satisfaction on their face because Paul had got his comeuppance—at least as much as I could see through my tears. But there were good times at church too: At Christmas, we got a small box of candy, an orange, and an apple.

Mr. and Mrs. Waller were part of this church; I believe he was a deacon in the church. I remember him with the collection plate going from row to row, passing it to the next person.

Another member was Mr. Graham, a nice old man and also a church deacon. Mr. Graham was the one to lead us in song ("Let's turn to page 350"), as our piano player, Aunt Ellen (who was not our aunt—that was just what everyone called her), gave us the introduction.

> *Oh what fellowship, oh what joy divine,*
> *Leaning on the everlasting arm.*
> *What a privilege, to go from day to day,*
> *Leaning on the everlasting arm.*
> *Leaning on Jesus, leaning on Jesus,*
> *Safe and secure from all alarm*
> *Leaning on Jesus, leaning on Jesus,*
> *Leaning on the everlasting arm.*

I guess I got carried away a bit as I still love singing that old song also.

Come to think of it I love all the songs we sang in church.

"Okay, let's all turn to page 69," Mr. Graham said, and Aunt Ellen started us with four bars on her piano.

> *Sing it over again to me, wonderful words of life*
> *Let me more of their beauty see, wonderful words of life Words of life*
> *and beauty, teach me faith and duty*
> *Beautiful words, wonderful words, wonderful words of life.*

Another good song.

Or maybe it would be Ocie Klump who would play the piano, because both Ocie, and Aunt Ellen played piano. I went to school with Hazel Klump, Ocie Klump's daughter. The Van Dorstens were also members of the First Baptist Church; they had two daughters, Marjorie and Joann. My sister Loreda was good friends with the Van Dorstens, and we still see Joann (now Grier) at school reunions from time to time.

In the fall, when the walnuts were falling from the trees, Mr. Waller would pay us to pick them. He had talked to my mother at church, and it seemed like a good way to make extra money. Mr. Waller knew we needed it.

"You can come out on Saturday or any afternoon you want," he said. "I need to get them in before it rains. You don't want water on walnuts—they start to mold inside. So on Saturdays, my mother, sisters, and brothers would all go to Mr. Waller's and pick walnuts.

One afternoon, it started sprinkling pretty good, and Orville, who was about six at the time, said, "I know where rain comes from!"

We said, "Where?"

"God's peeing!"

My mother slapped him so hard across the face. She did it hard and fast you didn't even see it coming. "You say anything like that again, I'll knock you clear into the middle of next week. I remember another time, he threw a spoonful of butter at my sister Alice (now she spells it *A-l-y-c-e* since she got all hoity-toity).

Mom grabbed a stick she kept for just such an emergency and beat him across his little legs until there were welts raised up on his skin and he was bleeding. He was only six.

"Don't you ever waste food again. There are people all over the world who are starving," she said.

We really had a loving mother, and she was such a good Christian lady too. Because she believed in "Spare the rod and spoil the child."

―⚏―

Mr. Waller had a house on about five acres of land with walnut trees on it.

In front of his home and just off Florida Avenue, he had a couple of gas pumps where he sold Polly Gasoline to the public. His home was a modern plan with a flat roof design. Along the left side of the house was a long gravel driveway.

At the back of the house, on the left of the driveway, was the swing to end all swings.

Mr. Waller worked for the electric power company. They had two older poles about forty feet long that they had taken out of the ground, and Mr. Waller bought them from the power company. He trucked them home to his place on Florida Avenue, and he then dug holes about six feet apart and set the poles into the ground. With the poles firmly in place, he put on his tool belt and climbing spurs, and, with a rope tied to the crossbeam, he climbed to the top of one pole, with the end of the rope in his hand.

At the top of the first pole, he pulled the cross beam up and bolted the cross beam into a predrilled hole in the pole. First, the bolt with a washer: he pushed it through the crossbar, then through the pole, then another washer and a nut. When this was tight, he threw the rope over the other pole and then climbed down. Then up the other pole. With the rope, he pulled the crossbar into position. And with a bolt from his tool bag around his waist, he took a bolt and washer and pushed it through the crossbar and into the pole. Now the last nut and washer with the nut tight, he checked the nuts on the two eyebolts, with their chains attached to make sure they were tight.

The eyebolts were fifteen inches each way from the center of the crossbeam, or thirty inches apart. With this done, back down the pole he came. He picked up the oak seat and attached a chain about twenty-four inches above the ground. Then with a two- foot level lying on the seat, he attached the other chain. The swing was all done and hanging level. What a great swing.

We could run very fast and throw ourselves into the swing seat with the long chains. The arc of the swing was very long, so when you would swing and pump hard, the travel was about thirty feet. What a great time we had on that swing.

A short distance behind the house was a drying shed for the walnuts.

There were bins with chicken-wire sides that he could dump the walnuts in to dry so the air could circulate around them. Behind that on two sides of the drying sheds was a fenced-off area. They had turkeys in it. The turkeys were kept for laying eggs, and Mrs. Waller sold turkey eggs to customers who came by for gas and also wanted eggs.

It seemed to me that this man had his hand in everything. I didn't think of it at the time, but writing this story, I admire him and the things he accomplished in his life. Mr. and Mrs. Waller were good Christian people, but very strict, as I found out later. We would walk down the long driveway going to the walnut orchard, and any noise would set those turkeys to gobbling. Orville and I would make some kind of noise just to hear them gobble. We would gobble, and the turkeys would gobble back. Gobble, gobble, gobble. Shoot, I'd do it right now if I could. Gobble, gobble. I guess it's a boy thing.

So after school and on weekends—no, not weekends, just Saturday, because, remember, Mr. Waller was Christian. I almost goofed Mr. Waller wouldn't work on Sunday. That day was holy. Someone from Hemet reading this story would have caught that. They would say I had told a falsehood—that's what Mr. Waller called a lie. I know because I was always being accused of telling a falsehood. Maybe I had just stretched the truth a little, who knows, certainly not me.

Here you boys take one of these five gallon buckets and help your mother and sisters pick up the walnuts. Mr. Waller had a long pole with a metal hook on it, about twenty or twenty-five feet long. He would reach up through the limbs, hook it around one of them, and shake the hell—oops, I mean heck out of it. The walnuts would fall onto the ground, which was covered with dead walnut leaves. The walnuts would roll under the leaves, and you had to move them around with your hands to find the walnuts. Sitting here now, I'm thinking, *Why didn't he rake up the leaves before we started?* The job would have been much easier with no leaves on the ground.

Now I know why in the fall, falling leaves, would just keep falling. ("Falling Leaves"—that would make a good title to a song. Ha! It's already been written. I'm always sucking the hind tit in everything I've tried to accomplish.)

We would pick the walnuts up in the five-gallon bucket and then dump them into a burlap sack. But we just called them tater sacks. But in this case, walnut sacks—same difference. It depends on if you're hoity-toity or not. Mr. Waller gave us a walnut huller to take the hulls off the walnuts. It looked like a metal hook with a leather strap, so as to strap it to your hand. Worked pretty good too. But the stain from the walnut hulls would turn your thumb and forefinger black. It would stay that way for a month, maybe more. Bear with me a minute, because I want to take a little side trip right here.

MAN TAN

I was in the army in 1959 and 1960. My very good friend Bob Mitchell and I were out one night driving around trying to see what we could find in the way of girls. We stopped at a store for a Coke, and they had some bottles on the counter by the register that said Man Tan. I picked it up. It was a clear liquid, so I asked Bob, "Hey, want to try it?"

He said, "I'll try it if you buy it, but I'm not spending my money on it."

"Okay, it's three dollars, you old tightwad. I'll buy it."

So I bought it, and we got back in the car and continued driving around. I would pour a little into Bob's hand and a little in my hand, and we would rub it on our face.

After a little bit I told Bob to look over here so I can see your face. "It doesn't look any tanner to me."

"Well, yours don't either," Bob said. "Well, let's put some more on."

"Okay," I said. So I dumped some more into his hand, quite a bit more, really. I thought we probably didn't use enough. I put plenty in my hand too. "If it doesn't work this time, it's probably no good."

After a half hour, I said, "Bob, do I look any tanner?"

"Not to me you don't."

"Well, you don't either. What a rip-off," I said.

"Well, I'll know better next time," Bob said. He was glad he didn't buy any.

After a while, we didn't have any luck finding girls, so we drove back to the army missile battery.

Next morning, I woke up and stretched.

What the hell is on my arm? I thought.

Through the back of my fingers and streaking down the back of my arms was a dark stain.

HOLY SHIT, I thought. *What the hell have I got all over me?*

About then, I remembered the Man Tan.

HOLY SHIT, I thought as I headed to the latrine (washroom). *I better wash this stuff off.*

I was down there trying to wash this stuff off, but it didn't want to come off. I looked like a Mongolian. My face was kind of a yellow-brown color.

HOLY SHIT.

My shirt would cover my arms, which were badly streaked, but I would just have to live with my face.

What a dummy, I thought.

So I took off through the barracks to find Bob and warn him before he woke up and had a stroke like I did. He was lying there all in a bundle, so I shook him.

"Bob!"

"What do you want?" he said, trying to focus.

"Look at your hand!"

By then, he was starting to wake up, and he turned over to look at me. He started laughing at me. "What in Christ's world you got on your face."

I said, "Don't look now, buddy, but you have it too."

"You're shittin' me," he said as he looked at the back of his arm.

"It's the Man Tan," I told him.

He threw the covers back and took off for the latrine, with me right behind him, laughing like crazy. His face was just as stained as mine. Washing did not help in the least.

Everyone at our formation that morning laughed at us. Then on the weekend, we went to Danville, a nearby town, to get a hamburger. The waitress was a cute girl named Jeanie. She said, "You boys got Man Tan on?"

We laughed and said yes. I knew we still looked like Mongols.

Bob and I are still friends fifty years later, and when we get together, one of us will say, "Hey, you got any Man Tan?" That three dollars was well spent because we had a million dollars' worth of laughs, I kid you not. Oh yeah, one of the ingredients in Man Tan is walnut stain.

Meanwhile, back at the ranch, we were picking up walnuts. Mom packed us a lunch to eat at noon. It was just something simple. We always had biscuits, I knew that, but she baked bread too. She had a big metal pan she would measure flour, salt, soda, yeast, and some sugar in, and enough water to make it into dough.

Mom would be into it up to her elbows, kneading it and punching it down.

Then she would lay a clean damp cloth over the pan of dough and let it rise. Then after it rose, she would punch it down and let it rise again. After doing this two or three times, she would tear off portions, put the portions in greased pans, and rub a little butter or oil on the top, and then bake it. What a good smell we had in the house, and oh, how good that bread was.

Hot bread and butter—you can't have it any better than that. I still love bread to this day. I can almost live on just bread. If I could, I would rub fresh-baked bread on the pages of this book just to keep you interested. But enough of the good life. We had to make a living.

We would work all day on Saturday and after school for a couple of hours.

Once in a while, usually on Saturday, we would go to Hammery's Market on the corner of Florida and San Jacinto Boulevard. We could have a soda or an ice cream bar. My sister Loreda said we were being paid two dollars a sack for picking up the walnuts, any extra income always helped.

When I was seven years old, my dad was living in a trailer in Allen's Motor Court, north on State Street and across from where the Hemet Turkey Show was held each year. I remember going to Dad's trailer after school, and he said he was making me a ring. He had a piece of pipe made of what he called nickel silver. He said it was going to be a horsehead ring, and he had scratched the likeness of a horse's head onto the ring and was filing the metal down so the horse's head would be raised up above the rest of metal. The hole in the ring was too small for my finger, so Dad put a punch into the hole. He was pounding the metal with a hammer to enlarge the hole and make the metal thinner between my fingers. I guess my mother was talking of divorcing my dad, and that was why he was living in the trailer in Allen's Court instead of in the house on Ramona Street where we lived.

Once the ring was done, Dad said I could take it and wear it, but he said, "Be careful, son, and don't lose it." I was so proud of that ring, and it was really shiny. Dad had polished it for me. I wore it until it wouldn't fit me anymore. Then I didn't know what had happened to it, and in time, I forgot about the ring.

In 1961, I had gotten out of the army and was at my mother's house in Long Beach, California. I was getting some things I had left for her to keep until I was released from the army.

"Here, son," Mom said and handed me a small box.

I asked, "What's this?"

"Well, open it, son, and see."

I opened the box, and there was my horsehead ring.

She had put it away for me and saved it all those years. I kept it among my things, and when my daughter Paula was about seven years old, I gave it to her. Paula loved horses as much as I did when I was her age, and she liked the horsehead ring my dad had made for me, just like I did so long ago when he gave it to me.

My mother and my father must have not divorced at this time because when we moved from the house at 123 North Ramona into the house at 704 East Central Avenue, they were still living together. But my sister Loreda said they fought almost every night when Dad was home about Mom running around with the church deacons. I can't remember my parents fighting, but I went to sleep early and slept like a log.

CENTRAL AVENUE HOUSE

I'm writing about events at the house we have rented at 704 East Central Avenue.

It's right on the corner of Thompson and Central. It was 1946 when we moved there from the house my brother Everett was born in at 123 North Ramona Street. Mr. and Mrs. Island rented us this house for twenty-one dollars a month. Our rent on the house on Ramona was seventeen dollars a month. The floor in the front room of the house has linoleum. There is a one-foot space between the edge of the linoleum and the wall. I remember my mother and sisters painting the strip a dark brown color, after we moved in.

There was an apricot tree growing about five yards from the side door on the east side of the house. Orville, Everett, and I liked to play cars and airplanes under the shade of the tree. Our sister Alice didn't play cars with us because she liked dolls, or paper dolls. She would sit there with a stupid doll on her lap, brushing its hair. Now I ask you, how much fun can that be? Purely from a boy's point of view.

One day my mother was ironing just inside this door on the east side of the house. There was a dartboard hanging from a nail on the right side of the door.

I had a metal dart that was pretty heavy, and I was throwing it into the dartboard. My mother was there in the doorway ironing. The spot gave her a lot of light and was probably cooler too. Needless to say, my dart missed the mark, but only by about three feet.

KTHUD.

The dart had stuck in my mother's head. She looked at me through the open door.

"Oh, Mommy, I didn't mean to," I said as I backed away, knowing I was going to be killed.

She looked like a unicorn, only her horn was a little to the right of center.

I kept repeating, "I'm sorry, I'm sorry."

She looked at me, like, *What are you sorry for?* She hadn't realized the dart was stuck in her forehead.

She reached up with the back of her hand to wipe her forehead and felt the dart. She grasped the dart with her right hand and tried to pull it out. But it was stuck tight. I went in to help her, still pleading for mercy.

My sister Ernestene, who was sitting at the kitchen table, came over to help. She caught hold of the dart, and with a twisting motion, the dart came free. With the dart out of my mother's head, I knew the attention would turn to me.

I don't remember what punishment I got, but I'll bet it fit the situation.

In the fall when the walnuts were dropping from the trees on our property, our mother would have us kids pick them in paper sacks. At night we would all sit around listening to radio programs and cracking the walnuts with several pairs of pliers my dad had in his toolbox. We had to crack the walnuts very carefully because the bakery she would trade them to wanted big pieces.

We would put the walnut meats in clean canning jars, then screw a clean lid onto the jar. When we had six-quart jars full, she would take them to the bakery and trade them for bread and cookies, even cupcakes. There were four walnut trees on the property we were renting. We also had a plum tree and a pomegranate tree. Unlucky for us because that was where our mother sent us to cut the switches to whip us with.

"You better not come back with a little one that breaks, or I'll send you for another one and I'll beat you to within an inch of your life."

I liked to cut a long switch because I would get as close as I could to her, then when she whipped me, the switch would hit her legs too. Of course, I always screamed bloody murder. I was hoping she would relent and show me some compassion. She didn't know the meaning of the word.

There was a vacant lot between our house and the next house east on Central Avenue. A man who must have worked for a potato grower or potato packer lived there. He brought potatoes home and sorted through them to keep the good ones and throw the culls over his fence toward our house. The culls would rot and smell to high heaven.

Orville and I started calling him Rotten Potato when we saw him coming into his driveway. We would say to each other, "Hey, Rotten Potato is home." Then we would yell, "Hi, Rotten Potato."

Well, one day he came driving down his long driveway, and Orville and I were watching him. He pulled up in the front of his house, opened the door on his '36 Ford sedan, and climbed out.

Orville and I hollered in unison, "Hi, Rotten Potato." And we waved to him like he was family. Welcoming him home from work, so to speak, since we didn't have anything better to do.

All of a sudden, he ran over to the fence, put his hands on top, and vaulted over. He was running toward us like a wild man. Boy, Orville and I took off for the side door of the house, which was just behind us. Rotten Potato was close behind us as we ran up the steps and into the house. Our sister Ernestene was coming out of the house about the same time we went flying past her. Rotten Potato bounded up the steps and into the house without even stopping.

Ernestene told him, "You get out of here. You can't come tearing into someone's house this way. Now you get out, you understand?" And she pointed toward the door.

"Well, those boys have been calling me names, and I'm tired of it," he said. "Now I want this to stop."

"Well, you go on home. I'll tell their mother when she gets home from work tonight, and she'll handle it." Ernestene had her arm on his shoulder and was trying to push him out the door. "Now you go on home."

Finally, he relented and left, walking back across the field to his house.

Orville and I were peeking out from under the stairway. Thank you, Ernestene, for saving our life that day.

Rotten Potato was out of breath, and I thought I saw drool coming out of his mouth. He might have had hydrophobia, the way he was slobbering, I don't know. You just can't tell about someone who chases little kids for no real reason. I was thinking he should be at the Patton State Hospital for the criminally insane.

"What do you think, Orville?"

"I don't think I'll wave at him anymore." Then he added, "I didn't know he was crazy."

I found out that day you can never be sure how your neighbor will react to a friendly greeting.

"I'm never going to wave at him again," Orville said.

Gee, the nerve of some people.

When our mother came home from work that night, Ernestene told her about the man chasing us into the house. So the next day, when Mom came home, we had to go cut a switch. Then we both got what for, but good, and with our bottoms red from the spanking, we had to go knock on the door and tell Rotten Potato we were sorry.

While Orville and I hid under the stairs while Ernestene (who I just called Stene, and still do) was pushing Rotten Potato out the door, saving us. Anyway, while Orville and I were sitting there waiting for Rotten Potato to leave, we saw a blue box, and we looked inside and found it was packed with bandages. I can't remember how long later it was that I stepped on a piece of glass and cut my foot because we were always going barefoot in the summer.

I came into the house crying, with the blood leaving tracks on the floor, and asked Stene to please put a bandage on it.

But she told me, "Honey, I don't have a bandage."

"Yes, sir, I know where there's some," I said, remembering the box under the stairs.

"Well, she said if you know where there is a bandage, you go get it and I'll put it on your cut."

So I went and got the box and pulled one of the bandages out and took it to her. She seemed irritated and said, "That's not a bandage. Now you go put that back in the box right now, and you get back outside, and don't you ever get into that box again."

I didn't understand why I couldn't wrap one of the bandages around my foot as they had plenty more in the box. It had two long ends, just right to tie it around my foot. Ernestene never did say why I couldn't have one of the bandages that I found in the blue box. I didn't know what they were until I had sex education in the seventh grade. I learned it was Kotex. Nobody explained things like that to children. I grew up very naïve, as most children did in the forties. Anything sexual was not even mentioned.

Looking back today, I don't think sex had been invented yet.

The field behind us was part of the same property because it was L-shaped. Across the field to the north of us was Mr. Byrd's house. Mr. Byrd at one time was the chief of police. One year at Christmas we didn't have much money and mom said she couldn't afford a tree. So one day I asked our mother if we could go ask Mrs. Byrd if we could cut a limb off the trees behind her house so we could have a Christmas tree.

"Oh, I don't care, son. Go over and ask if you want to," she replied.

We knocked on her door, and when Mrs. Byrd answered, I asked, "Mrs. Byrd, our mother said we could ask if we can cut a limb off your tree in the back to make a Christmas tree."

She said, "Well, I guess it would be all right, but don't you children get hurt! And, boys, they are only tamarack trees. They aren't pine trees."

"That's okay, we don't care," I said. "We just want a Christmas tree to put our presents under."

Orville and I got one of our dad's saws and cut off a limb that was low to the ground. It was five or six feet long. Then we carried it home, with Orville on one end and me on the other so as not to damage it. We had made red and green paper chains in school. We put the bottom of the limb in a bucket of dirt, and with a hammer handle, we packed the dirt around the trunk very tight. We stood it in the corner of the front room and wrapped the paper chains around it.

Mom gave us a few canning jar lids, and with an ice pick, we punched holes out near the edge. Then with a colored piece of yarn, we tied them on our tree. Alice and Everett helped too.

It's pretty, I thought.

It was dark by the time we were done. It was three in the afternoon when we went to ask Mrs. Byrd for the tree.

Now with the tree finished, it was six o' clock, and it had gotten dark outside. Mom had dinner on the table, and she told us kids to get in there and eat. "And eat everything on your plate because there are children in China who are starving."

"Okay, Mom."

We must live close to China because sometimes we didn't have enough to eat.

So we would go out in the field by our house and pick mustard greens to have more food on our table. I like them with salt and pepper and a little vinegar.

We had just finished dinner when someone knocked on our front door.

Mom opened it, and all she could see at first was a big Christmas tree. Mr. Byrd carried it into the front room and set it down.

Then he said, "I have some boxes of ornaments in the car. I'll be right back."

When he returned, our mother said, "Well, thank you, Mr. Byrd." We all said thank you too.

I stood there with my eyes as big as saucers. *Wow, that's a real Christmas tree*, I thought.

In 1946, a tree like this would have cost five dollars. We could buy a week's groceries with that.

What a nice thing to do for a needy family. When Mr. Byrd left, Mom had tears in her eyes as she thanked him. Today, as I'm remembering, I thank him too for his kind act. Thank you, Mr. Byrd. He made our Christmas really special because we had real Christmas ornaments to put on our tree. All we had to do was figure out how we were going to buy presents. I guess Santa would just have to take care of that problem as he has a gift for that kind of thing.

PILOT EXTRAORDINAIRE

"Okay, you guys back there, keep it closed up," the announcement came over the intercom.

I could see the skies starting to open up as I looked through the windscreen of the B-29 Superfortress. When we left the secret base in England this morning, the fog was so thick you could cut it with a knife. I lifted my microphone from the dash and said, "That's a Roger!"

We had to be on our toes from here on. Our fighter escort had reached their maximum range and had left us alone as they returned to base on the other side of the English Channel.

Lucky guys, I thought. I knew the Germans already had their Luftwaffe in the air as they did on our bombing run yesterday. We lost twenty-five planes on that mission.

Our commander said it wouldn't happen again today. I was listening to the drone of the big radial engines on this baby as she purred along, sending contrails behind us in the cold morning air as we reached our maximum altitude. There were contrails coming from all the planes as I checked the squadron one last time before we met the enemy.

"Hey, you guys, I see fighters coming at us from eleven o'clock high," I heard our commander say in the headset again. He encouraged the pilots to stay in a tight formation. "Don't anybody drop back. You guys keep it tight."

My copilot said, "There's one coming in fast on my right."

And I heard our .50 caliber machine guns open up from the waist gunner. I could hear the belly gunner open up as well. *Tat- tat-tat-tat*. I could feel their vibrations from the big Browning machine guns. He was really smokin' 'em.

"Get 'em, you guys," I said out loud to myself.

I heard the navigator tell me, "We are almost over the target. Shortly I'll open the bomb bay doors and make a big deposit in the German countryside."

I saw flak starting to appear in the sky just ahead of us. It looked thick enough to walk on. I heard my bombardier say, "You guys see what I see?"

I knew he was referring to the flak that had appeared in the sky all around us. I'd just told him this morning before takeoff to keep his mouth shut about the flak. I told him you scare everybody on board with all that talk about the flak.

I lifted my microphone from the dash of this monster I was flying. "What did I tell you before takeoff?" I asked.

"I didn't mention the flak," he said.

"I just asked if you see what I see."

"Well, hell, everybody knows what you mean!"

I would give him a reprimand when we got back to base after the bombing run. *Yeah, if we get back*, I was thinking. But enough of those kind of thoughts. I have to keep my head clear for the mission at hand and the safety of my crew—all young men depending on me to bring them back.

Everybody said I was as cool as a cucumber when it came to flying these big babies. I was the number 1 pilot in this squadron, but I'd had my share of close calls, though.

My thoughts were shattered by a flaming hot shard of shrapnel as it ripped through the side of my fortress. I called out, "Anybody hurt?"

I heard everyone trying to answer at once. It sounded unintelligible, with everyone talking in the headset at one time. I said, "Knock it off," as I tried to calm them down.

I guess they're okay, I said to myself. Somebody had to keep a sense of order here on this big bird if we were going to get the job done today without losing any of our buddies.

We were almost over the target now as I turned the plane over to the bombardier who guided the plane over the target. He was looking through the bomb sight when he said, "Bombs away."

I felt the airship rise as the weight of the bombs fell out of the belly of this big monster. I took the controls back from the bombardier, and I banked the big bomber as we turned for home.

"Take that, you pesky Germans," I heard one of my crew say. We probably snuffed a couple thousand of them, at least. My ship felt a little more agile as I checked our compass setting before lifting my mic and giving the men a "Job well done."

The sun shone in my face as the big Superfortress slowly came around and headed back to the English Channel. I lifted the microphone to my lips to tell my crew that they had done a good job. That's when I noticed the string on my tin can microphone had come loose from the nail in the tree.

My brother Orville on my right took the string and reattached it to the nail for me. Orville was my copilot today. My sister Alice had been our navigator as she navigated us to the target in Germany and safely back home.

I heard the enemy on the ground screaming at us. "You kids get down out of that tree and come in the house," my sister Rita called out from far below. "I'm going to tell Mom you kids have been in that walnut tree again. She told you to stay out of there before you fall and break your stupid neck. Besides, I have dinner ready. You kids want to go to the Hemet Plunge after we eat?" she asked.

"Hey, Orville, we're going swimming at the plunge."

"Neat," Orville says. I could tell he was excited. It would be good to get the sweat all washed off. It had been a harrowing day in the skies over Germany.

"Hey, Rita, what's for lunch? Not fried corn meal again, I hope!"

"No, we're having tamale pie," she told us.

"Oh boy!" Orville said as he started to run. He must be hungry too.

MY HORSE TONY

My dad had written and told me he had bought me a horse, an Arabian. "Son, he's big, and black as coal. I bought him for seventy-five dollars at an auction. Anytime your mother will let you come down for a visit, you can ride him. Now, son, you be thinking of a name, and the next time you write, you tell me what you want to name him."

"What do you want to name him son," he asked me in his next letter?" I remember listening to Tom Mix on the radio and his horse's name was Tony. So I wrote and told him "Tony". Dad said he was a big horse, about 15 hands high and was very gentle. I only remember hearing about my horse in letters from my dad over that year. My dad rode with Tom Wells on his ranch across the Colorado River from Blythe. Tom Wells's name is now on the Interstate 10 highway off-ramp east of Ehrenberg, Arizona.

The first time I saw Tony was when my mother took me to see Dad in Blythe. We rode the Greyhound bus down there, and for a little boy who always got car sick, it was a long ride.

It was getting late when we arrived. Tom Wells picked us up at the bus station in Blythe. He told us my dad was coming up from the lower ranch, down by Cibola, Arizona. Tom said Dad would meet us at the McCormick place.

The McCormick place was three miles north of the bridge east of Blythe over across the Colorado River. The road to Quartzsite and Phoenix didn't go straight east from the bridge like it does now. The road turned north through Ehrenberg, past the McCormick place, went on for a couple of miles, then turned east. Tom Wells had a bar on this road about seven or eight miles north and east of the bridge. A lot of military personnel were in Blythe during the war years, and many of the soldiers that were on maneuvers in the desert would frequent Tom's bar on weekends.

Tom drove us over the bridge and turned north. We had to stop at a quarantine station for inspection. They wanted to know if we had any fruits or vegetables. If you did, you had to forfeit them. Just beyond the quarantine station, we saw a couple of riders on the side of the road, and they were leading a couple of horses. It was my dad and another man, whom he introduced as Stony. I found out later that Stony's name was Ross Pennington, but they called him Stony or Stonewall. Sometimes they called him Stonewall Jackson. All that time, I didn't know there was a famous man and a president with that name.

My dad climbed down from his horse and sat me up in the saddle. If I had known what a climax was then, I would have had one. I was in heaven. My mother threw water on my dreams by saying I was too young to ride that horse by myself. My dad gave in and told my mother, "All right, you ride it with him."

So my dad helped my mother into the saddle, pushing me forward until I was almost sitting on the saddle horn.

"No, no," I kept telling my mother. "You'll make Tony sway back!"

My mother laughed and said, "Oh, for heaven's sake, son, I will not."

"You will too," I said. "Well, this is the only way you can ride Tony tonight—if I ride him too."

"So you want me to ride with you or give him back to Dad? Okay, but I know you'll make Tony sway back."

Dad had taken our place in Tom's truck, and when we rode into the McCormick place, he took the horses he and Stony had been leading and put them in the corral and started feeding them hay. Dad took Tony from my mother and unsaddled him. Then he hung the saddle from a rope in the barn. There were about eight other saddles hanging from ropes too. Mom went to the small house with a stove and a bed and fixed supper for all of us. I stayed with my dad as he put the horses away.

We left the barn and walked up to the house where Mom was fixing us supper. Dad had all the necessary things in a cupboard on the wall; the stove was a wood-burning stove. Tom Wells had gone on to his bar or saloon up the road a ways. It was dark by the time we were through eating. Stony said he would sleep in the barn. That way, my mom and dad could have the cabin to themselves. I was tired, and I went right to sleep. I'm sure my dreams were of the coming day and riding horses.

The next morning after breakfast, Dad said he and Stony had to take the horses to the river about a half mile away to water them. The McCormick place didn't have a well, so every time someone went to town, they brought back four or five cans of water. There was always a water bag hanging in the tamarack trees that the house sat under, where we could get a quick drink if we were thirsty.

Dad said I could ride along with them if I wanted to. He already knew the answer to that. Stony had Tony and two other horses saddled when we walked down to the barn. Stony asked me if I could get on by myself. I tried really hard, but I couldn't. I could catch hold of the leather stirrup, but I couldn't for the life of me get my foot up high enough to climb into the saddle.

Stony said, "I'll lead him over by the corral, and you can climb up the fence and swing into the saddle."

"Thanks, Stony," I said.

My dad came out of the barn carrying a rifle. He said, "We'll take this in case we see any rabbits." And he shoved it down into a scabbard on Tony. Jiminy, I've got a horse and a gun, just like in the movies. I was busting at the seams. "Okay, son," my dad said, "stay up beside me and take a tighter rein on that horse so you can control him."

"Okay, Dad!" I replied.

"Son, Tony's a gentle horse, but sometimes a paper will blow suddenly and spook him, and I've seen him jump sideways, so, son just keep your knees tight against his side."

"Okay, Dad," I said.

I was wishing I had a hat like Dad and Stony.

When we got to the river, we just rode right into the water up to the horses' bellies. They stood there sucking in the water. Once they had drunk their fill, they turned and came back up the riverbank out of the water. Dad was sitting there in his saddle looking up and down the river.

I asked him what he was looking for, and he said, "I was hoping to see some ducks, son. A couple of mallards, or a pintail or two, would have been nice," he said. "I was hoping to shoot a couple for your mother. Your mother likes baked duck cooked up with some kind of stuffing. I saw a bunch of mallards on a slough down at the lower ranch the day before yesterday. But no such good luck this morning." Then he said, "Maybe this evening, the Lord willing, or maybe we can get a nice cottontail going back to the McCormick place."

We were riding along the trail toward home when Dad said, "Son, get your gun out. There's a cottontail in the weeds by the trail." I was looking as I tried to pull the gun from the scabbard. It didn't want to come out because the sight seemed to be hanging up somehow. I kept pulling, but it wouldn't come free.

Then I heard Dad say, "Hold it, son. You took too long."

The rabbit ran into the bushes and out of sight.

Dad said, "Son, if you want to shoot a rabbit, you'll have to be quick. You won't be able to dilly-dally around."

"Dad, the gun wouldn't come out of the scabbard," I said. Then he told me to grab the son of a bitch with both hands and pull like hell.

I tried, standing up in the stirrups and pulling with all my might. Finally, it came free of the scabbard. He told me to lay it across my lap, and if we saw a rabbit, jack a round into the chamber, take a fine sight, and squeeze the trigger.

All the instructions were for nothing, because we didn't see another rabbit all the way back to the corral. But I was having fun. I was riding my horse Tony and had my rifle across my lap, so who cared? I wish I had a hat so I would look like a real cowboy.

That evening when we went back to the river to water the horses, Dad told Stony, "Let's tie up to these air weeds and slip out there and see if there are any ducks before we water the horses."

Stony had put a shotgun in his saddle scabbard before leaving the corral.

Dad pulled my gun out of the scabbard and said, "Take it, son, but watch where you point the barrel, and don't load a round into the chamber unless I tell you. I want Stony to shoot a couple of ducks if there's any here near the riverbank."

We got down on our hands and knees and crawled through the weeds out to the riverbank. Stony was leading the way, and as he got close to the riverbank, he lay down on his belly.

"Dick, I see some clear across on the other side, but I'd need a cannon to reach them."

"Nothing close?" I heard my dad ask.

"No, they're clear across the river. They look like they're feeding," Stony said. "Dick, there's a couple of mud hens in the tules below us."

My dad says, "I don't want a mud hen. Well, let's get the horses. Maybe we'll see a rabbit going back to the corral. I'd like to see Paul shoot a rabbit."

My dad or Stony always had to help me climb into the saddle as we mounted up, and then we rode back to the McCormick place. I looked close, but I didn't see one rabbit going home.

The next day, we saddled up and started for the river to water the horses. Once they were watered, we turned north, riding along the river for a couple of miles. Dad and Stony were looking for cattle tracks where the cows came to the river to water. They would follow the tracks that were going away from the river, hoping to see cattle.

Sometimes we rode up on eight or ten cows. Dad and Stony would look them over for brands and earmarks. Tom Well's property bordered the Indian reservation. I don't know if Tom Wells owned this property or was leasing it. He was running cattle in here because of the good feed all around us here in the river bottom.

Sometimes the brush would be thicker than hair on a dog, there were cottonwood trees, but mostly it was mesquite trees and what Dad called air weeds and salt cedar. Air weeds grew higher than a man on a horse's back. Riding through the brush, we would have to put an arm out to protect our faces from mesquite thorns, which are really sharp and hard.

After a day of this, I wasn't so keen on being a cowboy. Just riding down the trail, taking the horses to water was fun, but riding in brush to check on cattle was not fun. Besides, I wanted to chase something and shoot it with my rifle.

We were staying for only four days, and then my mother had to be back at work. It all came to an end too soon. My mother and I were on a Greyhound bus heading for home. My dad said he would send for me when school was out. I cried when it came time to say goodbye, and I was still crying when I waved goodbye out of the Greyhound bus window, but it had been a happy four days. Now I knew I really had a horse, and I knew what he looked like. He was big and black and as gentle as could be, and I knew it would be a long six months until June when I could visit Dad and ride my horse again.

For a boy of eight, six months is like ten years. After I was back in school, I told all my friends about going to my dad's, and that I had a horse all my own. Nobody believed me. "Ride it to school, then," they told me.

"I can't. It's down on the Colorado River."

My friends would say to me, "No, you don't. You're just lying."

I felt helpless as I stood there looking down at my feet. "Hey, at least I have cowboy boots."

For a little boy and his dreams of horses and being a cowboy, life was about as good as it could get.

WAR GAMES

Across Thompson Street on the west side of the Central Avenue house was a big field. That spring in 1946, they planted barley. It was about two foot high, so it must have been about June. The barley was green still, and the barley beards were a clump of seeds that had a four-inch tail off each seed. We could pull the barley heads off the stems and throw them at each other, like a dart.

Orville and I would pick a handful of the barley heads and attack each other with our arsenal. When we ran out into the field of barley and fell down, we could make paths that you could crawl around in so nobody from the street or walking by could see you. We had paths all over. What great fun!

The farmer was not happy when he came by to check the field, and there was so much barley flattened on the ground. Almost like the crop circles today made by aliens. In fact, they may have been considered the very first alien crop circles in history, or at least in Hemet. People weren't aware of aliens back then. The first flying saucer hadn't landed at Roswell yet. If the Roswell disaster had happened one year earlier, the rows of paths through the barley would have been blamed on aliens instead of on Orville and me.

But alas, the farmer came over and chewed our mom out real good. Not only were we pulling the heads off the barley, which was his crop to harvest, it was down on the ground instead of standing up, so the combine couldn't thrash it.

Boy, I was glad we weren't there when the man came over, because Mom said he was hopping mad. Mom said, "If he catches you boys in his field, he's going to report you to the police, and I won't be able to come see you. You'll be there till your sentence is served, and all they feed you is bread and water, and not much of that. So go cut me a switch because I told the man I'd tan your hide, and I'm a man of my word."

Drat.

Orville marched out to cut his switch, but I was not in any hurry. Orville liked to get punishment over with. I thought, *Let him get it over with first if he wants to. Maybe she will be tired after she gets done beating my brother.*

"Where were you boys when that farmer was here?" she asked. "I looked all over for you!"

"We were in the field behind the house digging a hole," I said.

"Well, quit dawdling and get me that switch, and don't come back with a little one!"

Orville stopped outside the door to let me catch up. "What'd we do?" he asked. "I guess it's because we crawled around in the field across the street and knocked the barley down. The guy was mad too, because we pulled the heads off the stalks and threw them."

"Nobody told him not to do it," I said. "I didn't know it was wrong, either. We were only playing."

I handed Mom the knife that she had given me to cut our own switches with. She started on Orville because he was closest. Orville had his hand on his butt, so the switch would hit his hand, so it didn't hurt so much.

"You ever going to get in that man's field again?" she was asking him. Her eyes were like two red coals of fire. The drool was foaming around her mouth, and I could tell she was really enjoying this as she dished out our punishment. She was like a demon obsessed. I shook my head no, even though she was asking Orville. I had started to cry too; maybe she would take pity on me.

She tossed Orville aside and grabbed me by the arm and started in on me. She didn't even use the switch I had to cut; she was giving it to me with the remnants of Orville's switch. "Ouchie, ouchie, ouchie." I was as close to her as I could get as I screamed bloody murder.

I was hanging from her arm with all my weight, hoping she would get tired and stop the punishment. She was panting, but I could tell she was enjoying it a lot. She was like a wild-eyed monster, even a raving maniac. Finally she turned me loose. Another couple of blows and I'd be dead.

Now I quit crying so hard because it was over at last.

I went outside and looked for Orville. He was out by the faucet in the yard with the hose between his legs, so he could get water in his hands to wash his face.

I had about quit crying as I said, "Orville, will you hold the hose for me too?"

The little snot put his thumb over the end of the hose and squirted me right in the face.

"Hey!" I yelled.

"Well, you said you wanted some water on your face, didn't you?"

He handed me the hose and went to turn it off. His hand was sore because he had taken all the blows on the palm of his hand.

He said, "I didn't know anybody cared if we ran through that field. Why didn't they tell us to stay out?"

"I don't know," I replied. "Want to go back to digging our hole?" I asked. "We'll just play in the field behind the house." Nobody cared because it was just weeds and stickers, which people called goat's head, and how they hurt if you stepped on one while being barefoot.

Charlie and David Gray came over on the weekend, and we got them some cans so they could help dig the hole. That was what we were digging the hole with—one-gallon cans. Mom brought food home in them from the Alessandro Hotel. The hole was about four feet deep.

Charlie said, "Hey, Paul, you guys, you want to play war?"

"This would make a good foxhole!" I said. "I know where there's a piece of pipe we can use to make a machine gun."

"Okay, go get it," Charlie told me. So I ran and got the pipe. "Neat," he said as I lay it on top of the mound of dirt

Somebody had dumped about six or seven palm fronds at the edge of the property by Byrd's house. So we went and got them to lie over the hole and our machine gun.

That way, the enemy couldn't see us because of the big mound of dirt we had dug out of the hole. We would be safe shooting at them with our old piece of pipe machine gun.

Orville and David would be the Japs and try to take our positions. Charlie and I were going to be machine gunners.

"Orville, you and David get some walnuts to use for hand grenades. Then you try to sneak up on our machine gun position and throw a grenade into it. If you get a grenade into our foxhole before we shoot you, then we'll be the enemy."

I was rubbing my legs together and holding myself because I had to go pee so bad. "Hey, Charlie, while they're getting walnuts, I have to go pee."

I wanted to just go in back of the garage and whip it out, but Mom caught me one time, and I got spanked. Mom would make a good Jap. She liked to sneak around and tried to catch us doing something she told us not to do. She was already a master at torture. *No use taking chances*, I thought as I went right on past the garage. I finished in the bathroom and went out of the front door to see if I could find anything else to use to play war with.

As I went past the front bedroom, Alice was facing the window; she and Everett were playing paper dolls, standing them up against the screen. That was all she knew, was stupid paper dolls. I went out of the screened-in porch and turned right to head back to where Orville and David were picking hand grenades off the walnut trees.

I came to the window and ducked down low, and as I did, I reached up and hit the screen really hard with my hand. Alice's paper dolls all went flying. I heard her say, "Umm, I'm going to tell Mom."

I ran out to Orville and helped pull a few walnuts in case Mom came out on the warpath. I thought, *I'll just tell her I've been out here all the time.*

Nobody saw me at the house. The wind could have blown those stupid paper dolls down.

We had gathered all the hand grenades we could reach, so I returned to the foxhole with Charlie. "Where are Orville and David?" I asked because my back was to them as I walked back to the foxhole.

Charlie said, "They went over by the garage.

I told him, "You watch the front and I'll watch the back in case they try to sneak up from there. Watch for the weeds moving, Charlie, because that will be them trying to sneak up on us." All of a sudden, a hand grenade landed in the weeds just in front of us, but about ten feet short.

"Hey," Charlie said. "I think they're under the pomegranate tree by the garage."

We were both looking at the pomegranate tree when one hit not two feet away on the side of our foxhole. I saw one of them was in back of the garage. It was Orville, and he was hiding behind a tree. They were getting our range, and we hadn't seen them long enough to fire a shot. Charlie swung our machine gun around so he could blast them if they showed themselves.

We didn't see David, who was crawling through the high weeds. He jumped up and was throwing grenades like crazy. Charlie started shooting the machine gun really fast.

Pow-pow-pow-pow-pow.

Charlie could make a really good machine gun noise. I heard Charlie say, "I got you, David. You're dead!" I looked over at David to see if he would fall down dead.

"Criminy." I got clobbered on my shoulder and my side, and Charlie got hit with hand grenades too.

Orville had snuck up from the back while we were shooting David.

"I got both of you," Orville said, all proud. "Now Charlie and I have to be the Japs." He said those weeds made him itch, and David was itching too. He wanted to go wash up so his arms would stop itching.

I told Charlie, "Let's pick up the grenades they threw at us while they go wash, else we'll have to pick some more." Our mother told us to stop picking the green walnuts, or she would skin us alive.

We had just finished picking the walnuts when Orville hollered from the house, "Mom said to come eat. She said to wash up outside."

Orville had a towel she handed him.

I told Charlie, "Tomorrow we'll be the enemy, and we'll sneak up from two sides, just like they did."

Charlie said he got hit hard by one of the hand grenades. He had pulled up his T-shirt and was looking at a big red bruise.

I told him, "Shoot, I did too, but we'll get them tomorrow. It will be payback time." After supper, we went back outside to play until dark.

Our mother called us into the house and said, "So you boys want to go see the new Disney movie tonight?"

"Oh, Mom, can we?"

"You go change your clothes. I won't let you go in those dirty clothes. Let Charlie and David borrow a pair of clean pants."

I ran out to the yard where Charlie and Orville were playing. "Hey, Charlie, Mom said we could go to the show."

Orville asked, "Can I go too?"

"Sure, Mom said we can all go. Hurry and get cleaned up."

"Charlie, you can borrow a pair of my pants," I told him.

Mom gave me a dollar to pay for the tickets. We went skipping to town to see the movie *The Three Caballeros*. It was a full-length cartoon. Also a movie called *Melody Time*, about Pecos Bill, Paul Bunyan, Jiminy Cricket, and Johnny Appleseed. Roy Rodgers was in it too. What a good movie for us to see, but I liked the part about Pecos Bill the best. Walking home after the show, we all had our arms on each other's shoulders, and we were singing the song from the movie.

We are the Three Caballeros.

We're always together in fair or stormy weather.
We are the Three Caballeros.

Another time, Charles and David Gray were over, and we were in the garage playing. There was a bed rail lying in the dirt floor. I picked it up and put one end on the opening that must have been a window at one time. There was no glass in it anymore. So I slid the rail as far as I could and gave it a push. It dropped, and I heard a scream from outside the garage.

Charles and I ran around to the outside and found Orville lying on the ground, knocked out cold, blood squirting from the top of his head. Charlie ran to get our mother, and I lifted Orville's head off the dirt as he was coming to. Mom ran up and held him and applied pressure to the wound. We didn't take him to the doctor, but Mom carried him in and laid him on the bed. She held cold compresses to his head.

Orville said in later years, x-rays showed that his head had been fractured. I didn't know he was out there when I pushed the bed rail through the opening, and I thought it had just split the skin on his head. Poor little guy. I was so sorry. He was standing there watching the rail come out of the window, not knowing it was to be launched right at him. He didn't know his dumb brother was about to crown him on the head.

One Saturday morning, we heard a commotion out behind the chicken pen, so Orville and I went to investigate. It was Mr. Anderson with a truck and a tractor. He unloaded the tractor with a disk behind it and started to disk the weeds that were growing waist-high in the field between Mr. Byrd's house and our chicken pen, or garage. Also, on the east side between our house and Rotten Potato's. Oops, I'm was supposed to call him that anymore, my mother said, and she had ears in the back of her head.

As Mr. Anderson drove past us on his tractor, Orville and I both waved to him, and he waved back. We knew Mr. Anderson because he would come over to our house sometimes and dig up worms out by our septic tank so he could go fishing.

Our septic tank was always full to overflowing and running right out on the ground. The earth was soft and wet, and when he shoved his shovel into the ground, he would turn up huge earthworms that would wiggle around like crazy. If we came out to watch, he would hand us a quarter, and say, "Give this to your mother," and we took it into the house and gave it to Mom.

She told us, "Well, heavens to Betsy, he didn't have to do that," as she pocketed the quarter and wiped the hair back off her forehead.

We sat down under the pomegranate tree to watch while Mr. Anderson drove his tractor in circles disking the field. He got to the middle of the field where the weeds were the highest, and all of a sudden, the tractor disappeared. Mr. Anderson had driven smack dab into our big hole.

I told Orville, "Maybe we better get out of here in case Mr. Anderson gets mad."

So Orville and I moseyed around to the front of our house, just in case he went to tell our mom. After a while, we went back along the other side of the house to see what was going on out back. Mr. Anderson and the truck were nowhere in sight. He had just up and left.

I said, "Hey, Orville, want to go see what happened to our hole?"

We walked out through the newly disked ground to where our hole was, with the tractor still in it, with its front wheels at the bottom of our hole.

"Hey, Orville," I said. "We better get away from here, because if he comes back, he might tell Mom about the hole we dug, and we'll catch it good for digging that hole."

So Orville and I moseyed back around the house to one of the big walnut trees and climbed up high where no one would see us but we could observe everything taking place. If there was to be punishment coming, I wanted to put it off as long as I could.

Mr. Anderson had a son named Willard, and our theater didn't open until three o'clock on Saturday and Sunday afternoons. But at noon, Willard would be standing in front of the box office window so he could be the first person into the theater on Saturday at three o'clock. So if you drove past the theater at any time after noon, you would be seeing Willard standing all alone at the box office.

We always claimed Willard was Loreda's boyfriend, which she, of course, denied. But it was great fun teasing her about him. If she said, "Well, Elsie Jenkins was your girlfriend," then I would say right back, "Well, Willard Anderson was your boyfriend." We would laugh about how absurd it was for both of us because we didn't like being associated with these people because they were simpleminded folks, not at all like us.

It must have been more than an hour before Mr. Anderson came back with another man and backed his truck out into the field.

He was hooking a chain onto the disk so he could pull it away from the tractor. Then they hooked the chain back onto the tractor. The other man got into the truck, and Mr. Anderson climbed onto the tractor, and with both of them driving, they got the tractor out of the hole.

Orville and I watched as they finished disking the field and loaded the tractor back up on the truck. They chained it down so it wouldn't roll off the truck. Then here came Mr. Anderson walking toward our house.

"Hey, Orville, I bet he's going to tell on us. Let's go climb up higher in the walnut tree in case Mom wants to whip us."

Mr. Anderson went into our house, and after a while, he walked out, got into his truck, and drove off with the other man.

Orville said, "I wonder what he told Mom?"

"Shoot, I don't know. Let's wait awhile. Then you go in the house and see if we're going to get whipped."

"No, you go find out," Orville told me.

"Come on, Orville. Just go look in the window and see if she's mad.

"Okay, but you gotta go with me."

And Orville started climbing down out of the walnut tree.

"Okay, let's go find out what he told Mom."

We looked through the window but didn't see anyone. "I guess we'll have to go in if we want to find out what he said about us."

I let Orville open the door and walk in first, in case Mom was waiting behind the door to beat us the second we walked into the house. Mom was stirring a pot of lima beans on the stove when we walked in, and she didn't look too mad.

She said, "Did you boys dig a hole out back of the garage?"

"Yeah, Mom, but Charlie and David helped dig it too."

I never saw her whip Charlie and David, so if she knew they had helped dig the hole, maybe she won't whip us either. But it was a good opportunity for her to beat the heck out of us—something she rarely turned down, as she liked to hone her skills at child beating.

"Well, tomorrow I want you boys to go fill the hole in," Mom said. "And don't you boys dig any more holes they could cave in and kill you."

"Okay, Mom," I told her. "But can we wait until Charlie and David come over? They helped dig the hole too!"

"No, now get on out of here and let me get back to fixing these beans for supper. And tomorrow, I want that hole filled in. You boys better hear me now. That hole better be filled in by the time I get home from work, or I'm going to skin you alive."

I told Orville as we walked outside, "I don't see why Charlie and David couldn't help us fill it in. They helped dig it too."

Charles and David were like brothers to us. When we were little kids, we called Mrs. Gray Mama Gray. Once we were big enough, about ten years old, we shortened it to just Gray. I felt that she loved us like her own children. Every time they came over, I would want to go spend the night with Charlie and David. Charlie was twelve days older than me. He just called my mother Huff!

Our mother had met Mrs. Gray at the church she attended in Blythe. They cleaned the church together after the service. Then when my dad moved to Hemet, at some time, they moved there too. My dad must have moved to Banning before going to Hemet. His brother Zenith Ernest Huff was living in Banning, a small town close to Beaumont, about twenty-five miles southeast of San Bernardino. That's where Zenith died in 1930, as I stated in a previous story. Betty, my sister was born in Banning in 1930, she is six years older than me. So I think they had come from Blythe to Banning before my dad moved his family to Hemet.

I would say, "Gray, can I come spend the night with Charlie?"

"Heavens to Betsy Paul, all we have to eat is cornbread and beans!"

"I don't care," I replied. "I just want to spend the night and play with Charlie and David."

"Well, if you don't care if all you have to eat is beans and your mother don't care, I guess it'll be all right."

"Can Orville go too?"

"Well, honey, we only have that army tent, and there's not much room. Even you will have to sleep on a pallet in the corner of the tent with Charles."

"That's okay," I said, thinking of the fun Charlie and I would have riding our stick horses all over the countryside.

So it was Friday night, and I would spend all day Saturday with Charles and David. We would take our BB guns and stick horses and ride all over playing cowboys or war. There was a tree on a knoll above where they had set up the tent. Charles and I were climbing the tree as we always did. I was out on a limb, which someone had wrapped a heavy wire around. At one time, there was a tire hanging from the wire for a swing, but now the tire was gone, leaving only the wire.

Mrs. Gray called out, "Dinner is ready. You boys come and get washed up."

We started to get down out of the tree, and Charlie was close to the trunk. I wanted to beat him and get to the tent first. I swung my legs down onto the heavy wire and wrapped my legs around it. I grabbed the wire with my hands and slid down.

"BAWAH," I started crying.

There was a hook bent into the wire on the end where the tire had hung. The hook had gone through the crotch of my jeans and penetrated my scrotum. I was screaming like all get out, on my tiptoes, my feet barely touching the ground.

Charlie didn't know what was wrong, he told me later. He tried to lift me up but couldn't. Mrs. Gray, who had just called us for dinner, came running up the hill as fast as she could. She lifted me up and was able to unhook me. She laid me down on the ground and opened my pants. My testicles were torn out.

She was crying almost as loud as I was. She said, "Oh my god, Paul, what have you done?'

She carried me down the hill to the tent, and she washed and cleaned me up. She pushed my testicles back in and put tape on the wound to hold it closed. We didn't have any money, so we couldn't go to the doctor. The tear was three inches long; I healed all right, I know it was hard to walk for about a week. Thank God, I don't remember the pain I must have been in until it healed.

Gray told me years later how terrified she was that day. She couldn't see where the hook on the wire was. She had to lift me and hope the hook would detach by itself, which it did. Not a good day!

CHICKEN BUSINESS

My dad came home about only once a month. He was working in Trona, in the high desert northwest of Barstow. He was driving a truck for a mining operation. He told us he takes the bus from Hemet to Riverside, then another bus to Trona. He told us he lives in a barracks with some other men and that he has a cot to sleep on. He sends my mother a money order each week, usually fifteen to twenty dollars.

I remember Orville, Alice, Everett, and me playing in the side yard of the house around the walnut trees. Mom told us, "I believe Dad is coming home this weekend," when we came home from school that Friday afternoon. I was so excited because I loved my dad. I always cried when I had to hug him and say goodbye. I remember big ol' wet tears running down my face each time he left. I knew it would be a long time before I saw him again.

It was about six o'clock as I looked down the street for him for the hundredth time when I saw him just coming off the school grounds at the end of our street. Our side street, Thompson, dead-ended at the grounds of my grammar school (I was in the fifth grade). He was carrying his big trunk. All four of us kids took off running down the street screaming, "Daddy, Daddy, Daddy!"

I got there first, and as I got close, he set his big trunk down and caught me as I leapt into his arms. "Daddy, Daddy, Daddy," I kept repeating as I hugged him and gave him kiss after kiss. His whiskers were rough because he hadn't shaved since this morning, but I didn't care. Daddy was home.

After my hugs, he squatted down and hugged the others. With all the hugs and kisses over, he stood up and pulled what he called a barber pole out of his big leather coat pocket. The leather coat had a sheepskin lining sown in. What he called a barber pole was a big stick of peppermint wrapped in cellophane. It was about an inch in diameter and about eight inches long.

"Here, you carry that," he told Everett.

When we got home, he said he would break it into pieces so we could all have a piece. He scooped Everett, whom he called Dinky, up in one arm and picked up his trunk with the other hand. I put my left hand on the front corner of his trunk, just so I could feel close to him. Orville had his left hand on the back of his trunk. I guess he wanted to feel close too. Alice walked on his left side under Dinky, with her hand in Dad's coat pocket, hanging on to him.

Then up the street we went toward home. We came up the street from the back of the house and into a trail from the back to the door on the east side. My sisters Ernestene, Rita, and Betty walked out of the house to hug Dad. We all happily went in through the side door.

"Hello, Fritz." Dad gave Mom a hug and a kiss. For some reason, Dad had always called Mom Fritz, and when she wrote to him, she signed it, "Love, Fritz."

Mom was just putting dinner on the table. Dad told Mom he had asked Jack Cross, the driver from Riverside and owner of the Hemet Bus Lines, to let him off at Thompson and Florida Avenue. Jack didn't usually make a stop there, but he pulled up close to the curb and stopped so Dad could get off. He opened the door, knowing it would save Dad five blocks of walking and carrying the heavy trunk.

When Dad stepped down from the bus, Jack said, "Good night, Dick."

Dad waved his hand and said, "Good night, Jack." He set his trunk on the curb and slipped his coat on.

I don't remember what we had for supper. I was too excited that our dad was home. I would linger on his every word; I just loved him so much.

"You children been minding your mother?" he asked. "How about you, Dinky, you been behaving too?"

Everett just nodded his head yes.

Dad was telling Mom he thought we should buy some baby chicks and raise some chickens for eggs while he was home. We could raise them in the old garage out back of the house. That way, we would have plenty of eggs when they start laying. I couldn't tell what Mom thought of the idea. She was already working two jobs. She worked at the Hemet Laundry during the day. Then when she came home, she would beat us kids for whatever mischief we had been involved in during her absence that night.

Then she worked at the Alessandro Hotel until eleven at night. The hotel management let her bring any of the food off the steam table that was left after they had shut it down. It was things like green beans, creamed corn, roast beef and gravy, sometimes rolls; and there was always mashed potatoes left over. Mashed potatoes and gravy are still a favorite of mine.

"Dinky, you go get that barber pole out of my coat pocket," he told Everett.

Everett went to the trunk and sat by the door where Dad had left it when he came in.

Dad had taken his coat off and laid it across the trunk. I watched Everett run his little hand into one pocket, but no barber pole. Everett was just five years old, and Dad told him, "Try the other pocket, son."

Everett's eyes lit up as he struck pay dirt.

"Bring it to me," Dad said. Everett handed it to Dad, and whack! Dad struck it on the edge of the table. It shattered inside the cellophane.

Then Dad tore the cellophane open, and the pieces fell onto the table. "Okay," he said. "Have at it—Hey, wait a minute," Dad said to Orville, who was into the pieces with both hands. Dad made him open one hand. "Hell, son, the other children want some too. Fritz, you want a piece?" he asked as he put a piece in his mouth.

Mom reached down, took a piece, and put it in her mouth to suck on. It was great to have Dad home!

The next morning at breakfast, Dad said, "I think I'll walk down to the feed store and see about some baby chicks.

"Okay, Dick," she told him.

I guess they must have talked about it after we had gone to bed last night.

"Oh, can we go too?" Orville and I chimed in.

"You boys know it's clear across town. If you get tired, I can't carry you if I am carrying a box of baby chicks."

"We can make it, Daddy," we said.

"All right, come on. Just remember, you have to walk."

"Okay, Dad, we will."

We arrived at the feed store, and I was surprised that they did have boxes of baby chicks.

Dad said, "Are these Rhode Island Red chicks?"

The man said, "They sure are!" I was looking through the holes in the box at the baby chickens. There were fifty in the box for five dollars.

Dad turned to Orville and me and said, "You boys think you can carry a sack of feed each?"

The bags were premeasured at five pounds apiece. I told Dad, "I can carry one."

Orville was quick to say, "Me too, me too."

I think that was Orville's favorite thing to say. When Dad said, "Me want some waddymelon," Orville was quick to say, "Me too, me too, me too!"

Boy, it was a long way home carrying five pounds of feed. Lucky for us, Dad stopped every couple of blocks to let us rest. As we passed by the A&P Market, Dad said, "You boys want an ice cream?"

Our faces lit up as we said, "We do."

I said, "I want a milk nickel," and Orville said, "Me too, me too."

When you ate your milk nickel and the stick said "Free" on it, you got a free one. Today we were unlucky, but the ice cream was great. In fact, I'd never had any bad ice cream. After our rest stop for ice cream, we felt we could make the six more blocks home.

Dad brought the baby chicks into the house and put them in a front bedroom. He dug through a closet and came out with an electric cord with a light bulb on one end. He set the box with the chicks in it on the floor. Then he went outside and came back with a piece of chicken wire. It was bent into a half-dome shape. He bent the half dome of wire in so the light bulb would lie on it without touching the box. Then he took a piece of old cloth and laid that over the bulb and wire.

This way, the bulb didn't touch the box or the cloth. The chicks were all clustered into one corner of the box, trying to keep out of his way. He returned the lid to the box and plugged the cord into the wall socket. He checked his work to make sure nothing touched the light bulb. We were all watching him, and he told us now they had heat, to keep them warm until they were a couple weeks old. He said he would get some newspaper to put in the bottom of the box and told my sister Betty to change it daily.

"Okay, Dad," Betty said.

Dad told Betty that since he wouldn't be here to take care of the chicks, she would have to be his little helper.

"When can we move them to the garage?" Betty asked.

"Your mother will tell you when to move them," Dad replied. Out in the garage, he got a couple of old pie pans and puts a little of the feed into them. He had a round pan with holes in it and a place to screw a quart jar into the center. The chicks could stick their heads in there and get a drink without falling in. He put it all down in the garage floor and then told Betty, "When your mother says it's time, you can bring the box of chicks out and dump them onto the garage floor." Which, of course, was dirt.

One day after school, Mom told Betty to take the chickens out to the garage and turn them loose because they were getting feathers and were starting to stink. Betty got the chicks two at a time and carried them out to the garage. She told Orville and me we could each carry one too. With all the chicks in the garage, Betty watched them for a little bit and then shooed us out and closed the door to the garage.

There was a window, really just an opening on the north side, toward Mr. Byrd's house. "The chicks will get plenty of light from there," Betty said. "Well, boys, it looks like we're in the chicken business," she told us.

"I'll help take care of them, Betty, if you let me," I told her.

"We'll see," she said.

Not much to tell about those chickens until they start laying eggs. The eggs are brown, and the stupid roosters are mean. They started to chase Alice and Everett. Mom told them, "Stay away from the chickens.

Those roosters will peck your eyes out, and I keep my distance too. Sometime that biggest rooster would run at me. He scared me a couple of times. I knew he deserved watching."

One day Mom was hanging wash on the line when she heard a commotion behind her. The mean rooster was up on Everett's chest and was trying to peck his eyes out. Mom had a stick nearby that she used to get the clothes out of the hot washing machine. She grabbed it and chased that mean old rooster away. The rooster was just out of reach, strutting around as though he was cock of the walk.

Mom went into the house, put a big pot of water on the stove, and then returned to hanging her wash. Boy, on a hot day, it was fun to run through those clean, damp sheets. They were cool and smelled fresh. She would tell us, "Don't you boys get your dirty hands on my clean wash, or I will beat you to within an inch of your life."

We knew she meant it too. But sometimes it was hard to turn the corner without grabbing a sheet to make a sharp turn if my brother was right behind me chasing me because I had flipped his ear with my finger from behind, and he was hell-bent on paying me back.

Mom went into the house and came out with the hot water in a bucket that was kept in a corner of the kitchen for trash. She carried it over to a stump where a tree had been cut down sometime in the past and set it on the ground. Then she went into the garage and came back with a hatchet. She laid it on the stump and turned toward the garage. She came out with a can of chicken scratch and started throwing some on the ground.

I was wondering why she was feeding the chickens so early. Betty usually did that later. The chickens all came running and clucking to get the scratch Mom was throwing on the ground. She set her can of scratch down and came up behind the chickens bent over their feed and, like a snake striking, she grabbed that rooster by his legs. He squawked and fluttered his wings for a minute and then was still.

Mom took him to the block, laid his neck on it with her left hand, and, with her right hand, she picked up the hatchet. WHAM! She gave that rooster a fling. It ran about three or four steps with blood shooting out of his neck two feet in the air. Then he fell over and flopped around. Mom walked over, picked it up by its legs, and stuck it in the bucket of hot water. She said mostly to herself, "I'll learn you to peck those children's eyes," as she started to pluck the feathers out of that mean old rooster. This was Saturday. On Sunday, we had fried chicken for dinner after church. Sure was good too!

Our grandmother came to visit us in the house on Central Avenue. I can barely remember her because she was there for only a couple of weeks. Her name was Alice Dunn, and she had a brother named Ellis Dunn, who was a rich oilman in Texas. Ellis Dunn and his wife wanted to adopt my younger sister Alice when she was about six years old and took her to live with them in Texas around 1946.

Alice stayed with Ellis Dunn and his wife, Odessa, for about a year, and then they returned her to us in Hemet. My sister Betty just told me that Ellis Dunn's wife, Odessa, was playing around with the pilot of their airplane, and Ellis decided not to adopt Alice because of the affair his wife was having. I don't know why my mother even considered letting the Dunns adopt her youngest daughter, unless it was because we were so poor and she felt Alice would have a better life with Ellis and Odessa Dunn. I don't know if my dad was in on this adoption. I remember when Alice came back to live with us, she had a lot of nice new clothes. I remember being jealous of her new finery. Most of my clothes were jeans with holes in the knees.

Over time, I guess we weren't able to pay the rent. Mrs. Island, who we had rented the house from, had died, and somebody wanted us to move out. I don't really know how it all came about, but someone decided to pour a concrete floor in the old garage that we had used for a chicken pen. They nailed one-by-twelve-inch pine boards on the walls and ran a gas outlet and one or two electric lights in the ceiling.

So here we were, living in the chicken pen. I only remember trying to go to sleep at night and my sisters keeping the light on so they could do their homework. I clearly remember how much a light would bother me as I tried to go to sleep with that stupid light on. If my BB gun hadn't broken, I would take care of the stupid light. I still could not go to sleep with a light on as I was fidgeting around, flopping first one way then the other trying to get to sleep.

My sister Betty hated this one-long-room house that had been the chicken pen that we were moved into. She was embarrassed by it and was very unhappy. She told me she had a date with a boy one night, and when he brought her home, she had him stop by the side of the house that we had to move out of. Then she went around the house like she was going in but ducked down and went out to the old chicken pen and went in without turning on a light and went to bed.

When she saw him at school the next day, he wanted to know what happened. He said he had waited for her to turn on a light in the house before leaving so he would know she was all right. She told him she had gone to bed without turning on the light so she wouldn't wake her sisters.

Betty was graduating in just a month from high school, and she had made up her mind that she was getting the hell out of that chicken coup. As soon as she had graduated, she packed her things and moved to Riverside.

This was the summer I went to Fresno with my dad, and when we came back, the rest of the family had also moved to Riverside. Betty had taken a job babysitting for a woman named Mary Armstrong. Betty had Everett living with her at Mary Armstrong's. Mary moved to Texas later, and Betty went with her, and us younger children were made wards of the court. Then we were put in a foster home.

THE SUMMER OF 1947

The summer of 1947, Dad was taking me with him for the summer. As soon as school was out, we caught the bus to Riverside from Hemet, then hopped on a Greyhound bus to Fresno. Dad was headed to a town called Riverdale, south and west of Fresno.

My dad knew a lot of people all over Arizona, California, and Oregon. He said, "You have relatives living in Washington State." He was going to work for Vera Statham. Vera had a farm outside Riverdale. He hired Dad to work all summer leveling land for him. He had a son who had just come home from Germany and had brought a German wife with him. She didn't speak much English.

I can't remember the son's name, but Vera had three daughters as well. The youngest was about seventeen; she was cute with big boobs. It seems that was all I noticed on a woman when I was young. I am writing this as accurately as I can, and that's what caught my eye back then. I was ten years old, and that's what I remember about her.

I still have a picture of her in my head. She still has big boobs and is wearing the same orange halter top. I can't change my memory of her, so I won't try. My dad told me, "I'd like to tell her she should wear a brassiere because without it, her breasts will sag as she gets older."

See, Dad was looking too! It must run in the family. But he was afraid she would take it wrong (duh). I'm glad he didn't say anything, because I liked to look.

She would tell me, "Com 'ere and give me a kiss." I would tell her no and start to run away. She would chase after me, and I would run out into the alfalfa field with her right behind me. She would grab me from behind and pull me down into the green alfalfa and smother me with kisses. I'd be kicking and screaming, but she would just kiss me more.

Finally, she would turn me loose and go back to the house. This was in the evening after work. Vera and his wife and the other two daughters would be watching all this. They would all laugh at my plight. I liked this family a lot. Vera would give me a couple of boxes of .22 shells, and tell me, "Paul, the damn cottontails are eating the hell out of my alfalfa. Shoot everyone you see. Is it any wonder I grew up a killer. I had the urge instilled in me at a young age. I loved it too!

I would see pheasants once in a while, but I never killed one that summer. Not because I didn't shoot at them, because I did. I would walk the bank of the slough that bordered Vera's property. The water was running low and fish would group together in low places where there was still water. The back of the fish was sticking out of the water and cranes (my grandson informed me they weren't cranes), which looked like storks, were pecking the backs of the fish. They eventually killed the fish and ate them.

We had a bed under a big tree about one hundred yards from the house, and that was where we slept. My dad always parked the big John Deere tractor under the same tree at night. He would just unhook from the big Fresno scraper he was pulling to level the land and then drive the tractor home. Our big double bed had two high bedsteads, and Dad had a mosquito bar (as he called it) stretched over the bed to keep the mosquitoes off of us at night. The mosquitoes were huge and would try to get at us under the mosquito bar. I would go to sleep listening to the buzzing mosquitoes.

After Dad had worked there for about six weeks. He asked Vera to take him to some wrecking yards over on Highway 99. He wanted to find an old Ford Model A that he could refurbish to drive home in the fall. So off we went and stopped at several wrecking yards. Finally, Dad found what he was looking for—a 1931 Victoria sedan.

It needed an engine, or at least for him to rebuild the one that was in it. It needed rings, and the cylinder head was cracked. Someone had sold the radiator for junk. Dad bought the Ford, and Vera towed it home for him.

Dad was willing to prowl through junkyards once in a while to find the missing parts. He would work on it in the evening after driving a tractor for ten hours. He got a head and had it resurfaced so it was flat.

He put new rings in the pistons, new connecting rods. He also found a good radiator. I remember him working on the brakes, which were mechanical. It took several weeks to put it back into shape.

When he finished, Vera hooked up a chain and towed it to start it. It started right away, and it sounded good too. Dad would drive it around after work, just to break it in. He didn't want problems taking me home. I had to be home the last week of August to start school in September. Mrs. Statham had bought a parachute at an army surplus store in Fresno, and she made me a white silk shirt from some of the material. It was a nice shirt, and I remember liking it a lot, although it was summertime and the shirt was hot from the tight weave of the material.

Sometimes we would go into the town of Riverdale to see a friend of his, Lec Statham. I guess he was some kin to Vera Statham. Now, I think his name must have been Alex. Lec, as Dad called him, must have had rheumatoid arthritis; his knees were swollen and hard. He let me touch them, and they were like stone with skin over them. He could only lie in bed if propped up. He just lay there all day looking out of the window. That bed by the window was also where he slept. What a dismal life he had lying in bed and just watching the world go by from his bedroom window.

My dad's theory was that when he was a younger man, he rode a motorcycle over rough roads and all the vibrations had caused him to have arthritis. My dad knew him before he had these problems. Dad stayed and talked to him for about four hours. When we left, Lec profusely thanked Dad for stopping by. Dad promised Lec he would come by again before returning to Southern California.

One day Vera was stepping down from his truck and said, "Paul, come help me a minute."

I ran over to the truck, and he handed me a package. The wrapping was clear, and I saw an airplane body. The plane was flat, but I could see the shape of wings through the wrapping.

Vera said, "Be careful when you open it. The wings are made to snap into place!" That is just what they did. It was a perfect plane, with the wings open. When you turned the wings up, they would fold back against the body of the airplane.

There was a stick six inches long with a heavy rubber band. A notch was carved in the nose of the plane where the rubber band could be hooked. Then with the wings in the folded position, I hooked the rubber band. Then I held the stick in my left hand into the air, and with my right-hand fingers on the tail, I stretched the rubber band tight. I turned the tail loose and launched my plane into the sky.

It went up like a rocket. Once it reached maximum height, the wings opened, and the plane went in a big circle. Round and round until it landed. What fun I had.

The balsa-wood plane was sturdy too, and how I loved that plane. That family treated me so good. I remember now the girl who chased me and kissed me so much was Betty Statham. The summer was drawing to a close, and we had to come home and get ready for school. But I remember that summer in 1947 like it was yesterday because I had permission to shoot everything in sight.

Dad drove us back to Hemet—to find no one at the house we lived in on Central. One of the neighbors gave Dad an address in Riverside, California. My mother was living in the Gail Hotel while my sister Ernestene and my brother Orville were living at the St. Elmo Hotel down the street. The hotels were a block apart on Eighth Street, east of Main Street. After we found my mother, Dad left me and returned to Blythe, but not without many tears from me. My dad explained to me that Mom had said I could go visit him come Christmas Vacation.

It had been a great summer with my dad. All summer I only remember missing my brother Orville. When I had that airplane that Vera had given me, all I could think was that Orville would like this plane. Alice and Everett were still too young to play war or cowboys with me. After dad left me with my mother at the Gail Hotel, she told me, "Son, Orville's at the Fox Theatre, if you want to go find him!"

Orville still remembers me coming in and finding him in the dark theater. We had a whole summer to catch up on as he told me about living in a hotel, and I told him about my summer with Dad. Orville was disappointed that Dad had gone on to Blythe without seeing him.

We only had one pair of skates in those days, so Orville would take one and clamp it to his shoe. I took the other one and clamped it to my shoe. It was the same principle that applied to skateboarders: Just push with one foot until you're moving good. Then pick up the other foot and coast.

Orville and I would go sailing along on one skate all over Riverside. We especially liked going to the Mission Inn at the corner of Seventh and Main Streets in Riverside. It had been converted into a hotel. There was a pond with live catfish in it, and another with big goldfish. We would walk through the old Mission and peek into rooms that weren't rented. Somebody told us there was a secret passageway from the Mission all the way to Mount Rubidoux west of Riverside. We looked long and hard but could never find the secret passageway, but it was fun exploring the old Mission.

THE WALLERS' FOSTER HOME

This was the time our mother brought up the subject of us going into foster homes. In another story, I told about being made wards of the court and being sent to live with Mr. and Mrs. Waller—people we already knew from the First Baptist Church of Hemet. They were no longer members of that church; now they were members of the Tabernacle Baptist Church, and Mr. Poole was their pastor. I guess Mrs. Dodge, our caseworker, must have taken us there, but I can't remember.

The Wallers had a grandson named Jerry Collins and a granddaughter Nancy Collins living with them. So with us four and their two, they had six kids to take care of. Mr. Waller had sold his house and acreage on Florida Avenue and bought one hundred acres on South State Street. He had built a house on it and called the place Echo Hills Ranch. It was a nice place that sat on a low hill just off State Street.

There were hills to climb, fields to roam, and caves to explore. For boys, this was good as it gets.

He had two milk cows and about 150 Karakul sheep. He sheared and sold the wool to someone. He also sold lamb pelts from newborn lambs. The lambs had to be killed and skinned within a day, or the natural curl wouldn't stay in the pelts.

This pelt was very desirable for women's bags, hats, muffs, and for collars. Sometimes they would sew a cuff on coat sleeves made from lamb's pelt.

The lambs that were to be kept had to have their tails docked—meaning the bottom portion of the tail was removed.

Mr. Waller gave me a quarter a week to come home from school and take the sheep out of their pen and let them graze on the hillside of their property. There was a lot of grass growing on the hillsides, as Hemet received more rain in the fifties than it does today. I let them graze for an hour and a half, and then I would herd them back into their pen. Then I would head for the house for supper after the chores were all done.

Right away, after moving there, Mr. Waller started to build a cement reservoir to hold water where the sheep could drink. Mr. Waller taught me how to mix concrete. He taught us how to drill a hole in rock with a star point chisel and a hammer. Hitting the star drill and rotating it at the same time would make a nice hole in the rock.

Then he showed us how to take a half stick of dynamite, push a hole in it with an awl, then take a cap and a short piece of fuse and put the fuse into the cap and bite it to crimp the end. Then insert the capped fuse into the dynamite and insert the dynamite into the hole drilled in the rock.

Mr. Waller told us, "If you want the blast to go down, put a gob of clay on the top to force the blast to go down."

We had to blast four or five big rocks out of the way of the road he was building, from his house down past the reservoir to the sheep pen at the bottom of the hill.

Off to the side of this road was where he had his two milk cows, Sally and Little Bit. Mr. Waller told us that when the reservoir was finished, we could swim in the cement pond where the sheep were to be drinking. But when it was filled that summer, there was moss and algae growing in it because of the hot summer weather. It was full of sheep slobbers. I did not want to get into the water. Orville said he didn't want to get into it either. Everett thought it looked yucky.

It turned out to be wishful thinking anyway because the well that he had dug on his property went dry when the water table dropped. I now wonder why he didn't have a well driller come in and drill a deeper well. All of a sudden, there was not enough water for bathing or using the bathroom.

So with the well dry, he bought a Ford truck and had a big tank welded up and installed above the cab of the truck. He already had a big water tank mounted on a hill just north of the house. The old well used to pump water to the tank, and then gravity would feed it down to the house. It didn't have much water pressure, but it worked all right.

With the well dry, he obtained a permit to take water from a fire hydrant close to town. He could fill the tank on the truck when he was on his way home from town.

He had a hose from a pump on the truck, which he would run to pump the water from the tank on the truck to the tank on the hill. They were strict about not wasting water. If us boys wanted to pee, we were to go outside. At least I learned to write my name real well. They also had an outhouse that we could use. We bathed only once a week to save water.

When we first arrived at the Wallers', they had an old '39 Buick sedan. After we had been there for about a year, Mr. Waller bought a 1949 Kaiser. It was neat, with push button knobs to open the doors. The Kaiser was a very modern-looking car for the time. He said it didn't have any wood in it except a piece over the spare tire in the trunk. He claimed this was very good because someone he knew had been in an accident in a station wagon, and a piece of the wood had impaled the person and killed him.

So to him, it was essential not to have any wood in the construction of the car, and the Kaiser was his choice. He drove it only on Sunday and Wednesday night, mostly to church or prayer meetings. We had to be in our Sunday best to ride in this car.

Mr. Waller would build box traps to catch rabbits. He had three traps set in holes where cottontail rabbits had a place to crawl under his fence. We would check the traps each morning and evening. The tin trapdoor would drop down when a rabbit tried to cross over it and deposit a rabbit inside. The weight on the back of the trapdoor would close the trap again. Sometimes we would have two or three rabbits in the trap when we checked it. We ate a lot of rabbit, and I still like cottontails. I prefer them over the white rabbit fryers you could buy in the stores in the fifties.

Mr. Waller fed us as cheaply as he could, but he also ate what we ate. He was just thrifty, kind of like how I've been my whole life. Maybe I got it from him; it doesn't hurt to be thrifty. With extravagance, you don't appreciate what you have. When you're conservative, you appreciate what you have more.

I think if you want something, don't go into debt or to your bank account to draw the money out for it. If you save for it, it will mean more because you worked to save the money to buy it. Sometimes after saving for something, I found out that I wasn't as crazy for it as I had been at the start. Maybe they came out with a newer or better version of what I wanted by the time I had saved the money. This is just one of the rules I've lived by. If you work and save for something, it will mean more to you in the end. Enough said.

Mr. Waller would drive into town every evening and go around behind the markets to pick up the green waste (lettuce, spotted bananas, apples with bad spots, celery, and cabbage that wasn't good enough to sell), just the trimmings from the produce of the market. He made arrangements with the markets to do this, and it helped the market too. They didn't have to pay someone to come pick it up before it spoiled and stank, because flies would be a problem too.

Mr. Waller's truck was a stake bed truck. Because it was used to pick up the trimmings from the produce, he had to enclose the truck. So he had nailed tin over the slats on the side of the gates. Jerry Collins, Orville, Everett, and I would ride inside of the enclosed truck bed. When we came to a stop, we would climb over the gates and down on the trailer hitch, which was about three feet wide. Then we would jump down on the road and run until the truck was going so fast we couldn't keep up. Then we would jump up on the trailer hitch bar and climb back in. At the next stop sign, we would do the same thing until we got tired.

One day Jerry Collins let the truck go too fast, and he fell into the street and rolled. "Holy smokes, someone should tell Mr. Waller so he could stop for Jerry."

No one wanted to tell him because we were afraid we'd get in trouble for jumping down from the truck and running. We just sat there looking at each other, wondering who was going to tell, but nobody told him.

When we got home, Mr. Waller pulled down by the sheep pen, got out of the truck, and then came back to unload the green waste.

"Where's Jerry?" he asked.

"We must have left him at the market," we lied.

"Well, why didn't you tell me?" Mr. Waller said.

"We didn't notice he wasn't here until just now," we lied.

Mr. Waller said, "Get back in and we'll go get him."

Shoot! We had to ride clear back to town, and it was cold by now. We got almost back to town, and there was Jerry, walking along the road heading home.

Jerry had to explain the scrapes and scratches, so he said he was running to catch us in the alley as we left the store, and he fell down and skinned his leg. Sometimes lies are good things. They save your ass!

When we came to the entrance to the Echo Hills Ranch, Mr. Waller would pull up by the mailbox and get out to see if it was safe to turn left into the driveway. His rearview mirror didn't stick out far enough to see back. To save him from having to get out and look back, we would start hollering, "NO CARS!" Then he would just turn into the driveway without stopping or signaling. He had a lever inside the cab that he could pull down to make a turn signal, but the arm extended only about three inches beyond the stake bed of the truck and wasn't very visible to anyone wanting to pass a slow-moving truck.

We felt as though we were handy little critters, riding in the back and shouting, "NO CARS!" Well, there was one occasion: We were coming home from town, and it was really cold. I mean, this was the dead of winter. All four of us were huddled together under a blanket down on the floor of the truck trying to stay warm.

We always knew when we were close to home because there was a small hill we went down, and Mr. Waller would start slowing down.

I said, "Jerry, get up and see if there's any cars."

Jerry said, "No way, I'm cold!"

"Well, I'm cold too. Orville, would you get up and look, please?" I asked.

"No, I'm too cold!"

Everett, who was little, didn't want to look either. I don't remember who hollered first. I think we just all hollered, "NO CARS!"

Mr. Waller started his turn into the driveway.

E R R R R R R T. BAM.

Suddenly we weren't too cold to stand up and see what had happened. Some people in a car thought we were slowing to stop at our mailbox, and the driver had started to pass since he didn't see any signal from the truck. Then when Mr. Waller suddenly made a left turn, the car went into the drainage ditch along the left shoulder of the road to keep from hitting us. There was a corrugated drainpipe for water to pass under our driveway, and that was the BAM we heard as the car hit that pipe.

Nobody was hurt, thank the Lord, but we all could have been killed, or injured in some way. Mr. Waller was hopping mad.

"Why did you children shout no cars?" I had already asked Jerry to take the blame. Jerry was their grandson—they wouldn't kill him like they would Orville or me, and Everett was too little to put any blame on. Jerry came through like a little trooper. He saved us all.

He told his grandfather he had risen and looked, and then he saw all open road behind the truck. But looking over the high gates on the back of the truck, he couldn't see the car following close behind us. All parties concerned were satisfied with the explanation. The couple in the car were pretty shaken up, and their front end was out of alignment, but they were able to drive on. Needless to say, Mr. Waller never trusted us again. Thanks to Jerry Collins, we were spared a sudden death that day, and I lived to write this story.

"You children want to go on a hike today with me", Mr. Waller asked us at breakfast one morning? I'm going to hike up to the ridge behind the springs, to cut a Mountain Laurel. We'll bring it down with us and decorate it for Christmas. "I'll go" I said. Orville and Jerry wanted to go too. Jerry's sister Nancy, our sister Alice, and Everett were too young to make the hike. Mr. Waller had some snacks in a bag and a canteen of water. He also had a small saw to cut a limb off a mountain laurel.

When we left the house going toward the springs, we had to climb over a stile. Mr. Waller had built a stile so you could climb over the fence as though with a ladder. When you came to a fence on each trail around his property, instead of crawling under or over the wire, you could climb right up the steps of the stile and down the other side. I was impressed. And you didn't push the fence down and make it sag.

As we went past the natural springs, there were young willow trees growing below the springs. In the spring, the willows had buds on them called pussy willows, they were pretty cut and put in a vase of water, but this was winter so no pussy willows.

As we were leaving the spring behind, the hiking became steep. We would pause often to rest and look out on the valley. West was Winchester, south was Aquanga, and north was Hemet. We got to where the mountain laurel was growing by about 10:30 a.m. Mr. Waller chose a limb about six feet long and cut it off.

We ate our snack and drank most of the water on the way up, but going downhill back to the springs would be a piece of cake. What took more than a couple of hours to climb you could descend in twenty or thirty minutes. If you were thirsty, you were motivated to get to the spring for a cold drink of water.

In the spring and summer, there were tadpoles and mosquito larva in the springs, but this was winter, so there were no little critters about. The water was cold and clear. Mr. Waller was always talking about improving the springs and maybe selling spring water. Sometimes we would help him muck it out down to bedrock, but even then, it was only a foot or so deep.

He also talked of blasting it, to see if the stream of water would improve. He was also afraid it would damage the granite base and the spring would dry up. After we left there in April 1950, he did have a little hut by his gate where you could purchase spring water by the gallon, so he had piped it down after all.

We were back with our mountain laurel Christmas tree. It looked really nice decorated. After supper each evening, with chores and dishes done, Mr. Waller would read a chapter from the Bible. He would often pause and talk about a certain passage we were reading about this or that.

He would say, "It was two thousand years from Adam and Eve until Jesus, and then if Christ is consistent, it would be two thousand years until Christ's return. But also, no one knows the day or the hour except God. If someone says God or Christ will return on a certain date, you can be absolutely sure that Christ won't return on that date. As God has said, no one knows the day or the hour." I wondered why the secrecy.

Mr. Waller was also Orville's and my Sunday school teacher at Tabernacle Baptist Church. There was one boy, Lawrence Whiting, who would sit down at the piano and play the boogie-woogie. We loved it, but church members frowned on it, believing it was the devil's music. Still it was fun to hear the boogie-woogie being played in church until it was stopped.

One Sunday, we arrived at church a little early, so Orville, Jerry, and I and some other boys were in the gravel parking lot playing. Someone saw a bee's nest hanging from the eave of the church. So us boys got some rocks and started throwing them at the nest. We had hit it a few times, and the bees were really mad. Honey was dripping from the honeycomb. Church members would drive into the parking lot, but the bees were so thick that they had to go find a place on the street to park.

After Sunday school and church, the bees had pretty much settled down. We were all reprimanded but good. They said it was the work of the devil, and I guess maybe it was, but boys just have to have something to throw at or launch a spear, arrow, or a bullet at. I think it all started with the cavemen. It's just that our weapons have improved today. I could have really done a number on the bees with my slingshot, but it was home awaiting my return.

Once a month, different churches around Hemet would hold what was called a Singsperation. It was gospel groups, quartets, trios, and duet singers singing good old gospel songs for a couple of hours. I loved to go, and I still like good old-time gospel music. Our choir at the church comprised of Mr. and Mrs. Waller, Dorothy Adams, LaVie Adams, Jerry Adams, and another young man whose last name I think was Todd, I can't remember for sure. I believe he was a bass singer. I thought they sounded great.

Pastor Poole always preached a good sermon. But he was always preaching to one wall or the other, never really looking at the congregation. Alice Poole, his wife, played the piano, and my sister Alice was named after Alice Poole. I liked this church. Mr. Poole later on had a radio program that aired on Sunday evenings, but since it was a local station in Hemet, we couldn't get it in Riverside.

I forgot to mention that the swing to end all swings was moved from the house on Florida Avenue to the house at the Echo Hills Ranch. I would have liked to see how he pulled the telephone poles out of the ground and reinstalled them at the new house. I didn't think to ask him how he accomplished this feat. I do know this: from the things I saw him do, he was plenty capable. When he set his mind to something, he could do it. Maybe he put a hole down beside the two poles, inserted some dynamite in the two holes, and blasted them into the air. Then while they were airborne, he could pull his truck under them and they would land in the back. And then he could haul them to the new location. To this little boy, it could be possible for him to do this. I just didn't think to ask him to find out if that was what he had done to move the poles out to Echo Hills Ranch.

BARBARA WEBB

We are living with the Wallers in Hemet in 1949 and going to school there. I was in the seventh grade, my first year of junior high school, and Mrs. Mary E. Willy was my homeroom teacher. I found it hard to get used to changing classes every period. The bell would ring, and we would grab our books and head to our locker to put those books away and grab the ones for the next class.

Life seemed more hectic. Run here, run there, don't forget your notebook, take notes in class, and write down homework assignments. I'm out of breath, and I'm only writing about it fifty-five years later. Aaaah. I'm ready to quit school all over again. I missed grammar school already, and it was only my first day of junior high. I didn't realize how smooth and uncluttered my life was until now. I wish I could go back to the old days and the old ways. Junior high doesn't even have recess.

What do you mean there's no time to play anymore? I just played all summer after graduating from the sixth grade. I was not ready to grow up. I was just playing cops and robbers a few days ago with my brothers and shooting up the countryside with our cap guns. Now all of a sudden, I had to act like an adult and look studious. I didn't think so. I didn't know if I was ready for this fast-paced world I was suddenly thrown into. Oh well, what was my teacher saying? Sex education. Well, now we're getting somewhere.

Mrs. Willy was going to teach us sex education in addition to homeroom. I thought, *Finally we're getting to the good stuff. Maybe this adult stuff won't be too bad.* I had already noticed that Mrs. Willy was pretty and had an hourglass figure to boot. *Life is good.*

"You boys and girls feel free to ask any questions you want to."

I noticed we were boys and girls for the first time. Just three months ago, when we graduated from sixth grade, we were called children. Finally we were making the transition from children and were on our way to being adults, and I was noticing the boys were getting whiskers on their faces.

Richard LeVan, who I had gone through grammar school with, raised his hand.

"Yes, Richard, you have a question?" Mrs. Willy asked.

Richard asked, "What's Chinese blue balls?"

Everybody laughed. "No, no, class, don't laugh," she told us. "Richard has heard someone say this, and he's curious about what it refers to, isn't that right Richard?"

Mrs. Willy said, "There are many different venereal diseases. This is something that has made a man's testicles swell and become large." I'm not going to write about everything we learned. The fallopian tubes, uterus, ovaries, menstruation, pregnancy. For Christ's sake, you already know all of this stuff. I don't need to draw you a picture. Oh yeah, how to achieve pregnancy. I mean, we learned it all. I was ready to go out into the world and start reproducing.

I felt a good place to start was Barbara Webb. She rode our school bus, and she was slim and very pretty with blond hair. I was in love again, and this time it was real. Not like the puppy love I'd known before. This was a heart-stopping romance. I hadn't even told Georgia Powell or Erlene Owen how much I had liked them.

Here was Barbara Webb riding our school bus, and I mean, she was right behind me. I would be able to tell her how much I liked her; all I had to do was turn around. So I turned around just to say hello.

God, she's pretty, I was thinking. I mean, she was a real live doll.

Before I could say anything, about how I felt, she spoke to me.

"Paul."

Oh my god, she knew my name already.

"Aren't you friends with Bobby Todd?"

"Yeah, I've been friends with Bobby since first grade." Bobby's parents had a home across the street from the Hemet laundry where my mother worked, and since we were friends, I would stop by to play from time to time. I had also played marbles and bottle caps with him in grade school.

"Why?" I asked.

"Well, would you give him this note?"

"Sure," I said. I saw Bobby all the time, and I was happy to do anything for Barbara.

She said, "Don't read it, okay?"

"Okay," I said.

"Promise?" she asked.

"Barbara, I promise I won't read it." But I had my fingers crossed. Everybody knows a promise is not good if you make it with your fingers crossed.

I got off the bus with my brothers and my sister Alice and Jerry and Nancy Collins. As I walked up the hill to the house, I opened the note and read it. The note was short and to the point. She told him how cute she thought he was, and what did he think of her? She liked Bobby, so I folded the note and lifted it to my face to see if it had any perfume on it. Then I put it into my pocket.

I'll give it to Bobby tomorrow at school, if he's lucky.

Harry Peacock, Bobby Todd, and I were pals in the seventh grade. Harry always wore a navy peacoat when it was cold. When we went through the cafeteria line to get milk at noon, we could get it for only five cents for a small carton. While we were in line to pay for the milk, we had to pass the cooler that held the ice cream. We would each take an ice cream and stick them in Harry's pockets. His coat had really big pockets. At least we would have dessert after we drank our milk. That's when I found out stolen ice cream tastes just as good as bought ice cream.

The next day, I saw Bobby Todd in the hallway.

"Here, Bob, Barbara Webb rides my bus, and she sent you this note."

"What's it say?" he asked.

"I don't know, read it," I lied.

I thought, *I guess I'll never have a girlfriend. All the boys have grown tall over the summer, and most have whiskers, to boot. I don't have jack shit, not even peach fuzz. The girls are attracted to these tall hairy guys. They want a man that can sweep them up into their arms and run away with them. Heck, I can barely carry my books. I'm just too small for my age.*

Still, my eyesight was good, and I could appreciate a good-looking girl. Barbara was the kind of girl a boy wanted to put up on a pedestal. Some of my friends were actually dating. They were taking girls to the movies and talking about buying them popcorn and Cokes. Heck, I didn't even have enough money for lunch. I was still brown-bagging it. I couldn't afford to go to the show by myself, let alone have money for the girl's ticket.

But I did go to a show when I visited my mother once a month in Riverside. My mother never had any money either. She told me, "Son, if you want to go to the show, you'll have to go ask Don for a quarter."

Don Garner was washing the dishes for a restaurant down the street from the Riverside Grill.

Mom got to know him in Hemet while working at Tahquits Café, where Don was washing dishes at the time. My sister Betty also worked there as a waitress. I think now what a nice man he was. He was just washing dishes for a living and didn't have much change he could spare, but he always came through with a half dollar or so for the movies. He had been an alcoholic, and he said he would rather give us show money than spend it on liquor.

Mr. and Mrs. Waller didn't approve of going to the movies. They had a radio, but I never heard them turn it on. The church frowned on such things. No lipstick or rouge either. Mr. Waller told me not to waste my time reading fiction: "That is just a lie someone thought up and not worthy of your time."

I guess I must have listened to him because I prefer nonfiction. In school I liked books about mountain men like Kit Carson, Jim Bridger, and Lewis and Clark. I liked to read about exploring and trapping. I loved the thought of living off the land, more or less like the Indians did. Nothing permanent like the Indians did with the teepees.

If it got too hot or too cold, you could just drag your home someplace else. If a neighbor gave you trouble, just drag your home over the next hill, out of earshot. Unless the neighbor had a cute daughter, then just move in with him and learn to live with it.

In junior high, we had to suit up for sports. My mother had to come up with money for shorts and, excuse me, a jockstrap.

Where the heck does this weird-looking thing go? These elastic rubbers look like they would make a neat slingshot, I thought.

Our shorts were maroon, with a gold stripe down each leg. The class sweaters were the same color, and you could win a school letter if you were good in sports. Guess who didn't have a sweater or a letter? No cheating now!

The school sweaters were about fifteen dollars. That was fourteen ninety-nine more than I had to my name. I guess we weren't broke, but we were badly bent. Foster parents couldn't care less if you had a class sweater. We were lucky to get lunch money on a rainy day.

I remember Bob Todd riding, or falling, through Brandon's candy shop glass door. I can't remember how it happened, but I remember the scar on his nose. The broken glass must have sliced it, either when he went into it or when he fell down. I saw Bob Todd at a school reunion in about 1994; he said he didn't remember me.

He was selling real estate up around Santa Barbara. He looked different; I noticed he had his hair permed. He didn't marry Barbara Webb. What a waste.

I saw John Bartlett, another friend from Hemet in 1975, and he told me Harry Peacock (of stealing ice cream fame), drowned in a pond outside of Hemet. John said Harry was trying to retrieve a duck he had shot, and the cold water had given him cramps so bad he drowned. Anyway, that's what John told me. Another friend from grade school, Tommy Level, had committed suicide, they told me at that same reunion.

Tommy explained the f-word to me in third grade. When he used it, I asked, "What's that mean."

He told me, "That's when your dad gets on top of your mother naked."

I thought, *My folks don't do that. I've never even seen them with their clothes off. I think he's wrong about this. How sick! His parents must be weird if they do it.*

When in grammar school, I never had a baseball mitt. Some kids would bring their mitts to school and use them while playing ball. I remember Tommy Level asking me as we were leaving school one afternoon if I would like to hang around and catch some flies. I said, "Sure, what will we catch them in? Want me to run home and get a jar?"

"No," he said. "I'll hit the baseball into the air with my bat, and you catch it and throw it back."

The first time I tried to catch the ball, it stung my hands so bad I dropped the ball. Tommy said I needed a baseball glove. "Why don't you run home and get it," he said since I lived only a block away. I was embarrassed to tell him I didn't have any stinking baseball glove. Instead, I said okay and went home. But I never went back to play with him. I never owned a baseball glove, a football, a basketball, or a tennis racket. If someone had asked if I wanted to shoot some hoops, I would have said, "Sure," and then run home to get my slingshot or BB gun.

The only thing my brothers or our friends Charles and David knew how to play was war games or cowboys and Indians. I never owned a baseball bat either. I didn't own a bike until I was thirteen years old. When we were living at the Wallers', I got a job one summer cutting apricots for Mrs. Baron. She had a big goiter on her face and neck.

In the past, my mother and my sisters had cut apricots for her, and she was always happy to have help getting the apricots cut and laid out to dry. We cut the apricots and placed them on big wooden trays. Men would pick up your tray when it was full and place it on a cart. After the cart got so high, they pushed it to a house where sulfur was burned. Then they were left in the sulfur house overnight before they were placed in the hot sun to dry the next day.

We were paid by the field box to cut the apricots. Big apricots you could cut pretty fast, but if you got a box of what we called marbles, it would take twice as long to cut that box. When your box of apricots was empty, they would bring a full box, punch your card, and take away your empty box.

After your trays were four high, you called, "Trays away," and they came and took away the four trays, and then you started over. I worked there three weeks in 1949 and made thirty dollars. I found a used Schwinn bicycle for thirty bucks and bought it. The Schwinn bike had knee action forks on it, and I took it home and removed the front and rear fenders. I had spent my whole three weeks' wages on that bike, but it was worth it.

I loosened the handlebars and took them out and turned them over. Only sissies rode their bikes the way a girl did. I was in hog heaven; I could not believe I finally owned my own bike. A Schwinn bike was the best you could buy, in my opinion, even if it was used.

After working cutting apricots that summer, Mr. Waller had bought a field of corn from some farmer. He cut the stalks of corn down and tied them into bundles, and we carried them up a plank and loaded them into his truck. We were hauling it home to feed to his sheep. There were tomatoes growing under the corn stalks—big beef-steak tomatoes, six or seven inches in diameter.

Mr. Waller had a lot of lug boxes that he saved from picking up the green waste behind the markets, so he would carefully cut the tomatoes loose from the vines and pack them into the lug boxes. Jerry, Orville, and I carried them up the plank and stacked them in the truck. Once the truck was full, Mr. Waller would put the tailgates back into the truck.

Upon arriving back at the ranch, he would stop past the house to unload the boxes of tomatoes. Then he would go down the hill to the sheep pen to unload the stalks of corn. If the sheep hadn't cleaned up what we dropped off the day before, we stacked it in the barn for later use. Mrs. Waller had the tomatoes wiped off and looking good in the lug boxes. Some of the lugs of tomatoes were sold around town to smaller markets, but some were sold at a stand at the entrance to the ranch on State Street.

They sold them on the honor system. Take how many you wanted and put the money for them in the slotted box that was there for that purpose. Mrs. Waller said there was usually more money than there were tomatoes missing. Someone probably didn't have the right change, so they left extra.

I think it took about a week to cut all the corn down and truck it home. But at least he had a good reserve laid in for winter. He also had rice hulls to feed to the sheep that he had purchased somewhere. And remember, I was taking them out to graze on the hillside each day after school. We had a lot of milk from the two cows, Sally and Little Bit. Mrs. Waller churned butter from it and also made cottage cheese.

She would let the milk turn to clabber and then pour off the liquid. Then she would take the clabber part and put it into a clean cloth and hang it from the wash line to let the breeze blow through it. That would dry out the curds as she turned it throughout the day. It didn't look anything like cottage cheese you buy in the stores today. It was dryer, and with a little salt and pepper, it tasted really good. And if you wanted it a little wetter, just add a little milk back into it.

I had bought six white baby ducks to raise. When they were big enough to lay eggs, Mrs. Waller paid me thirty cents a dozen for them, and we ate the eggs for breakfast. I also had guinea pigs; I just really liked to raise animals and birds. Selling the eggs to Mrs. Waller gave me the money to buy feed for both the guinea pigs and the ducks.

SNOW IN HEMET

The winter of 1948–49, it snowed in Hemet. We came out of the house one morning, and there was three inches of snow on the ground. We had to line up in the kitchen for our daily dose of vitamins and minerals. Mr. Waller would buy Cal-O-Dine by the carton, and four gallon jugs to a carton. Cal-O-Dine was essential vitamins and minerals that helped to sustain a strong body. God, what an awful taste it had. We would just chugalug it without stopping so we wouldn't gag.

You can tell how good something is for you by how bad it tastes. I mean, this crap was *nasty*, so it should have been the fountain of youth. Mr. Waller drank his and smacked his lips like it was good.

"You children sit down and eat. You got up late this morning," Mrs. Waller said. Then she added, "You don't want to miss the school bus."

If we were coming down the hill to the bus stop, Sally would stop and wait for us while we would run on down. But if we hadn't left the house yet, he would just sail right on by. He claimed he had a schedule to meet and he couldn't dillydally, while we dillydallied.

Boy, this morning was colder than a witch's tit. We were waiting for the school bus, waving our arms and jumping up and down—anything to keep warm. My younger brother Everett had sandals on with white socks. His little feet were freezing as he stood there in the snow. He saw an old cardboard box that someone had thrown out beside the road and went over and got it to stand on. At least his feet were out of the snow, but they were wet and cold. He told me his feet were freezing, and I told him maybe the bus would be here any minute. I was looking down the road, and we could see three or four miles, and no sign of the bus. So it wouldn't be a matter of minutes, and they still had to stop for the kids on Mission Valley Road.

There was no traffic on State Street at all this morning, although I did see a couple of car tracks in the snow. But there were no cars coming from either direction, especially from the south where our bus would come from.

I looked once more just to be sure, and then I told everyone, "I'll run up the hill and tell Mrs. Waller the bus isn't coming. You guys watch in case you see it coming up the road! If you do, just holler and I'll come back. Okay? I'll see if we can come back to the house to get warm. Everett, maybe you can change your socks."

Everett nodded his approval as he told me again that his feet were freezing. I got back to the house, and Mrs. Waller wanted to know why I was back. I told her, "The bus isn't coming. Can we come back to get warm?"

"No, you'll miss the school bus," she told me.

"But it isn't coming!" I told her again. "And Everett's in sandals."

"Well, that's what your mother bought him, so he'll just have to make do with what he has," she told me.

"Well, could Mr. Waller drive us to school in the car?"

"No," she told me. "Dad can't get the car down the hill because it's too slick." Yes, she called him Dad. "He could lose control and wreck the new car. Well, heaven forbid he wrecks the new car. It's okay if we freeze, but let's not wreck the new car. You children will just have to start walking." She was all heart.

"If the school bus makes it through the snow, they will stop on the road and pick you up."

"Can't we stay home today?" I asked.

"NO! Now go on and start walking, and I'm not telling you again." I could see her face was all red because she was irritated with me. I knew better than to argue with her because she lit into me more than once, and I knew she would be happy to do it again. I didn't feel like giving her the pleasure today, so I started back to the bus stop.

Everett had a problem with wetting the bed. He just slept so soundly he wouldn't wake up. We had a coffee can by the bed so we didn't have to run all the way to the fence just to pee at night in the cold. I would wake him every time I woke up, but that wasn't enough. They tried giving him a nickel every time he didn't wet the bed, and that would work once in a while. But when he had an accident, they claimed he was just too lazy to get out of bed. Like anybody was so lazy they would wet the bed and then have to lie down on it.

Mrs. Waller would get angry because she had to wash extra bedsheets. Remember, water was a problem. We had to haul it from town. She would yank the sheets off the bed and put it around his shoulders and fasten it with a clothespin. She would make him wear it until it was time to go to the bus. One morning, I'd had enough of their crap.

They were ranting and raving about him wetting the bed because he was just lazy.

I said, "Why don't you leave him alone? He can't help it." Orville was also standing there.

Mrs. Waller shouted, "GET HIM, DAD. Don't let him talk to you like that."

Mr. Waller grabbed me and lit into me and gave it to me good. He told me not to ever interfere in this again. "Your brother is just lazy."

At least when they determined I was the real bad guy, they left Everett alone. Everett doesn't remember this happening, but Orville and I do. Everett was pretty small, so I'm not surprised he can't remember. I'll bet he remembers walking to school in those sandals, though. When your feet are cold that long, you remember it for a long time.

Okay, I' was back at the gate, and I told everyone, "She said we have to walk."

It was about two miles into town, then another mile to the school. Everett's school was a little closer; it was on the south of town. But the junior high was on the northeast side of town. I remember getting to school cold and late. I just can't remember anything else about that day at school except the bus was there after school to take us home. I think the snow had melted by then. NOT A GOOD DAY!

Okay, so Orville and I got into some trouble while we were still living in the Wallers' home. Orville and his friend Donald Schofield broke into a sporting goods store and took a couple of guns and some ammunition. They brought them out to the Wallers', and I helped them shoot up the ammunition.

Our dad was in the general hospital in Riverside for something that was wrong with him. I can't recall what was wrong now. Orville told Dad about robbing the store, thinking Dad would be pleased. Our dad was always talking about something he had stolen somewhere.

Well, Dad told Mom, and she said, "As soon as you boys get back to Hemet, you go to the police station and turn yourselves in."

I was fourteen, and Orville was twelve years old. We were put in juvenile hall in Riverside, California.

We spent three weeks there before we were placed in new foster homes.

There were some fishing licenses that had been stolen and burned. The state of California wanted seventy-five dollars for the missing license. Part of our probation was that we had to repay the seventy-five dollars. Our dad was the one who had to pay it. We were asked if we wanted to return to the Wallers', and we said no.

I for one was too ashamed of being in juvenile hall to want to return to the schools in Hemet. I guess I wanted to start fresh someplace else and not face my classmates in Hemet. I loved the town of Hemet, and I would go back from time to time. It was no longer the little sleepy town it once was. It was congested and crowded just like the rest of Southern California. But for me, it will always be my hometown. What a great place for a boy to grow up. I could walk a mile out of town and shoot rabbits, or even quail.

My sister Loreda would drive Dad's car while Dad and I sat astraddle of the headlights and Dad shot cottontail rabbits that would be sitting beside the road. We would take them home, and Dad would clean them, and Mom would cook them for supper. I'm sure there must have been some crime in Hemet while I was growing up, but I never heard of child molestation or a murder in the years I lived in Hemet. Oh, and except the break-in my brother did at the sporting goods store—they called that a crime.

A NEW FOSTER HOME

Orville and I were finally getting out of juvenile hall. Mrs. Dodge, our caseworker, was coming to pick us up. We got in her car, and she said she was placing us into new foster homes. Juvie, as we called it, was in Arlington, just a few miles south of Riverside. I didn't see my sister Alice or my little brother Everett. I guess they were already at the new foster home. We had all been together in Hemet.

I was riding in the front seat with Mrs. Dodge. "Your mother couldn't come today because she is working," Mrs. Dodge said. "I'll be taking you to your new homes and introduce you to your new foster parents. I missed the part *homes*.

We were driving north on Market Street and had already passed the Fox Theater on Seventh and Market, our favorite theater in the whole world. I thought it was beautiful inside. The carpet on the floor was a medium red color. There were big chandeliers hanging from eight-foot recessed circles in the ceiling. Dark heavy wood outlined the recesses. In the center of the lobby, the steps leading to the balcony had the same red carpet and dark wood on the handrails. I liked to sit in the balcony of this theater. On the left, just before the balcony steps, was the snack bar.

It was always lit real good. The lobby itself was dimly lit by the light of the chandeliers. I had seen *Colt .45*, *Mighty Joe Young*, and *The Gunfighter* here, as well as *The Boy with Green Hair*. When we lived with the Wallers in Hemet, Orville, Everett, and I were allowed to go spend the weekend with our mother in Riverside. Not all at once—we might get into trouble—but one at a time. I could hardly wait for school to be out on Friday night.

The week that it was my turn to go, the school bus seemed to just poke along. We lived about three miles south on State Street. The

Wallers had about a hundred acres on the left side called Echo Hills Ranch. Our address was Star Route Box .01. The bus pulled up to our mailbox and dropped us off.

We would get off, and Sally, our Indian bus driver, would get out, look both ways, and then walk us across State Street, the main highway south toward Anza and Temecula on down toward San Diego. Don't ask me why our driver was named Sally, because he was a man. I liked him a lot, and he was always fair if he had to settle squabbles or when kids got rowdy.

We crossed the street carrying our books, and once we were across, we would run like crazy up the hill. I would say it was about three hundred yards to the house on a level spot on top of the hill. I would leap out of the bus and run as fast as I could up the hill if it was my week to go to my mother's in Riverside. I would have my clothes all laid out on my bed so all I had to do was shower, put on my fresh clothes, and be ready to go.

Mr. Waller had a stake bed Ford truck that he would drive to town to pick up green waste from behind several stores for his black karakul sheep. I would ride into town with him to the bus station.

"Well, have a good time and tell your mother hello for me," he said as he let me out of his truck at the station.

"Okay," I said.

Wilbur, the bus driver for the Hemet bus lines, had the bus sitting at the curb; my mom had purchased the ticket in Riverside. Wilbur had my ticket on his clipboard so she had given it to him at the station in Riverside before he started back to Hemet that morning.

"You can go ahead and get you a seat," he said. I liked to ride up front because I got carsick on curvy roads. "We won't be leaving for a few minutes," he added.

Only about eight people were on the bus. I looked, but I didn't know any of them. Oh well, I didn't like to talk to people anyway. After a while, Wilbur came out and did a quick headcount to make sure the number of heads matched the number of tickets. He sat down behind the wheel, reached over to a handle, and closed the door. Then he looked in his rearview mirror, turned the wheel, and pulled away from the curb.

It was just a half block to Florida Avenue where Wilbur turned right; we were on our way, and it was none too soon for me. Our first stop was in San Jacinto (San Jack for short), about four miles away, then on to Gilman Hot Springs with its tree-lined drive and big golf course where people with money played golf and basked in the sun. Wilbur was in the bus station only a short time as no one was getting on or off here. Wilbur came out of the little station and sat down in the seat, closed the door, and we were on our way again. The road ran along the foothills coming out of the Hemet valley, and there were no more stops to make before Riverside. The bus started to descend into the town of Riverside down Box Springs grade.

It's a separated highway here; soon we were on Seventh Street passing the Golden State Theatre that was just across the street from the Riverside Grill where my mother worked. I was at this theater once on a Saturday morning because they had ten cartoons and two serials, then two western movies, all for a dime. After the cartoons, out walked Bill Boyd, who played Hopalong Cassidy. He was dressed in his western outfit, which he wore in all his Hoppy movie roles. He spun his six shooters a couple of times and told us to be good boys and girls and to mind our mothers and fathers. He said he hoped we would enjoy the movie today, and, "Tomorrow you children go to Sunday school or church."

The lights in the theater were bright, and I was amazed at how freckled Hoppy was. In his movies, you couldn't see his freckles because of the makeup. What a good cowboy he played. This was the second time I had seen Hoppy as we were up in the mountains at Idyllwild on the road to Palm Springs, and Hoppy was filming a movie. We were standing by a fence that had Hoppy's horse Topper in it, and my dad lifted me up and sat me in Hoppy's saddle.

Later that day, when they were shooting a scene, my dad hollered at one of us and ruined the scene, and they were upset with my dad because they had to shoot it all over again. They didn't mind you watching, but they wanted you to be quiet.

After passing the Golden State Theatre on Seventh Street, we passed the Fox Theatre on Seventh and Market. Wilbur turned left into an alley in the middle of the block and pulled up behind big Greyhound buses.

"Riverside," he said as he opened the door, "everybody have their ticket ready." And he collected the tickets as we climbed down from the bus.

"Good night, Wilbur," I said as he took my ticket.

Wilbur said, "Have a good time with your mother." He knew why I was coming to see my mother—because my mother had bought my ticket and given it to him to give to me.

I walked out of the bus station heading toward the Fox Theater and turned right on Seventh Street. I was going to the Riverside Grill where my mother was still working because they didn't close until eleven o'clock. It was seven thirty, and a boy was standing on the corner hollering "GET YOUR HERALD PAPER," but I walked by, and I didn't want any stinking paper. I wanted to see my mom, and maybe get something to eat.

I walked in and headed to the kitchen at the back.

"Hi, son, did you have a nice bus ride?" my mother asked me.

"Yep!" I said.

"Are you hungry, son?"

"Yeah, I'm starving, Mom."

"Well, go sit down at the counter and I'll be along to serve you in a minute, son."

"Okay, Mom."

"You go ahead and start looking through the menu, son".

Mom came up behind the counter, wiping her hands on her apron. "See anything you like?" she said.

"Yeah, I want the jumbo fried shrimp."

"You want a malt with it?" she asked.

"Can I have a Coke?" I asked.

"Sure, son, I'll put your order in."

"Okay, Mom."

Someone had put money in the jukebox, and Vaughn Monroe was singing, "(Ghost) Riders in the Sky." I liked that song then, and I like it now.

An old cowpoke went riding out one dark and windy day,
Upon a ridge he rested as he went along his way.
When all at once a mighty herd of red-eyed cows he saw,
Plowing through the ragged skies,
And up a cloudy draw, yippee I ay
Yippee yioo, ghost riders in the sky....

"When I'm done, can I go to the show, Mom?"

"Well, son, there is a midnight show at the Fox Theater. If you run up to my room and take a nap, I'll come wake you up when I get off work and we can go to the midnight show together." She had a room at the Gail Hotel on Eighth Street, which was just around the corner.

"Okay, Mom. What's playing?" I knew it wouldn't be a cowboy picture because Mom liked scary ones.

"*The Mummy* and *Abbott and Costello Meet Frankenstein*, I think, son."

"Okay, I like Bud Abbot, the fat, one he's funny."

"Son, that's not Bud Abbot. The tall thin one is Bud Abbot. Lou Costello is the little fat one."

"NO, SIR!"

"Son, it is. I know it should be the other way around. Bud Abbot is the tall one."

"Well, I am going to ask somebody else."

"Well, go ahead, but you'll find out I'm right."

"Okay, Mom, but don't forget to come get me."

"Okay, son, I won't," she said as she returned to washing dishes.

"This is the place," I heard Mrs. Dodge say as she turned into a driveway on the left. She had waken me from my daydreams. "Let's get out and go in and I'll introduce you. They are really nice people. I think you'll like them a lot."

I wasn't so sure. I looked at Orville to see what he thought, and he just shrugged.

He seemed kind of indifferent, like, "We'll see." Orville adjusted to changes better than I did.

When Mrs. Dodge rang the bell, an older woman came to the door. "Come on in," she said. "Paul, this is Mrs. Schwartz."

We went into the house, and it was kind of dark, with only a couple of lights on. The lady was smiling. She said, "I have a boy. He is in school right now, but he will be home soon. You can put your things in this room with David.

Things. I don't have any things, I thought.

Mrs. Dodge said she had gone to Hemet to the Wallers' to get my clothes and things. "Well, I'll leave you and Paul to get acquainted, and I'll take Orville over to his new home."

"Orville's not staying here?" I asked.

"No, Orville is being placed in another home. Paul I'm sure you will get along fine."

"NO, I WANT TO GO WITH ORVILLE!" I was really upset.

"I don't want to stay here." And I started to cry. Mrs. Dodge was telling me this is your new home and you'll get used to it. "NO! I WANT TO GO WITH ORVILLE!"

"I'm sure when David gets home and Paul has another boy to talk to, things will be fine," Mrs. Schwartz was saying.

Mrs. Dodge said, "Well, I must run. I'm running late already." She opened the door, and she and Orville went out to the car and got in. They drove off, and I was having a hard time trying not to cry. I walked back into the house. I didn't like the smell in here. It smelled of strong spices, garlic or something I wasn't used to. I didn't like it.

"Paul, you can put your things away," Mrs. Schwartz told me. She walked over to a dresser on one side of the room. "This will be for your things, and David's things are over here."

"Tomorrow I will take you down and enroll you in school. We'll get along fine, you'll see, and David is such a sweet boy. I know you will like him."

When David came home, I could see that he was kind of studious. He didn't look like he was ever dirty. I thought, *He won't play army or cowboys.* He didn't look any too happy to have to share his room either.

After he said hello, he mostly ignored me. He spoke mostly to his mother. I put my things away and just sat down on the bed. I didn't know where to go or what to do. I wish my dad would come and get me. I was wondering what Orville's new home was like. Orville said recently that he doesn't remember too much about it.

He said the home they put him in was out on La Cadena Avenue, toward Colton, but in the same vicinity as I was in, just farther out.

Orville remembered only that he slept in a bunk bed, on the bottom. The kid above him would pee the bed, and it ran through the mattress and trickled down on him. So Orville didn't take crap off nobody. He put his feet against the bottom of the boy's bunk that was sagging from his weight, and he pushed with all his might, pushing the kid high into the air.

The kid came down on his side and hit the edge of the bunk bed and went sprawling onto the floor. Orville doesn't remember more than that about the place, but he was sent back to juvenile hall. I think he must have been deemed incorrigible at the ripe old age of eleven.

Mr. Schwartz came home from work. "Dave, this is Paul. He will be staying with us for a while."

Dave said, "Hello. What do you like to do, Paul?"

I said, "I don't know."

"You like to play ball?"

"I don't know," I said.

"Well, David likes to play ball. Maybe you boys can go outside after supper and play catch. David has a couple of mitts around here somewhere. Do you know where they are at, David?"

"They are in the garage," David said.

"Well, after we eat, why don't you see if you can find them."

"But I have to study, Dad."

"You boys get washed up. Supper is ready. David, why don't you show Paul where to wash up."

I hated the smell in this house. *I wonder what Orville is doing?*

The next day, Mrs. Schwartz took me to school, someplace north and east of Market Street in Riverside. My mind was blank about the school or anything I did there. I went for three days. Then one morning, I started down the street toward downtown Riverside. I knew I couldn't wander the streets because a truant officer would pick me up and I'd be back in juvie—maybe even prison next time, who knows.

There's a billboard sign across Market Street where the road turned and went east to La Cadena. So I walked over to look at it; there were a lot of high weeds around it. I walked through them to the billboard. *Boy, that sucker is high*, I thought.

There was a ledge up on the sign a ways; I thought I could climb up there. I climbed up on the supports for the sign and was able to zigzag up to the ledge where the sign workers stood to replace the sign. I was on the back of the sign so no one could see me.

I was up there about four hours, I had already eaten the lunch that Mrs. Schwartz packed, and I was getting thirsty. I was careful climbing down. There were homes across the street with a hose lying in the yard. I didn't see anyone around, so I turned on the hose and got a drink. Then I went back to the sign and climbed up. The school let out at three thirty, so then I could go back to Mrs. Schwartz. She always asked me, "How was school?"

"Okay," I would reply.

"Got any homework?"

"Not yet," I told her.

This went on for about a week. The school called, wanting to know why Paul wasn't in school. I was busted. Oh well. I don't remember anyone saying anything to me at the foster home. I'm sure they must have asked me questions, but for the life of me, I don't remember any. Within two days, Mrs. Dodge picked me up and said all of us children were going to be put in a foster home together again.

I'm not sure, but I think Orville, Alice, and Everett were already in the car.

Mrs. Dodge said, "I put you with some people on a farm with cows, chickens, and pigs."

I said, "Do they have any horses?"

"I don't think so," she said.

We were in an area southwest of Riverside. It was orange trees and pastureland. I liked it, and I could tell Orville liked it too. At least we were all back together. Mrs. Dodge turned in to a gravel driveway. There was a barbed-wire fence on the left with hog wire over that and about eight young walnut trees on the right. The driveway was about two hundred feet long with a big red barn at the end of the driveway. In front of the barn was a big turnaround area, and over to the right was the back door to the house.

I was excited but also apprehensive. What were the people going to be like? I guessed we would find out soon enough because a tall woman with a pleasant smile greeted us at the back door.

"Children, this is Mrs. Carter," Mrs. Dodge was saying.

I thought, *Wow, she has big knockers.* I was at an age when I noticed things like that, and as I looked around the place, I thought, *I like it here already.*

We could handle anything as long as we were together. We survived our mother's beatings, didn't we?

LIFE AT THE CARTERS'

The Carters lived at 6312 Streeter Avenue, Riverside, California. I loved it at the Carters'; they treated us really well. When we first got there, we were given bedrooms upstairs. Later on, they moved the boys into a bunkhouse at the back of the main house.

Mrs. Carter said, "We have a television."

What's a television? I thought. "This is my son Robert, or Bob, if you want to call him that."

Robert shook hands with me, and I noticed his left arm and hand were crippled. Also, his left leg and foot were turned in a little. His walk was just a little strange.

Mrs. Carter said, "Robert had polio as a boy."

Robert could move his arm, all right, but his hand was turned down and didn't work well.

He showed us around the place. On the left side of the barn, as you came out the back door of the house, was a room where the chicken feed was kept. The hog feed was in here too.

In the middle of the barn, behind two large sliding doors, was a shop where Mr. Carter (Blackie) kept his tools and his truck. Here he had welding tanks because he was going to school under the G. I. Bill. He was also an ex-fighter. That's where he got the name Blackie; his given name was Clifford, but I never heard anyone call him Cliff. It was always Blackie. On the right side of the barn was a room where they candled the chicken eggs to look for blood spots in the eggs. They were also graded or sized here.

The driveway went around back on the right side of the barn. And right away, there were arched openings in the wall of the barn. As we walked past the arched openings, about every six feet, you could see chickens in cages.

Bob told us, "Stay out of this part of the barn where the chickens were because they would excite easily, understand?"

"Yes, Bob!" I could tell he was very firm about us staying out of the barn.

"If you upset the chickens, they will stop laying. If you excite them, and they stop laying, I'll have your ass. Now you got that?" He seemed tough, but I liked him right away.

He took us to the back of the barn where they had a lean-to built against the back of the barn. Under the lean-to, they had stacked hay that they could feed to the cattle.

"How many cows you got?" I asked.

"Well, only two milk cows, but we have about twenty in the permanent pasture."

"What's a permanent pasture?" one of us asked.

"Well, you see all that green grass growing out there beyond the fence?"

"Yeah!"

"Well, that's pasture for cows."

"Oh," I said, looking out at the pasture.

Bob said they rented pasture out to farmers to feed their cattle without buying expensive hay.

Farther out back where the road stopped, there was a strip between the back of a corral and the back of a shed where he told us they milked the cows. We turned in an opening and there on the left was a pen with a sow with piglets. In the next pen was another hog. Bob said they were getting ready to take him to the slaughterhouse.

On the right was the pen with a roof and one light for milking the cows. The pen also had stanchions to hold the cow's head while they were milked. That way, the cow couldn't move around while you were milking her.

"I'll teach you boys to milk starting tomorrow," said Bob.

Sounds like fun to me, I thought.

This was May of 1950. Orville and I enrolled at Central Junior High School. We rode a bus to school each morning and home again in the afternoon. I was just about to graduate from the eighth grade—heck, I was almost grown. I had transferred in from Hemet JR High. I had been in school for only six weeks, before the school year ended.

Yeah! We were out for the summer, and we could go barefoot. I loved being barefoot. Oh, happy days! But their gravel driveway made your feet sore until they toughened up. Then you were okay for the summer. Unless you stubbed your toe. Oh, how that would hurt. If you ever stubbed your toe on asphalt or cement, then you know what I mean. It hurts just to think about it. The only thing that hurt me worse was to stubbing it while it was still scabbed from the previous stubbing.

We have learned to milk the cows, and I developed arm muscles from squeezing those udders. I guess I could have called them teats; either way, both are correct. Orville was milking one cow, and I was milking the other.

"Lukie Bob." That's what we called Robert. He had been doing the milking before we came. Now he was able to devote most of his time to those chickens. I really think he was worked to a frazzle before we came to live at the Carters'.

I thought he was very easy to learn from, unless he caught you running through the chickens. I know because I decided to take a shortcut one day. I was in a hurry and was running from the back of the barn along the north wall, turning left down an aisle between the chicken cages.

The stupid chickens started squawking like crazy. I hadn't seen Lukie Bob over in a corner working on the chickens' water system. "HEY, GET YOUR ASS OUT OF HERE BEFORE I RUN THIS HAMMER HANDLE UP YOUR ASS."

I had no doubt he would do it too. "Sorry," I said as I kept going.

The first night I was there, I found out what television was. *Wow, this is neat. It's like having a picture show in your home.* Well, not quite. There was a lot of what they called snow on the screen. But it was pretty neat, although there wasn't anything on until around three or four in the afternoon, except a test pattern. But on Saturday, you could find kids' programs around noon.

Besides, we couldn't turn it on till all the chores were done and we had eaten supper. I really didn't mind doing chores except we had to get up early to milk the cows each day at six o'clock. In the afternoon, we milked at about five o'clock in the summer and around four thirty in the winter. Cows liked to be milked at the same time every day.

They would be there mooing and waiting for you. We fed them good alfalfa hay while we milked them, but we would put some oats in the trough before putting the hay in, kinda like dessert when they got to the bottom. And it made their milk rich.

I had a one-legged stool to sit on, and I would lean my head into the cow's flank. It would steady me, and I could feel the cow start to move. I needed to know as soon as possible if she was going to lift her leg. They could stick it in your bucket so fast you'd be amazed.

Then I have to dump it in the hog slop, wash out the bucket, and start again. Not a good thing if you want to get done and washed up for supper. And of course, I had to say a few choice words; I was almost an adult. "Son of a bitchin' cow." I mean, who was going to hear me out here?

"Hey, knock that shit off," I heard somebody say.

"Screw ya." It was only Orville. He cussed too. Well, why not. Blackie and Lukie Bob talked that way. Dad-gum it, I should clean this up. This could turn out to be a children's book. Maybe I should have said blankety blank. Shoot, I can't find my eraser.

There are always a million flies around when you're milking, so old Bossy was always flicking her tail and hitting Orville and me upside the head. Orville thought of putting a wire around a brick, and then wiring it to her tail.

I said, "Shit, that won't hold her tail. She'll just flick her tail and hit you with the brick and knock you clear into the middle of next week."

He said, "You know, I think you're right."

And then I told him, "Hey, it was a good idea, though!"

Then there were always the cats, coming around wanting milk. Orville and I would spray a stream of milk at their faces. If I could hit them a couple of times really fast with the stream of milk, they would be soaked. They would start licking themselves or each other. They were very happy cats. Afterward, we would let the cows out of the stanchion and head for the house with our buckets of milk.

As we came into the kitchen, Mrs. Carter said, "Just set them on the floor by the counter and I'll get some cheesecloth and strain it. You boys wash up and we'll eat. Then you can watch television. It's Wednesday night, so wrestling is on.

When we lived with the Wallers in Hemet, and it was our turn to visit our mother in Riverside, "we would catch a Pacific Electric bus and go to the Olympic Auditorium in Los Angeles to watch wrestling. I can still remember some of the wrestlers we saw: George and Bobby Becker, Enrique Torres, the Swedish Angel, Gorgeous George. My mother loved wrestling. When the matches were over, we caught the PE bus back to Riverside, arriving about midnight. Then up to the hotel and into bed.

On Saturday, the television started about noon. I remember the Cowboy Theatre, brought to you by the big three car dealers of Southern California: Fletcher Jones Chevrolet, Ray Gould Chrysler Plymouth, and Yeakel Oldsmobile. They had the Three Mesquiteers with Ray "Crash" Corrigan, a young John Wayne, Max "Alibi" Terhune, Lash La Rue, and Colonel Tim McCoy, just to name a few.

Movies had to be seven years old to be shown on television in the forties. These movies must have been at least fifteen years old. If you hadn't seen the movie, who cared? Certainly not me. Being a kid, this was all new to me. In fact, television was new to everyone in the fifties. Notice I'm not calling it TV. In the early fifties, it was television. TV came later. I liked *The Art Baker Show*, brought to you by Chevrolet. They sang in their commercial,

> *Drive your Chevrolet, through the USA*
> *America is asking you to call.*
> *Drive your Chevrolet, through the USA*
> *America's the greatest land of all.*
>
> *On a highway, or a road along a levee*
> *Nothing can beat her; life is completer in a Chevy*
> *So make a date today, to see the USA,*
>
> *And see it in your Chevrolet.*

On Saturday night, about seven thirty, we would watch a show we all liked: *Hometown Jamboree*, with Cliffie Stone as the host. The group consisted of cute little Bucky Tibbs, Eddie Kirk, Gene O'Quin, Les "Carrot Top" Anderson, and Tennessee Ernie.

"Come on out, Ernie."

"Howdy, Cliffie!" Ernie would be in bib overalls.

"Will you sing a song for us, Ernie?"

"I'll be glad to, Cliffie." He would swing his arm in a loop and start to sing.

> *Well, there it stands in the corner with a barrel so straight,*
> *I looked out the window and over the gate.*
> *The big fat rabbits was jumpin' the grass*
> *Wait till they hear my old shotgun blast.*
> *Shotgun boogie, I don't need but one shot*
> *Look out, bushy tail, or tonight you'll be in the pot.*

Herman the Hermit, who was Cliffie Stone's dad, would play the cowbells—not the title to a song but real cowbells. Speedy West played steel guitar.

A frequent guest was Terry Preston (who was really Ferlin Husky). Jimmy Bryant played guitar with Speedy on some numbers. Eddie Kirk and Bucky Tibbs sometimes sang duets. Cliffie Stone introduced them all.

As a kid, I thought television was wonderful, but today the magic is gone. It's just an everyday occurrence; its everywhere you go. I seldom see any real creativity, just the same old crap day after day. I think we've gotten too big for our britches, and one of these days, God will give us a slap in the face to wake us up. At least I hope so. The world seems so uncaring now. This is just my opinion. My wife was just reading over my shoulder. She said, "That's enough of your opinions."

Another great show was *Ina Ray Hutton and Her Melodears*. What a ball of energy she was, directing the band and tap-dancing. Seems I remember her dress strap breaking and exposing a little too much on television, as it was live television. Sometimes she would be all out of breath from all the dancing and directing her all-girl band. I found a

YouTube video of her performing "Doin' the Suzy Q." Anytime I want a lift, I just click on it, and there she is, looking like she did so long ago as she directed her all-girl Orchestra.

"The name of this song is "Doin' the Suzy Q," and she would start singing,

> *It's just a waltz and a shuffle*
> *Then we're off to Buffalo*
> *It's a big improvement*
> *On the truckin' movement*
> *Not too fast and not too slow.*

One more thing before I leave the topic of television: The one we were watching in 1951 was a 7-inch job. Maybe there has been some creativity, after all. I now watch a 40-inch set. I'd say there was some creativity there.

Roy Fochet (pronounced *Foe*) was Mrs. Carter's uncle, and he had a ranch just up Streeter Avenue from Mr. and Mrs. Carter's ranch but on the west side of the street.

Sometimes he would come get Orville or me to work for him. We would mow his grass or rake his yard, for which we were always paid. (Reading this story, Orville said he only remembers getting fifteen cents.) He had a permanent pasture and ran a few heads of cattle. He also grew alfalfa for hay.

He would cut and bale it. After the hay was baled and laid out in the field, Orville and I would go to his place after school and on weekends, get in his '37 Chevy truck with a four-speed transmission, hook up to a flatbed trailer that was about sixteen feet long, and then drive through a gate down along the bales of hay. I had to sit on a cushion to be tall enough to see out the windshield.

I pulled the truck up until the front of the trailer was even with the first bale. Orville and I get out with the hay hooks Mr. Fochet had in the floorboard of the truck.

We would both stand a bale on end and then reach down and slam our hay hook into the bale and, leaning back at the same time, lay the bale on the trailer. Then we would drive on to the next two bales of hay.

We would work a couple of hours in the evening after school. We would only put one layer on the trailer because it was too high for us to lift. They were two wire bales of hay, which weighed about seventy-five pounds. Three-wire bales of hay would weigh 125 pounds. We could not lift those; we were just too small. I liked to do this because I got to drive the truck, but Mr. Fochet would also drive. I wasn't as motivated when I couldn't drive.

In September, my brothers, my sister, and I were back in school at Central Junior High School. I was in the ninth grade, and I don't remember much about my ninth grade. The only thing I remember is being in Mr. Tydus's electronics class and making a crystal set. Pretty neat too. A crystal set is a primitive radio, but it worked. Oh, and a girl that sat next to me in English class. She and I would talk about a television show that was on every weekday at four o' clock. Her name was Regina Johnson.

Space Patrol. ABC presents high adventure in the vast regions of space; missions of daring in the name of interplanetary justice. Joining us now, Buzz Cory, commander in chief of the Space Patrol. Regina Johnson and I both watched it faithfully every day. Then we would discuss it the next day. I don't remember too much more about going to school here. I graduated from the ninth grade in June of 1951.

The days were growing short after we went back to school in September 1950. The cows that Orville and I milked before school in daylight we were now milking in the dark. There was one light overhead, but it didn't give off much light. As winter set in, when it rained, we were in mud up to our eyeballs. Well, almost.

From where the driveway ended going left, we passed the big manure pile and continued into the shed where we milk, we've had to lay some boards down to walk on. Otherwise we will have mud all over us. In the morning it's up at 6:00 milk, taking the hog slop with us, milk the cows, come back to the house with the milk get washed up and sit down at the breakfast table. Something sure smelled good and the kitchen was warm and cozy.

Mrs. Carter was a good cook, and there was always plenty. They raised their own hogs and cattle. They had a cold storage locker someplace and a large freezer at the house. When they slaughtered a hog or cattle, the meat went into the cold storage locker. We had eggs from their chickens and pork or beef from the freezer. We had butter we churned ourselves, milk from the cows, and plenty of chicken fryers, so life was good.

LIFE ON AN EGG RANCH

On the Carters' chicken ranch where they sold eggs and fryers. My brothers and I would help pick up the eggs from the wire cages that were hung three feet off the ground where the chickens were kept. We would help candle the eggs to look for blood spots in them. They had a candling machine, and after the eggs passed over the light, they would be sized by going through the proper slot in the candling machine—small, medium, large and extra-large. Mrs. Carter also had an egg route at the March Air Force Base outside of Riverside California.

The Carters had a 1939 Chevy coupe, with its trunk lid removed. They built a pickup-type bed in its place. We would load up the back of the car with cartons of eggs, and then off we would go to sell their eggs at March Field. She had a bag she would put four or five dozen eggs into, and she would go door to door in the housing area selling eggs. She sold extra-large eggs for 95 cents a dozen in 1951.

We would park at the curb, and she would get out and start walking from house to house. When she needed more eggs, she would walk out to the curb. I would drive up, and she would refill her bag of eggs. I loved doing it because I was driving. Life didn't get better than that for a thirteen-year-old boy. Meanwhile, back at the ranch, there was always something to do. Morning and night, there were two cows to milk; my brother Orville milked one while I milked the other.

They had a couple of hogs to slop, which was made from grain and leftover milk from the cows that we used in the house. Robert Pierce was Mrs. Carter's son, but we called him Lukie Bob. The reason we called him that escapes me now. Lukie Bob was twenty-four, and he did all the feeding of the chickens. He had feeding the chickens down to a science.

Layer mash is the only one I remember but it had to be done at the same time each day, usually at three o'clock in the morning, and then again at three o'clock in the afternoon. He would get upset if we hollered or made any loud noises. The chickens would get upset and stop laying eggs, and this was his livelihood. He would threaten us with bloody murder.

There were two other boys living here as well: Robert Wright and Roy Hansen. The Carters kept us all active in 4-H too. I was raising a day-old calf I had bought at the auction in Pedley for six dollars. The Carters also had a permanent pasture.

They had their own few heads of cattle, plus, they would rent the pasture out to other people whose cattle needed somewhere to graze. The pasture had to be irrigated every week or two.

I would hear Mrs. Carter say, "Bob you have water coming at two tomorrow morning." So Bob would have to be up and out at the standpipe to open the gates by 2:00 a.m. He would irrigate one section of the pasture and then close the gates and open them on another section. Not all the sections were watered at once because they didn't want the cattle in the wet sections.

After school and on weekends, we would have to remove the manure from under the chicken cages. It would stack up really high, so it was a never-ending job. We would be out there long after dark. Orville, Everett, Bob Wright, and I were doing this very smelly task when Bob Wright bumped Orville with the wheelbarrow, getting chicken manure on Orville's pants.

Now this was not the thing to do. Orville was two years younger than me—eighteen months, really—and he didn't take shit off nobody (no pun intended).

I was in front of the wheelbarrow, and I was standing there with a shovelful of manure, waiting for Bob to set the wheel borrow down so I could dump my manure in it. I could tell Orville was pissed, Bob was probably three years older than Orville but that didn't make any difference to Orville. I saw Orville reach down and grab a big handful of stinking wet chicken shit and then let fly with it at Bob, hitting him on his head and back. The remnants hit the side of my head too.

Bob had already grabbed a handful of manure and was throwing it at Orville. I had a big handful and threw it at Orville, but Bob, being in between, got clobbered too. He started throwing chicken shit like a maniac. He didn't know I was hit by Orville. So he must have thought we had ganged up against him, so he turned and started throwing at me. Now I was getting it from Orville and Bob, who were getting it from me.

We had chicken shit in our eyes, hair, and all over our clothes. The manure burned like crazy. I was hollering, "KINGS, KINGS."

When you hollered Kings, they were supposed to stop.

Finally, we stopped throwing, and I was going to get in the shower so I could wash this shit off. So I lit out for the house with Orville and Bob right behind me. I went to a room, apart from the one that we slept in, that had a shower; and as I reached for the doorknob, Mrs. Carter was just coming out of the house with a bucket of extra milk. We always put the table scraps and anything else a hog might eat in the hog bucket and poured the extra milk over it. Whenever we went to milk the cows in the morning, we carried extra milk to the hog pen and dumped it into the hog trough.

Mrs. Carter said, "What do you boys have all over you?"

Bob said, "Orville threw chicken manure at me."

And Orville said, "No, I didn't. He put it on me first."

I said, "Bob hit Orville with the wheelbarrow and got manure on him."

"Well, I don't care who did what. Don't any of you boys go in that room until you're all washed up. And leave all those clothes outside."

So we got the hose and started squirting each other. That manure was really burning our skin by this time. I hosed Orville and Bob and then said, "Hey, Orville, would you hose me?"

I could see the delight in Orville's eyes at the thought of getting to hose me. When we had washed most of the manure off our clothes, we stripped down to our shorts and finished the job.

Everett was the lucky one. When I got hit, he took off. Mrs. Carter had a look of disgust on her face, but I also saw a smile as she turned away.

HOT ROD

Blackie had a son—Wayne—from a previous marriage. I believe he had graduated from high school in June the year we arrived at Mrs. Carter's in 1950. He was best friends with Raymond Hamm. I knew Raymond Hamm from the school in Hemet. He had lived in Hemet before his family moved to Riverside. I was surprised to see him there at Carter's home.

He pulled up in a green Ford Model B roadster. No top on it, no fenders on it, but it was cute as could be. I would notice because I've always loved cars. Raymond had flaming red hair, and Wayne called him Hambone. Hambone got out and raised one side of the hood on the roadster.

He reached in and pulled the dipstick out. Then he walked to the driver's side, took a rag, and wiped the dipstick. Then he stuck the dipstick back in and pulled it out again. He put it to his face so he could see the oil on it and said, "Hey, Wayne, you got a quart of oil?"

"Yeah, my dad has some in his shop over there." He pointed to the open door of the barn.

Raymond walked over to the shop while Orville and I were looking at the engine. It was a flathead V8 engine. Raymond had it painted chrome yellow, with chrome acorn nuts on the bolt heads. There was an aluminum intake manifold with two Stromberg 97 carburetors, topped off with two chrome air cleaners. A teenage boy's dream.

Hambone came back with a quart of Royal Triton motor oil with a pour spout sticking out of it. He reached into the engine and pulled the oil breather cap off. Then he stuck the pour spout into the breather hole and poured the oil into the engine.

While it was draining, he said, "I have to run get gas at the station on Jurupa Avenue about a mile away. Wayne, you want to ride with me?"

"Okay!" Wayne told Hambone as Hambone pulled the oil can out and shut the hood on the roadster.

Then Wayne got in, and Hambone turned the roadster around in the driveway, Orville and I were standing by the back door looking at them. I was jealous. What a cute little hot rod.

Hambone stopped beside Orville and me. "You guys want to go for a ride? I'm coming right back".

I could have fainted and fallen over. I ran around to the passenger side where Wayne was getting out.

"Go ask my mother," he said.

Oh shoot, would she let us go? I wondered. We ran into the house to ask Mom. We had started calling her Mom. Wayne and Lukie Bob called her Mom, and so it was just natural for all of us to call her Mom too.

"Can we go get gas with Wayne and Hambone?"

"Well, I don't know. Raymond drives pretty fast," Mom told us.

"We'll drive slow, Mom," Wayne says from behind me.

"Well, all right, but you children be careful and stay sitting down."

"Okay, Mom, we will," we would say together.

I ran around to the passenger side and jumped in. Orville climbed in but had to sit on my lap. Wayne got in and made us scoot over. Hambone got in, clutched it, and I moved my leg so he could get it into first gear. We're packed in like sardines in a can, but I loved it.

At the end of the driveway, Hambone turned right up Streeter Avenue, pushing the gas pedal down. The rear wheels were still on gravel, so they spun like crazy. When the tires hit the asphalt, they squealed as Hambone peeled rubber, leaving smoke on the street.

Wow! I like this car.

It was really fun with the wind blowing in our faces. Hambone had the windshield cut low, so there was quite a bit of wind as he speed-shifted into second gear and we picked up speed.

We went by Roy Fochet (Foe), and I saw him looking at us as we went by.

I hope he doesn't call Mom, I thought. Because that was her uncle, and we were really cooking it by now. The curve at Streeter and Jurupa was coming up fast, and Hambone let off the gas. Around the corner we went, and it was a short distance to the filling station.

Hambone got out and pumped the gas. Then he went inside to pay.

Wayne said, "I'm going to get a Coke. You and Orville want one?"

"Sure." *Do we look crazy?* I thought. *Of course we want a Coke.*

These guys were treating us like adults. Finally we were not kids anymore, and we were living the good life. I smiled at Orville, who was grinning too.

Wayne handed us a Coke, and we all climbed back in. A little more rubber as we peeled out for home. Even Orville sitting on my lap didn't feel heavy. This was so neat. I can't believe Hambone took us with him to get gas. He turned back in the driveway. Shoot, the trip was over to soon.

Orville and I climbed out, and then Wayne got back in and they turned around and pulled up beside us, where Orville and I were standing finishing our Cokes.

Hambone said to us, "If you guys ever have a date and want to borrow the car, you can."

Right, I thought as I watched them pull out of the driveway and peel out, leaving burnt rubber as they turned left down Streeter Avenue.

Orville said, "I think he was kidding. What does Orville know? He's just a kid."

I thought he meant it. All I had to do was find a date. Shoot, I didn't even know any girls. I bet if I had Hambone's car, I could find one, but I would need some money if I was going to show her a good time!

"Hey, Orville, got any money!"

TRAIN WRECK

"Robert, you have water coming at 2:00 a.m."

"Okay, Mom. I'll go shut the gates on the standpipes in the backfield and open them on the ones in the front where there are no cattle."

That way, it can run in the front pasture until I finish feeding the chickens in the morning, Bob told his mother.

Lukie Bob had the chickens fed and the water moved to a different part of the pasture by the time we got up. He had just sat down at the kitchen table as we finished breakfast and was getting our books and heading out the driveway to the street. We tried to be early for the school bus. If we missed it, we couldn't stay home. Mom would have to drive us to school. That would be a big hassle for her, and time wasted, really. She was so busy all the time. After the children were off to school, she would do the dishes, dust the house, and then start a load of wash and head out to the room in the barn to candle the eggs and then place them in the cases for shipment to the stores.

When Bob finished with the irrigation that would move the water from field to field, he would then be in the chicken barn collecting the eggs. Each coop had a card attached. If you picked an egg from a chicken, you made a mark on the card under the day of the week it happened to be. This had to be done faithfully.

If a chicken went very long without laying an egg, she was replaced with a new one.

The Carters had five thousand chickens, so there were a lot of eggs to pick up and cards to mark. The hen that was removed because she wasn't laying was killed, dressed, and sold as roasting chicken. Chickens had to be productive, or they met their demise. When Bob finished collecting the eggs in baskets, he carried them to the room to be candle and grade them for size. With the eggs candled and put into cases, Bob could relax for a while. He could eat lunch then take a nap because he had gotten up so early to receive the water that morning.

We were out on the street waiting for the school bus when I heard the train whistle blow. I looked south on Streeter Avenue to the train crossing. There were no gates or arms to come down to stop traffic. The engineer would blow the whistle, and cars would stop, following a kind of honor system.

Just then, the train came across Streeter Avenue. BAM! The train engine hit a car whose driver hadn't heard the whistle. As the train crossed Streeter Avenue, the tracks started to curve from west to north. We started running to the crossing about three hundred yards south. The train tracks bordered the Carters' property on the south.

When the train hit the car, a little boy being driven to school was in the passenger seat. He was torn from the car and dragged down the tracks. There was flesh and body parts along the track for about fifty yards. There was metal inside the tracks that his head had hit. There were brains and flesh all over this sharp metal.

A man told us, "Go back. You boys don't want to see this."

It was time for the school bus, so we had to run to catch the bus. It wasn't a pretty sight. I remember telling everyone on the school bus what had happened. Not a good day.

Writing this story, I still feel sorry for the parents of that little boy. I never even knew his name, as we didn't read newspapers.

We still worked a lot cleaning under the chickens and doing chores. Blackie had finished the work he and Doug Jones were doing in El Paso.

They had been driving to El Paso in Doug's 1950 Hudson Hornet. They had a contract with the army to paint the barracks there. They came home only every other weekend. I believe it took three or four months before the job was done.

When Blackie was finally back home, he started fixing an International truck he had bought. It was a flatbed with stake sides. He had bought it used and painted the cab red and the bed and stakes black. They put a compressor and spray tanks on it, and Blackie was shooting Gun Tex on houses. It was a thick grainy or sandy mixture. He had contracts to shoot Gun Tex on some apartments in Los Angeles.

So on weekends, Orville and I would go with Blackie and Doug Jones to help mask windows so Blackie could spray the gun texture on without getting it on the windows. After it dried a little, we could pull the tape and paper off, and the job would be finished. He was paying us $1.25 an hour for this, but it seemed it lasted only two or three weekends.

Blackie was still contracting painting, but I don't remember going to work with him anymore. He built pens inside the barn in an area away from the chickens. We went to the livestock sale at Pedley and bought day-old calves for about five dollars. Then with the excess milk from the two cows Orville and I were milking, we would mix it with Calf-Manna that was purchased from a feed store. Then with the mixture in a bucket with a nipple on it, we would feed the calves.

Sometimes the calves got the scourers (the shits). Then we would add a junket tablet to the mixture before they drank it. Junket tablets were used in the making of homemade ice cream. This seemed to help. Scours can kill a calf if not remedied in time. When the calves were about three months old, he took them to auction and sold them. He kept replacing the calves as the older ones were sold. It was a never-ending cycle.

We had some calves that died from various ailments. Mostly it was the scours that did them in. These people were into anything that they thought would make them money. They were really hard workers; we were very fortunate to have been placed in their home.

HITTING A MOVING TARGET

Blackie and Evelyn Carter had a sporting goods store in Carlsbad (or Oceanside?), California, before they bought this chicken ranch in Riverside. On the right side of Blackie's shop was a room that backed up to the room where they graded their eggs. They had all the stuff that was left over from closing the sporting goods store in this room. There were fishing reels, new in boxes; new fishing poles all for deep-water fishing; and nets for lifting fish from the water.

Also what caught Orville's and my eye were the boxes of shotgun shells. We were always shooting at birds using slingshots with rocks, but I don't remember ever killing one. But it was fun to shoot at them. If it scared them away, that was good enough. Well, we found that if you pried the wad out of the end of the shotgun shells, you would find BB's inside.

The ones marked 00 had a big shot inside, about one-quarter inch in size. We would take three or four of these pellets and put them in the pouch of our slingshots. Then we figured that it was like shooting a shotgun at the bird. The idea was good, but the pellets didn't hold together very well. The pellets scattered too much, but it was fun shooting at a cardboard target, or a Coke bottle.

One day I heard Hambone's hot rod pull into the driveway, and I didn't want to get caught in the storage shed, so I hightailed it out of there and went out through the barn where I was not supposed to be. Here came my sister Alice coming around from the back. She looked as though she was looking for someone. She was dressed in a red sunsuit and looking all hoity-toity. She had just passed the arch in the barn to my left. I grabbed an egg from the chicken cage I was standing in front of when I first saw her.

I timed it just right when I thought she would step into the opening and threw the egg. She stepped into the opening just as the egg was launched and hit her high on the head above her right ear. She was looking into the arched opening to see who had done such a dastardly deed, and there I stood.

"Aumm, I'm going to tell Mom!"

I knew I was in for it if Mom found out. We weren't supposed to be in with the chickens, but throwing perfectly good eggs was a no-no.

I ran down the aisle as fast as I could, trying not to excite the chickens in case Lukie Bob was around.

Alice was walking just ahead of me with her head leaning to the left so the egg wouldn't fall off. She wanted to get there with the evidence still intact.

"Oh, Alice, don't tell. I'm sorry. I was just throwing away a cracked egg," I lied. "Hey, you want my funny books? I'll give them to you. Please, Alice, don't tell on me. They'll kill me."

I mean, I was pleading for my life, and Alice was heading straight to the house as though she didn't hear me pleading right behind her. She seemed unconcerned that I was going to be killed when we reached the house and she told on me.

"Please, Alice, I'll give you anything you want. Hey, you want my cap gun? You can have it."

Shoot, she was at the back door, and without even pausing, she opened the door and marched right in. Mom was working in the kitchen.

"Mom, Paul threw an egg and hit me with it."

Mom walked over and looked at Alice's head with the egg on it.

"Paul, did you hit your sister?"

"Yeah, but I didn't know she was there," I lied. "I was coming to get a basket so I could help Bob gather the eggs." That sounded pretty good. Who could be mad if you were just trying to help? I said, "I was coming down the aisle and there was a cracked egg lying in one of the pens, and I threw it away," I lied. "I didn't see Alice coming, and when she stepped in the doorway, the egg hit her."

"You children know you're not supposed to throw eggs, now you go out there and help her clean it off."

Alice wasn't happy with the outcome, but she let me help her clean it off. I kept telling her how sorry I was as I washed the egg out of her hair. Finally, she let the whole issue drop. She told on me, but I had it coming. We laughed about it today, but I still apologize for that dastardly deed so long ago. At least she didn't want my funny books and my cap gun. That would have been a real tragedy. I would have never forgiven her if she had taken my funny books and my cap gun. Just kidding.

I told Alice I was writing a book, and she said I had done things like that to her many times. I suppose she wanted me to recall all my mischievous deeds. I really don't think she thinks clearly anymore. She'd had too much brain damage from being hit with eggs. I'm truly sorry, Alyce. Hey, I spelled it the hoity-toity way she spelled it.

HAMBONE'S LITTLE ROADSTER

When she was all cleaned up, Alice grabbed a towel and began drying her hair. She had egg in her hair and also her ear. That was probably why she couldn't hear me pleading with her not to tell. I know it must have been something like that, because she loved me. And who could blame her? I treated her so well. With Alice on the road to recovery, my attention turned to Hambone's car in the driveway. I thought, *Where is he? Maybe he's here to see if I've found a date yet? He's probably anxious to loan me the car.*

Orville came up from the barn area.

"Orville, have you seen Wayne and Hambone?"

"They were in Wayne's room when I came out a while ago," he replied. "I was headed into the house to find them when they walked out the back door, laughing."

"Hey, Paul, you got your driver's license yet?" Hambone asked.

"No, I'm not old enough yet."

"Too bad. I was going to ask you to take my car to the filling station and fill her up for me."

"I could do it," I said. "I drive the car on Mom's egg route."

"Better not," he said. "I saw a motorcycle cop just before I got here. I don't want you to get a ticket."

"Oh, let me. Oh please! I'll drive careful."

Wayne said, "Go ask Mom if she cares if you drive Hambone's car over on Jurupa Avenue to get some gas."

I run up the steps and in through the back door. Mom was putting cream in the butter churn.

"Mom, can I drive Hambone's car to the filling station to get gas for him? He said I could."

"No! You're too young!"

"But you let me drive on your egg route."

"That's different—you're just driving along the curb. I wouldn't let you drive in traffic. You don't have enough experience."

"Oh, Mom, please."

"No!" she said.

So I turned, and I went back outside feeling sad.

Wayne and Hambone had the hood on the roadster up; they were looking at something. Orville was standing behind them, watching. I walked up to see what they were doing. Orville looked at me and pointed to Hambone's back. Hambone was wearing his pants really low, and we could see the top of his crack, with red hairs sticking out.

Orville leaned forward and snatched those low pants clear down to his knees. My jaw dropped. I couldn't believe what I just saw. Hambone was standing there in his shorts, with his pants around his feet.

Wayne started laughing while Orville took off running. Hambone reached down to pull his britches up. He told Wayne, "Let's get that little bastard."

Orville had already gone through a hole in the fence and was running across the pasture. Wayne and Hambone tried to crawl through the hole in the fence. Wayne's pants got hung up on a piece of the broken wire.

Hambone said, "He's already on the railroad tracks. Let's get the car." Hambone helped Wayne pull his pants loose from the wire, and then they start running back to the car. They jumped in and started it, spinning a brodie right there in the driveway. Dust and gravel flying everywhere. I thought, *They better hope Mom don't see them because she has clean wash hanging on the clothesline.*

They tore out of the driveway, and I saw Wayne rise up in the seat, looking toward the tracks to see which way Orville went. Hambone peeled rubber when he came out on Streeter Avenue, going south to the railroad tracks.

I ran to the opening in the fence so I could see where Orville went, but I didn't see him anywhere.

Boy, Hambone's going to kill him when he catches him. I wouldn't want to be in Orville's shoes right now.

I saw Hambone driving slow along the railroad tracks, looking for Orville. The ditch along the railroad tracks had high weeds growing in it. Wayne got out of the car and started walking up on the tracks. Orville must be hiding in the high weeds.

Wayne shouted, "I see him." He must have been thinking that if Orville thought he had been spotted, he would jump up and run.

But Orville didn't fall for it. *He must be hidden real good*, I thought. Hambone was driving slowly along the road by the ditch. After about a half hour, I saw them give up and get into the car. They turned around and headed slowly back to the house, with dust boiling up behind the little car.

The little roadster pulled up and stopped by where I was standing. Wayne got out and stood there, looking toward the railroad tracks, to see whether Orville had come out of hiding yet. Hambone walked over to the fence, put his hands to his mouth, and hollered as loud as he could: "YOU HAVE TO COME OUT SOMETIME, YOU LITTLE BASTARD."

They laughed and went into the house to get a drink. I was still looking for Orville, but I didn't see him. *Boy, they are going to kill him*, I thought. I sure wouldn't want to be in his shoes. They are right; he had to come home sometime.

Wayne and Hambone had told Mom earlier that they were joining the Air Force, meaning, they had already signed up. They both came back out of the house, they were still laughing about Orville pantsing Hambone. They looked toward the tracks once more but didn't see Orville. So they got in the roadster, slowly backed up and drove out the driveway. I was watching from the back of the house, I yearned for a little roadster just like that one. I saw them turn down the ditch line one more time. They took one last opportunity to find Orville. *He must be hiding in a really good spot if they didn't find him*, I thought.

The car turned around again, and I saw it speeding back along the tracks toward Streeter Avenue, with dust rising behind them. They turned south toward Arlington and then were out of sight. I went into the house to get my milk pail because it was almost time to milk. *If Orville don't come back for days, I'll have to do all the milking.* I started around the corner of the barn, thinking, *Hambone won't ever loan me that car now.*

"Hey are they gone yet?" I heard a voice say from the barn. It was Orville.

"Orville, they are going to kill you if they ever catch you!"

"Shoot, I don't intend to get caught," he replied. "Hey, Paul, let me have your milk bucket and you go get the other one so I can help milk the cows."

"Okay," I said as I handed him the bucket. I headed back to the house to get Orville's bucket. *At least I won't have to milk both cows tonight*, I was thinking. *But what about when they finally catch him? With Orville dead, I'll be the only one left to milk the cows. Just my luck*, I thought as I headed for the house.

Orville sure ruined my chances of ever getting a date, without Hambone's car. *I'll probably die without ever knowing love. I have nothing to look forward to. And all because my dumb brother wanted to pull somebody's pants down. Why couldn't he have pulled Wayne's pants down. Wayne don't even have a car. If he did he wouldn't loan it to me.*

Hambone was going to be my salvation on the road to romance.

DRIVING A COMBINE

Orville was raising a calf that he got at auction for five dollars. I was raising rabbits and selling rabbit fryers. Everett had a goat that he milked twice a day. He had a platform about three feet high that the goat jumped up on and puts its head in a stanchion with hay she could eat, while Everett milked her. The goat gave about a quart at each milking twice a day. Everett encountered a lady who couldn't drink cow's milk but could tolerate goat's milk, and she bought Everett's goat milk and was really happy to get it because it was a very mild-tasting milk.

One day the lady arrived a little early, and Everett was just starting to milk the goat. It was always lifting its hind leg trying to step sideways and, in the process, stepped into his milk pail. Everett grabbed the goat's foot and lifted it out of the pail. The lady was standing there watching all of this. Everett knew the lady needed him to finish.

He said, "I'll have to go strain the milk because there is crud in it from the goat's hoof." When Everett came back with the milk all strained, the lady paid him and left, but she never came back. Everett was only twelve years old; he didn't think to throw the milk out and start over.

My sister Alice had several ducks for her 4-H project. She had them in a pen behind the candling room. Sometimes, in the evening, my brothers and my sister would play a game called Shoot the pin. It was a game where one person was It. You drew a circle on the ground, and the one who was It hid his eyes while the others went off to hide. It was somewhat like hide-and-seek, except that when you found someone who was hiding, you would point your finger and say, "Shoot the pin." That person then had to go get in the circle.

Now, while the It person looked for someone else, the person in the circle would try to get someone to run and touch them and say, "Safety." If you have been safety-ed, you both could go hide again, and then the It person had to start looking all over again. The It person would try not to get too far out of sight of the circle. If the It person couldn't find you after a little while of looking, he would holler, "Whistle and shout, or I'll send my men out." His men being the people he had captured and put in the circle. The people from the circle were then able to shoot the pin until everyone was captured. It was a fun game.

Orville had raised his calf and took it to the auction in Pedley. It sold, and he had about fifty dollars from the sale. He told me he was going to run away and go live with our dad. Orville seemed to have a lot of affection for our dad at this time, as I did too. I wished I was brave enough to run away too. Dad was always saying, "Me want some waddymelon," then repeating what Orville had said when he was about four years old. "Me too, me too, me too."

Our dad would repeat that a lot. There would be roadside stands selling watermelons, and sometimes as we stopped, Dad would say to us, "Me want some waddymelon?" Then he would mimic Orville with "Me too, me too, me too" in a silly voice like Orville used when he was four years old.

In the summer of 1951, Blackie Carter had a combine and a tractor. A Ford tractor with dual wheels on the rear. Dual wheels gave it more traction. Tractor tires are filled half full of water to give the tractor more weight, thus more traction. Blackie had contracted to thrash a field of wheat in Sunnymead (now Moreno Valley). So he took Orville to drive the tractor and pull the combine and thrash the grain. Orville was told to thrash the field in a square. When he came to a corner, he made a big circle so he could come back and start the other way. That way, you kept a square corner. Well, I guess Orville was making one of these corners when he didn't leave enough room and hit an irrigation standpipe.

The standpipe was concrete; the mower cycle bar had hit the standpipe, damaging the mower bar. Blackie came home that night and said, "Paul, I want you to go run the combine." Then he explained that Orville had run the combine into the standpipe. He said maybe Orville was too young to drive the tractor pulling the combine. Orville was thirteen, and I was fifteen, and I was excited to get to drive the combine and felt I should have been asked first.

So early the next morning, Blackie got me up; Mrs. Carter had breakfast ready and our lunches packed. After eating, we loaded up, drove out to Sunnymead, and I climbed aboard the Ford tractor that was still sitting in the grain field. Blackie had started the engine on the combine. So with the beater blades turning and the cycle bar sawing back and forth to cut the grain, I put the tractor into gear, let out on the clutch, and away I went, running the cycle bar right along the last cut Orville had made the day before.

The beater blade would pull the grain stocks into the belt, carrying the grain up to the thrasher. The cycle bar would cut the grain stocks off so they could go up the belt.

I had really looked forward to this the night before. I had pictured how fun it would be to be driving a tractor all day. Well, it wasn't as I had dreamed. It was really hot sitting on that iron tractor seat in the hot sun, in the summertime. The chaff from the grain would get all over me. I itched; I had it in my nostrils, and it went down my collar, making me itch all over. I even had it in my eyes.

The grain that had been separated from the stems of grain went into a hopper. There was a truck parked in the field with wood sides. When the hopper was full, I stopped the tractor and then I went to drive the truck under the chute from the combine.

Then I started the auger from the combine attached to the hopper, and the auger would start emptying the hopper into the big truck. Then I would get back on the tractor and start driving again. I did this all day, day after day, for about a week. I was sure glad when the job was finished.

I was excited for my tractor driving to start that first day, but I was even more excited when the job was finished. Blackie drove me out to the field that last morning. He told me on the way out to drive the tractor back home. He said I should be home by noon, so I didn't take a lunch. I drove out of the field and started down the road at a snail's pace. The Ford tractor in high gear would go only about twelve miles an hour, but pulling the combine, I couldn't go that fast. So with stop signs and pulling over to let traffic pass, it was slow going.

If I didn't let the cars pass, they would be blowing their horns. I drove down Alessandro Street about eight miles and then turned left over to Van Buren, then turned right on Van Buren Avenue heading to Arlington. I turned right off Van Buren onto California Avenue so I would go through Magnolia Center.

There was a big canyon to cross. It was a paved street, so when I started down into the canyon, which was about one hundred feet deep, I thought I would kick her out of gear and let her coast. Wrong thing to do, I found out too late. The weight of the combine was pushing the tractor too fast the front wheels started to shimmy. The steering knuckles were just at the bottom of the steering column.

I had the brake pedals locked together and was standing on it with all my weight, which was all of 110 pounds. It wasn't working; in fact, it was getting faster. I sat back down in the seat and put both feet on the steering knuckles and pushed with both feet to try to stop the front wheels from shimmying. I was scared. This thing was going faster. I clutched the tractor and tried to jam the damn thing back into gear.

The gears were grinding every time I would try to engage the shift lever. I was hanging on to the steering wheel for dear life. Finally, the stupid rig was at the bottom of the canyon and starting up the other side. The rig slowed down enough that I could engage the transmission. With the tractor back under control and going up the other side, life returned to normal. I didn't have a mirror, but I'll bet my face was white.

I had been scared to death in this ordeal, and I learned a very important lesson: Don't ever take a tractor out of gear to coast down a hill. If that hill had been longer, I would have been dead. Look at all the loving I would have missed out on in my lifetime if I had died that day way back in 1951. Thank you, God, for looking after a dumb kid.

So it was on through Magnolia Center, where I had to cross a busy intersection at California Boulevard and Magnolia Boulevard. Finally, with the tractor and combine home, I was safe. But that day and episode stayed with me all my life. Nobody today can picture how really scared this little boy was. I can't say it enough: THANK YOU, GOD, FOR LOOKING AFTER A DUMB KID.

MISDEEDS

I came in from milking one morning and put my bucket of milk by the sink. I heard Mom talking to Lukie Bob, something about New Castle disease. I knew chicken ranchers were always talking about New Castle disease—a thing that chicken ranchers had to worry about because if you got it in your chickens, the state or county would kill all your chickens.

Mom was standing in front of the little gas stove in the living room, as always, on a cold morning. She had her dress pulled up behind her to her waist. She liked the heat from the fire to go right on her bottom. She stood talking to me like this; I wondered if she had any panties on. Really, it was none of my business. I didn't want to see—I was just curious. She said, "Blackie said to ask if you boys are stripping the cows out really good when you milk? If you leave any milk in the cow, she will slowly give less and less milk." They wanted Orville and me to make sure to get it all out.

I was late getting done one day, and I was still milking when Blackie came in and checked the cow Orville had finished milking. He pulled on a teat to see if there was any milk left in the cow's bag. He saw me and said, "Make sure you get all the milk out."

"Okay, Blackie," I said. That was a few days ago. She probably didn't know he had checked and was using his name to be sure and strip the cow's bag out good.

I raised rabbits, which I butchered so I could sell rabbit fryers.

I had a sign out on the front of the house saying, RABBIT FRYERS FOR SALE. I would dress them out, clean them good, and wrap them in white freezer paper. Then into the freezer they went. People would pull in to purchase eggs. Then they would see my sign and say they would like a rabbit fryer too. Or maybe it was a chicken fryer they wanted. If Mom sold a rabbit fryer while I was at school, the money went into my jar in the kitchen.

If I had a lot of fryers in the freezer and another batch was big enough to be dressed out, we would call a guy with a truck with cages on the back. He came and bought all I had. I had twelve does and a buck. After the young rabbits were taken from the doe, after two or three weeks, I would breed her to the buck.

I kept cards on the hutches with the date she was bred, when she gave birth, and how many babies she had. It was all part of my 4-H program. In a feeder between the cages, I would put a flake of good leafy alfalfa hay. But they were also fed rabbit pellets. By selling rabbit fryers, I always had money in my pocket even after buying hay and rabbit pellets.

On Saturday afternoon, Mom would take us into Riverside to the Fox Theater, where we would see a double feature. We would run up to the ticket window and ask what time the movie would be over and then run back and tell her. She would be there at that time to take us home. We would get back just in time to start our evening chores. Sometimes we would help dry the dishes, but mostly, that was Alice and Mom's job. Alice didn't have outside chores to do, nor did she help with the livestock. Everett helped with the dishes too.

With the chores all done and supper eaten, it was time for television.

Remember, our television was a big seven-inch square. *Hometown Jamboree* was my favorite program on Saturday night. I loved anything with music. By eight or eight thirty, we were off to bed. In the early fifties, the television stations stopped their programs at midnight. They would play the National Anthem with a flag waving. Then they would cut to a test pattern. If the television was turned on before programming started, all that you would see was a test pattern. We always went to bed early because we had to be up early to milk.

Bob Wright of chicken shit fame, the one who started the whole mess by wiping the wheelbarrow on Orville's pants, was really into boxing. He was always reading *The Ring Magazine*. We read comic books, and he read his *Ring Magazine*, which was all about boxing. I couldn't care less about boxing. I didn't want to clobber anybody.

"Come on, put the gloves on," he would say.

I was close to fifteen, and Bob was close to seventeen. Orville and I were both small for our age. At sixteen, I was still getting into the movies as being under twelve. So you can see Orville and I were small for our age. Orville had always had more heart than me. It seemed as though he put the gloves on with Bob willingly.

Bob would dance around on his toes, punching him upside the head. After Orville had had enough getting knocked around, Bob would tease me into putting the gloves on. "Come on," he would say. "I'll just spar with you. I'll just hit you on the shoulder."

Use me for a punching bag, he meant.

I wasn't good at punching or keeping my guard up. I was an easy target for his blows.

He would give me the old one-two, usually really fast, right in the face. I remember having my nose bloodied once. I had seen kids at school with broken noses, and I didn't want one. The ones I saw at school had a piece of stainless steel taped over their nose, I guess to keep it straight while it healed. After doing this with Bob a few times, I figured I would never make a fighter. I didn't have the heart for it; besides, I didn't want to hurt anybody, especially me.

When they made a bunkhouse out of a room where they had a cream separator, we all had bunk beds. Roy Hansen, a new boy at the Carters', slept under me. Roy was a nice kid. He was tall for his age; he wore thick glasses and was kind of quiet. Roy and Everett got along well, except when Roy had Everett put the boxing gloves on with him. Roy knocked Everett for a loop over some hedges that grew beside our patio area.

After a few times getting clobbered by Roy, Everett figured he didn't want to be a boxer either. Bob Wright and Roy Hansen did not want to teach us the fine art of fisticuffs. They just wanted to knock the shit out of us. Bob got the gloves on me a few more times that summer, always with "I'll only hit you on the shoulder." Then letting you have it, right in the face again. I realized Bob was a liar; a house didn't have to fall on me.

I found out there always has to be someone who wants to run the show. Usually, he was the big kid, and being big, he could make the other kids do what he wanted. Make you bring him a drink or snatch your comic books when you were reading them. Anything to show he was boss. Finally, I got tired of it.

So one day, he wanted to slip out of the house to see a movie about boxing. That was all he thought about. I told him that Orville and I sneaked out and had gone to a movie one night. I said there was no screen on one window in the bay window upstairs.

Bob was sleeping in the room Orville and I shared upstairs before he arrived at the Carters'. They had turned the creamery room into a bunkhouse. We just opened the window and went out on the roof of the bay window. There were two decorative posts sticking about a foot above the roof, and we just climbed down. Then after the movie, we walked home and climbed the post and then came back in through the window. No one knew what we had done. In reality, I climbed out the window to go get a jar of albacore that Mrs. Carter had canned and stored in a pantry off the kitchen. We had done this a few times, so that was how I knew how to escape, and since Bob was in our old room, he could do it too.

That night, Bob said he was tired and was going up to do his homework and then go to sleep. It was barely dark, but on a ranch, you get up early, so you go to bed early too. For some reason, I don't remember Bob Wright having to milk a cow. When I finished milking, I was coming by Bob's calf pen, and I got the idea to open his pen and let the calf out. I knew Bob was planning on going to that show because I told him how to sneak out.

I came into the house with my bucket of milk and said, "Mom, Bob's calf is out, and he must have left the gate open. Shall I go put it back in?"

"No! You go upstairs and tell Bob his calf is out and to go put it back in the pen."

"Okay, Mom!" So I went upstairs, knowing Bob wasn't there. But just in case he didn't go, I would tell him his calf was out.

I looked around, and I didn't see him, so I went back downstairs and told Mom, "He's not up there."

"He's not! Did you look in the bathroom?"

"Yeah! I didn't see him."

She went up and looked, and she couldn't see him either.

"Maybe he ran away," I said.

"No, he's probably out in the barn with Robert," she said, meaning her son. She never called him Lukie Bob like we did. She went out to ask Robert if he had seen Bob. Robert said he hadn't seen Bob.

It seemed that we looked for the better part of an hour.

Finally, Mom said, "Well, he'll have to come back. All his clothes are here."

I went to bed out in the bunkhouse with Orville and Everett on one bunk and me and Roy on the other.

I closed my eyes and was thinking, *I hope they send him back to juvie.*

Bob was there at breakfast the next morning. He didn't go to school because his probation officer was coming to talk to him.

When we came home from school, he was gone. Mrs. Carter didn't say much, just that his probation officer had Bob pack his clothes and took him away. Personally, I was glad he was gone. I don't remember what they did with his calf.

Looking back now, I know I was wrong. I'm seventy-one years old going on seventy-two. I made mistakes, and this was one of many. Bob Wright was just like us. We were in foster homes; we weren't living with our mothers and fathers. He just wanted someone who cared. A family to be part of. We were all in the same boat. Maybe in a prior foster home someone had treated him like he had treated me. Bob coped by getting tough. My dad told me, "Son, life is short." And looking back at seventy-one, I can see he was right.

When you're a kid, you rate time by how long the school year is. It takes forever. If I could have pictured how time would fly in the summer or Christmas vacation. I could have envisioned how fast time would pass. I dwelt on how slow the school year went, or how long it was from Christmas to Christmas. That's how I gauged time.

No one came to visit Bob Wright or Roy Hansen at the Carters'. My sister Rita often came to visit us, and would even take us home overnight a few times. She lived in San Bernardino, and one time, she picked us up and asked, "Could you get a chicken? We can take it to my house, kill it, and cook it for supper."

I said, "I'll go see."

Nobody was around, so I got an old feed sack, took a chicken from the cage and shoved it in. I came out from the barn, stopping to see if anyone was around. When I didn't see anyone, I walked over to Rita's car and got in.

"Keep it down while I turn around," she told me.

We drove to her house, where I killed the chicken and cleaned it. Rita baked it in the oven, and then she made mashed potatoes and gravy to go with it. She took her knife and sliced into the chicken.

"Eww!" I heard her say. "What's this?"

I had forgotten to remove the chicken craw. "Don't say anything about this to Truman," she said, meaning her husband.

I said, "Just slice it off."

It was contained in a pouch and didn't hurt the rest of the bird. It didn't bother me, but I noticed Truman and I were the only ones eating chicken that night. Rita mostly had mashed potatoes and gravy.

My dad came and took us all to see *Red River*, featuring John Wayne, at the Arlington Theatre. It was summer, and that theater was stifling hot. I was a kid and loved westerns. My dad told us he was trying to get custody of us. He said he would let us know how it went.

I went to the sale at Pedley with Blackie and was able to buy a day-old red calf at auction for six dollars. I bought Calf Manna to mix with milk to feed my calf. He grew strong and was never sick like some of the day-old calves that Blackie bought. When the calf was three months old, I took it back to Pedley with some calves that Blackie was selling, and it was auctioned off for fifty dollars.

I wanted to buy a motorbike so I kept watching the paper and found one. It was a Whizzer Motorbike on a Schwinn frame, and the ad said fifty dollars. Mrs. Carter took me to look at it, and I bought it. I wished Orville was here to see it, but he had run away. They caught him, and he was living in another foster home now.

Allen Pierce, a boy at school, had told me to take the head off of the Whizzer engine and mill it down so it would have more power. So I removed the head, which was made out of aluminum. I put it in a vise and carefully filed it down about a sixteenth of an inch. Blackie had a flat grinding stone, and I laid the filed engine head flat onto the stone and pushed it back and forth.

When the file marks were all gone, I knew it was flat. I reinstalled it on the engine, and I might be crazy, but it seemed to have a lot more power because I had increased the compression. I took Everett and Roy for a ride on it, and they thought it was great fun. Roy said he would like to buy one someday, and I saw him reading the want ads in the paper after school.

Roy Hansen's folks were dead. We were all just trying to get through childhood and become adults. Then we could take care of ourselves. I dreamt of owning a car, just driving down the open road, not a care in the world. Kind of like I was doing with my Whizzer bike. I hope Bob Wright and Roy Hansen had a good life. We were all just a matter of circumstance. I feel that I have been very blessed in my life, and working in construction was one of the highlights. I loved to build things. I wish Orville, Everett, and I had got into building homes when we were young as I think we would have been good at it.

ORVILLE RUNS AWAY

"I'm going to run away," Orville said. I thought he sounded just like Br'er Rabbit in *Song of the South*: "I'm gonna leave my old briar patch!"

"Are you? Where are you going," I asked.

"I'm going to Blythe where Dad is!"

I don't remember if I believed him, but Orville wasn't afraid to do anything. He had more guts than a government mule.

We just got up one morning, and he was gone. He just packed his clothes and left. He had about fifty dollars from selling his calf at auction. I didn't remember what took, place so I called Orville. He said he called the Greyhound bus depot and got the time the bus for Blythe left at night. It would leave at 11:00 p.m. He didn't remember how much the ticket was, but he called a cab to pick him up in front of the Carters' at about 9:30 p.m.

At the bus depot, he purchased a ticket and boarded the bus and was on his way to a life with Dad. No more schooling, just watermelons, guns, and hunting. All the carefree things in life a boy dreams of. He said he would get in touch with me when he was grown and had a phone. He took the Carters' phone number so he could check in from time to time, to let me know how the good life was, so to speak.

Orville doesn't remember much about the trip to Blythe. He said he slept most of the way. He remembers it was really hot—no air-conditioning on buses back then. The window by his seat he had open as far as it would go, which was about six or eight inches. The night air was stifling hot by the time the bus reached White Water Pass, beyond Cabazon. He woke up covered in sweat. When it's hot like that you doze off, then wake right back up. You sleep a little, but you don't get a good rest.

The bus took all night and into the next day, about noon, to get there. The bus would stop in Beaumont, Banning, White Water, Palm Springs, Cathedral City, Indio, then Blythe. The bus stop in Indio was at a café. The driver said, "Indio! We'll be here for forty-five minutes for breakfast. Our bus number is 1349. Be sure to look at the bus number before boarding again." Sometimes passengers boarded the wrong bus.

Orville sat at the counter, looked at the menu, and ordered a stack of hotcakes and a bacon side. There was a bowl with matchbooks in it for smokers; Orville put three packs in his pocket.

He figured he might need a match for something; besides, they were free. The waitress brought the hotcakes and side of bacon, four pieces. *Great*, he thought.

"You want something to drink with that, honey?" the waitress asked.

"I'll have a glass of milk," Orville said.

She brought the milk and put his check down by the glass.

"If there is anything else, honey, just let me know!"

Orville finished the hotcakes and milk and went to the cashier to pay. The bill was ninety-five cents. Then he walked back to the counter where he had sat and put a dime tip for the waitress. She saw him and smiled. "Thanks, honey."

Orville went to the bathroom and then got back on bus number 1349. After the bus was loaded, two new passengers, both men, got on.

Once in Blythe, Orville took his suitcase and started walking east on Hobson Way. About a half mile out of town on the right-hand side of the street was a sporting goods store. Orville went in and looked at some .22 rifles. One bolt action Remington .22 with a clip that held 6 rounds caught his eye. He was only thirteen, but kids could buy a gun then without any trouble. Children were raised around guns then. If a gun was standing in the corner of a room and you knew it was loaded, you knew it wasn't to be touched under any circumstances—no *if*s, *and*s, or *but*s.

So with his new rifle and a box of shells (which the storeowner threw in for free) but sixteen dollars lighter in his wallet, Orville, with suitcase in hand, was again headed east to Intake Boulevard. He decided to stop at a market for a few things to eat. He bought six cans of sardines, a box of crackers, a chunk of cheese, and a big bottle of soda pop.

Orville was once again on his way east toward Intake Boulevard. A man in a pickup stopped and asked him if he wanted a ride.

"You bet," said Orville, and he climbed into the truck.

Then the man asked Orville if he would like a job.

"Doing what?" asked Orville.

"Well, a couple of days ago, it rained on my hay bales lying in the field. They have dried on the topside, and I need help turning them so they dry on the bottom side, or they will mold if I don't turn them over."

"Sure," Orville told him. So the man drove out to a field, and they started turning the hay bales over.

Orville said it was so hot and humid that sweat was pouring off him. Finally, after two hours, they called it quits for the day. The man asked if he could drop Orville someplace. Orville said, "Sure," and directed him to a place on south Intake Boulevard, where our dad lived. A man who owned the five-acre property lived in Los Angeles. He gave our dad permission to stay there and look after the place, just so people didn't use it for a dump. If people start dumping trash on your property, a lot of trash can accumulate in a short amount of time. And it can be costly to have cleaned up.

Orville walked down the long curving road into the property. As he walked along, each footstep caused dust to rise up around his legs. It was a powdery, alkaline dust. By the time Orville reached the lean-to shed that Dad had built on the property, the sweat on his legs had turned the powdery dust to a type of mud. Orville was afraid going on the dusty road that Dad wasn't there because there were no recent tire tracks. Orville's fears were confirmed when he got to the makeshift shed. The plywood door was locked, and there was no sign of activity.

He sat down on an old bench that Dad had placed in front of the shack. He set his suitcase and the new rifle he had purchased down on the bench beside him. *Shit, it's hot*, he thought. The area around the shack was all air weeds six or seven feet high and as thick as hair on a dog. No air stirring at all. He sat there pondering his predicament, with sweat from his armpits running down his sides. One good thing, though: the sun was going down. What a long day this had been, he was thinking. He pulled the key from a can of sardines and opened them up. He began eating the sardines with crackers and washing it all down with the pop, which was warm by now.

He was really tired and started looking for something to lay down on to get some sleep. Dad had left an old tarp rolled up on a chair to the south side of the shed. He picked it up and started looking for a place out of sight where he could lay down. He didn't want to go to sleep where the police could find him (if they were looking for him).

He walked out into the high air weeds and found a mesquite tree in a little opening. He thought, *This looks hidden enough. No one can see me through the high weeds.* He kicked a few weeds out of the way so the place wouldn't be lumpy. He took out his pocketknife and cut some of the air weeds off to lay down for a mattress.

When the air weeds were about two inches thick, he rolled out the canvas tarp and lay down. He took the .22 rifle out of the box, took the magazine out, and, with the box of .22 shells the store clerk had given him, he put six shells into the magazine, worked the bolt on the rifle, and put a round into the chamber.

He was ready to do some business if anybody gave him any shit.

He lay there with his suitcase at his back and his new rifle cradled in his arms. *Shit, it's hot,* he thought as he closed his eyes to get some much-needed rest. *I should have waited for cooler weather to leave home.* He wondered where Dad was as he lay there listening to the crickets chirping before he finally dozed off.

The sandy silt in Blythe does not cool off at night. The sand holds the heat. The temperature might change by ten degrees from day to night; it was still about ninety-eight degrees. He woke in the morning with the sun already up. At least the air weeds were shading him from the hot sun. He knew as the sun got higher in the sky that the mesquite tree, with its little leaves, wouldn't offer much protection from the sun.

He felt as though he had cotton in his mouth. *Boy, I need a drink bad,* he was thinking. *I hope my dad has some water at the shack. If he don't I'll have to walk to the river about a mile away. I'll take a pot or a can and bring some back. But right now I'll go see if dad came home last night, as that would end my troubles, and dad would hide me from the police if they were looking for him too.*

He started for the shack and there in his tracks from last night was a snake track. It had crawled right over his track, no telling how long ago. And it was big too, about four inches wide. That's a big snake. He hadn't thought of snakes last night. Hell, he was used to living in a house, not the wild desert. But he wasn't concerned, as he had his newly bought gun to protect him from any pesky critters that came snooping around.

Dad wasn't at the shack this morning, but Orville found a five-gallon plastic can of water at the back of the shack. There was a piece of plywood leaning against the plastic can so the sun wouldn't shine on it. He picked up a porcelain cup nearby, took the lid off the can, and slopped a little water in the cup to rinse it out. He couldn't wait to fill the cup and get a cold drink. He put the cup to his lips. Shit, the water was warm as pee.

After pausing for a minute to think how he could cool it down, he put the cup to his lips and drank it dry. *I'll just pretend its hot coffee*, he thought. The sardines and crackers didn't fill him from the night before, and he was hungry. Thinking Dad would be here and would have food, he had bought the sardines for snacks, not for a meal. *Who wants sardines for breakfast anyway*, he thought, looking around at the sack of food.

He was thinking he had better start walking back to town—something he didn't want to do in the heat of the day. He looked, and there in the pasture, where Dad had a couple of horses at one time, was a cottontail rabbit. He thought that rabbit looked like breakfast. He picked up his .22 rifle, which already had a bullet in the chamber.

He clicked off the safety, drew a bead on the rabbit behind his front leg, and squeezed the trigger. *Pow*, the rabbit fell over, kicked a few times, and then was still. Orville walked over, picked it up, and thought, *My new rifle shoots real good*. He looked for a place to hang the rabbit so he could skin the hide off the little critter.

The mesquite tree in the back of Dad's shack was a good place to start. He found a short limb that had been broken off. He pulled the skin down on the rabbit's leg to expose the tendon and push the leg onto the limb. With the rabbit hanging from the limb, he was able to completely skin it. Then he cleaned the insides out. He took it to the water can, splashed some water on it, and the rabbit was cleaned.

There was a lot of wood lying in a pile where Dad had trimmed the trees. He broke some of the small limbs and laid them crisscross-style on some newspaper that was stacked by the corner of the shack. Then with a match from the book he had taken from the bus stop in Indio, he lit the paper. As the fire caught, he added bigger branches.

There was a metal screw jack handle from some car in a junk pile in the back of the shack. With that and a couple pieces of wire, he found he was able to attach the rabbit to the jack handle. He sat down and put the rabbit into the fire. He kept turning the rabbit slowly. The mesquite wood is a hardwood and makes a hot fire with very little smoke. The fire pops a little as he keeps turning the rabbit. He can hardly wait for it to cook.

Orville always had an ear turned to the road coming in. He wanted to hear if a car was approaching from the road. He said to himself, I should have gone out to the pasture to cook the rabbit. In case anyone came in, they would see the fire. *Oh well, too late now*, he thought. *If I hear someone, I'll just drop the rabbit and run.* And he looked for something to throw on the fire, maybe cover it up, but anything he saw would burn up.

The rabbit looked done, so he pulled a leg off and bit into the meat. *Mmm, this is good.* He quit worrying about the fire because he was hungry. No bread, just rabbit and crackers and warm water. Even the soda pop was warm this morning. He sat thinking about the turn of events. He had never once thought Dad wouldn't be here.

He remembered just a few short nights ago he was watching a comedy on television. It was Laurel and Hardy. Ollie said to Stan, "Another fine mess you've gotten us into." Well, that was how he felt now—a fine mess he had gotten himself into. *Where did I go wrong?* he was thinking. I thought Dad was always in Blythe, as the letters he wrote came from there.

Later that day, Orville heard a car coming down the driveway, and he hightailed it into the brush just in the nick of time. It was a police car, and an officer got out and looked around. He walked over and tried the door on the shack, but it was locked tight. He looked around once more and then got into the patrol car and left. Good thing Orville had scraped some dirt over the fire when he finished cooking the rabbit.

Orville was watching it all from his hiding spot back in the brush. He waited a half hour before he came back out. He knew the policeman hadn't seen the ashes from his fire, but he walked over and kicked a little more dirt on them. *Can't be too careful when you're hiding out*, he thought. He was thinking he would have to be very careful after this. Police officers were pretty smart; they might try sneaking back in just to see if anyone was here. Then he thought they were looking for him, all right. *Better be careful.*

He stayed far out in the brush for most of the day, but he occasionally came to see if Dad had returned to the house. *It's so hot and humid*, he was thinking. So he rolled his rifle up in his canvas sleeping tarp and placed his suitcase nearby. Then he started making his way out of the driveway and headed for the river to swim. He was careful not to walk in the dusty road so he wouldn't leave any tracks for nosy cops to see. *Maybe there will be watermelons on Homer Johns's place beside the river. Boy, a ripe watermelon would sure taste good*, he was thinking.

As he walked the mile to the river, he was wondering what his brothers Paul and Everett had told the Carters when they found he had run away. *No more school for me, I'm just going to shoot game and live off the land just like my dad.* He was wondering where Dad could be. *Maybe he went over to Riverside to visit us at the Carters'. Oh well, I can't be worrying about that right now because I'm going swimming.*

Oh boy, look at all the watermelons, he almost said out loud to himself as he walked out onto the edge of the field of melons and picked one. He lifted it up and dropped it, splitting the melon open. Then he dug his fingers into the heart and ripped it out and lifted it to his mouth and took a big bite. *This is really good*, he was thinking as he returned to the road to finish the trip out to the river. The river's water was flowing too fast, so he decided to swim in the slough that ran back from the river. Besides, the water in the slough was warmer.

What a way to spend the day. *Paul and Everett should be here*, he was thinking. *They will have to milk the cows before long because the sun is getting low. I better be heading home too before it gets dark. Maybe Dad will be there by now. Won't he be surprised to see I've come to live with him. We can just hunt and fish together. I bet he will like my new gun. I might even let him shoot it if he's good. Hope he's home now.*

As soon as he turned into the dusty road, he knew Dad hadn't returned. The tracks of the cop car were the last ones on the road. He walked in the weeds beside the road, going back to the old shack. He didn't want to leave any tracks for the law to see. It was still light, but he was tired from his walk to the river, so he went out in the brush and unrolled the canvas and took his rifle out and lay down with the rifle nearby. He kept wishing dad would come back. *There's nobody to talk to*, he thought as he patted his rifle. He felt this rifle was his one true friend that would always stand by him.

Orville sat around in the brush just waiting for his Dad to return. The cops, he found out, always drove into the driveway about three o'clock in the afternoon. The cop would get out, look around, and then leave. After the cop left, Orville waited for a while before he started walking to the river to swim and eat another watermelon.

By the time he reached the river, his legs would be all dusty, almost up to his knees. Once he dove into the slough, it all washed off, and did it ever feel good after another hot day. Another watermelon wasn't bad either. He was thinking he would eat another heart out of a melon on the way home. He was kind of tired of sardines and crackers with cheese. In fact, the cheese had started melting a little and was tasting stale from the heat.

The next day, he was sitting by Dad's shack, eating sardines and crackers again, when the officer walked back down the road and caught him sitting there. "Are you Desmond Huff's son," the officer asked.

"Yeah."

"Well, I have to take you in, son. You've run away, and you can't just stay here by yourself. You got any clothes with you?" he asked.

"I have a suitcase and my rifle out in the brush," Orville told him.

"Well, let's go get them," the officer said. Then he asked, "Were you looking for your dad?"

"Yeah, but he's not here," Orville told him.

The officer told Orville he had seen his tracks in the dirt, so he knew he was here. That was why he parked out on the pavement and walked in on foot. He told Orville, "I figured you heard my car coming in and ran and hid, am I right?"

"Yeah."

"Well, I have to take you back to Riverside." They got in the car and made the long trip through the desert back to Riverside, California. They placed Orville back into juvenile hall in Arlington California. After a week in juvie, Orville was placed in a foster home on Van Buren Boulevard east of Arlington. The foster parents' names were Drake, and they attended the First Baptist Church of Riverside.

We had all attended the church in the past, so I started going there again so I could see Orville and hear about what happened when he ran away from the Carters'. He told me about the rifle he had bought and said Dad wasn't in Blythe, and that he was glad to get caught. I told him about buying a Whizzer Motorbike with the money I got from selling my calf. It's really neat, you'll see.

Then I said, "I'll bring it to church next Sunday, and I'll give you a ride." I also told him about coming along the dirt road that ran alongside the railroad tracks on my bike where the boy had been killed while we waited for the school bus. I said that I would have my motorbike going really fast, and as I came up the grade onto Streeter Avenue, I could jump my bike off the ground. I told him, "I have to watch the traffic really close so I don't hit a car on Streeter Avenue. You'll see how much fun it is when I bring it next week and give you a ride.

Orville told me that Harvey Sanders was in the foster home at Drakes where he was now living. Mother and Dad were friends with Harvey's mom and dad, Martha and Emmett Sanders. I think our parents were friends with Emmett and Martha in Hemet where we were born.

I think I've said this before in this story, but I'll say it again. My mother was living at the Gail Hotel on Eighth Street, and my sister Ernestine was living down the street at the St Elmo Hotel.

Emmett and Martha Sanders lived around the corner a block south on Main Street in still another hotel. Orville had gotten to be friends with their son Harvey during this time, so he had a friend at the Drakes' when he was placed there.

Orville told me when he first arrived at the Drakes' home that he walked outside and saw there were some boys walking toward him, coming from a bunkhouse. He said the biggest boy he could tell was kind of a bully and was bossing the other boys around.

Orville said he knew this was a boy who would give him trouble if he didn't nip things in the bud. So Orville said he was ready. When they got close enough, he smacked the biggest boy right on the end of his nose.

Blood flew everywhere. The other boys were amazed someone would be crazy enough to take on this bully. Orville was a hero to these other boys from then on, and the bully never gave him any trouble while he lived there. This was where Harvey Sanders had been placed as well. Orville got to keep the rifle he bought in Blythe, so he and Harvey would take it out on weekends and shoot up the countryside.

Orville said Harvey liked to ride their bikes to March Air Force Base down the road from where they lived, and they would lie on their backs and shoot at B29 airplanes as they came in for a landing at March Field. Not too smart, but the aircraft were high enough that they didn't hit any as all they had were .22 shorts. I would hate to think what could have happened if they had.

On Sunday, I arrived at church to find Orville standing on the sidewalk in front of the church with other boys from the Drakes'. As I pulled up by the curb, Orville walked over to my motorbike and said, "Neat. Come on, I'll take you for a ride. We have time before church."

Orville sat down on the gas tank, and I gave the motorbike the gas as we headed south toward the Riverside Poly High School, where I had started the tenth grade in the fall of 1951. The high school sat in the foothills south of Riverside. The football field was a flat field in the valley. And the school up on the hill overlooked it.

I turned left off the road going up to the school buildings and picked up speed with my motorbike pretty fast as it was going downhill toward the football field.

As I came across the end of the football field, there was a sharp turn to the right, but it was banked a little, and I wanted to give Orville a thrill, so I kept my speed up pretty fast. I noticed the road was a little wet but didn't think it would be a problem for this daredevil who had been jumping this bike off the ground just days before.

We came into the turn, and I leaned the bike low. All of a sudden, we were sliding sideways on the muddy asphalt. Good thing there were no cars coming from the other direction, or we would have slid under them. Holy shit, our Sunday suits were all muddy on the right side. I told Orville how sorry I was. We couldn't go back to church now with mud all over our clothes. I rode the bike up in front of the church and dropped Orville off and said I was sorry again, and I lit out for Carters'.

When my clothes had dried, I tried to brush the mud off and wiped them with a washrag, but they never did come clean. I finally rolled them in a ball so the mud didn't show and told Mrs. Carter to send them to the cleaners. I can't remember getting into trouble, but Orville wasn't allowed to leave the church grounds after that. Another fine mess I'd gotten us into. Three months later, our dad had gotten custody of us, and we went to live with him in Blythe.

NO MORE FOSTER HOMES

In February 1952, Dad came to pick us three boys up at the Carters' home in Riverside, California. We had been told he had gotten custody of us, and we were told to get our bags all packed as he would be there that day. Dad came, and Everett and I were excited to be going with our dad. We knew we would be picking Orville up and we would all be back together again and living the good life with our dad.

Our sister Alice was going to be living with Aunt Ellen from the First Baptist Church out in Hemet again. When Dad showed up to get us, he was driving a maroon 1941 Willys coupe. He had a wooden pickup-looking box built into the space where the trunk should have been. I had been worried about being able to take my Whizzer motorbike with us because of limited room.

Dad was able to get it into the car with all our things. But we still had to go to the foster home where Orville was living and get him and his bags, and anything else he had. We said our goodbyes to the Carters, who were very nice people. If it wasn't that we were going with our dad, I would have been sad.

Mrs. Carter said, "You boys write and let us know how you're doing."

I said, "Okay, we will." And we waved to them when Dad turned the car around and started out of the driveway. We drove out to the Drakes' where Orville was staying out on Van Buren Avenue. After he loaded his things into the car, we were on our way to a life with our dad.

Dad said, "We'll go out to your cousin Doris's home in Beaumont." She and her husband, La Rue Meredith, had a home on a big wash a couple of miles west of Beaumont. It was Friday, and Dad had to wait until school was out before picking us up in the afternoon. Since it was late in the afternoon, he had decided to see Doris and La Rue and spend the night with them.

When we got to Doris's house, she was glad Dad had stopped by. She fixed us supper and made the beds for us to sleep in. The next morning at breakfast, I asked Dad if I could get my motorbike out and ride it around through the hills. He asked if I had any gas in it, and I said I did. "Well, after breakfast, we'll get it down from the car since we will be staying Saturday night and going home on Sunday," he told me.

I was riding my bike all around their property when I came up a steep hill and saw La Rue was standing at the top of the hill watching me ride the bike. He said, "Paul, can I take your motorbike for a ride?"

"Sure," I told him. I got off and watched him ride off on the bike. He rode down the steep grade I had just come up and made a turn at the bottom of the hill and gunned the bike. He took a run at the hill, and up it he came.

I was wondering if he could climb the hill because he weighed at least two hundred pounds. But climb it he did, and he was smiling as he rode past me. He rode the bike out to the paved highway we had turned off of to get to his house last night. He was gone fifteen or twenty minutes when I saw him coming back, and he was going wide open. Wide open, it would go thirty-five to forty miles per hour.

I watched him circle the bike and come back still smiling. He pulled the bike right up to me and said, "You think you'd want to trade this bike for that Ford Model A over there?"

I turned around and looked at a black Model A sitting out by the barn.

"Are you kidding?" I asked.

La Rue said, "No, I'm not kidding. Go over and check it out." The little car was clean and had all the glass in the windows. My heart was racing as I wondered if he was teasing me. Then he said, "The key is in it. Take it for a spin. So I climbed into the little coupe and started the engine. It started right up. I sat there waiting for it to warm up with a big grin on my face. I was thinking, *If he's kidding, I'll kill him when he starts to laugh at me.* I watched him as he walked back over to the motorbike and started it up and went barreling down that steep hill again.

He was as excited as I was. I shifted into low and took off on the road out to the blacktop. This was similar to the little roadster that Hambone let me ride at the Carters'.

This car had a top; Hambone's was a convertible. *Oh well, can't have everything all at once.*

I turned around at the pavement and drove back to the house. Dad had walked out of the house and was standing in the driveway. I pulled up to him and said, "La Rue wants to trade this car for my motorbike, and can I trade him, Dad?"

"Hell, son, if you want the car, go ahead and trade." Dad walked to the side of the car, raised the hood, and looked the engine over. He closed the hood and opened the door and sat down. He said, "Drive up the road apiece and let me hear how it sounds."

We turned around at the pavement again, and Dad said, "Hell, son, I don't think you can go wrong. You'll have to drive it all the way to Blythe Tomorrow."

"That's okay." I was really excited. "Well, let's talk to La Rue and make the deal, just so's he don't want any money to boot. The trade has to be straight across, no money exchanged."

I swapped my motorbike for the car, and we exchanged pink slips. I spent the rest of the day cleaning everything on it. I wanted it to be as clean as Hambone's car was. I wished Hambone was here so I could show him my car. I wished mine had a V8 like Hambone's did, but I was happy anyway. I took Orville and Everett for a ride in it too.

"Hey, Orville, maybe Dad will let you ride with me tomorrow when we drive on down to Blythe."

Orville said he would ask Dad if he could ride with me.

The next morning, we left Doris and La Rue's and headed on down to Blythe.

Orville was in the passenger seat, and I had traded for my first car. Dad said he would lead the way and for Orville and me to follow him. I had turned sixteen only a month ago. I bet the Carters wouldn't believe I had a car already and was driving it to Blythe. Shoot we only left there two days ago.

Lukie Bob didn't even have a car, but he used the '39 Chevy that I drove on Mrs. Carter's egg route. I wish Lukie Bob could see me with my 1931 Ford Model A and me driving it to Blythe.

Dad wanted to stop at a market in Indio to buy the fixin's for sandwiches. He said, "Let's get a loaf of bread and some lunchmeat and a few slices of cheese. Then we'll hit a gas station and fill the gas tanks, as that Model A only holds ten gallons. Then we'll head on out past Chiriaco Summit, and we'll pull over under a palo verde tree and eat. You boys want a carton of milk?" Dad asked no one in particular.

"I do," I told him. "We need something to wash the sandwiches down with."

When we left Indio, we were going up steep hills with only a two-lane road. There were a lot of trucks climbing the grade, and they were in low gear and not going very fast. We just fell in line behind a gasoline tanker because we didn't have enough power to pass. I think it took more than an hour to get to the summit. My Model A would go only about forty-five miles an hour on the flat highway. The trucks we were behind were doing only fifteen miles an hour.

There was a filling station at the summit, and we pulled in to check the water in the radiator. I saw steam coming from it as we neared the top, and it made sprinkles on my windshield, so I knew it was low on water and was getting hot. We had to pay twenty- five cents for the water because they had to truck it out to the summit from Indio.

We had our radiator full, used the bathroom, and were on our way to the spot where we would pull over to eat. It couldn't be too soon for me as I was really hungry. It was almost way past noon by now. Doris had made us hotcakes before we left Beaumont, but they were gone long ago.

Finally, Dad turned off the road and stopped under a big palo verde tree. We got out and spread the sandwich fixin's out in the back of Dad's car with the pickup bed. Each one of us made our own sandwich, and Dad put out some cups to pour milk into. I was surprised the milk was still cold. But there was a cold wind blowing, and it was cold even in the sun. As I sat and ate my sandwich, I watched the cars on the highway.

They went whizzing by, some going seventy miles an hour, and they probably had heaters in their cars too. I was jealous, but I hoped to have a new car someday myself.

Dad brought me back to reality when I heard him say, "Well, boys, we better get this show on the road, and we want to be in Blythe before sundown. How's your car running, son?" he asked me.

"Good, since we stopped for water," I told him.

"Well, get in your buggy and let's get on down the road," Dad said.

We were making better time now because the steep grades were behind us. It took us an hour to reach Desert Center, then another hour to get into Blythe. Dad pulled into some old apartments where he had rented one of them for us. That was part of getting custody of us: he had to have a home for us to live in.

I don't remember much about this time, but we enrolled in school. I was in the tenth grade. I rode a school bus out north of town each morning, which was quite a ways out to the school. We attended the school for maybe only four weeks. I hated the school in Blythe.

Dad said, "Son, if you boys don't go to school, they'll come and put you back into a foster home, and there won't be a damn thing I can do about it. If you want to quit school, we'll have to leave the state and hide out."

I was ready to do anything because I hated to be the new boy in school. The students didn't act friendly at all. Dad didn't like paying rent each month either, so we moved out of the apartment down on South Intake Boulevard. Dad sold his Willy's, and we loaded my Model A with our stuff and left Blythe one morning without a goodbye to anyone. Dad was headed to Casa Grande, Arizona, where he hoped to find work on a farm.

One of us had slammed the door on my Model A and broke half the glass out on the driver's side. It was raining going from Yuma toward Gila Bend, Arizona, and whenever we met a semitruck, it would splash water into the broken window and drown me as I was driving. It was a long way to Gila Bend traveling forty-five miles an hour with dim lights on my model A Ford at night when you're cold and wet.

Well, we finally made it to Gila Bend, and we just pulled over and camped out in the brush along the highway. The next morning, we were on the road again. At least I had changed clothes and was dry. It rained off and on all the way to Casa Grande, and when we arrived, we pulled into a stockyard just outside of town. It was still raining, so we had to just sit in the car. Thinking back now, I wonder why Dad didn't rent a cabin someplace. At least we would have been dry and comfortable. But Dad hated to spend money on rent.

I don't know how much money Dad had, but it couldn't have been very much. I do remember he walked into Casa Grande and an Indian man approached him and said he would give Dad ten dollars to buy him a quart of Four Roses whiskey. Indians couldn't buy whiskey at this time in the early 1950s. Four Roses was the only whiskey that was sold in a quart bottle. All the other whiskeys were sold in four-fifths quart. We hung around Casa Grande for about a week as we looked for work. One rancher whom Dad stopped southwest of town said he would like Dad to do some plowing for him when the weather got better.

My Ford was burning oil pretty bad on one cylinder and was fouling the spark plug. Dad said he thought the rings might be broke on that cylinder.

Dad told the rancher he would stay a few days and work on his car while waiting for the weather to get better. The rancher said we could stay in one of his cabins if we liked while Dad worked on the car.

So we finally had a roof over our heads. Dad drove into town and bought a set of rings for the motor. He came back and started pulling the head off the motor and dropped the pan as well so he could get the connecting rod and piston out. The rings were indeed broke, so he replaced them with new ones.

The process took two days to finish, with me watching everything he did. I loved mechanics and wanted to learn all I could from my dad. The farmer still wasn't ready to work the fields, so Dad said, "Let's get the hell out of here and go over around Buckeye."

The next morning, we loaded up and flagged Old Brownie out of there. I don't even think dad told the rancher we were leaving.

WADDELL RANCH COMPANY

I was driving my Model A coupe going up a dirt road from Perryville just north of Buckeye, Arizona. Dad, my two brothers, and I were driving north toward a ranch where Dad had worked in 1945. We were about out of money. It was early spring 1952 in Arizona. There was not much work going on this time of year. The cotton had been planted but wasn't high enough to chop.

Dad had been to a couple of ranches down around Casa Grande and Eloy. They were all six weeks away from needing workers. We had left Casa Grande early this morning.

Dad said, "Boys, we are low on money. If we go over around Buckeye, maybe we can find some cotton to chop."

We didn't know what he was talking about because my brothers and I had never chopped cotton.

He said, "When we get to Buckeye, we'll drive around and look for a group of cars parked at the end of a field. If we find them, they will be cotton choppers." We were driving through fields planted with young cotton plants, but nothing high enough to chop.

Dad looked worried when he said, "Hell, son, I don't see work here either. The cotton is just too young to chop. The plants are only about three inches high. They have to be six or eight inches high before they'll want workers in the field."

"What do you mean by chopping cotton, Dad?" I asked.

"Well, son, a tractor drags a planter behind it, and it lays down a solid row of seeds. Then when the plants are six or seven inches tall, cotton choppers walk along with a wide hoe, chopping out the plants. They leave them spaced about twelve inches apart. They pay twenty-five cents for a quarter-mile row."

"Will we all be able to work?" I asked.

"Well, you two older boys can, but I don't know about Everett. We might have to keep Everett hid out. If they see Everett's not in school and I don't have a good reason for him being out of school, there will be all hell to pay. You and Orville are big enough to be out of school, but Everett isn't," Dad said.

We'd been driving around Buckeye, and Dad said, "It's just too early. A couple of weeks from now, there will be plenty of work. But in the meantime, we have to find work. I mean pronto. You boys be looking for a tractor parked in a field so we can get some gas after dark."

"Okay, Dad, we'll watch."

"I was working on a ranch over here in 1945, about three or four miles north of Perryville, just on up ahead," Dad told us.

We pull into Perryville. It had only a Reds Market and a filling station (Flying A Gasoline). North across the street was a bar where they sold liquor. We didn't stop in Perryville; we started north on an old gravel road. It was washboardy and rough.

Dad said, "In 1945, I was working for the Waddell Ranch Company. The foreman over the livestock was Ershel Mothershed. I don't know if Ershel is still working for them. I got hurt while working there in 1945 and was laid up for a couple of months. I was drawing disability checks while I was laid up. I got a wild hair in my ass one day and saddled my horse and leading a black mare that was with colt, I flagged Old Brownie out of there.

"I still had two checks coming. They were supposed to send them to me in Blythe, but they never did! I know old Scott Libby, Waddell's son-in-law, and the ranch superintendent cashed the checks and kept the money. I know they forged my signature to the checks. If they did forge my name, I got them by the balls. They'll have to come up with that money. Forty-five dollars will hold us until work breaks." Dad said.

"This is the ranch we are coming to up ahead. This is old man Waddell's house here on the left," Dad told us as we were passing a cement blockhouse. It had a nice lawn and a big driveway, with a Cadillac sedan and a Ford station wagon in the driveway.

"This is the ranch where they keep Waddell's racehorses. I had changed my name while working for the Waddell Ranch Company because your mother had a warrant for my arrest for non–child support. She said she did it to get state aid. I didn't want to be arrested, so I changed my name to Buck Thorne. You boys need to think of an alias too since your mother probably has the police looking for us."

What the hell! I thought. *I don't know what to change it to. I'm Paul. Nothing else would sound right.*

Orville said, "Well, I want to be Jessie Thorne." Orville could always adjust to anything.

I thought awhile and then said, "Okay, I'll be Frank Thorne. If Orville's going to be an outlaw, I will be too."

I could tell Dad was pleased. One hundred years ago, we could have started our own gang. Dad said Everett would be Lee Thorne.

Dad said, "This is it, son."

I turned right into a dirt driveway with a fence on either side. There was a big barn straight ahead. It was open, with rooms on the left and right sides of the opening going clear through the barn.

Dad said, "This is Waddell's stables."

We drove around the right side of the barn, or stables as Dad called it. There's was a little white house on the right side of the driveway with a green door.

Some man walked out to see who had pulled into the driveway. Dad stepped out on the right from the passenger seat.

"Well, goddamn! Howdy, Buck! What's it been, four or five years?"

"Along time, Ershel!" was Dad's reply.

Some little girl playing in the yard came over and put her hands in her daddy's hip pockets. Ershel said, "These your boys, Buck?"

Dad said, "Well, let's say they got caught in my trap." And they both laughed.

The little girl, about six years old, kept bending her knees and was still hanging from her dad's pockets, almost as though she was trying to pull his pants down. This girl was Verel Ann Mothershed, and she is now my wife, some forty-nine years later.

The man leaned and twisted around, catching her by the arm. "What are you doing back there?" And he chuckles.

My dad told the man why we were there. Ershel said, "I don't know, Buck. I remember Scott came here with a check for you, but you were gone. I don't know what they might have done with the check. You say there were two checks owed to you, Buck?"

"Yes, and they were supposed to send them to me in Blythe, and I could sure use the money as I'm having trouble finding work."

"Well, I have to go up to ranch headquarters tomorrow, and I'll ask Scott if he remembers. Hell, that was a long time ago, Buck. Six or seven years, at least!"

"I know, but those two checks were due me, and I really need them and could use them about now."

"Well, I'll see what I can find out, Buck. Are you staying around here?"

"Well, we just drove in from Chandler. Me and the boys will just drive up toward the White Tank Mountains and pitch camp."

"You say you're looking for work, Buck? Mr. Waddell has been wanting a fence built from the stables east toward Pugh's Store. I haven't had time to do it myself. I'll tell you what, let me ask the old man if I can hire you and your boys to build that fence."

"I'd sure appreciate it if you would, Ershel!"

"Okay, Buck, I'll see what I can do. You come by tomorrow afternoon and I'll let you know what I've found out."

"I'll sure do that, Ershel. Thanks. Come on, boys! Let's load up and we'll go find a place to camp for the night."

The next day, we drove back toward Buckeye, still looking for someone with cotton high enough to chop, just in case Mr. Waddell wasn't ready to build the fence yet.

"Keep your eyes open for a tractor sitting in a field someplace," Dad said. "If we don't spot a tractor soon, I have to spend what little money that's left on gas. I'd rather keep it for food." When we were in Buckeye, Dad said he would go to a couple of bars and see if anyone knew of any work going on. He was driving because I didn't have a driver's license. Anytime we were in town, he drove. He didn't want the police to stop me and question us about me and my brothers not being in school.

He pulled up in front of the bar and said, "You boys stay in the car. I'll go in and inquire about work."

He came out of the bar after a few minutes, walked up to the driver's side, and put his foot on the running board. Leaning his arms on the window opening in the door, he said to me, "No such good luck." He said the bartender had heard ranchers talking and saying the cotton was just now coming up. "I'll have to break down and buy five gallons of gas, I guess. We don't want to run out. Then we'll head back to Waddell. Maybe Ershel has found out something."

Dad drove to an independent gas station, where the gasoline was cheap, and put in five gallons. He told me to check the radiator. "But be careful, son. It's hot."

Orville and Everett got out and went to use the restroom. Dad checked the oil in the engine.

"It's a quart low," he said. When your brothers get back, I'll pull over under those trees up ahead and put a quart of oil in." Dad carried a two-gallon can of oil with us. Gas stations sold it for about 50¢ a quart, so he bought it at Pep Boys—$1.25 for two gallons. And this old Model A I had traded my Whizzer Motorbike for was using oil pretty bad. Dad said it needed rings. The radiator was full; oil in the engine was full. We got gas, and everything was hunky-dory.

"Let's drive up to Waddell and talk to Ershel."

Dad pulled into the driveway; Ershel was in the opening to the barn. "Howdy, Buck! Pull on over by the house while I put this mare away." He was holding the mare with a halter on by a short nylon strap.

We drove back to the house, and a woman with black hair came out with three small girls just as Ershel walked up.

"Buck, you remember my wife Viola?" he asked.

"Howdy, Buck. Ersel said you came by yesterday. How have you been?"

"I've been pretty good," my dad replied. "I finally got my boys. They gave custody of them to me around the first of the year."

"Well, good," Viola said. "They look like nice boys!"

"These your girls?" Dad asked.

"Yes! We've added a couple since you left. This one's Verel," she said as she put her hand on the little girl's head. "That one over there is Donna. This one behind me is Gail." The two bigger girls were blond, but the baby in training pants had brown hair.

"You still cowboying?" Dad asked the woman.

"Yes, you know me! I try to give Ersel a hand now and then." I noticed she mispronounced Ershel's name. Maybe she had a speech impediment. She called him Ersel, but Dad said his name was Ershel.

Then I saw him bend over and on the back of his belt was carved the name "Hershel."

"For crying out loud, what the heck is his name?" I asked Dad.

He said his name was Ershel, pronounced *Er-shel*. Okay, that was cleared up, but his wife still called him Ersel. Who knew? He looked or answered when I said Ershel. Later, I found out that *Er-sel* was right, but I never changed the way I pronounced his name.

"Buck, Mr. Waddell said for us to get started on the fence, but it will be a couple of days until I can get the lumber for it ordered out. We have a television if you and your boys want to come down about dark."

"Oh, can we, Dad," we all said together.

"Okay, we'll see," Dad said. He hadn't watched television. He had seen them in store windows in town but had never sat down and watched a program.

We told him how neat it was; I told him we watched television at Mrs. Carter's. We would have to leave our camp unattended while we watched television, though. But I guess no one would bother with it at night for a couple of hours.

Later, after we had eaten supper and the dishes were done, Dad said, "Well, you boys load up and we'll go down to Ershel and Viola's for a little while. Ershel didn't mention if he had talked to Scott Libby."

We drove down to Ershel's, and he came outside and greeted us. "Howdy, Buck. You and the boys come on in."

Viola asked us if we would like a glass of iced tea. We all nodded our heads yes.

"Buck, I talked to Scott. He said to come up to ranch headquarters, and he would get you to sign a check, then give you the money."

Dad said he would run up there tomorrow.

The television station in Phoenix was KPHO. There was another one, but I can't remember it. We stayed for about an hour and a half. Then we got tired, so we said good night and left.

Ershel said, "I'll get that lumber ordered out tomorrow, Buck."

"Okay, Ershel. I'm taking these boys home and putting them to bed.

Next morning, we were up early, and with breakfast out of the way, Dad said, "Let's load up and go see Scott Libby."

As we drove by Ershel's we saw his 1951 Chevrolet flatbed truck was not in the spot where it was parked last evening. "He must be working," Dad said. "Sometimes he would go over and chauffeur Mr. Waddell around. Sometimes he would drive the old man to Phoenix on business."

We drove on past, and I saw the three Mothershed kids playing in the yard. One looked like a boy, and I noticed there were four children, not three. I asked Dad, "Do they have a boy?"

"No, just three girls," he said.

Oh well, I know I saw a boy about Everett's age of twelve years old.

We drove by a migrant farm workers' camp. There were about twenty one-room shacks under some cottonwood trees. Then to the east end of the shacks was an area fenced with chain-link fencing.

Dad said, "Martin, the ranch foreman over their agriculture operation, has an office there." There was a gas pump for company trucks. Then joining that on the east side was Pugh's Store.

"Pugh's Store is where ranch employees go for their checks, and cash them too. But he hassled you to buy goods from his mercantile store. He has clothes, hats, dry goods, and groceries. He will also give you credit if you're working steady at the ranch. A song 'I Owe My Soul to the Company Store' comes to mind. Seems like if you get a line of credit with one of these stores, you just get deeper and deeper in debt. Better hang on to your receipt. They're famous for padding the bill. Meaning they would add a few things you hadn't bought."

We turned left at Pugh's Store and headed north. Within a mile or so, the road was lined on both sides by grapefruit trees. Orville said, "Let's stop and pick some grapefruit."

"Son, we can't just walk out into the man's orchard and start picking grapefruit in the daytime. They'd haul our ass to jail. But we could pick some at night."

Everett said, "They won't haul our ass to jail at night, will they?"

"Well, son, they have to catch us first. At night we'd be mighty hard to spot."

About four miles north, we came to the ranch headquarters on the west side of the road. Dad turned into the driveway. "You boys stay in the car while I go talk to Scott Libby."

It was only a short time before Dad came back out.

He had his wallet out and was putting money into it. "I got it," he said as he opened the door and climbed in behind the wheel. "I knew I had them by the balls if they had forged my name on those checks."

"You think they did, Dad?" I asked.

"Hell, yes," he said. "You think they would have given me this forty-five dollars if they hadn't?"

Dad backed the car out, and we headed south toward Pugh's Store. "Let's head into Litchfield Park, and we'll pick up a few things from Abraham's Market."

"What about getting it at Pugh's Store?" I asked.

"No, son. He's too damn high," said Dad. He stopped at Abraham's Market on the northwest corner of Litchfield Park Boulevard and Camelback Road. It was a good-sized market for a small town. We all went in, and Dad wasted no time putting groceries into a basket.

Over on the right side of the store I saw some shelves with ammunition on them. I walked over to Dad and asked him, "Dad, can I get some .22 shells?"

"Yeah, go get some. They are seventy-five cents a box."

I wanted three boxes in case I got trigger happy. I had a Remington pump-action rifle. Dad had told me, "If you take your time when you draw a bead on something, you won't need a second shot." *I know*, I thought. *But I just like to shoot.*

"Let's load up," Dad said after paying for our things. "We'll flag Old Brownie back out to Waddell."

As we drove by Ershel's, his truck was still not there. We didn't see a living soul at the stables. Dad just kept driving west. As we passed Waddell's racetrack on the right, Dad said, "That's new since I worked here in 1945."

There was a pond on the left where a pump with an eight-inch discharge pipe was pumping water into the pond. From there, the water flowed into an irrigation ditch.

"Martin must have some irrigators working today," Dad said.

Farther up the road, there was another cement ditch about four feet wide and two feet deep. It also had water running through it. The road crossed the ditch, but a sign on the other side said, CATERPILLAR PROVING GROUNDS. KEEP OUT.

GOOD SHOW

Ershel said, "Buck, the lumber for the fence came in, if you want to start building the fence tomorrow!"

We were sitting in their living room watching television. We had come to their house about 5:00 p.m., but Ersel wasn't there. Viola said he had driven Mr. Waddell to the racetrack and should be home very soon. "Buck, you and your boys want to come in and watch television?"

So that was what we were doing when Ershel came into the room. He and my dad discussed building the fence, but we were just watching the Ray Odom show, and there was a new singer on it—Marty Robbins.

The next morning, we started building the fence. We set the first post into the ground after digging the hole. Ershel wanted them twenty-four inches deep. That way, if horses rubbed up against the fence scratching themselves, it wouldn't lean over. Mr. Waddell wanted a nice straight fence. We were digging the holes with posthole diggers. Once the first post was in and tamped into place good and plumb, we just laid one of the fence rails on the ground and centered our next hole on the end of the rail.

We also measured top and bottom to make sure the post stayed plumb.

The rails were sixteen feet long, so each post was going to be eight feet apart. We had a string line stretched tight. We were using the existing barbed-wire fence for our alignment. With a hundred-foot tape, we could pull our tape off of the iron stakes that the barbed wire was strung onto. Once the string line was set and eyeballed as straight, we were on our way.

Ershel said, "Buck, let's set the first rail eighteen inches to the bottom of it when we start our second row up." Ershel wanted to cut the rail in half so that all the joints wouldn't be on one post. He said this would make a strong fence.

Sounds good to me, I thought. I'm glad were taking turns with the posthole diggers because that was work that none of us was used to.

Orville and I had quit school about only two and a half months before, and Dad hadn't been doing hard labor either. Ershel didn't push us, but he wanted us to keep working. He said he was sure old man Waddell would drive by to check it out. He didn't want the old man to see us loafing. Everett was mostly watching us work.

At about four o'clock, Ersel said, "Let's go over and sit in the truck, Buck. I want to catch the race from Turf Paradise."

So every day, around four o'clock, we would head for Ershel's truck and listen to a recap of the day's races. He kept a log on win, place, and show, writing down each horse's name. We thought this arrangement was neat because we got paid until five o'clock.

Ershel was very knowledgeable about racehorses. Only thing is, he had a bad habit of saying, "Paul, last time out, this old horse win it by a nose," or "some other horse win it by four lengths." I wanted to say, the horse *won* it, not win it.

Viola came out to see how we were doing, and I'll be goddamned if she didn't say "win it too." She told Ershel, "I remember that horse win it last time out."

I gave up. I guess that's the way they talk in Arizona, far be it from me to correct them. Shit, I can't keep from saying ain't.

It was Friday evening, and we were listening to the horse races with Ershel, and he told my dad that Viola wanted to go see that new movie *The Will Rogers Story*. It was playing in Phoenix."

"Buck, if you and the boys want to go, come on down to the house about three on Saturday and we'll drive over to Phoenix and see it."

"Can we, Dad?" we asked. Ershel said, "I think we can all get into the cab of his truck." "The boys might have to sit on someone's lap." "Three o'clock Saturday you say? Okay, we'll be here," Dad replied.

Saturday afternoon, we drove to Waddell Stables, and we all loaded into the flatbed truck and drove to Phoenix. We saw *The Will Rogers Story*, starring Jane Wyman and Will Rogers Jr. What a good movie. Viola talked about it all the way home. I was jammed up against Viola with Everett on my lap, and I was very much aware she was a woman, not some bony man but a real soft woman. I liked the feel of her at my side, and she was pretty too!

If she were alive today, she would be my mother-in-law. I was just a kid with stupid thoughts. Now I'm too old to remember what those thoughts were, but I didn't mind being pressed up against her. Too soon we were back at Waddell, and we got into our old car and headed for camp.

The next morning, bright and early, here came Viola again in the truck. "Paul, Ersel wants to know if you could work a horse again over at the track?"

I said, "Sure." I was excited that he wanted me to ride with him. I went with Viola, and Dad said he would come along in the car. We drove up to the racetrack just off the main road. Ershel was still down the road a ways, riding a horse and leading two others. Two of the horses were bays, and one was a dappled grey. Seems like it was Viola who called it Spook. Spook and one of the bays had a jockey saddle on it, but the other bay had a western saddle.

Ershel said, "Paul, I'm going to let you ride this ol' gray horse, and Viola will take the other horse and go down the back side of the track, and when we come up the back stretch, she'll catch your horse by the reins and stop him. Viola, why don't you go ahead and get into position. Then Paul and I will mount up and see what these horses are made of this morning.

"Paul, I'll give you a leg up. Then you walk ol' Spook away from the track, and when I get on, turn your horse and come back to me. I'd like to get lined up, but if you can't hold that horse, just let her go like we did last time," Ershel told me.

I saw Dad pull up in our car and park next to Ershel's truck. Ersel said, "Viola's almost there. Let me give you a lift."

I settled into the saddle, and as I did, I turned my horse, the gray one they called Spook, toward Dad and my brothers, but I was watching Ershel. He kind of sprung from the ground with his waist in the saddle. Then he swung his leg over the horse and came to a sitting position. I saw he had a crop in his hand, which he quickly stuck into his belt in the back.

His horse was fidgeting and tossing its head. This gray I was on seemed to be pretty calm. Ershel was walking his horse out of the curve at the end of the track, and he said, "Paul, bring that horse up alongside of me! I think I can hold this horse if you can try to come even with me. I was only a horse length behind him, and already, Spook was ready to run. Ershel had me on the inside close to the rail. His horse was ten feet or so from the rail. Both horses wanted to run.

My horse's head was about even with Ershel's body when I heard him say, "Let 'em go!"

As soon as I released pressure on the reins, my horse took off. By the time I was at full speed, my horse was a little ahead. Ershel's horse's head was right by my right elbow, and we were flying. The turn looked a long way away when we were trying to get the horses even, but the curve was coming up already.

Again, I had tears in my eyes from the wind driving into them. This horse went a little wide in the turn, and Ershel took advantage of it because he was still on the rail. His horse was strong and carried more weight.

He didn't pass me, but we were pretty even. I was on the outside for the rest of the race. Coming out of the turn, I saw Viola start to gallop her horse in anticipation of my horse coming abreast of her, and she reached out and caught my horse's reins. Viola was a good rider, and very confident in the saddle. My dad liked her and spoke of what a good hand she was at cowboying. I'm sure he noticed how pretty she was too. He might have even had a fantasy or two. I know I did. But enough of fantasy. That was long ago, and the memories of a maturing kid who had hormones pumping through his veins.

Ershel took the jockey saddles off of the two racehorses and wiped them down with an old rag. He put the jockey saddles in the back of his truck while we all talked for a while, mostly about the race and the building fence. Before we left, Viola said, "Buck, you and the boys come on down and watch television tonight if you want to."

"We'll do that," Dad said. I think he liked television.

We worked all throughout the following week building the fence, and we were close to getting it finished.

"Buck, you remember that Russian kid Rusty?"

Dad said he did.

"Well, I talked to him in town today, and he said he has a new Winchester model 70, in .270 caliber. He wants to come out tomorrow, Saturday, and try it out. If you and your boys want to come along, bring some guns down about nine o'clock in the morning and we'll go drive down the canal bank in my truck."

Dad said, "We'll be there."

Oh boy, we get to go shooting.

The next morning when we drove into Waddell Stables, Ersel and the Russian kid were sighting down the barrel of a gun. We got out of our car and walked over to them.

Ershel said, "Buck, you remember Rusty, don't you?"

"Yeah, I remember him. You've grown up," Dad said."

Rusty Tregaboff was scarred badly on his face, and he had fingers missing on both hands. Ershel had told us that Rusty's mother was doing the wash with lye soap in a huge pot of boiling water when the stand collapsed and scalded Rusty, who was about three years old. He was literally cooked: His face, arms, hands, feet, and a lot of his body were deformed. He had only two fingers on his right hand; it looked like a crab claw. But he was very strong with those deformed hands, and nothing stopped him in his life.

Ershel, Rusty, and Dad got into the cab of the truck. Orville, Everett, and I got up on the flatbed of the truck. The truck had two gates at the cab, so we were standing and holding on to the gates for support. I had my double-barrel shotgun with the stock resting on my boot so it wouldn't slip around on the wood bed of the truck. Orville had Dad's single-barrel shotgun. I had a couple boxes of shotgun shells, and we took some out and put them into our pockets. We wanted to be ready if we needed to load up in a hurry.

Ershel headed toward the Caterpillar outfit, and after we crossed over the small cement lined canal he turned right. He was driving really slow, and we were watching for any critters we could shoot. Since he was driving slow, we went ahead and put shells into our guns.

Ershel said, "Orville, if you boys see anything, just pound on the top of the cab, and I'll stop."

It wasn't long before a cottontail ran out of the brush, and as it crossed the road, Orville shot it, and it was going pretty fast. It just rolled right on across the road. The rabbit came out of the brush so fast we didn't have time to pound on the cab. Ershel stopped, and Orville jumped down and retrieved his rabbit. With his rabbit in hand, Orville got back into the truck as I gave him a hand up.

"Nice shot, Orville," I said! *Maybe I'll get the next one*, I thought.

Down the road about a hundred yards and out of reach of our shotguns, a jackrabbit had come onto the road, and he was sitting up. Ershel stopped, and the passenger door opened. Ershel said Rusty wanted to try his .270 on that jackrabbit up ahead.

Rusty took a rest between the doorframe and the cab and shot, but missed. But it only took about two jumps and stood up high again. Rusty already had another round jacked into the chamber and took aim again. This time he was dead on. The rabbit was no longer among the living. Ershel drove on up to the rabbit and stopped so Rusty could get his kill. The .270 had done a number on the jackrabbit, and there wasn't enough of the rabbit left to clean. He said the gun shot good, and he thought he might have jerked the trigger the first shot.

Some quail flew across the road, and Orville and I both got one apiece.

We got down and picked them up, and about four more flew out that had hung tight in the brush. Orville and I got two more. My dad climbed out of the cab and said, "Let me clean the four quails so the shot through their insides wouldn't flavor the meat. He didn't pick the feathers off; he just skinned them. He ran his finger inside and had the bird cleaned in less time than it takes me to write about it. He also cleaned the rabbit that Orville had shot, and all the critters went into a brown paper sack. I knew we would have them for supper.

We were able to get two more cottontails before we headed home. Orville and I both missed a couple of shots at quail and also a couple of rabbits, but we had a good time. Back at Waddell, we got some water and washed the quail and rabbits. Viola loaned us a pan to carry them to camp in. All in all, it had been a fun day.

Rusty was loud but was always laughing and in good humor.

He had his wife, Patsy, with him one time when he came out to Waddell. She was very pretty. I was wondering how someone scarred as bad as Rusty was had married such a pretty woman. I guess it's true it's what's inside that counts. They seemed happy together.

Viola said next time, "If you boys get enough quail for all of us, I'll cook them up, because we like quail too."

Dad said, "There you go, son. That's an offer you can't refuse."

Orville and I said we would try harder next time, but the quail would have to cooperate too. Just being a good shot isn't enough if you don't see any quail. Dad said, "Next time, son, take the horses. You can ride right up on them, and they won't flush so quick. Try to get three or four lined up, and you can get them all with one shot." Dad called it ground sluicing the sons of bitches.

He wanted all the birds he could get with one shot. I think because once you shot, they took flight, and you had to walk a long ways to find them again. Unless we were horseback, like he said, but once you shot off of a horse, he would fidget around, making it hard to get a decent shot the next time.

"Okay, next time out, we'll try to get enough for everyone," I said. "But that's another day and another story. Right now we have to get that fence finished and painted before Mr. Waddell comes along and fires us all. Where did I leave my hammer and nails? Hey, Everett, have you seen the nails?"

PHOTO GALLERY

Dick and Ureda Huff about 1923

Everett and Barbara Huff Dick Huff Paul and Bonnie Huff. Children in front are Tim and Phillip Rhodes

Dick, Rita and Orville Huff

Alice Chapman holding Alice Huff. Earnestine Rita holding Everett Elizabeth holding Paul and Betty Huff

Paul Orville and Everett Huff about 1946

Paul Huff about 1947

Orville and Paul Huff about 1959

Paul Huff and his mother Elizabeth Huff about 1947

Paul Huff about 1955

Dick and Everett Huff

Paul Huff and Tim Rhodes

Paul and his mom Elizabeth Huff

Dick Huff

Dick Huff

Tim Rhodes and his grandfather Dick Huff

Orville Huff

Paul Huff

Dick Huff

Dick Huff

Dick Huff holding Rita Huff

Paul Huff 1959

Dick and Elizabeth Huff about 1945

Dick Huff holding Betty, Elizabeth Huff with Rita and Earnestine Huff

RACE DAY

We were up early, and Dad was fixing breakfast. I looked up, and here came Ershel's truck. Viola was driving, and she was by herself. She stopped and climbed down out of the green truck.

"Howdy, Buck," she greeted my dad. "How are you boys this morning?"

I wondered why she had come up here to find us so early in the morning.

Viola said, "Ershel is bringing a couple of horses up to the track this morning. Buck, you think Paul would want to ride one of them alongside Ershel?"

Dad asked me if I wanted to go ride one of the racehorses. "I can ride one," I said.

Viola said, "Well, you go ahead and eat your breakfast."

"If I'm going to be riding, I'd rather not eat anything because I always get a side ache," I answered. I had eaten before and then rode, and right away, I had the worst side ache imaginable.

"Dad, can I eat when I get back?" I asked.

"Well, go ahead, son. This food will keep until you get back!"

We piled into the truck and drove a quarter mile to Mr. Waddell's racetrack. Ershel told me as he adjusted the stirrup to fit my legs, "Paul, this ol' horse is hard to hold back, so we will just have to play it by ear. He is gonna want to run as soon as we try to get them lined up. Now he'll be hard to hold, so you can just pull on one rein real hard and keep him turning. I'll try to maneuver this ol' horse into position. Now if you find you can't hold him, just let him run. I'll give this ol' horse its head. I can tell how we do after the race, by how far apart we are after the race."

This horse I was on was walking sideways, fidgeting around and tossing its head. I never rode a jockey saddle before. My knees were up under my chin. Ershel had me hold the reins in a crossbar effect.

"Paul, this horse is a bullheaded son of a bitch," he said. He could tell I had my hands full. My horse was already trying to run as Ershel said, "Let him go!" I dropped my hands to give the horse its head, and in about four jumps, we were at full speed. All I could hear were the hooves on the track and the wind in my eyes and ears. I was leaning forward, and my face was right alongside its neck.

I was right on the rail, coming into the turn, and I just let my body go with the horse's movements. It felt as though we were both leaning, and we were well into the turn now. I didn't know where Ershel was, but he hadn't passed me anyway. I went by a pole as I came out of the turn and headed down the back side of the track. I heard Ershel say, "Paul, pull him up!"

I hauled back on the reins as hard as I could, but this ol' horse just seemed to run harder. I had tears in my eyes from the wind. I was straining to stop this horse, but it didn't want to stop.

The horse was starting into the far curve and was slowing down pretty good now. Wow, what a ride! I'd never ridden so fast in my life. Ershel came alongside and took the reins at the bit and got the horse under control.

"The horse is breathing really heavy," I told Ershel. "I just couldn't stop him!"

"Yeah, these racehorses just want to run, and it takes a strong hand to stop them. It was a good race, though," he said. "Paul, you handled that horse really well through that curve.

"I think the horse handled me. I was just hanging on." What a fun ride.

"Paul, if we do this again, I'll have Viola at that pole on the backstretch to catch your horse and help to stop it."

"I could use the help," I told him. I knew I just wasn't strong enough to stop the horse.

"Paul, I have some horses at the stables, if you boys want to ride them. They could sure use the exercise, and there's a lot of country around here to ride in," Ershel said. "If you want to come on down in the morning, I'll saddle them up."

Ershel told us he was still waiting for the lumber to be delivered so we could start building the fence.

"I don't know what my dad wants to do tomorrow," I said.

When I told Dad, he said he didn't care because he needed to work on the car. He thought the spark plugs were fouling because of the excessive oil it was burning. He hadn't done much to it since working on it in Casa Grande before we came out here to Waddell.

After breakfast the next morning, Dad drove us back to the stables at Waddell.

Ershel saddled us a horse apiece and handed me a canteen, saying, "You boys might get thirsty before you get back."

Good thinking. I didn't think to take water with us, and this was the desert and not a place to be in winter or summer without water. He told us, "There is a canal that runs north and south almost at the foot of the White Tank Mountains. So if for some reason you need water, just head downhill, and you'll find water.

"Okay," I told him, and we headed out of the gate and turned west at the corner of Camelback and Perryville Roads.

We were riding on sandy gravel next to the dirt road we were following toward the Caterpillar proving grounds where Camelback Road ended. When we came to the Caterpillar outfit, we turned north along the irrigation ditch Ershel had told us about. There was a lot of wildlife back in here. Right away we saw rabbits running across the road. I didn't even think to bring a gun; we could have shot a rabbit for dinner. We turned into a really big wash heading west. There was a lot of brush, I noticed, and mesquite trees, some with mesquite beans hanging from their limbs.

I saw a big covey of quail, maybe twenty or thirty of them. I tried to count them, but they moved too fast. Some even flew up on the side of the canyon. I heard Orville behind me say, "Hey, you gonna keep all that water for yourself?"

"I might," I said. "Why, you and Everett thirsty?"

Orville said, "No, but my throat is kinda dry."

"Okay, if you're going to start whining, let's have a swig. It's on my saddle, so I get to be first," I said. We reined the horses in, and I helped myself to a cold drink.

I handed the canteen to Orville, and as I did, a roadrunner came out of the brush and stood there in the road looking at us.

Everett said, "Hey, I think he wants a drink."

So I told him, "Well, why don't you give him some of yours?"

By then, the roadrunner flipped his tail and took off running like the devil was after him.

"I guess he must have heard them ring the dinner bell," Orville said.

"Maybe there's a coyote after him like in the cartoons," Everett opined. "Well, maybe he did seem to be in a big hurry."

We were just walking the horses because we weren't in any hurry. We just liked to ride horses. Sometimes if we stopped too long to look at a canyon, the horses would try to turn and head for home. We came around a corner in a wash we were riding in, and there stood big mule deer just looking at us. We thought it was a doe, but it could have been a buck that had shed his horns. Probably not. They should be getting new ones by now. He wasn't at all excited, I guess because of the horses. I'm calling it a he; I like to think of it as a buck. But I know deep inside it was a doe. But it could have been a buck! Enough already.

I noticed the sun had dropped below the hill, so I told my brothers, "Let's have another drink and head back home. I was getting a little sore from riding most of the day. I knew when we got back to the stables and climbed down that we would be tired. These old horses, once they were going toward home, you had a hard time holding them back. Just a few minutes earlier, they were just plugging along. Now they acted like I was using a quirt on them.

I was thinking how much I loved to ride horses. This was what I had dreamed of staring out of the window at school. I still wanted to be a cowboy! Just riding the range with my bedroll tied behind my saddle and my trusty gun in the scabbard. I might even run into Hopalong Cassidy or Roy Rogers out here, riding around someday.

Stranger things have happened. "What do you think, Orville? You think we could run into Hoppy or Roy Rogers?"

"I think I'm hungry," Orville said.

"Now that you mention it, I'm hungry too. Let's head for home."

We were about an hour from the stables. We would be darned hungry by the time we got back. I asked Orville if he wanted to trot, but he said his side hurt.

The horses were walking fast, as though they knew we were going home. As we came back by the irrigation ditch, we let them drink. They were thirsty. "Might have one myself. You want one, Orville?"

"Sure," he said.

Finally, we were back at the Waddell Ranch stables. Viola came out and said she would unsaddle the horses for us. "You want us to curry them?" I asked.

"Naw, I'll just rub them a little bit with this old towel," she said.

Dad had stayed there the whole time we were gone, talking to Ershel. "Well, you boys ready to head back to camp so I can fix supper?" he asked.

"Yeah, we're hungry."

Heading home, Dad told us that Viola said the horses hadn't even broken a sweat. He said, "That's why Viola came out to help unsaddle the horses. She wanted to see if we had been up there on the desert running them or racing them. He said she was impressed that we hadn't. I hadn't even thought of running them. Whenever I had ridden with my dad, we always walked the horses unless we wanted to rope something.

Dad said, "It's not like Gene Autry in the movies. If you run a horse like that, he'll give out in a short distance. You can walk him all day, but you can't run him more than a mile, not hard anyway. I had learned to ride when Dad said he bought me a horse in the sixth grade. I must have been eight or nine. It seems that, that was all I thought about growing up. Some people say I never grew up, but that's beside the point.

PEAR PICKERS

We were in Kingsburg, a little town twenty or so miles south of Fresno. Arizona was just too hot for us to stay there in the summertime. Dad always camped out, not wanting to pay rent. That was just money wasted, he said. The only shade we had was a mesquite tree, and their leaves are tiny and don't offer much shade.

The farmers had all their cotton chopped by June. We had even gone back on some fields to chop out Johnson grass. Bermuda grass also was a problem for farmers; one farmer called it devil grass. I was chopping old devil grass halfheartedly when he came up behind me, took my hoe out of my hands, and said, "You have to go at it like you're killing snakes. You can't just lightly hoe this grass, and you have to get down and get all the root out. Otherwise, it will just grow right back.

He took my hoe and showed me the fine art of hoeing out Bermuda grass. With my hoe just a-flying, he showed me how to be really motivated chopping that old devil grass. After two minutes of fast and furious chopping and with the sweat pouring down his face, he said, "Now that's how it's done."

Well, I'll be damned, I thought. *He's so good, why's he paying us to do it?* I wondered.

He said, "Get it all chopped out and leave it lying on top of the ground and we'll come back and pick it all up after it dries. You have to get every root and piece, or when it gets wet, it will grow back. What he wanted me to do was chop for ten hours the way he had for two minutes. I noticed he was huffing and puffing as he started walking back to his car at the end of the field. I thought his legs looked a little wobbly too. I watched him in case I had to go help him get back to the car.

I bet it didn't take long for him to get to a bar for a tall cool one. *Asshole*, I thought. He wanted the grass picked up after it lay on the field and dried. Seemed like we just needed a bag and could pick it up right now. *If you're going to pick it up, why does it have to be dry?* I guess he had his reasons, but they were beyond me. What do I know? I was only sixteen! I've learned from my own lawn that he was right about one thing: If you don't get it all, it grows back. Even the smallest root—once it gets wet, it starts to grow.

The second week of June, we were having a tough time finding work. It was hotter than hell, so Dad said, "The fruit should be getting ripe in California. Let's load up in the morning and flag Old Brownie out of this godforsaken place."

Sounded good to me. At least we would have a break while driving over to California from Arizona.

After sleeping all night, Dad had a change of heart. "Son," he said to me, "we need to trade this car off and get another one. I know it's your car because you traded your bike for it, but, son, it's worn out. It needs a whole new engine. And we need an oil well just to keep it supplied with oil. Everett and Orville are jammed in like sardines. We really need a bigger car. So what do you think?"

"Hell, let's trade it, Dad," I said.

"Okay, we'll drive into Phoenix and see what we can find."

The next day, we drove into Phoenix and looked in car lots. We found a nice 1938 Chevy, a sedan, and all the glass was good. It had nice tires; it was painted black and seemed to be in great shape. But the part I liked best was it had a Smithy's Glasspack muffler on it. It had the neatest sound. People always asked, "Do you have dual pipes on that?"

"No, just a Smithy muffler," I would reply.

When the deal was finalized, Dad took the rear seats out and threw them away. He wanted room for our bedroll behind the seats. Boy, this sedan had a lot more room for our stuff. Plunder, Dad called it. "I've heard some people's stuff is shit, but our shit was stuff." I think George Carlin said that. We put the bedroll behind the seat with our suitcases and guns. Then Orville and Everett climbed in on top of them. The little Chevy had two bucket seats up front, so Dad and I climbed in as I was driving. I was in love with this little car. What a neat sound from the exhaust, and the glass didn't rattle in the frames like the old Ford Model A did.

Finally, we were on our way to California. But no banjo on our knee (it's okay to chuckle). We stopped in San Bernardino to see a movie. It was Randolph Scott in *Bad Man's Territory*, a western. It couldn't get better than that for me. After the movie, we drove up Cajon Pass to Highway 138, then northwest to the little town of Little Rock and Pear Blossom.

Up by Palmdale, Dad said, "Take the next road to the left. We'll drive out by the Little Rock Dam. And we'll spend the night there."

We unrolled the bedroll and crawled in. I was tired, but look at all those stars! The night sky was alive with them. I saw shooting stars streak across the sky every few minutes. And the night air was cold here in Little Rock as I pulled the covers tight around me and snuggled in to stay warm.

"Okay, you boys, vacation's over." Dad had a fire going and was fixing to cook breakfast. "You boys get washed up. How you want your eggs?"

After eating, we loaded the car back up and drove into Little Rock to look for work. Dad had worked here many times over the years, so our first stop was a place he had worked before. Turned out it was the last stop too. It was on the south side of the Pear Blossom Highway. So we were hired to pick pears. After two days, they asked me to be a swamper on one of the trucks. I told them I would and started loading boxes of pears onto a truck and hauling them out of the orchard. Dad, Orville, and Everett were still picking the pears.

After work, we ran into Cecil Ward and his three sons—Kenneth, Donny, and Dale. Cecil Ward was the brother-in-law of Dad's brother. Dad's brother Ernest had been married to Cecil's sister, Iva Ward. Ernest and Iva were my aunt and uncle. My uncle Ernie died in Banning, California, in 1930 and was buried in Riverside. He died of typhoid fever after drinking water from a contaminated well he had cleaned out and thought was safe. On this same year, June 9, 1930, my sister Betty was born in Banning.

Cecil Ward was here in Little Rock working on the pears just like we were.

Cecil and his boys would all work very hard all spring and summer, just camping out in the orchards that they were working in. They would save their money and then go back down to Blythe and camp on the Colorado River and fish and hunt all winter. Cecil had a trailer house that he towed to wherever it was they wanted to live. Cecil liked to loaf all winter, just hunting and fishing as he enjoyed life, as did Dad, because they were two of a kind.

Before Dad got custody of us three boys, he and Cecil would prowl the desert around Blythe in the wintertime looking for anything in the way of junk that wasn't nailed down that they could sell for the scrap metal to junk dealers in Blythe.

Dad would tell us stories about going out to old mines that had been abandoned, kicking open the door, and ransacking the place. They always strapped their pistols on before going in to the place. Dad said when they had finished ransacking the place and were walking back to the car, he would glance at Cecil out of the corner of his eye and catch him undoing the strap over the hammer on his pistol. So Dad would drop his hand down to his pistol in anticipation of what was coming next.

Cecil would holler, draw, and spin around while drawing his pistol, as Dad did the same thing. Both guns firing almost as one as they shot from the hip at the doorknob on the door of the old mineshaft. If they both missed the doorknob, they would both fire again until the knob had been blasted off the mine door. Then they would look at each other and laugh and argue over who had blasted it first. Then they would talk about who was fastest on the draw. Dad always talked about what fun it was, and he liked Cecil like a brother. He told me he thought Cecil was quicker with a pistol than he was with his pistol.

The first time I met Cecil, Dad and I were driving toward the river outside of Blythe on a narrow dirt road. I was about ten years old and was down at Blythe visiting Dad, it must have been wintertime because it was cold.

We were meeting a car coming toward us, and all of a sudden, it turned off the road a little into the weeds. Some man opened the door and climbed out, and as I watched him, he quickly pulled a gun from behind his seat and walked toward us. At the same time, Dad had opened his door and reached for his gun in the back seat.

I was scared as I thought these crazy men were going to shoot it out, just like I had seen cowboys do in the movies. They were walking toward each other. Then they started laughing and lowered their guns and shook hands.

Dad said, "Howdy, Cis, what are you doing over here?"

"Oh just down to the river trying to shoot a mess of ducks, Dick. This your boy?" he said, looking over at me. Dad said, "Well, that's one of them. There's two more over in Hemet."

Cecil was kind of scary-looking and had only one good eye. Come to think of it, he was downright ugly. I found out later he was really a nice person. Except when he was drinking. He would tell us, "Boys, I'm mean when I'm drinking, and I'm drinking a little bit all the time."

When I was in the army in 1959, my sister Rita used to go down and camp on the Colorado River with her sons. One time in the 1970s, they ran into Cecil Ward, who was camped nearby. Cis would cook up a mess of catfish and have my sister and her boys over for supper.

Cis made a beer batter for the fish, and Rita and her son Christopher talked about how good it was. I always liked fresh catfish cooked up for supper too.

I haven't mentioned Cecil's brother Ed. He came over to where Dad was living in Blythe while I was there visiting one year. Dad said, "Show Paul how you can dance, Ed." Then he said to me, "Son, you watch him because this man can really dance."

Ed got up and started to dance, kind of like a mixture of clogging and tap dancing.

My dad really liked Cecil and his brother Ed Ward. I think it was because they were all outlaws. "Scoundrels, really."

QUARTZSITE

We are picking cotton around Buckeye, Arizona, in the fall of 1952. We had been to California all summer picking fruit around Fresno. Our hands we're chafed from picking the cotton. It was cold, and I thought we had lost our motivation. Anyway, Dad said, "You know, I've been thinking lately about that military range over north of Quartzsite."

He said it was a good place to go spend the winter. "There's not going to be much work around these farms till spring, and most of the cotton has been picked. There's always quail and dove along the washes north of Quartzsite. Sometimes you might even spot a deer if you're lucky. There is plenty of firewood in the washes too. What do you boys think? You want to go out there and see what we can find? It's a good place to spend the winter where no one will be looking for us.

"Remember, your mother probably has the law looking for us. If we don't find any shells enough to pay us to pick them up, there's another military range east of Bouse, between Hope and Parker." Then he said, "There's another one north of Desert Center in California. I think the best place to start is Quartzsite, and we have enough money to last us through the winter if we find a place and stay put."

Orville and Everett liked the idea, and so did I. My brothers and I hated to pick cotton. We could barely pick enough to pay for our soda pop and something to eat on the lunch wagon. A Black lady had the lunch wagon, and she sold pop, chips, sandwiches, cigarettes, and I think you could even get a bottle of wine if she knew you.

The cotton wagon where we took the cotton we had picked to weigh up was where she had her lunch wagon parked nearby. Dad called the woman Queenie.

I can't remember if other cotton pickers called her that. She was a nice lady, very jovial, always laughing. Some of the cotton pickers could pick three hundred pounds of cotton in a day; some would have one hundred pounds by noon. I could pick around 70 pounds all day. The pay was three dollars for one hundred pounds. So you can see we weren't getting rich, but it kept us from digging into our savings and ammo money.

Dad would pick about 125 pounds. I don't remember Orville or Everett picking any more than I did. We had a sixteen-foot cotton sack around our neck, down our chest and between our legs. It was laid out behind us as we dragged it up the row, picking the cotton on both sides of the row and putting it in the sack.

Early in the morning, the cotton was damp from the dew. It made it hard to get off your hands. When you pulled it off of one hand, it would stick to the other hand.

What a pain it was, even when the cotton was dry after the sun came up. I had chapped hands and dry skin, and the cotton would hang on to my dry skin. I hated to pick cotton. Once I came upon a citron growing in my row. It probably weighed eight to ten pounds. I put the melon in my sack and kept on picking cotton. When I weighed up at noon, I had sixty-five pounds; they deducted eight pounds for the weight of the sack.

Everett and I climbed the ladder to the wagon we were dumping our cotton into. There was a wide board you could step onto to dump your cotton sack. The cotton was all in the bottom of the sack. I held the bottom end and dropped the top of the sack into the trailer. Everett was standing beside me; we heard the melon go zip as it slid down the inside of the sack. We both laughed. You couldn't see the melon because it was covered with the cotton. It was dishonest, but what the hell. That's not the worst thing I ever did.

We were still camping on the desert west of Waddell Ranch. That night, Dad said, "We will drive to Buckeye in the morning. We will stock up on groceries, then hit the road to Quartzsite. When we get there, we'll see what we can find in the way of brass shells."

My brothers and I could have hugged his neck. No more picking cotton. YIPPEE!

We arrived in Quartzsite in the early afternoon and turned into a dirt road heading north through a wide wash. The road was just car tracks from people driving around. I mean, it wasn't a graded road. We passed by a windmill and a large galvanized tank full of water.

The windmill was turning, so there was a steady stream of water running into the tank. Dad said, "Stop here and we'll fill our two water cans."

A steel ladder was attached to the side of the tank, so a person could climb up and look in, which I did. The tank was probably eight feet high by fifteen feet across.

The water was cold and clear; all sediment had sunk to the bottom of the tank, and it looked like green moss at the bottom. We didn't linger here, just long enough to fill our cans. Then we were on our way again.

The wash was really wide. Sometimes we would come up out of the bottom of the wash onto higher ground. It was almost like an island of hard-packed sand. The roots of the mesquite and cat claw trees had kept flash floods from washing all of it away. After several hundred feet, the road went back into the bottom of the wash. The farther we got from Quartzsite, the less visible the road became. I hear Dad say, "It doesn't look like anyone has been in here in a long time. In winter, sometimes we get flash flooding in the hills east of here, and it washes away all roads. Then you just have to hunt and pick a new road in through the wash." Dad remembered the general direction.

Sometimes he would stop and say, "We need to get out and do a little doctoring on this road with shovels. I can't be sure, but I think the road we are looking for is a little west of here." He turned left and said, "There's a road that goes out of this wash into the sand dunes. The road is probably washed out in the bottom of the wash, but it will probably be visible on the sides where water hasn't run. If no one has been here and it doesn't look like there has been, we'll have to doctor the road a bit to climb out of the bottom of the wash."

In a few minutes, he stopped and looked over toward me, but out the window on the passenger side. "I think that's it right there." And he pointed to where I could see a road going up out of the wash!

My brothers went out of the back of the car. We all piled out and followed Dad up the old road, going up the bank out of the wash. He said, "This is it, son."

The road out of the wash was hard, but as soon as you broke out on top, it was sandy as hell. We followed the old road a ways, checking to see what kind of condition it was in.

Dad said the salvage people in 1947 took a Caterpillar bulldozer and cut a road up the bank and up through the sand dunes. "You can still see a berm of dirt on each side of the road that they had dozed in." The road itself was full of what Dad called blow sand. The berms on either side had desert grasses growing in them, so you could see both edges of the road.

Dad said the sand was soft but felt solid enough to drive on as long as we kept moving. If you stopped in this blow sand, the wheels would dig down when you started to drive on. "It's just this stretch of road right here we have to worry about," he said. "Let's go get the car and see what we can do. Paul, you and Orville climb on the back bumper just in case it's not as solid as I think. Everett, you can ride up front with me. First, though, let me take the shovel and dig the bank down a little. Everett, you want to get the shovel out of the trunk for me? Paul, you and Orville help me throw some rocks against the bank where it's washed out."

I was eager to do anything. It was a long ride from Buckeye that morning. I was stiff and needed to work the kinks out, so to speak. We had the road looking fairly decent, at least where our wheels would go.

Dad said, "I'll turn the car around till it faces up the road where it goes up the bank. Then you boys jump on. I'll have to give her hell in order to climb out of the bottom of this wash. "Okay, Dad," I said. "If you come out on top and start to get stuck, Orville and I will jump off and push."

"You boys will have to hang on tight now," Dad said from the driver's seat.

"You boys all get set to go?" Dad hollered out the window.

Orville and I said, "Yeah."

Dad said, "I'm gonna back up a little so I can get a run at it."

Orville and I both had one hand in the rear side windows and the other hand on the top of the car.

"Okay, here we go." Dad took off fast, the car moving so fast the car bounced quite a bit. Orville and were hanging on for dear life. BOOM. We hit the side of the wash where we had just fixed the bank. I heard Dad gun the engine, and up the bank we went flying. *Piece of cake*, I thought as we came out on top.

We didn't stop until we were on solid ground out of the blow sand. Dad said, "Doesn't look like anyone has been in here in a long time." He looked ahead and said, "Up the road a ways, I see a group of palo verde trees. We'll drive up there and make camp."

"Okay, Dad."

"What are you waiting for? Let's go!" Orville said.

We drove through the sand dunes for a quarter mile. Dad turned right and went over to the trees. "This is as good a place as any to make camp. The sun being low in the sky, it's time to get supper," he said.

While we ate, Dad said, "We'll go out in the morning and see what we can find in the way of shells."

I could only guess what he meant. My brothers and I had never been in a gunnery range before. One good thing: I didn't see any stupid cotton stocks. That was a welcome sight. Just greasewood and desert grasses.

"Paul, you get that tarp from under the chuck boxes and lay it over the hood of the car after I undo the ground strap. It's going to be cold in the morning, boys."

I had figured that out myself. As soon as the sun went down behind the hills, it turned cold.

"If you boys roll your shirts and pants up and put them under your pillow tonight, they'll be nice and warm in the morning."

"Okay, Dad."

"Son, this desert is cold. I'll bet there will be ice in the wash pan in the morning."

Orville and Everett had placed the tow targets over by the palo verde tree and unrolled the bedroll on them. They had gathered up some wood and brush and had it ready to strike a match to it in the morning. That way, one of us would jump out of bed, light a match, and touch it to a little paper. Then we would jump back into bed until the fire was burning real good.

When the sun went down, there was nothing to do but go to bed when you camped out. What a clear night. No wonder dad was forecasting a cold morning. Man, there were a million stars. Not too many shooting stars, but I saw a few. The stars were twinkling bright tonight.

"Okay, it's Everett's turn to start the fire," I heard Dad say. I threw back the canvas and saw it was already daylight. Hell, it seemed as though I had just closed my eyes.

.50 CALIBER MACHINE GUN SHELLS

The sand dunes we were in was due north of Quartzsite. It was all blow sand—not as bad as that down at Yuma, but bad enough. The sand blowing over the years would pile up around greasewood bushes, now called creosote bushes. But greasewood was what Dad called them, so that was good enough for me. Anytime the wind would blow in the fall and winter months, and that was a lot of wind, the sand dunes would get higher and wider, so over the years, these dunes would reach about ten feet high and thirty or forty feet wide and there were valleys in between the dunes.

During the war years, this was a gunnery range for army fighter planes to practice aerial gunnery. The army had built pyramid-shaped targets spaced about three hundred yards apart on a line running north and south through the sand dunes. Since I wasn't there, I'm telling Dad's story of what they were used for.

He said fighter planes would practice strafing the targets. So as a result, the spent brass shells were dropped from the machine guns on the fighter wings.

They did a lot of practice, those pilots. So you can imagine the spent brass shells littering these sand dunes. Dad said the government sold the rights to reclaim the spent brass shells to scrap dealers at the end of World War II. The scrap dealers brought in a Caterpillar tractor to bulldoze a road through the sand dunes so they could bring in trucks and workers to salvage the spent brass shells.

There were fences and signs marking the boundaries to the target area. These were big signs with warnings: PELIGRO—DANGER, DO NOT ENTER. But I guess after the salvage, people left, and it was more or less abandoned. The signs were there, but people pretty much ignored them. A lot of junkies, my dad included, were out there picking up the brass shells to sell to junk dealers in Blythe.

They pretty much had it cleaned up in 1948 or 1949. Seems that no one went out there anymore. So as we didn't like picking cotton around Buckeye, Dad wanted to go see how we would do picking up the brass .50 caliber shells. Anyway, he wanted to check out the shooting range once more to see whether the wind over the years had uncovered the brass shells that the salvage people didn't get because they were buried.

The next morning, we crawled out of our bedroll, and Dad fixed breakfast.

He was a good cook; gravy was usually on the menu. "Today let's make a dido up through these sand dunes and see if the wind has uncovered any shells," he said. He told us the salvagers had cleaned it up pretty good three years ago. That was the last time he had been in here prowling around. He said an acquaintance, Frank Bearden, liked to prowl the desert with his kids, looking for scrap; and if he had been in here, it would all be cleaned up. "But we'll take a look-see anyway."

We drove north on the old road the salvagers had bulldozed up the center of the sand dunes. Dad stopped the car after a hundred yards and said he saw some shells sticking out of the sand on his side of the car. "Let's take a look-see." Dad picked up several black .50 caliber shells that were right in front of him. I could see only about two inches of the shell as the rest was buried in the sand. When he pulled the shell from the sand, we saw that only the top two inches were black. The part that was buried was still brass colored.

Being exposed to the sun for years was what turned the brass black.

Dad turned them with the open end facing down and clacked them together, knocking out the sand inside. My brothers and I started picking them up too. I heard Dad behind me blow on one of the shells, creating a keen whistle. Soon all of us were doing it. Kinda fun too!

"Boys, knock them together and get all the sand out. Salvage yards won't pay top dollar unless the shells are clean."

Shoot, they were all over the place. In just a few minutes, we had our hands and pockets full. "Let's go back to the car and empty out our pockets and get some bags to put them in." Dad said.

Back at the car, Dad pulled several old gas mask bags from the wheel well under the spare tire. "Boys, it looks good. I wouldn't have believed there would be this much brass still out here." While he was getting the bags out, I went to the passenger side and reached in and pulled my holster with the Iver Johnson .22 pistol in it out from under the seat. I strapped it on my hip; if there were any critters to plug, I wanted to be ready. Orville walked up from behind me and reached in for his new Colt Woodsman. It was a .22 automatic he had picked up from the O. S. Stapley hardware in Buckeye.

What a nice gun. I hated to admit it, but I was jealous. What a neat little gun. Mine was only a revolver, but it held nine shots. It was lots better than a slingshot. But still, it wasn't automatic.

Dad told me, "Hell, son, you don't even need another shot if you put the first one on target. Besides, those bullets cost money.

True, I thought, *but still, rapid fire is fun.*

Orville had his clip out and was pushing .22 shells into it. As he finished and shoved it into the holster on his hip, I said, "Hey, let me have some of those .22 shells."

I had looked in the glove box but didn't find any. That's because he already had them in his pocket and his hot little hand.

He said, "Well, if you want some, why don't you make your daddy buy you some?"

"Okay, wise guy, I'm the oldest. I should have first dibs on them." I'd have taken them away from him if he weren't so tough.

The little shit would fight at the drop of a hat. He was ornery as shit. He would kick ass and then take names later. Besides, he was packing a pistol. I didn't want to have to shoot him just to have my way. And then he could draw that pistol pretty fast too! I guess it was better to just take what shells he felt like giving me. It was better to live to fight another day.

"Okay, boys," Dad was saying, "two of us can take the gas mask bags. The other two, take these ore sacks." So we started back, picking up shells. Every once in a while, we would find a loaded round. Most of the loaded ones had a black tip painted on the bullet. This meant it was armor piercing. Bullets painted with a red tip were tracer bullets, meaning you could see the bullet's path through the sky because of the fire burning at the back of the bullet. The iron rings that held the shells together in a belt form, so that they would feed into the machine gun, were lying all over the place. In fact, it was hard to tell the iron clip or ring from the black brass shells sticking out of the sand. We often walked over to an iron ring thinking it was a brass shell.

It wasn't long before we had our first gunnysack full of brass shells, and we estimated it to weigh 125 pounds. Not too bad!

Sometimes we would find a half of a belt of loaded ammunition, which our Dad called bandoliers. A full bandoleer was 250 shells all clipped together in a belt. I once found a bandolier of 248 shells—meaning only two had been fired. Dad told us some of the soldiers he had talked to at Tom Wells's saloon told him they were trained that if a belt jammed going through the machine gun, they should release it and start a new belt into the gun.

We took all the live ammunition and stuck them into the hole in the trailer hitch where the ball was supposed to be and bent it back and forth until the bullet came loose enough to remove it from the shell.

Then we dumped the gunpowder into one of the ore sacks. I think the ore sack held about a cubic foot of gunpowder. Then in the morning when it was cold, we would take a handful of the gunpowder and put it into the wood when we wanted to start a fire.

We left a little trail of powder from the handful of powder about ten inches long. The next morning, we would just strike a match and touch it to the trail of the powder.

It would burn up the trail to the handful in the woodpile, and in a blaze, our fire would be started. It would burn so hot and fast that there was no need for kindling. What an easy way to start a fire on a cold morning.

This scene unfolded every day for the next week or so. I got to throw one of the loaded shells into the sand and sticking it like a knife. But one day it hit on the wrong end. It landed on the primer end, and the primer must have hit a rock. BAM! The shell exploded, scaring the hell out of me and, in the process, giving me powder burns through my pants and into my legs. It also blew sand into my eyes. Not a good day!

After getting the sand out of my eyes and pulling my pants down to look at the powder burns on my leg. I decided not to try to stick the shells into the sand anymore. Dad thought it was a good object lesson, and he didn't have to say a word.

After a week or so, we had about ten sacks of shells. Dad said, "We'll take them to Yuma." That town was the closest to us. Going back out across the wash to Quartzsite, we had to be very careful. We didn't worry about getting stuck because of the weight in the car from our sacks of shells, but it tended to drag on every wash we went into. Also Dad was worried about busting a tire with all the weight in the car because the tires had only a 4-ply rating. Finally, we were on the highway headed south to Yuma.

"Son, don't get over forty-five miles an hour. If a tire blows, you won't be able to control the car."

I was driving very carefully, and all of a sudden, POW, FLOF, FLOF, FLOF.

A tire had blown, and I pulled the car to the side of the road. It was a good thing Dad had a two-ton jack, or we might have had to unload the car to jack it up. With the tire changed, we loaded into the car, and we were on our way again.

"Goddamn, son, drive careful. If we blow another tire, we'll be in deep shit. Our spare is on the ground."

One of us will have to hitch a ride on down to Yuma and buy a tire. When we get there I'm going to put two six-ply tires on the rear. The six ply tires will handle the weight, these four ply are just too light for this kind of hauling.

We had left most of our plunder, as dad call it out on the desert covered with brush because there just wasn't room for it all with the sacks of shells.

We had gone about ten miles when another POW, *flof, flof, flof.*

"I hate to say this, boys, but we're in trouble with a capital *T*!" Neither tire could be salvaged. The whole sidewall had blown out of both tires when they blew out. "Well, we can do one of two things," Dad said. "We can sit here and cry, or we can walk down the highway a ways and see if we can find something we can salvage." We were always seeing tires thrown out along side of the road—maybe we'd be lucky.

Dad said he and Everett would go up the road and for Orville and me to go down the road. One of us on each side of the roadway. Orville and I walked about a half mile when we saw an old army Jeep tire lying out in the brush. It was smooth, but there were no breaks in the sidewall of the tire. We could barely see Dad and Everett, so it wouldn't do any good to try and holler. So we started rolling the tire back to the car. By the time we got back, we saw Dad and Everett were also returning. They hadn't found anything we could use. I heard Dad ask if the casing was broken. I said, "No, it looks pretty good to me, Dad."

"Well, let's get this tire off the car."

Thank God dad had an extra inner tube, because both of the tires that had blown out had ruined the inner tubes. Dad had his tire irons out and was tearing down the spare while Orville and I jacked the car up and got the wheel off. Dad had the Jeep tire on our rim, and he and Everett were starting to pump it up. It was a six-ply casing, which was good.

We still had about twenty-five miles to go to make it to Yuma. "Okay, boys, let's roll, but keep an eye open for another tire, just in case." We stopped a couple of times to look at tires along the side of the road, but nothing was any good. We made it to Yuma with that old Jeep tire.

It was late when we got to the junkyard and sold the brass shells. If I remember right, we got $135 for them. That wasn't bad for a week's work. We couldn't make that kind of money picking cotton. Besides, they wouldn't have let me strap on my pistol picking cotton. They would think of me as some kind of crackpot. Instead of a boy who just wanted to tote a gun.

With our newfound wealth, I bought a new hat. We saw a couple of shows and then replenished our grub boxes. We went to a wrecking yard and dug through a bunch of tires until Dad found just the right tires we needed. They had good tread, and both were six-ply. They were six dollars apiece. For a dollar more, he threw in the inner tubes. He charged another dollar for mounting them, which Dad told them to do since we were rich.

Going back to Quartzsite with our new used tires, I felt as though I was driving a Cadillac. I had even bought a big bar of rocky road chocolate. *Life is good.*

After about two months of this, the pickings were getting slim. We had just come back from San Bernardino, where we had taken a load to Alex Novack and Son in Ontario, California. They gave us more per pound for them than they did at Yuma. We got two hundred dollars for that last load. We saw every movie in town, filled our chuck boxes again, and lit out for Quartzsite. Dad had come up with a novel idea.

He said he had been finding a lot of shells in the bunches of dry grass that was everywhere. So when he was buying groceries, he bought about six boxes of kitchen matches. We'll just walk around picking up shells as usual but carry a pocket full of matches, strike them, and drop them into the bunches of grass.

It worked well too, but with all four of us striking matches, it looked as though the whole desert was on fire. Nowadays, they would have been out there with a helicopter to see what in hell was taking place. Back then, nobody paid any attention, if they even noticed at all. The next morning, we would walk to every bush that we had burned the day before and picked the brass shells out of them. We got a lot of shells that way after the brush had burned and turned the spot black.

One morning, we awoke to a very damp canvas tarp over us. It had rained during the night, not enough to make us roll up the bedroll and scramble for the car, but enough to wet things pretty good. We threw fresh gunpowder into the wood for a fire, and soon it was blazing. We weren't running the car enough to keep the battery properly charged. With all the starting the engine and killing it in a short time, the battery kept going dead.

So every afternoon, when we came in from picking up shells all day, we parked the car on a small hill nearby. That way, we could just give it a little shove to start. Six-volt batteries didn't have much power in them, and so it was easy to run them down. Once we started it in the morning after it had set all night, it would start fine; but just in case, we still looked for a place on a downhill slope to stop it.

This morning, for some reason, we had gone south on the road instead of north. We were heading back to the wash we had crossed coming in to here. I was out with Everett on the left side of the road with my bag on my shoulder, to hold the shells as I picked them up. As I reached for a couple of shells, I noticed fresh deer tracks in the sand. They were made after the rain had fallen, because each step turned over dry sand underneath.

"Everett," I said, "here's fresh deer tracks. I'm getting the gun from the car and see if I can get it. Tell Dad I'm going to track it. If I lose the trail, I'll come back."

I got my .22 rifle out of the car. It was already loaded, but I stuck a box of shells in my pocket just in case. I lit out, following the tracks in the sand, which were easy to follow.

I must have tracked it for more than an hour when I heard a noise on my right and ahead of me. It took me a minute to see it, but there was a big buck running up a small mound down in the wash. I dropped down on my right knee and took a rest across my left knee and squeezed the trigger.

I was holding just behind his left front leg. POW. He jumped sideways and stopped again. I knew I had hit him the first time, but he didn't go down. I took the same site a little higher on his shoulder, but still behind it. POW. This time when the gun cracked, he went down. I started down into the wash with my heart beating like crazy because this was my first buck. I'd killed a doe before, back when I was twelve years old, behind the McCormick place that Tom Wells owned.

I went over to him, thinking, *I've never dressed out a deer by myself before.* I had watched my dad many times do this procedure. I had a picture of it all in my mind. I had every confidence I could do it. I reached into my pocket and took out my knife and opened it up. So I cut off the head first and tried to get the deer lying downhill, so the blood would drain out of the animal.

Don't try to pack out a head. You can't eat those damn horns, Dad had said. *Then go around each hoof with the blade of your knife and then slit the hide to the knee. Peel the hide down to the knee, go around the center of the knee, and, with your knife blade and with both hands, lift the knee until it pops. Then cut the lower leg and hoof free. You have to repeat this four times.*

Now slit the stomach, skin, and remove the insides. Then take the left front leg and right rear leg, then tie the skin together. Do the same to the right front leg and the left rear leg. Now you can get into it like a pair of suspenders. Okay, now you're ready to pack a deer out.

It was almost as though I could hear Dad talking me through the procedure.

Shit, I had my arms through the legs, but no way in hell could I get up. The buck was just too heavy. I lay there for a moment, sizing up my situation as I wondered what to do. I looked around, and there was a big rock down at the bottom of this mound I had killed the buck on. The rock was about four feet high, and it was embedded into the bank. I dragged the deer down on top of the rock with the legs facing the outside of the rock.

Once I jumped down into the wash, I was able to lean back against the rock. I slid the deer to me and got back into the legs I had tied together. I found this way was easier to get the deer on my shoulders. It was heavy, but I made it, but by no means was it a piece of cake. I thought I could handle this. Boy, it's hard to walk in loose sand and gravel with so much weight on your back.

I made it about one hundred yards. Then I gave out. I just let the deer drop off my shoulders to the ground, and I fell down beside it, exhausted. I hated to do it because I knew I could never get it on my shoulders again. I just wasn't man enough. I wasn't a man at all; I was only sixteen years old. I had always heard about how many deer my dad had packed out, but I just wasn't capable of this feat. I lay there on the deer, thinking about how far the car and camp was. The blood of the deer had dried on my hands, and it felt like a big scab. I wanted to wash my hands and get the blood off.

After a few minutes of lying there and getting my strength back, I got up and started to look for something to clean my hands on. I had tried to rub the dried blood off with wet sand. That helped, but I wanted it to be all off. I found a kind of flat rock with a depression in it, and there was enough water in it to get my hands fairly clean.

I didn't have any drinking water with me or anything to eat. I thought if I could find another rock with water in it, I would lay down and drink it. I looked around, but I didn't see anything but wet rocks—not enough to sip a little water out of. I returned to the deer and assessed my predicament. I was still at the bottom of the wash.

The walls were about twelve foot high, but there were places that the walls were sloped. I just needed to find a place that I could drag the deer up out of the bottom of the wash. I would pull the deer to me then back up a couple of steps and drag it to me again. I'd do that over and over for about a half hour then fall down and rest wondering what the hell I was thinking. I should have brought Everett with me.

I found a small ravine going up out of the wash, where water had made a slopping gully. I could tell this was as good a place as any to try to get the deer out of the wash. Maybe when I got on top, I could see my dad or my brothers, but this wasn't to be. I got the deer on top of the wash, but I couldn't even see the car, let alone a person.

While I was getting rested, I walked along the edge of the wash, looking for enough water in a rock to get a drink. I found two and got about a half a teacup out of them. Hey, anything at all was more than I had. What to do? What to do? I could walk back to camp to get help, but then I would have to walk all the way back to show them where the deer was. I didn't think I had the energy to walk out and then return.

I knew the road went west from our camp, but I didn't know how far. I untied the deer's legs and then retied the hind legs together. That way, I could stand between its legs, and with the tied knot at my stomach, I was able to lean into it and drag it much easier.

And the sand away from the wash was firmer and much easier to walk in as I dragged the deer toward the road. I won't go into how much misery I went through to drag that deer to the road, but I'll tell you this: The sun was down when I came to the road. I left the deer lying on the road; there were no car tire tracks on the road, so I knew my kill was safe.

It was maybe a quarter mile to camp; I could see Dad's fire going as soon as I came over a little rise. I walked into camp, and Dad was looking at my hands for blood. "You got one?" he asked.

"Yeah, I left it on the road running east and west," I replied.

"Hell, son, sit down and eat. You must be hungry!"

"I'm thirsty, Dad," I said.

Everett asked me where I got it. I told him over in the big wash. After I had eaten, we loaded up in the car and went to get the deer. We loaded it into the trunk and drove back to camp.

Dad said, "Sit down and take it easy, son. I'll hang it right here in this tree and get the hide off. Then we'll just let it hang until morning."

I let Dad, Orville, and Everett take care of skinning the deer because I was so tired. I just washed up and fell into bed. It had been a long day, and I lay there thinking. I must have started tracking about 8:30 a.m. or 9:00 a.m. Now it was way after dark. What's that? Was it worth it? You bet! I loved to hunt, but if you had asked me when I was dragging the deer up the slope coming out of the wash, I might have said, hell no, it wasn't worth it. I would have parted with that buck pretty cheap. Looking back on it today, I wonder how I did it.

The next morning, Dad was up butchering my buck. "I'll cut us off some steaks and fry them up for breakfast."

I was so sore from dragging the deer I could hardly move as I tried to get out of bed. There wasn't a muscle in my body that didn't hurt. It was another cold day, and the wind had started to blow a little this morning. That was good because meat keeps better when it's cold. After Dad got the steaks cut off the hindquarters, he wrapped the rest of the meat in a clean sheet and a canvas tarp and then hung it in the shade on a limb of the tree.

Dad had a good fire going, and he floured the steaks and had them frying in a skillet of hot grease. He had a lid on the skillet so that ashes from the fire wouldn't blow into his cooking. Like I said, the wind was blowing this morning. Dad made gravy again, and the steaks sure smelled good cooking. He was frying potatoes in another skillet, and when the steaks were done, he laid them on top of the potatoes and put a lid on it. Then he set the skillet on the small table where we ate.

Dad had a bowl, which he poured a can of milk into. Then he poured some water in it too. He was browning flour to make the gravy in the skillet he had cooked the steaks in. He dumped the milk into the skillet, stirred it, and said, "You boys get a plate. This will be ready in about two shakes."

Everything sure tasted good after starving yesterday. Dad said, "Son, you can lay around camp this morning if you've a mind to, and your brothers and I will go out and pick up some shells. When we get back at lunchtime, if you feel all right, maybe you can help us this afternoon. You've earned a well-deserved rest, son."

"Okay, Dad," I told him. "I am still tired. Maybe I will go back to bed and sleep for a while."

"Okay, son. See you at noon," Dad said.

And with that, they climbed into the car and headed out to the sand dunes to pick up shells. I sat around for a while. Then I just crashed back into bed. All I could think of was how tired and sore I was. And of course, I lay there reliving how I had killed my first buck.

Soon I was fast asleep and woke up only when I heard our car pull up into camp.

Writing this story today and remembering it, it's like it all happened only yesterday. I never outgrew my love to hunt. I never felt that I had to kill something, just being out in the forest or out on the desert and having my gun on my shoulder was a little bit of heaven. Setting up against a tree in the woods when you're cold and seeing the sun coming up and feeling those first rays of sunlight hit you and feeling the warmth from it—it's such a good feeling. Just wondering what the day will bring in the way of game, or if it will bring anything at all. Sometimes as the sun warms me, I would doze off, and when I awake, I would wonder if any game had walked past while I slept. I would open my thermos and pour a cup of coffee and feel around for a candy bar in my pocket, thinking, *Life don't get better than this.* If you haven't hunted, you wouldn't understand.

PROSPECTORS

We had just pulled into the Shell gas station in Quartzsite Arizona. The station was run by Dave Scott, whose mother and family owned a gold mine west and a little south of Quartzsite. The mine, with its tailings pile, was visible from the station.

Dad wanted to pick up a few things from the tiny store in the gas station and to top off our tank before heading off into the desert west of where we had been picking up brass shells. Dad knew the Scotts: Dave and his brother who owned the station. Dad had lived in Blythe, about twenty or twenty-five miles west, for about fifty years.

Our car at the time was a '41 Chevy sedan. Before we bought it, someone had painted it a godawful green. But we had traded our 1938 Chevy for it in Phoenix, Arizona, two or three months before.

Anyway, to get back to what I was saying about the car.

On the back bumper wedged between the car and the bumper guard on one side, we had a white army surplus water can, and on the other side, in the same spot, we had a red army surplus gas can. When heading out into the desert, you better have extra gas and water. We always had two water bags hanging from the side rearview mirrors. That way, we always had a cool drink of water available. And we would refill it from the water can on the back bumper.

Dad had gotten some peaches, some flour, and Rex Pure Lard and salt pork from the store, which we would now call a mini market. With our tank full and having lard to cook with, we were ready to go. So we loaded up, and I turned the car around, and we headed back toward Blythe. It wasn't far, maybe a half mile before we turned onto a dirt road on the right and headed somewhat northwest into an old road running along a dry wash.

This road was well traveled. Dad said it went out to a still-active mine. We were going to explore a mine Dad knew about, which was about ten miles out. The road was really washboardy, and if I was driving too fast, the rear of the car would start to fishtail, or the car would start to turn sideways. Dad kept complaining about how fast I was driving. Even thirty-five or forty miles an hour on a rough road can be dangerous. But what did he know?

"Goddamn it, son, slow down. You're going to bust a tire."

Tires in 1953 weren't constructed very well; they were made from rayon instead of nylon. If you got ten or twelve thousand miles out of a set of new of tires, you were doing good. Besides, Dad didn't buy new tires,

We always went to a wrecking yard and purchased used ones. Same with a car battery. A new one was ten or twelve dollars, but one from a wrecking yard cost around three dollars. Of course, we were taking a chance on whether the one we bought was any good. Dad would take a pair of pliers and short it across the post, and if it threw sparks everywhere, it must be good. He figured if it had been sitting in the junkyard and still had life in it, it would see us through.

The road stretched along a dry wash, and a couple miles up ahead, if Dad didn't kill me first for driving too fast, I would be turning right and crossing the wash. You had to be careful and choose your way when crossing the wash because it was loose gravel and very sandy. It was really easy to get stuck. Then we would have to jack up the car and cut some brush and put it under the rear wheels, sometimes for twenty or twenty-five feet.

At least until you reached solid ground. Then we would be on our way again, until we got stuck again in some sandy wash. Sometimes Orville, who was seated between Dad and me, and Everett would just climb on the back bumper and ride. That way, if I got stuck, they would jump off and push.

If the sand was really soft, we could get stuck, even with them pushing, if the road was going uphill.

Dad was always complaining. "Goddamn it son, if you would have gunned the motor like I told you to, we wouldn't have got stuck again." He said a few choice words—cussing, really. "Are you trying to kill your brothers on the back bumper?" He said next time I got stuck, he was going to drive. So with a little pushing and a lot of cussing, we were on our way.

After coming out of the wash on the other side, the old mine road we were following was pretty hard. Once we were on good ground, Dad said, "Stop up ahead a little bit, son."

I want to get out and get some weeds and brush out of the tracks. That way, if someone came along snooping around, they wouldn't know we were back in here. Dad told Orville and Everett to drag a log or two into our tracks. He threw a few rocks into the road just to discourage anyone from following us in. We were heading almost north now, but there were small washes that were no more than a dip to cross as we wound our way north through one ravine after another.

The country was mostly palo verde trees, some cat's claw vines, some small desert grasses, and some ironwood here and there. Ironwood is really hard. You can't chop it with an axe. You have to lay one end on something and then try to break it with the back of the axe. If you build a fire out of ironwood, it is really hot. The coals from the fire will still be there the next morning. You can just set a cast iron skillet on them and get to cooking.

Anyway, I was still driving since I hadn't gotten stuck again. Everett in the back seat said, "Hey, there's a deer."

I was looking around to my left, but I didn't see anything. Orville and Dad were looking too. I asked Everett, "Are you sure?"

Everett said, "Ya, he's laying right out there."

I looked where he was pointing, and sure enough, there was a buck out about fifty yards lying there looking at us. Dad had a .32 Winchester Special between him and me, and I said, "Hey, Dad, let me shoot it."

Dad said, "Go ahead, son, and shoot it." He still hadn't seen the deer;

I laid the gun out the window and drew a bead on the deer's forehead because that was all I could see besides his horns since he was lying behind a downed log. I squeezed the trigger, and *kaboom!*

The gun kicked me back into the car from where I was resting it out of the window. I felt someone yank the gun out of my hands and heard Dad say, "Give me that son of a bitch."

I had missed the buck slick and clean. Dad had to lean all the way forward and into the steering wheel to get a shot. *Kaboom!* Man, that buck went ass over teakettle.

Dad had shot him on a full run. As he hit the ground, he broke off one horn. We walked out to where he was lying and saw that Dad had shot him in the back of the head, knocking off both his horns. What a shot! I remember that shot like it was yesterday. Dad could cuss like a son of a bitch, and he could shoot like a son of a bitch. And on top of that, it was a nice buck too.

Dad had his pocketknife out and was sharpening it on a whetstone. He would be doing the honors of gutting the buck. For those with a weak stomach, think of it as cleaning the buck out. In the heat of the day, it's good to get the animal cleaned and get the hide off as soon as possible. Otherwise, the meat can spoil. But this being winter, there wasn't much to worry about as the days were cool.

Dad told my brother Orville and me to both grab a hind leg and spread the buck out so he could perform the operation. He split the stomach and reached in and pulled the insides out. He was still holding the heart and the liver so as not to get them in the dirt. Dad told Everett to go back to the car, open the trunk, and get a clean pan big enough to hold the organs.

Everett came back with the pan and also a lid, since flies were a problem. Anytime we killed a deer, we always had the heart and liver that night. We got a short rope from the car and tied the buck's hind legs over a limb of a palo verde tree. Then Dad started skinning the buck. He was pretty fast. Of course, he had to stop now and then to sharpen his knife. The job is much easier with a sharp knife. With the job all done, we wrapped the carcass in an old clean sheet Dad had for just such an occasion.

Dad seemed to always be prepared for things like this. He got under the buck and with it on his shoulder, I untied the rope so he could carry it to the car. Orville picked up the pan and carried it to the car. Everett had to take the gas and water cans off the back bumper in order to get the pan out of the trunk. Dad laid the deer across the chuck boxes that we carried in the trunk with all our food and cooking utensils inside. We shut the trunk and put the gas and water cans back on the bumper.

We loaded back in the car and were on our way, feeling pretty good about the turn of events. We always had canned goods, lard, flour, salt and pepper, and, usually, bread. But because bread doesn't keep well in a hot car, Dad would just make biscuits, or what he called corn pone. It was a mixture of flour and cornmeal and an egg that he would dump into his Dutch oven and cook. The finished result was about two inches thick and as big as the bottom of the Dutch oven. It had more flour in it than cornbread, and I liked it a lot.

We were still headed north toward Parker, Arizona. There were still a lot of washes to cross. Some had a sharp drop-off where a cloudburst had sent a flood down the wash, washing out the sides. We would have to shovel the sandy bank down, so I was able to drive the car off without hanging the rear bumper on the side of the bank. But at least we weren't stuck anymore. Lucky for me, because I was still driving. I was seventeen, and I loved to drive. Except when I screwed up and incurred Dad's wrath, but even that was bearable as long as I was driving.

We finally reached the canyon we were looking for and turned into it, heading a little southwest. The bottom of this canyon was sandy but packed pretty hard because of the damp ground. As long as I kept moving and didn't gun the engine, so as to not spin the drive wheel, we were okay. In fact, the bottom of the canyon was pretty flat. The last cloudburst had left it pretty smooth.

A lot of the time, when we were driving along the shoulder of the wash, we were driving in the old mine road. As you may remember, we were heading to an old mine that Dad knew of. The canyon ended abruptly as the mountain rose up in front of us. Up on our right, about seventy-five feet above the floor of the canyon, I could see some old shaft, and Dad said that was where the mine was.

It was late in the afternoon so the car was in the shade. I was able to get the car turned around because there was a wide space.

But I did break through and was partly stuck, but Everett and Orville stepped up on the back bumper to give it a little more weight, and I was able to finish the job. We opened the trunk and got the buck out and laid it on some brush. That way, the meat would cool down much faster.

I couldn't wait to climb up the old road that went up the side of the hill to where the old shack stood, and Orville, Everett, and I started up to go exploring. Dad had the trunk open and was fooling around with the heart and liver. He dumped some water from the water can into the pot as my brothers and I went out of sight up on the side of the canyon. The mine shaft was about fifteen feet by fifteen feet, and the wood was bleached out to a grayish white. It still looked pretty stable.

On the side we walked up on, there were sixteen lead acid storage batteries, so at some time, they had a power plant at the mine. Maybe the miners had an old gas generator to charge the batteries so as to have electric lights in the mine. There were plenty of drill points and pieces of metal lying around. Close to the mine shaft was an old rusty bedspring, and off to one side were a few five-gallon cans of carbide. The miners used the carbide to put in their lamps, and when water was mixed in, you had acetylene gas.

The lamp was small made out of brass; it had a chrome reflector with a tube from the tank for the acetylene gas to pass through. You would take a match and light the gas, and there was your light. We walked over and opened the door to the shaft. Against the back wall was a nearly new cast iron cooking stove. Dad would be in his glory; he had a real stove to cook on.

Dad had followed us up to the old shack, and he said the mine itself was a little farther up. I could tell he was pleased when he saw the stove. "Goddamn, would you look at that!" he said. "I can hardly wait to get a fire going."

But right now, we wanted to go exploring that mine. We all walked up to the mine opening and looked in. You couldn't see very far inside, and Dad didn't want us back in there until he could check it out the following morning. And we would have to get the carbide lamps working first.

There was no sign of anybody having been there in years, probably because the road in was so deteriorated. And we had to do a lot of road repair just to get there. So we headed back to the car. Dad said, "You boys get some firewood gathered up and I'll build a fire in the stove and start cooking the heart and liver."

I told my brothers, "That sounds good to me." So off we went down the wash a ways, gathering wood.

It wasn't long before Dad had the wood in the stove burning, and the lard was sizzling in the skillet.

Dad had floured the meat and was ready to put it in the hot grease with onion. The aroma was starting to make me hungry. I couldn't wait for it to be done. Soon Dad said, "You boys get your hands washed and grab a plate."

I got washed, grabbed my plate, and Dad laid two pieces of liver and a piece of heart on it. There was a table in the back of the shack, but no chairs.

We all went outside and grabbed an empty carbide can and carried them in to sit on. I brought one for Dad. We all sat down and started to eat like we were starving. It was really good with gravy, just heart and liver, bread, and gravy. Dad had made a pot of coffee too. Boy, as hungry as I was, I could have eaten the ass out of that deer since we didn't have anything else to eat since Quartzsite.

After supper, we all went out to scrounge for more wood for a campfire. It was better to have too much than not enough. We would need to keep the fire going until we felt that we were ready for bed. Dad always had his fiddles with him, and after dinner, while the dishes were being done, Dad would get the fiddle case from the back window of the car where he carried it. Then he would sit down on the chuck boxes that Orville and I had carried up from the car, and he would tune the fiddle and rosin up the bow and give us a tune. He knew quite a few tunes:

Red River Valley

From this valley they say you are going,
We will miss your bright eyes and sweet smile.
For they say you are taking the sunshine
That has brightened our pathway awhile.
Come and set by my side, if you love me,
Do not hasten to bid me ado.
But remember the Red River Valley,

And the cowboy who loved you so true.

I can still hear those strains from Dad's fiddle. He had made it himself, and he had also taught himself to play the fiddle.

Down in the Valley

Down in the valley, valley so low,
Hang your head over hear the wind blow.
Hear the wind blow love, hear the wind blow,
Hang your head over, hear the wind blow."
Write me a letter, send it by mail,
Send it in care of the Birmingham jail.
Birmingham jail love, Birmingham jail,
Send it in care of, the Birmingham jail.

We would stand around the campfire with our hands outstretched toward the fire, warming our hands and kind of diverting the smoke from the fire away from our face. No matter which side of the fire you were on, the smoke always blew in your face, especially your eyes. Another thing you learned was not to stand too close, or the fire would change direction and singe your eyelashes. Then for days, every time you blinked, your eyelashes would stick together. Almost like Velcro.

When wood was plentiful, we always had a big fire. Dad always said, "White man build big fire and stand way back, Indian build little fire and stand up close."

Well, we liked a big fire. This was winter, and winter in the desert is cold, especially down in this canyon. In the desert, no place is hotter in the summer or colder in the winter. Besides, if you were facing the fire, you were hot and your back side was cold, so you turned around to warm your back side, and the front side got cold really fast. It was never-ending turning around, especially to keep the smoke out of your eyes.

It was starting to get dark, so Dad said, "You boys go get the bedroll out of the car while I put this fiddle away."

Orville and I went back to the car and started moving things around so we could get the bedroll out from behind the seat.

The bedroll was our blankets rolled up in a tarp that was double length. That way, there was protection from moisture from the ground, or, should it start raining, we were protected from the weather because the tarp was folded back over us. I mean, you couldn't stay there in a blinding rainstorm, but in a light rain, you were okay.

We usually had a couple of tow targets we had picked up on the desert west of Phoenix to use for a mattress. F-80 Shooting Star jets would fly out of Luke Air Force Base northwest of Glendale, Arizona, going down to a gunnery range near Ajo, northwest of Tucson.

Target-towing planes would leave earlier. They were prop driven jobs. Then the F-80's would practice aerial gunnery at the targets. Sometimes the cable attached to the target would be partially severed by a bullet from the F-80. The plane with the target would drop it before landing back at Luke Field. But those with weak cables, the cable broke, and down would come the target wherever it happened to break.

So we had found some of the targets that had been shot loose and found they made a good mattress used under your bedroll. Anyway, Dad said, "Let's bring the old bedsprings down to the car. Better to sleep in the car with the bedroll than carry everything to the mine."

So Orville and I fetched the springs and laid the targets down on the springs rolled out the bedroll, and we were ready for bed. We were all four sleeping side by side on that bed, but I don't remember being crowded. We were just snuggling in when Dad said, "Did either of you boys put anything over the hood of the car?"

In the wintertime in the desert, that's standard procedure. You don't want the radiator to freeze because it would split the radiator. Then Dad said, "We would be shit out of luck, and one of us would have to walk back to Quartzite to get another one from the wrecking yard, and that was a long way to walk. You would have to carry the water bag because you couldn't walk it in a day. I don't remember anyone putting antifreeze in cars in the fifties. Maybe back east they did, I don't know."

So he got back up wearing his long underwear.

In October, Dad put on long underwear and wouldn't take them off until the weather warmed up in about April, except to wash them. He sat back down on the side of our bed and lifted his feet so he could brush the sand off and crawled back into bed. "You boys better listen to the old man, or they will find your bleached bones out here on the desert one of these days." I could barely hear him as I was dozing off. Tomorrow would be soon enough to worry about such things.

I woke up, and Dad was up with a fire going already. "You rascals gonna sleep all day?" I said, "Not me." Dad had a pan of water heating so we could wash up. So with my clothes on and my teeth brushed, I was ready for breakfast. Dad had laid the deer up on top of the car when he covered the hood the night before. That way, it would be cold in the morning, and he would wrap it up to keep it cold all day. He had sliced off some steaks, and that was what we were having for breakfast, along with potatoes and gravy.

He had gone to the mine shaft and started a fire in the stove. "I'll have these steaks cooked in two shakes of a lamb's tail."

Everett had done the dishes the night before, so with clean plates set on the table, we were ready for bear.

Those steaks couldn't be done soon enough for me. And they smelled real good too.

We had a Coleman stove that Dad would cook on, but cooking on this big cast iron stove with wood saved us money. This way, we didn't use up our white gas, which was more expensive than regular gas. And we always liked to live as cheaply as we could. That way, we had more money for ammunition, and to sustain us before going back to work.

Dad said, "You boys grab a plate because this meat is ready."

We had instant coffee to wash the food down with. I didn't like it black, so there was some canned milk left from making gravy, so I put cream and sugar in mine. *Aaah, life is good.*

"Hey, Everett, you ready to go back up to the mine?"

Dad said, "Not so fast. Everett's gotta do these dishes before anybody is going anywhere."

Orville and I said we'd help because we wanted to get back up to the mine. So Everett washed, and I dried, and Orville put them away. Dad was moving the chuck boxes and repositioning everything.

"Son," he said, "I'll go down and move the car as close as I can. That way, we won't have to carry things so far."

We were finishing the dishes when I heard Dad calling for us to come down to the car. The battery was almost dead, and the motor would just barely turn over. That stupid cheap-ass battery that Dad bought at the junkyard was almost dead.

The only good thing about this turn of events was Dad always told me to park the car with the nose headed downhill. That way, if you had to push the car, it would be easier downhill. Dad slipped in behind the wheel, and, with Orville, Everett, and me pushing, we tried to push it fast enough to start the damn thing. We pushed, but I could tell the ground was just too sandy to make it roll very fast. I hollered try it. Dad popped the clutch. The car jerked a few times but wouldn't start.

Dad got out and said, "Let's push it back to where it was," because we were starting to go over a little rise where the old road went out of the bottom of the canyon. So we all three started pushing. Boy, pushing a car in sand that has been disturbed was not easy; and going the other way was uphill.

Orville and I had our back to the car. Everett was in the middle, and we were pushing with everything we had. We would make about seven or eight feet and then have to stop and rest to catch our breath. Finally, with a lot of pushing and some cussing too, we were back where we started. We had the wash all torn up behind us because our feet had dug into the sand as we pushed the car. The sand was just too loose now to try again. Besides, I was pooped.

Dad was kicking his own ass because he didn't disconnect the ground strap to the battery. I said, "It's that old cheap battery," but Dad said, "No, the car must have a short in it someplace." Then he said, "I'll tell you what, Paul. You and Orville run up to the mine and see if you can get some boards to put under the wheels while Everett and I smooth this sand out."

So up to the mine we went, and we found a lot of timber and decaying boards lying around. We grabbed three that looked like we could carry, and with Orville on one end and me on the other, we went back down the side of the hill to the car.

We laid them end to end in front of the tires on one side. Each board was about twelve or fourteen feet long, so that would give us about forty feet of board to push it on after we brought down three more boards

We got the other boards under the wheels and were ready to start pushing. Dad told me to get in and he would push this time. He said, "Try second or third gear so the engine would turn over easier."

They got it going, and I popped the clutch out, and the engine caught right away.

Aroom. The car started. Dad was beside me saying, "Keep her running, son."

I thought, *Yeah, right. I'm going to kill it then have to push it again.* I was idling the engine pretty fast so it wouldn't die. We needed to let it charge for about an hour so it would start the next time. I backed it up the boards just in case it wouldn't start and we could push it again down the boards.

Dad said we could take off prowling around if we wanted, but we should stay out of the mine until he had a chance to look it over, and he would stay with the car. When it was charged, he was going to shut it off and disconnect the ground strap so the short wouldn't run the battery down again.

"Everett, you ready to go back up and do some poking around?"

"Yeah, let me grab my hat." Orville and I already had our hats on. In the 1950s, we all wore straw hats. It was unusual to see a man without a hat. That hot sun was murder. So with me leading the way, we started up the hillside to the mine. I mentioned the batteries before, with their clear glass case, but there were several ore cars turned upside down too. I think they were upside down so that if it rained, water wouldn't stand in them and rust them out.

They were good ore cars, and being upside down, their wheels were on top, so I gave one a spin just to see if it was free and would turn. It did so I gave the other three a spin. All worked perfectly, and I was wondering why the people, or, I guess, miners, had gone off and left all this behind. If they were abandoning the mine, why didn't they take all this stuff with them? The tracts from the mine were in good shape, so I asked Orville and Everett if they would help me put one of the ore cars back on the track. They came over, and we flipped it back on its wheels and set it on the track and gave it a push. It rolled pretty good. I told Everett, "Jump in and I'll give you a ride."

You have to remember we were kids and always looking for something fun to do. So I pushed him down the track toward the tailings pile. There were two metal pieces clamped to the rails at the end of the tracks so the ore car would stop and not run off the end of the tracks.

There was an overhead cable hanging from three round poles tied together with some cable and cable clamps in an A-frame configuration.

One end had a large hook on it, and the cable ran through the hook and was braided back into itself. Someone had done a nice job. The other end went to an old gear-driven wench that you cranked with a long metal handle. The miners would hook the cable to an eye on the rear of the ore car then turn the wench handle so as to dump the ore car into a chute that a truck was parked under down in the wash. I wasn't there to see all this happen, so I'm assuming they trucked the ore out to a smelter someplace, maybe down to Yuma, Arizona.

I knew firsthand there were foundries and smelters there. Back in the twenties and thirties, $6 million worth in gold had been taken out of the Chocolate Mountains west of Blythe and the Trigo Mountains across the Colorado River in Arizona. And the back side of those mountains being Quartzsite. The $6 million was at a time when gold was about $11 an ounce. Our friends, the Grays, had a gold mine in the Chocolate Mountains west of Blythe.

"Hey, Orville, help us push it back up the tracks and I'll take a ride." The tracks were on a little downgrade. That way, when the ore car was full, it would push easier. Then empty, it would be easy to push with a little upgrade.

"This is fun. Too bad we don't have more track I could really get it going fast," Everett said. "Hey, let's push it back into the mine. Then we can really get it going."

So I said, "Why not?"

So we started pushing the ore car up the tracks, and it was curving into the entrance to the mine.

"Thought I told you boys to stay out of that mine until I've had a chance to check it out," I heard my Dad say from somewhere behind me.

"We were just going to push it right up to the entrance," I lied.

"We wanted to see how fast we can get it going," Everett said.

Dad said, "Did you ever think how the hell you're going to stop it if it's really going fast? The son of a bitch will jump those stops on the track and whoever is in the car will go down the chute ass over teakettle. And then I'll have to dig a hole and bury you right here. Did you boys ever think of that? You boys better start listening to the old man."

"Okay, Dad!"

I thought, *He's so smart.* I didn't even think of that. We could have gotten our crazy selves killed. "Well can we go into the mine now, Dad?" I asked.

"No, I came up here to get you boys to help me dump the gas from the can into the tank of the car. I couldn't find the siphoning hose. I think we left it at our other camp north of Quartzsite in the sand dunes."

That was where we were camped before starting out on this excursion to the mine.

Dad went on, "So if one of you boys will hold the funnel for me, I'll try to pour gas into the tank. I was just ready to come up to the mine where you boys were when I noticed that gas was escaping from around the rubber seal on the can." Dad kept going. "I guess the heat from the sun is causing the gas to expand and leak out. I noticed yesterday on the trip in that the sloshing of the gas was causing us to lose a little bit, and I don't want to lose any more."

"Okay, Dad, I'll help," I said, "but then can we go look in the mine?"

"Well, just so you know," said Dad, "there are more important things to do besides poking in some old mine where you might get hurt. Besides, you boys ever think there might be rattlesnakes back in that mine?"

Shit, why'd he have to bring up rattlesnakes? I hate snakes of any kind. Rattlesnakes will crawl back in a place like that to hibernate or to get out of the sun. This being winter, I would say they were hibernating, so I would say snakes aren't a problem for us today. Anytime I stared into a dark hole, I thought about snakes. I remember being over around Safford, Arizona. We were looking for work, and we had pulled off the road into some brush so we weren't seen from the road, and we camped for the night. The next morning, Orville had taken his .22 rifle and had walked south.

Everett and I were walking out through the bush, in the other direction, just kind of prowling around to see what was there, and Everett damn near stepped on a good-sized rattlesnake that was laying there sunning itself. It was cold, so I thought that was the only reason it didn't strike. The snake was the same color as the ground he was laying on and really hard to see. Then that time over at Buckeye, Dad was out quite a ways ahead of us walking up a dry wash, and my brother Orville said to me, "You hear that rattlesnake singing?"

I said, "I sure do. I think it's up there by Dad, and he can't hear it because he's hard of hearing."

We hurried up to where Dad was and hollered, "Dad, stop! There's a snake there someplace!"

I mean, about one more step, and that snake would have struck. Dad just couldn't hear the rattles on a snake anymore.

Orville had my .22 automatic, and he shot and killed the snake. So we walked on farther ahead, and here was a cement culvert about twelve by twelve and about six feet deep.

There was a corrugated pipe in the bottom about a foot in diameter, and there was a rattlesnake with his tail and rattles visible because the pipe went into the bottom of the culvert on an angle. But before I could get a shot off, the snake disappeared into the hole.

Orville said, "I'll get a stick and climb down there and poke him out."

I said, "Okay, but be careful."

He said he would and for me not to shoot him. He said, "Make sure to shoot the snake." He knew how trigger happy I was.

As he got down there and stepped on that pipe, man, the singing started. That snake sure was making a lot of noise. Orville was poking the stick in the hole, and out came a snake. He stepped back, and I shot it. Orville tried to lift it out of the hole so we could see it. And out came another one, and I shot that one too.

I said, "Hey, is there any more in there?"

Orville got back on the pipe and probed, and out came more. I was in hog heaven. Boy, I was shooting the shit out of those snakes. I believe I killed eleven. Dad said they had probably fallen in and enough rats or mice, maybe even a rabbit, had fallen in for them to eat enough to keep them alive. What a good day of shooting I had.

I guess I got carried away talking about the snakes. I just hope I haven't lost my place! We had the gas in the car and went back up to the mine. We put fresh carbide in three of the lamps and then took them over to our water can and poured a little water in each lamp so it would start to make acetylene gas.

Dad pulled out his Alka-Seltzer bottle, where he carried his matches so they wouldn't get wet. That way, he always had dry matches for starting a fire in any kind of weather. Dad struck a match on his boot and lit each lamp. Now we were ready to look into the mine.

Dad was leading the way. The shaft went straight back into the hillside. It was about five or six feet wide and about seven feet high. We could walk standing up okay.

The tracks for the ore cars were running up the center of the mine shaft, and we were walking on the wood ties that the steel rails were nailed down to so they didn't move as the ore cars moved over them.

I started thinking maybe we should be pushing an ore cart ahead of us in case there was a boogeyman in the mine. Just kidding. I knew if there was any body in here, we would have seen his tracks. So I wasn't afraid. Everett, who was walking behind me, said, "Maybe we should be pushing an ore cart in front of us."

I figured Everett must be scared. So I asked, "Why, you afraid of the boogeyman?"

He said, "No! So we can bring out the gold."

I liked his thinking!

"If there's any gold, I'll go get an ore cart. Don't you worry about that," Orville said.

About every fifty feet or so, there were eight-by-eight timbers shoring up the mine. Two upright timbers, with one across the top with wedges driven in between the upright post and the header to make them tight to the roof of the mine. The timbers looked strong. Somebody knew what they were doing. Dad said this was a gold mine because there was quite a bit of quartz here and there.

Sometimes a vein of quartz would run out to the side of the main shaft. The miners had followed it to the end of the vein. The quartz rock was gone, so they had trucked it out. But you could see the remnants of the ore still on the sides of the shaft. Dad said a lot of gold is found in quartz rock. Quartz doesn't always have gold but it's a good place to start if you're prospecting.

We kept pushing deeper into the mine always stopping to examine any side tunnels. I felt something bump my shoulder and heard something going past my head. I turned my light so I could see up ahead. Dad was looking too. There were bats by the hundreds going past us. I saw a one-by-four board leaning against the wall, and I picked it up and started swinging. I could feel the board hit one now and then. Dad and Everett had just stepped to one side of the mine. Orville was right behind me.

"Let's don't go any farther in." Dad said. "We might get bit by one of these bats, and they carry rabies." Shining the light back in the mine, we could see the bats hanging from the ceiling. Dad said bat shit (guano) could give off a poisonous gas that could kill us.

He didn't want to take any chances because he still had money in his wallet he wanted to spend. "And who's going to eat that deer if anything happens to us?"

It was so musty in the mine, maybe from the bats or their droppings, that I was ready to head back out. I wish I had that ore car because Everett and Orville still owed me a ride. Oh well, the walk would do me good, and I was getting thirsty. Besides, it was kinda scary when you think about how it could cave in. Then we would be buried deeper standing up in the mine than we would be outside lying down.

"Hey, Dad, you got anything to eat, 'cause I'm hungry."

"We have those peaches, or I can cook some more of that nasty old buck. But right now, I'm going to go lay down and take a nap. Don't you boys get into any trouble."

"Okay, Dad!" I said. "Hey, Everett, want to get the ore car and see how fast we can make it go before it jumps the tracks?" Orville said he would help.

"What did I tell you, boys?"

"Okay, Dad!"

That night at supper, Dad said, "We are almost out of water. We have to think about getting the hell out of here tomorrow. I don't want to drain the water can dry because if we broke down and had to walk out, we would be shit out of luck without water to drink."

"Well, Dad, do you want to load up tonight?"

"No, son, but try to use as little water as possible. If we just slice some meat off that deer's ass, then we can have sandwiches. That way, we won't have dishes to do."

"That sounds good to me," Everett said, since he would have to do the dishes. Dad's rules not mine. Orville and I tried to help him, but I knew it wasn't often enough. We still had a lot of wood gathered up, so we got a fire going.

Dad said, "I'll cook on the Coleman stove. That way, I won't have wait for the stove to get hot."

Dad got the Coleman stove and was pumping the tank up with the little hand pump. I got the deer out from where Dad had wrapped it up and put it in under the bedroll. It was wrapped up real good, and with the bedroll lying on it all day, it stayed really cold. Dad had camped out most of his life and knew how to keep food from spoiling. Always hang the meat out at night so it would get cold, then wrap it back up in the daytime. Dad never washed his skillets. He would dump the grease he was cooking with back into his grease bucket, then take a clean cloth to wipe it out. Then stick it into a big paper sack and put it away.

Sometimes Everett would forget and wash the skillet, and Dad would be fit to be tied. "Goddamn it, son. If you wash my skillet one more time, I'll kill you. Now you better listen to me 'cause I'm just as serious as the day is long. Now, you wash that skillet, and you're dead meat." He went on, "That skillet will stick when I try to cook in it. I'll have to get some bacon and re-season it, but you won't know about it 'cause you'll be dead. Now you better listen to the old man."

I had the bedroll rolled out on the homemade mattress and was crawling in. I was sick of hearing Dad complain about that stupid skillet.

Boy, if you have never slept under the stars way out in the desert, you don't know what you're missing. You can't believe how the heavens with all the stars look.

Shooting stars everywhere: The Big Dipper, the Seven Sisters, and the Little Dipper. I could lie here all night looking at the stars. They were beautiful.

"Come on, quit playing with your peters," I heard Dad say. I had fallen asleep lying there looking up at the stars, and the air was crisp this morning.

"You boys get out of bed and let's get the car loaded up and we'll flag Ol' Brownie out of here." That's what Dad called getting packed up and leaving here. "I want to get back to Quartzsite, and another thing, I'm not fixing anything to eat. We will grab something to eat at Dave Scott's store. So get with the program, or I'll leave you behind."

That's how my dad was: no patience. *Patience, hell!* I thought. *I want to kill something. My dad!*

Oh well, we were on our way, and I was driving. Life was good. "Now, son, some of the washes we crossed coming in here, the back bumper will drag on going out, so if you think we might get hung up, stop, and we will get out and throw some rocks under the bank and shovel some dirt on to them. If the back bumper hangs up and the rear wheels don't have enough contact with the ground, we'll be stuck. Then I'm gonna make you get out and jack the car up while Orville and Everett and I sit here and watch you."

"Okay, Dad, I'll be careful."

Dad said, "Well, just see that you do. I'd hate to kill you right here in front of God and everybody."

So I drove up on a wash that we had come up all right coming in, but going in this direction, it looked like I might get hung up. I asked Dad, "What do you think?"

He said, "Let me get out and take a quick look." Dad got out and said, "I'll get the shovel out of the trunk and do a little doctoring on the road."

I was watching him through the windshield, and I was thinking, *My dad's getting old.* He was sixty-five on his last birthday. He was born in Burr Oak, Kansas, in 1887, to my grandfather, Daniel Samuel Huff, and my grandmother, Barbara Baughman, who were from Ligonier, Indiana. My grandfather was a farmer and had come out to Kansas looking for cheap farmland. I guess things weren't too good on the Nebraska border, so at some point in time, they left Burr Oak and moved to Coffeyville, Kansas.

Dad said that in 1892, he was with his mother and father in Coffeyville, and the Dalton Gang had robbed the bank the day before and the townspeople had their bodies lying out on the plank sidewalk. Dad said there were flies all over the bodies. He was only five years old, but he remembered them all his life. He thought because of the flies, it must have made a hell of an impression on him.

In 1898, they were traveling in a covered wagon from Coffeyville to Arapahoe, Custer County, Oklahoma Territory, when my grandfather, Dan Samuel Huff, became sick after traveling three weeks in the moving wagon. He died there in 1898. My grandmother, Barbara Huff, was able to return to Coffeyville, but without my grandfather's body. He had been buried in the town of Summit, Custer County, Oklahoma. She wrote this letter to her mother-in-law, Ruth Ann Huff, back in Ligonier Indiana:

March the 19 1898
Direct 15
Arapahoe, Custer Co. O T (Oklahoma Territory)

Dear mother and brothers,

With a sad heart i write to you once more to tell you of the death of my Dear beloved husband and oh mother it seems as tho i just can't give him up it is so hard to bear all alone no one but me and my three children out hear among strangers but one family that we was acquainted with. but the neighbors was so good to us in his sickness he only lived a week and two days and till 20 till 2 the next morning he died March the 12 at 20 till 2 Saturday morning and was buried Sunday the 14. At 2 o'clock in the afternoon there was a nice procession for to be among strangers there was about twenty teams in all. we buried him in a very nice place but not where he requested to be, he wanted to be buried west of Coffeyville in the robins grave yard but i could not take him now but will sometime as soon as i can.

Oh dear mother i washed today his clothes with the rest, but they was washed with many a tear. oh if you only could have been hear. He ask me once where is mother i said i don't no why did you want to see her. He said no i guess not and that was all. But i understand him to call for Pa the last word he said but these folks hear thinks i was mistaken they think he was calling me and i was with him all the time and when i wasn't he would call for me. Oh mother you don't no how the dear one did suffer, he died on my breast. Oh dear mother i no it will kill me we are hear among strangers and I don't know what to do. they say i can't move him for two years and i haven't got the money now that i can do it. i will send you a little of his hair. i got him a coffin for 22.50 it was the best i could do for we are 65 miles from any railroad. And this is as soon as I could let you know about it. He always said if he ever got a home it would be a 2 x 6 and sure enough it proved to be that way. he went in the house from the moving wagon we came in and never left the house or went out again, i mean until he was carried out. Poor soul is at rest now mother rite to me and tell me what would be the best for me to do i can't go back up there and leave him, and they say i can't move him for two years B H to dear old mother good by rite soon, we are left in a bad shape now i tell you.

She remarried eighteen months later in Coffeyville, Kansas, to a man named Frank Oram. My dad said he didn't get along with his stepfather, so he ran away at the age fourteen and went to live with his aunt Margaret in Ligonier. Margaret was married to a man named John Schlotterbach. He was on the 1900 Census, living with them in Ligonier, Indiana.

Sometime after that, my dad moved back in with his mother and his stepfather. Frank was a violinmaker, and my dad learned the trade from him.

"For Christ's sake, son, are you dead or just deaf? I've been yelling and waving my arms around trying to get your attention. The road is passable now, so if you're awake now, start the car, and I'll watch the rear bumper." Dad kept grumbling, "Hell, you made me walk all the way back from the other side of the wash. And there's not that many miles left in these old legs."

"I guess I was just dreaming, Dad," I told him. "I'm sorry."

"That's okay, son. I thought something was wrong with the engine again. Next time, stay awake and do your sleeping at night," he told me.

I was able to get down the road and off the side of the wash without getting the rear bumper hung up. I was careful. Dad would be proud of me. He got back in, but Orville and Everett got on the back bumper, and I drove on across the wash and out the other side. Soon we were back on the main road, which was still being mined.

I stopped to let Orville and Everett get back in the car. We turned left and headed back to Quartzsite—and none too soon, either, because I was hungry. Hey, I didn't get stuck, so I think God was looking after me. Probably figured he had enough trigger-happy kids in heaven. I can't remember seeing one critter to shoot at coming out from the old mine. We came to the blacktop highway and turned left heading to the Shell station. Dad said better top off the tank again and fill the gas can. That way, Dave won't care if we fill our water cans from his hose.

Everett got the gas can off the bumper while I got the water can and went to fill it. Orville took the gas cap off and started pumping the gas. The air and water hoses were off to one side of the station. As Dad was heading into the station, he said, "Let the water run a little, son, so it won't taste like the hose."

"Okay, Dad," I said.

"You boys want a soda water?" I heard Dad ask from the station.

"Sure," I said.

"What kind you want?"

"I'll have a Barq's Grape, and Orville and Everett want a Barq's Orange."

"Want an ice cream too?" I heard him ask.

"I'll have an Eskimo pie," I said. Orville and Everett said they want a Popsicle.

Dad brought out the pops and ice cream, and I drank my pop while the water can filled. Orville already had the gas can filled, and Everett put it back on the bumper. He came over, and we drank our pops and finished our ice cream.

I said, "This water hose sure is running slow."

Everett said, "I'll go see if Dad's getting something to eat."

"Hey, tell him to get a quart of Knudsen Buttermilk too."

"Okay," he said.

Finally, the stupid water can was full, so I carried it over and put it on the bumper. Dad and Everett came out of the station with a sack, and we loaded it into the car. I started it up and then turned around and headed back the way we had come.

Dad said, "Let's drive out to that windmill, and we will eat lunch there."

I didn't care because I was full of pop and ice cream.

"Dave is higher than hell on all the shit he sells in his store," Dad said.

I said, "It's cheaper than driving all the way to Blythe."

"I know, but he's still higher than a cat's back."

"I think after we eat at the windmill, we'll head on out to the sand dunes. We need to get back to work picking up shells to replenish our nest egg."

"Okay, but can we start picking up shells tomorrow? I'm kinda tired."

Everett said, "Me too."

I said, "How can you be tired, Everett? You're just lying back there on the bedroll."

Orville said, "Well, I'm tired, if anybody is interested."

Dad said, "Okay, but let's hit it early, boys."

We were back on the mine road, and it wasn't far from the turnoff to the windmill. The Scotts owned most of the country we were driving through.

Dad said he thought the old lady Scott had homesteaded this land. "They run a few head of cattle in here. From time to time, she ships some to market. Well there's the windmill son pull up over there by that mesquite tree."

"Which one?" I said.

"That big one over there." He was pointing to it.

"This good enough?" I asked.

"Pull up a little more until we're in the shade."

I killed the engine and opened the door.

Dad said, "I'm going to sit right here and eat."

Everett, in the back, said, "Well, I want out. I'm sick of laying back here on this bedroll."

"Oh, quit bellyaching," I said.

"Well, it's cramped back here, and I've rode back here all the way."

Orville said, "Well, if he's going to cry like a baby, let's let him out."

Everett said, "Okay, thanks."

I hadn't opened my door yet, so I said, "Say please."

"Oh, for Christ's sake, *please*."

"Dad, Everett's cussing."

"Well, he better knock that shit off, or he won't get any lunch," Dad said.

Everett said, "Well, Paul won't let me out of the car."

"Son, let the crybaby out."

"What did you get for sandwiches?" I asked as I opened the door and got out.

Everett was right behind me. I guess he was really glad to get out.

"I've got bread and bologna and a jar of mustard and a jar of dill pickles—that's all I saw fit to eat."

"No telling how long Dave has had it in that meat counter, but I figure if it don't make a turd, it will push one out."

"No dessert?" I asked.

"You see those cow pies laying out there on the ground, well that's dessert," Dad said with a grin.

"I guess I'll pass on dessert," I said.

We were sitting there eating and watching some old skinny cows that had come in to drink from the trough. The windmill pumped the water into a tank—a big one about twelve or fifteen feet across. Then a pipe ran out to the trough. It had a float setup on it, and when the cattle drank from the trough, the water level went down; and as the float lowered, it turned the water back on.

We saw a few doves coming in to water from the tank, so I got in the back of the car and pulled my .22 rifle out. I put some shells in, and I told Dad, "I'll see if I can shoot some doves."

He said, "Okay, but be careful."

I walked about twenty-five yards to the tank and squatted down by a mesquite tree. I sat there for quite a while, waiting for some doves to come into water. I was sitting there minding my own business when this old skinny cow came walking toward me. I said, "Hi, Bossy," and stood up, and that dumbass cow started pawing the ground.

Dad said, "Better be careful, son. That old cow might charge you."

"She better not," I said. "I'm not doing anything to her."

About that time, that stupid cow charged right at me. She couldn't move too fast because she seemed kinda sickly. I stepped aside, and the cow stopped and started pawing the ground again. She started to charge me again. I just lowered my gun at the cow.

I heard my dad holler behind me, "SON, DON'T SHOOT THAT COW!" I ran out of the way of the charging critter.

"Goddamn, son, what the hell were you thinking? You can't just go around shooting people's cattle even if they are half dead. Jesus Christ, son, we'd have everybody in Giles County looking for us. Hell, son, I don't want to spend time in prison for some old sick cow. Goddamn it, son, what were you thinking?"

I said, "I don't know. The stupid old cow was after me."

"Well, don't do it anymore."

"Goddamn, I still don't know what the hell you were thinking of, or if you were even thinking at all."

"Well, let's load up and get the hell out of here. That old lady Scott would put us so far in jail they would have to shoot beans to us with a shotgun."

I climbed in, and I started the car, which had been starting pretty good since dying on us at the mine. I guess the battery must be fully charged by now, and Dad wasn't taking any chances because he was still taking the ground strap off the battery at night.

I was feeling very dejected on account of Dad getting so mad at me. That old cow would have probably run a horn right through me. I guess Dad would have figured that was all right. I drove on across the wash, and as I was approaching the bank where the road went up out of the wash back into the sand dunes, I saw a jackrabbit sitting in the road.

I said, "Hey, there's a rabbit. Everett, quick, hand me the gun. I want to shoot it and use it to bait my traps with when we get back to camp."

The rabbit was still sitting there as I drew a fine bead on him and squeezed the trigger. *Pow!* And down he went. "I'll go get him," I told

Dad as I opened the car door and got out. I carried it back to the car and laid it behind one gas can on the rear bumper. I told Dad I wanted to see if I could catch some of the little swift foxes we had seen once in a while as we picked up the shells.

We pulled back into the camp we had left at least a week before in the sand dunes to go exploring the mine. Everything looked just as we had left it, so no one had been here snooping around. I got my rabbit, and I told Dad I wanted to go set some traps before it got dark. I got eight traps and walked out through the dunes to look for good locations to set my traps.

I'd put the bait back in a bush and then set my trap back a foot from the bait in a shallow depression. Then I put a piece of paper over the pan of the trap and sprinkled dirt on the paper. That way, the fox would be looking at the bait he was smelling and not see the buried trap and step into it.

Dad had shown me how to set the trap just so. I remember catching four or five foxes a night. I would have to skin them and stretch the hides each morning before heading out to look for shells. Usually, Orville and Dad would help with this chore most of the time. We were paid three or four dollars for each fox hide when we shipped them to the furriers. I liked to trap and wished I could have done more of it. I didn't always catch a fox because sometimes they would get the bait without stepping into my trap. But that was a challenge for me—to outwit the fox.

One day I had a fox in a burlap sack, and Dad was trying to get it out.

The fox had his muzzle in the bottom corner, and when Dad put his hand down there to get it loose, the fox bit him through his finger. We couldn't get the fox to open his mouth, so Dad took a pistol and shot the fox in the head right through the burlap sack.

Dad said, "Boys, this fox could have rabies. If I start foaming at the mouth and acting crazy, you take the pistol and shoot me, as I will be beyond any help. Then just dig a hole here in the desert and bury me, and don't ever tell anyone what you had to do."

I'm just glad he never started foaming at the mouth, as I don't think I could have shot my dad. Now for his acting crazy, that was another matter, as that was an everyday occurrence. (Just kidding.)

CADIZ DRY LAKE

"Boys, I think we should move this operation to the gunnery range on the dry lake north of Desert Center in California," Dad told us three boys one evening around the campfire. I asked him if he thought there were any shells out there.

"Well, I don't know, son, but at one time, you could pick up a gunnysack full in a three-foot circle." He was telling us that one of the men who had worked for the salvage company told him the brass shell were that deep on the dry lake. They were in Tom Well's bar drinking when the man was telling some men at the bar about his job. Of course, you can't believe all the things you hear in a saloon. Liquor gives you a great imagination and will make a person stretch the truth a little.

Dad had gone out there with a friend one time, and he was able to see the operation. He said back then, there were still a lot of shells, but the salvagers had run them out of the area. He said they had a permit from the government giving them the right to all the metal they could retrieve from the gunnery range. The men who had stopped them were armed and said, "So you boys turn your vehicle around and leave, and be quick about it."

"Cadiz Dry Lake is in the middle of nowhere," Dad told us. There's not a tree in ten miles in any direction. There's only brush and greasewood and some desert grass, just like here at Quartzsite. "If you think there are more shells, let's go find out."

"Okay, in the morning after breakfast, we'll load this camp into the car and go have a look-see."

I knew I'd be happy because I'd be driving. We were almost out of water anyway, and when we stopped for gas, we could get a Coke.

As we crossed the bridge over the Colorado River, Dad looked at the water running under the bridge and said, "It looks like they have had a flood up on the Bill Williams River." The water looked as if it were pure muddy sand. "If there's a flash flood, it washes mud and debris down all the washes in the area, and it comes shittin' and gittin' down the river," Dad was saying. "Lord help anybody that gets in the way."

Once we were into Blythe, we filled up with gas, and we all got a pop. The Safeway store was just beside the gas station, and Dad wanted to buy a few things for his chuck boxes. He told the station attendant he wanted a gallon of white gas for our Coleman stove as well. We checked the water in the radiator and got our windshield cleaned.

"Might as well go first class," Dad said.

I told Dad I was going to walk down the street a ways while he bought groceries. I liked to window-shop to see what was new in the store windows. In 1953, Blythe was only about six or seven blocks long in town. Then there were shops and car dealerships and vacant lots going east. Then you were in east Blythe. The whole town was only a mile long from start to finish.

After I had looked in the store windows, I returned to the car, and Dad was putting things into his chuck boxes. He said, "Get your brothers and let's hit the road."

Orville and Everett had bought a bag of gumdrops and a licorice twist. As we headed out of town, we were already into the gumdrops because we all had a sweet tooth.

In Desert Center, we turned north on the road going to Rice and Vidal Junction, then on to Parker, Arizona. A few miles out, there were mesquite trees and ironwood trees and gnarled-looking trees that Dad called cat's claw. We came to some foothills, and the road went around them, and the road turned to the northwest for three or four miles. Then it turned north again.

This is where we left the paved road heading west down into a valley. Maybe a half a mile then we came to a canal, which Dad said was bringing water from the Colorado River to the Coachella Valley and even Los Angeles. It was the Metropolitan Water District Canal. It was cement lined, and after stopping to look we continued on another mile to the bottom of the valley.

As the road started to go uphill from the valley, Dad said, "Let's turn off the road here on the right."

I said, "I don't see any road," and Dad said we would make our own road. He told me to just drive out across the desert and he would look for the army road he had taken when he came to investigate with his friend years before. He was looking, but he said the wind over the years had filled in the tracks. "We will have to see if we can make our way out to the dry lake."

We were just driving where we could, around greasewood and brush, where there was enough room for the car to get through. The terrain was mostly hardpacked sand and gravel. After a mile, we came to a sand dune about eight feet high, and as we approached it, I was looking for a place where I could get through the brush and over the sand dune. Dad told me to gun the hell out of the car once I had started, but I knew that if I got stuck, it would all be my fault.

"Son, if you would have come this way a couple of feet, it would have been clear sailing. Goddamn it, now we have to dig the son of a bitch out."

"Well, shit, then why don't you drive the son of a bitch if you're so good at it," I told him. "Hell, I just picked the place that looked like it was solid and gunned it like you said to do," I told him. "I don't even want to drive anymore. I'm sick of getting chewed out."

Dad got out and walked to the back of the car and opened the trunk and pulled out one chuck box so he could get the axe and shovel out. He stuck out his arm with the axe in it and told me to cut some brush while he dug the sand from the back of the tires.

He also told me to quit complaining, that he thought I had picked a good place to cross and that he couldn't have done any better.

"Well, why do you always blame me?" I asked.

"I don't know, son. Just old, I guess."

"Hell, I wasn't trying to get stuck," I said. "You think I like to cut greasewood and pack it under the wheels?" I asked.

"I know it, son. Let's forget it and get the son of a bitch unstuck. This isn't the first or the last time we're going to be stuck out here, so just do the best you can."

Orville and Everett didn't say anything; they just went on gathering brush. They probably thought that while he was chewing me out, he was leaving them alone.

It wasn't long before we had our car back on solid ground. Dad had told me to get in and back it up, but I said, "Hell, no, you do it."

"Okay, I'll drive, then, but you boys climb on the back bumper for weight."

Dad lined the car up again only a little farther south and said, "Hang on." This time we made it okay, and I was content to just ride on the bumper. Sometimes, though, when Dad hit a big bump, it would throw us off the bumper. But it was easy to run and jump back on. We thought it was fun.

It was maybe five miles from where we left the graded road to where Dad said, "We could set up our camp." We were on the south side of Cadiz Dry Lake, and the lakebed itself was flat, with no sign of water. Just a plain ol' dry lake bottom with nothing growing in it. Salt crust was all there was as far as the eye could see. After we unloaded our chuck boxes and bedroll and gas and water cans, we started driving along the south side looking for shells. By now we were experienced shell gatherers.

When we saw shells sticking out of the sand or lying on the sand, we would just step off the bumper and run to pick them up. We were young and barefooted, and it seemed as though we could run all day in the soft sand. We had so much energy. Oh, to be like that again. But today all I can do is remember, and sometimes I can't do that very well.

Dad was just driving along slowly, and if we found a lot of shells and couldn't get back to the car, he would stop and get out and pick up shells around him until we got back to the car. We dumped everything we had picked up into the trunk and then went back to looking. We might be a half mile from the car if we were following a line of shells that the planes had dropped.

The shells fell out of the plane about twenty-five feet apart. If you picked up two, look ahead twenty-five feet, and there would be two more. That is, until the gunner stopped shooting, because that would break the sequence. But another plane might be right behind it laying down another row of shells, and they were crisscrossing one another as well. Maybe not in the same day, as the training went on for three years.

Out here, north of Desert Center, there were tank tracks, and there were a lot of iron bullets lying everywhere that had been shot from the guns on the tanks. They were six inches long and two inches in diameter, but there must not have been an explosive in the bullets because they were all unexploded. Anyway, we didn't find any that had exploded. Dad said they were probably practice rounds for training the soldiers.

Still, Dad said, "Don't touch them, they might blow up."

I said, "Why don't we just pick one up and throw it and see if it explodes."

"Goddamn it, son, what did I just tell you? Leave the sons of a bitch lay right where they are. I don't want to hear another thing about it."

Then I told him, "I could get my .22 and shoot one and see if that would make it blow up! Or I could hit one with a hammer." I was trying to get him riled up.

"What did I just tell you?" Dad said through clenched teeth. "Leave those unexploded shells alone, and I don't intend to tell you one more time. Now you got that through you thick skull?" he asked.

I just wanted to give him something to gripe about. It was easy to make Dad testy, and kind of fun too.

The brass part of the projectile must have remained inside the tank. We would have liked to have found some because that would have been a lot of brass.

I mean, it would weigh way more than the .50 caliber shell weighed. Probably six to ten times as much as a .50 caliber one did.

One morning, just at dawn, the wind started to blow with the force of a hurricane. I mean, it started with a big gust and didn't stop until three days later. We were still asleep, and all of a sudden, a gust of wind took the canvas that we had folded back over us and blew it out straight. It couldn't go anyplace because we were all four sleeping on it.

We jumped up in our shorts and started to roll our bedroll up, which was hard to do with the wind blowing so hard. And it felt as though we were being stung by bees. It was from all the sand that the wind was carrying with it. It was burning our eyes too, but finally, the bed was rolled up and put away in the car.

Dad put the chuck boxes into the trunk and shut the lid. And we climbed into the car, and there we sat for three days. The car rocked with each gust.

I said, "Can't we go someplace else where the wind isn't blowing?"

"Son, when the wind blows in the desert, it blows all over. We might have to drive as far as Phoenix to get out of it. We better just stay put for now and let the wind blow itself out."

It was very boring just sitting in that car for three days with the wind howling and rocking the car, with nothing to do but read some old comic books. We had a deck of cards, so we played crazy eights and a little poker. That got boring too. Just try going to the toilet with the wind and the sand blasting your bottom. Better hang on to the toilet paper too, or it would be blown away.

Finally, after the third day, the wind slowed and then stopped altogether. Dad said, "Well, the wind has laid who wants to go find the egg?"

Funny, I thought. *If the wind never blows again, it would be too soon for me.*

When we got out of the car the next morning, the tires looked brand new. The sand had cut all the old dead rubber off of them, and they were black as could be.

One day we decided to drive up to the convoy of cars that the army had placed in a long line for the machine gunners to shoot at. They were all old cars from the twenties and the thirties. I think I counted sixteen of them all in a long line. They were all shot to shit. Nothing could be salvaged from this stuff, but we found a few shells lying here and there.

On our way back to the camp, we found an unexploded eight-inch projectile from a cannon. It had a timing mechanism on the pointed front part. The timing mechanism must have stopped when the projectile hit the ground. About six inches from the back end was a one-inch-wide band of brass that had the rifling marks on it, so it definitely had been shot from a cannon. It was about twenty inches long.

One day Dad stopped at the unexploded cannon projectile. "Okay, if you boys want an explosion, I'll show you one. Let's all get out and gather up some brush, and we'll pile it on this damn thing, and I'll show you an explosion."

We set to work gathering brush like little beavers and piling it on the projectile. Soon it was six feet high and six feet wide, with a teacup full of gunpowder put underneath the brush. Dad whipped out a match from his pocket and struck it on the sole of his shoe and threw it into the powder. It started the brush to burning, and Dad started for the car, saying, "Let's get the hell out of here, boys."

We drove off a hundred yards, and I stopped the car. Dad looked over at me and said, "What did you stop the car for?"

I said, "I want to get out and watch it blow up."

Dad told me, "We sure as hell don't want to stop this close to the son of a bitch. You kick this son of a bitch in the ass and let's go another half mile."

"A half mile, we won't even be able to see it go off," I said.

"Son, don't take the time to argue with me, just get the hell on up the road. When that thing blows, I don't want to be in the same county."

"Well, I want to see it blow," I said.

"You can see it blow just as well from up there by those old cars."

"Okay, for Christ's sake, I'm going," I told him.

Finally, I stopped the car, and we climbed out and walked around back. We were standing there leaning against the car with our foot on the bumper, watching the smoke rising up into the sky.

"I hope we can see it go off from here," I said. After maybe a half an hour, I said, "I think the fire went out, Dad?"

"No, let's wait and see. There's still smoke there."

"Dad gum it, Dad, it didn't go off," I said. "Let's go back and put some more brush on it."

Dad told me a flat "No."

"Why?" I asked him.

Dad said, "There's still heat from that fire in the ashes that are all around the shell."

"Yeah, but hell, Dad, if we go back and pile more brush on the fire before it cools down, it still might blow," I said.

"Goddamn it, will you listen to the old man. We're not going back there today, and that's it!"

"Well you don't have to go. Me and Orville can go pile more brush on it," I said.

"Goddamn it, for the last time, we're not going back there today, and you might as well forget it. Now you got that straight?" Dad asked. He said, "The coals on that shell might keep that son of a bitch hot all night. It would be just our luck to drive back there and it would explode."

We were all still standing around looking back at the little smoke that was rising up into the air. I said, "Hey, what about going back and dumping some of our gunpowder on it?"

"Will you listen to me! We're not going back, and that's final!" Dad told me. "Tomorrow or the next day will be soon enough to drive by it again."

"But it will take an even bigger pile of brush if this one didn't set it off," I told Dad. "I don't see why we can't do it now."

KKKKA BOOM.

Holy shit. A mushroom cloud went up into the air, and it looked like a newsreel of an atomic bomb. I saw two pieces of metal flying through the air: one went past us on the left side of our car and another hit the dirt about a hundred feet from the back of the car. It was on a straight line from the shell, so if it had come another hundred feet, it would have hit us.

I kept my eyes right on the spot it hit, and I ran out to the place and started digging with my hands so I could get the piece of shrapnel. The dirt was powdery, so it was easy to dig. When I grabbed the metal, wow, it was hotter than hell, and it burned my fingers, which had clamped around it. Nobody had to tell me to let go of it; I lost interest in that piece of shrapnel really fast with my fingers burned. I was licking my fingers and blowing on them as I went back to looking at the big mushroom cloud. I hadn't thought of the metal being hot from the fire when I dug it up. I'll bet the cloud was visible from 29 Palms Marine Base, but no one came out to look.

Dad said, "Now we can go back and look at the hole it made when it exploded."

I lost interest in the thing when I burned my fingers.

Dad said, "Let's go have a look-see."

It had blown a hole about thirty inches deep and about five foot in diameter. I was sure glad Dad didn't let me talk him into going back to put more brush on the damn thing. *He is so smart*, I thought.

If it had been left up to me, I would have been right there piling brush on the unexploded shell when it went off, and I would have been hamburger.

I'd be playing harps right about now, I thought.

I guess other shrapnel pieces went in other directions, but we didn't see them. The only one we found was the one that I burned my fingers on. I had it in the back of the car for a long time.

One day Dad asked me what I wanted to do with it, and I said, "Aw, just throw it away, Dad."

The piece was about ten to twelve inches long and had split into a fork on one end. It was really jagged and blue from all the heat.

I still have the picture of that mushroom cloud in my mind after all these years, and I can still see the piece of metal that went whizzing past the car on the left side. It went way beyond where we had stopped, thinking we were safe. There were so many dumb things I have done in my life where I could have been killed. I know God was looking after me for some reason. We probed the hole, and even dug out some of the powdered dirt and sand, but there wasn't any more metal in the hole. I think we did find the aluminum timing mechanism, but not in the hole.

After we returned to camp, Dad had some Cuticura Ointment, and I put some on my burned fingers. They hurt, but not as bad as I would have had I been piling brush on the shell when it went off. That would have been me sailing through the air. I always did want to fly. We were on this gunnery range for a couple of months during the winter of 1952 and into 1953, maybe longer.

We had picked up most of the brass shells that were visible over about a three-square-mile area. One day we drove into the dry lake itself, about a quarter of a mile. We got out and walked around looking for shells. They weren't like the ones in the sand that had turned black from the sun. Once we had adjusted to the new look of them, we found them sticking up everywhere. They were encrusted in an alkali salt, and a lot of the shells had been eaten away from the salts. They weren't black anymore—they were red-looking once the alkali had been removed.

Just knocking them together wouldn't knock the salt crust loose because the salty sand on them was wet.

Dad said, "We have to get them clean, or the salvage or scrap dealers won't give us much money for them."

We had picked up about six gunnysacks of the crusted shells when Dad said, "Let's take them over by Desert Center where there are trees. We'll gather up a bunch of wood and dump the brass shells into the woodpile and set them on fire so they will dry out." Sounded like a good idea to me. Maybe there would be some quail that I could hunt as the dry lake didn't have anything for us to hunt.

Dad thought the heat from the fire would make the salt turn loose of the shells. We got to the place where Dad wanted to go, just north of Desert Center but off the road so we would not be seen if someone came snooping around. These trees were high, so all anyone from the road would see would be a glow in the night sky, and there really wasn't much traffic on this road at night anyway. My brothers and I set to gathering wood and brush. We dumped out the sacks of shells on the ground and then piled the wood onto the pile of shells.

It was getting dark by the time we had everything ready. "Get me that sack of gunpowder," Dad said. The gunpowder was what we had saved by removing the bullets on the loaded shells and dumping the contents into our ore sack.

Dad dumped a couple of handfuls into the wood and brush and then struck a match on a rock and touched it to the gunpowder, and in a minute, it was burning pretty good.

The weather was cold after the sun had gone down, but Dad had fixed supper while my brothers and I were gathering most of the wood for the fire. Sometimes we would make eggs and bacon for supper. I don't really remember what Dad had fixed, but I'll bet it was good. I liked the things Dad cooked up. After eating, we just mostly stood around the fire that was burning pretty hot by now. We even had some big pieces of ironwood in the fire.

We were talking and warming ourselves and always turning because one side was always hot and the other side was cold. Dad said we were killing two birds with one stone, keeping warm and burning the crust off the shells at the same time. The fire had been burning for more than a half an hour and was really hot, and it felt real good too.

POW, we heard from the fire, and hot coals and ashes flew all over the place.

Dad said, "That was a live round, boys. I guess we missed one when we were extracting the bullets and dumping the powder.

POW! ZING! went another round that sounded like a .22 caliber shell.

Dad said, "That was a primer going off from the loaded rounds we had pulled the bullets out of." We didn't think about the primers being still in the brass casing.

POW! POW! POW! Shit, they were going off like a machine gun.

The primers were like bullets coming out of the fire. We started backing away from the fire when I heard one primer hit out car.

Dad said, "Boys, we better duck our nuts out of here before one or all of us gets shot. Paul, you jump in the car and back it up out of the line of fire," Dad told me.

Every few minutes, another primer would go off, and live rounds were still exploding too.

The live rounds weren't dangerous, but they blew fire all over the place. But those damn primers were shooting out of the back of the shells like they were in a rifle barrel. If one hit you in the eye, you would be shit out of luck. Best to just start looking for something to make a patch out of, because that eye would be a goner.

Needless to say, we stayed far away from that fire the rest of the night. And since we couldn't see well enough to hunt more wood in the dark, we rolled our bedroll out and climbed in. Man, there was a lot of stars out tonight. I could almost believe we were in a war zone someplace with the enemy shooting all around us. Every time a loaded round exploded, it sounded as though a bomb had gone off and was blowing cinders everywhere.

The fire was out the next morning, except for some ironwood coals that were still hot. We got some dead limbs that were lying around and brushed the shells out flat so they would be cool enough to pick up. Dad's idea worked really well because when we knocked them together, all the salts and dirt just fell right off. We just knocked them together and then threw them into the gunnysacks.

In a couple of hours, we had them all cleaned and sacked up. The shells were clean, but they were a copper color now instead of a brass color. By noontime, we were done, and the car was loaded up, and we were on our way to San Bernardino to sell them. I don't remember how much we got for the shells—it was usually between one hundred and two hundred dollars. We saw all the newest movies, especially the westerns, and checked out the sporting goods stores for ammunition, or to see if they had a new gun we couldn't live without. With our chuck boxes full again, we were on our way back to the dry lake.

We returned to the lake once again, since we had done so well on the last trip and now we knew we could clean them pretty easy. But each day we would move farther and farther out into the lake.

"You want to stop where we did yesterday?" I asked Dad.

"No, drive on farther out, son," he told me. So I drove on another hundred yards, but once in a while, I could feel the rear wheel spin a little.

"Dad, it feels like it's getting slick. We should have got out and checked to see how far we were breaking through the crust."

But Dad said, "Just a little farther, son."

By now, the rear wheels were spinning, and we couldn't move forward. We were stuck—and I mean stuck good. I didn't have a good feeling as we got out of the car to look.

Orville and Everett were on the back bumper, but they didn't say the ground was muddy. They were probably just looking for shells. We looked at the front bumper and saw it was pushing muddy crust ahead of it. That was how low the tires had sunk into the lakebed. Shoot, the front bumper was scraping the dry crust ahead of the bumper. That was what had finally stopped the car from moving ahead. That and the mud under the wheels was what stopped us. Another fine mess we were in, and this didn't look good.

There was no way to see under the car, but we knew it was down on the frame of the car. We could also see a little water oozing from the sides of our tire tracks. I looked around, wondering what the hell we were going to do, and saw the ends of .50 caliber shells sticking up all over.

Suddenly I wasn't interested in the brass shells anymore. I thought the bumper looked like it was deeper into the crust of the lake. *Shit, our car might sink out of sight*, I thought. Damn, it was forty miles at least back to Desert Center. That would be one hell of a walk. I guess we could hitch a ride once we got to the paved road, but somebody would have to stay with our things in camp. We couldn't hitchhike carrying our guns. I think we had sixteen guns in the back window of the car.

We would look like Pancho Villa's army. We could walk to the canal that we crossed coming in here that first day. So we would have plenty of water. If our car didn't sink completely out of sight, maybe we could get somebody to drive us back and hook a towline on the car and pull us out.

I heard Everett say, "I don't think we'll ever get out of here."

We had been stuck a lot of times, but never like this.

Orville said, "You ever been stuck this bad, Dad?"

"Yes, son, I have," Dad told him.

"Son, when I first started driving, there were no roads like there are now. The roads were just cow trails with deep ruts a foot or more deep.

When it rained, the ruts would fill with water so the road would become a mud hole. Sometimes the ruts were so deep you couldn't turn out of them. If a car was coming at you in your set of ruts, one of you had to back up until the other could get out of the rut so the two cars could pass. Dad remembered a sign that said, "Choose your rut well, because you'll be in it for the next twenty miles."

Damn, I thought. *What are we going to do?*

Dad said, "Let's walk back to camp and see what we can find to put down under the wheels. We have those pieces of plywood we picked up one day to use for a fire. We'll get those and anything else we see lying around to use under the wheels."

We were starting to walk back to camp when Dad said, "Let me get the axe out of the trunk." He walked back, opened the trunk, and took out the axe. We just stood there and waited for him to come back. He said, "We'll need to cut some greasewood to lay in the car tracks because the plywood won't take us far. We'll have to carry the greasewood in bundles out to the car."

When we got to camp, Dad said he would fix us something to eat while my brothers and I cut down some greasewood and tied it into bundles that we could carry on our shoulders. After eating, we all picked up what we could carry and headed out to our sinking car. We had a couple of jacks in the car and a shovel, but how the hell were we going to get the jack under the car with the frame sitting on the ground. Dad got the shovel from the trunk and started to dig a hole under the front bumper. He was digging a big hole.

"Why you digging it so big?" I asked.

"Hell, son, I have to get this two-by-two piece of plywood deep enough to put a couple of blocks on as a solid base for the jack. Otherwise, when I try jacking the car up, the jack will just sink down without lifting the car."

"You want me to do anything?" I said. "Well, one of you boys can get a stick and clean the mud off this shovel. That would make it a lot easier on the old man and drag some of this dirt away from the hole I'm digging. That would be a big help too."

Soon Dad had dug the hole big enough to get the piece of plywood into under the bumper and put some blocks on top of that.

The first time, the jack wouldn't fit under the bumper, so he removed the boards and dug out a little more dirt. Then he tried it again. The jack would barely fit this time.

He told Everett to get him the jack handle out of the trunk. The jack lifted the car only about six inches, if that. But at least the bumper came off the ground, and Orville and I wedged a couple of boards underneath both sides so Dad could let the jack down. Then he took the blocks and the plywood out and packed the hole with dry dirt from the top of the salty crust.

Dad was using the jack for a tamp so he could get the bottom of the hole hard again to lay the plywood onto. After he had the dirt tamped solid, he placed the plywood and blocks back into the hole and jacked the car up once more. This time the front wheels started to lift off the ground and out of the ruts.

"Block the bumper again," Dad told us because he would have to go through this procedure one more time to get the undercarriage to clear the ground.

Once the undercarriage was clear, we packed some of the top dry crust into the tracks, leaving just enough room to get the plywood underneath the tires.

"Hey, Dad, it's starting to look good," I told him. I was starting to feel that this operation was doable after all.

He told me, "We are only halfway. We still have the back of the car buried in the mud."

"Yeah, but it's working, Dad," I told him.

Orville and I went to the back of the car and started to dig the hole for the plywood so Dad could rest. We dumped the dry dirt in front of the rear wheels until it started getting too wet. Then we threw it over to the side of the car. It wasn't long before we had the hole looking deep enough, with Orville and me both digging.

Dad placed the plywood just the way he wanted it and jacked the car up again. He kept repeating this maneuver until the rear wheels were clear off the ground by six inches. Then we tamped more dry dirt into the tracks until they were about level with the top of the lakebed.

"You boys get the greasewood while I put the plywood under the rear wheels."

Everett and Orville were filling our tire tracks with the dry crust and walked it in good so it was packed down. "Lay the greasewood in the tracks as far as it will go," Dad told them. I was rubbing dry dirt on the tires to get the mud off so they wouldn't spin when the car started to move.

"Okay, boys, let's give it a try," Dad was saying as he got in behind the steering wheel.

My brothers and I were in front, ready to start pushing when Dad was ready.

"Now don't let me back off the plywood," Dad said, "or we might be stuck again."

The car moved back a couple of feet, and Dad stopped and asked us, "How does it look, boys?"

"Looks good, Dad," I told him. "Pick up the plywood in front of the tires and move it to the rear."

Dad then moved the car back a little more.

Orville and I were moving the plywood each time Dad moved back and Everett had the shovel and was filling in the tire tracks with dry dirt and walking it to pack it down. *What a team*, I thought as I was becoming thrilled at our progress. I would rather do this for a week than have to walk out to the highway and hitchhike to Desert Center.

Finally, we had gone a long ways when Dad said, "This time when I start, I'm going to go as far as I can go."

"Okay, Dad, you want us on the front to push or on the back for traction over the wheels?"

Dad said, "Get on the front in case you need to push because the weight on the back wheels won't help much in this mud."

My brothers and I got on the front bumper and had a handhold on the hood emblem with one hand and a handhold on the inside front edge of the fender well with the other hand.

"You boys set?" Dad asked out of his window.

"Yeah, let her go," we all said at once."

Once the wheels started to turn on the plywood, Dad gave it the gas.

"YEEHA!" we hollered. The rear wheel on my side was throwing mud all over my hand and arm that was holding on to the fender well. "Keep it going, Dad!" we hollered, as though we thought he might stop, which he wasn't about to do. Dad couldn't turn to look back because his neck was stiff from old age. The ruts of our tires kept it going straight without turning the wheel at all.

"Hot diggity," I said because we were rolling along pretty good. Dad was able to back onto solid ground again, where he came to a stop. "Shall we go back and get the plywood?" I asked.

"It will wait until tomorrow," came Dad's reply.

Suits the shit out of me, I thought.

"Let's flag Ol' Brownie for camp. We've done enough damage for one day," Dad said. "YEEEHA." I was glad to be unstuck.

When I saw our car settling down into the frame and with both axles buried, I thought our car was a total loss. I never dreamed we could dig it out the same day. I could tell Dad was happy too. He said he would rather dig it out if it took a week than to have to walk clear back to Desert Center to get help.

We had mud on our clothes, our arms, our hands. I even had mud on my head from the wheel spinning and throwing it everywhere. Once we were back at camp, we got all washed up and changed our clothes. We felt much better, and we still had a car to drive around. Life was good. We used a lot of water getting ourselves clean, so Dad said, "Let's go to the canal we crossed coming in and refill our water cans."

"Now?" I asked, because it was getting pretty late in the day.

"No, it would be dark by the time we drove out to the canal," Dad said. "I meant in the morning after breakfast. We have enough for tonight."

I asked Dad if I could stay and walk over to the north side of the lake to see if there were any shells there.

"No, son," came Dad's reply. "We all need to stay together in case we run into any trouble. "If you want to go there, then go. But wait until we get back with the water."

"Yeah, but it will be late in the day," I told him.

He said, "It's better to stay together, son."

"Okay, Dad," came my reply.

The next morning, we just left our camp with the bedroll and chuck boxes and stove and all our shells sitting there and headed out through the sand dunes toward the canal. Dad had gotten water from the canal when he had been here a few years ago. He told us we needed a rope to go down the canal bank. At least we had our tracks to follow going back out, but we still got stuck once on a dune that was pretty steep. I don't think a day went by without us being stuck at least once.

Once we reached the canal, we got out with our water cans and rope and walked over to the chain-link fence. Dad reached down and lifted the bottom of the fence so Orville and I could scoot underneath it. Then we pulled the two five-gallon water cans under the fence, and Dad handed us the rope.

"You boys hold the fence up while I crawl under," he said.

After Dad crawled underneath the fence, Orville and I both took a water can and the rope and walked to the edge of the canal.

Quack! Quack! Quack!

Shit, six teal ducks rose up off the water.

They had been right against the bank, and as soon as we walked up, they were gone. I didn't think to bring a gun with us up on the canal. I could have gotten a duck or two if I had thought to bring a gun. I would have needed a shotgun. No such good luck today. I would have been happy just to shoot my gun into the air. Gun smoke in the cold morning air has a good smell to it, I think. Rifle powder doesn't have much of a smell after it is fired but shotguns do.

Oh well, I took a five-gallon can, and Dad held the rope while I walked down the canal bank and put the water can into the water. As the can started to fill, it sank deeper into the water. It was heavy too.

"Don't slip in, son," Dad told me from the top of the bank where he had his end of the rope around his waist.

The can wasn't quite full, but I pulled it out of the water and screwed the cap on. Dad and Orville pulled me up the bank, as walking and carrying that can of water was difficult.

We had a big pan with a handle on it, and Dad put the rope on Orville and told him to go down and get a pan of water so we could top off the can that I got that wasn't quite full. Then I went down with the last can and filled it. Orville got another pan of water to top this can off. We wanted them as full as we could get them. With our cans full—and we checked the radiator too—we headed back down the valley to the dry lake, but without any ducks. I was still kicking my behind for now, crawling out on the canal bank to check for ducks.

It was noon before we returned to camp. I told Dad I would wait until the next day to walk into the foothills on the north side of the lake.

Dad said, "Let's look at the south side again, where we had been picking up shells for weeks."

If we weren't picking up shells, then there was nothing to do—only sit around camp, which was very boring. There was nothing to hunt. We had seen only a couple of jackrabbits in the month or so since we had been here.

The next morning after breakfast, Dad said they would drive me around the lake so I wouldn't have very far to walk to get to where I wanted to prowl through the foothills.

Dad stopped the car and said, "Okay, son, go look if you want to, but I don't think you'll find much. The maneuvers were mostly on the south side and east from the lake where they had the convoy of old cars sitting."

I had my .22 pistol strapped to my hip just in case I saw any critters that needed killing.

My pistol was loaded, and I also had a box of fifty .22 shells in my shirt pocket. Just in case I needed to blast my way out of an ambush. I never knew when a posse might light out after me. There might be a reward out for me. After all, we had quit school when we were on probation. I didn't want to wind up in juvenile hall again.

If they tried to take me back, there was going to be a shootout. I knew I was safe in thinking this way since we hadn't seen a soul in the month or six weeks we had been here.

I had been gone from the car for about an hour, and I had seen a lot of tank tracks that were blown full of sand. Dad said Patton trained in here early in World War II. I saw a hole over on my left that looked pretty much like the hole the atomic bomb blew in the ground when it exploded. I walked over to it, and it turned out to be a machine gun nest. Some soldiers had their machine gun set up here and had shot one hell of a lot of bullets.

I estimated about two sacks of .30-06 ammunition was here in this hole.

I felt as though I had struck it rich. I'd hit the jackpot. Dad would be proud of me. He didn't figure I'd find anything. *Won't he be surprised*, I thought. I marked the spot in my mind on a line from where I knew camp was to a peak of a hill right behind me. As I walked back out to the lake, I kept kicking marks in the soil with my boot so I could return to the treasure.

When I got back down to the lakebed, Dad and my brothers were busy walking around picking up shells. As I came walking up, Dad said, "It was a wild-goose chase, wasn't it, son?"

"Not really, Dad." And I told him about finding all the .30-06 shells in a foxhole.

"The hell you did," was Dad's reply. "Are they a long way from the lake?" he asked.

"Not if we drive as close as we can get to them," I told him.

"How many you figure there are?" he asked.

"About two sacks, I think, Dad."

"Well, hell, let's go get them," was Dad's response.

"Well, right now I need a drink of water," I told him.

"Well, the water bag is at the car, so we started toward it, still picking up shells.

Orville and Everett came over, and I told them about finding the hole with all the machine gun shells in it. I said there might be two sacks full in the foxhole. Then after we all had a drink of water, we loaded into the car and drove across the lake to where I had come out of the foothills. I told Dad to just head towards that high peak I was pointing at. "The place is up there, dad."

Dad was turning this way and that, trying to get the car as close as he could. Finally, we couldn't get the car any closer there were too many rocks and ravines. We got some gunnysacks from the car and walked another hundred yards over the ground that I had kicked boot marks into. But knowing where the high hill was and just going towards it was the best guide for me.

Once back at the hole, we all started scooping the empty brass shells into our gunnysacks. Dad said this must have been a place where they had trained machine gunners in, because there were so many the shells in one place. To carry them out, we filled the sacks about only a third full, so they weren't so heavy.

But once we were at the car, we dumped the sacks. All together, we had two and a half sacks of .30 caliber shells. It was a good day's work, and Dad estimated them to weigh three hundred pounds. We kept the clean shells separate from the dirty ones that we had picked up on the dry lake with the salty crust all over them.

Dad said we would stop again on the way out to burn the crust off. We had three sacks of the crusty ones, but this time, we wouldn't make the mistake of making camp at the same place where we were going to burn the shells. We were lucky to not get hit by the primers shooting everywhere the last time. Maybe God was looking after us.

It was spring, and the desert cactus and grasses and brush were turning green.

On our way out this time, Dad told us we won't be coming back here again because the pickings had gotten so slim. He said it was time to go over around Buckeye and chop some cotton. We did go back, though, but it wasn't until 1956 that we did. I had bought a 1942 yellow Jeep in San Bernardino for $550.

So one day we all decided to take the Jeep out to Cadiz Dry Lake and go four-wheeling. My brothers and I were living at 1880 Highland Avenue in San Bernardino.

Dad had remained in Blythe. I was working at a Chevron Gas Station on Fifth and L Streets. But that's another story.

ORVILLE RUNS AWAY AGAIN

In the spring of 1953, we were chopping cotton over around Buckeye Arizona, and Orville told me he was going to leave and run away. He had done it before when we were at the Carters' house when we were in foster homes. This was before Dad had custody of us three boys. Dad was always on to Everett about anything and everything.

I guess he had Everett down one day in the dirt and was hitting him. Orville must have taken notice because he said that if Dad ever did that to him, he would kill him.

I can't ever remember seeing Dad hitting Everett, but I do remember one time on an abandoned airfield west of the town of Perryville, Arizona. Dad was griping about something Everett had done. As I remember it now, it had something to do with washing the dishes or his skillets, and Everett didn't get them clean. Dad pulled out a .32-20 revolver and shot into the ground close to Everett's legs.

I remember saying, "Hey, knock that shit off. You could hurt him!"

"Well, I'm going to hurt him if he don't get these dishes clean." Dad was always complaining about those stupid dishes. We were chopping cotton ten hours a day, so Dad had Everett do the dishes after breakfast and supper. He didn't let Everett chop cotton because Everett was supposed to be in school, and if the authorities found out, we could be put back into foster homes.

I didn't know of anything else to say to Dad when he shot the pistol except to stop it. I never felt that Dad wanted to hurt Everett; he was just making his point about getting the dishes clean, and to impress upon him that he was serious about what he was saying. But shooting right under his feet wasn't the right thing to do. I tried to get the story from Everett the way he remembers it, but he said it was long ago. "Let's forget it."

I can't remember if I could have done anything else at the time. I would like to think I did all I could.

We looked for Orville for several days. Then Dad gave up looking for him. He said, "Well, if that's what he wants, he'll just have to get by on his own."

It was hot again, and the cotton we were chopping was about finished. Dad was angry that Orville had left when he said "Let's get the hell out of here and go work in California."

We drove up to Hollister, where Dad had worked on the apricots in previous years. The nights seemed to be cooler here than in Fresno, where the nights were very hot. We got a job cutting apricots for a shed owned by a Dr. Holstein. I cut only the apricots for one day. Then the shed foreman named John asked if I would want to work hourly taking the trays away as the cutters filled them up.

"Sure," I said.

I was happy to do that, knowing I made more money doing that than cutting the apricots. You always had mushy apricots on your hands, or you would cut your finger with the cutting knife. I was paid a dollar an hour for taking the trays away and stacking them on carts to be rolled to the sulfur sheds.

I was seventeen, and a young girl cutting apricots with her brother and sisters Began flirting with me. She was very cute; she had brown eyes with gold flecks in them. She was wearing a man's shirt with the sleeves rolled up. My dad was still going by Buck Thorne, so I told everyone my name was Frank Thorne, and Everett was Lee.

I was working with another young man who said his name was Tex (I found out later that his name was Albert), but they called him Tex because he was from Texas. He had come out to California to stay the summer with friends. He had decided to work in the fruit to make some extra money.

I found out the girl's name was Shirley Gibbs, and her dad was the foreman over the cutting shed operation. Shirley also had a stepmother who was working cutting apricots.

Whenever Tex and I came to pick up the trays that Shirley and her sisters had filled, she would put her hand on my arm as I was straining to lift the heavy trays and say, "Hey, Muscles." No one had ever called me Muscles before as I was skinny, but if she thought I had muscles, it was all right with me because, like I said, she was really cute.

Tex was going out the coming weekend with Nadine, Shirley's stepsister. I knew Shirley liked some boy from school, and she was seeing him on weekends. That's what Tex told me when we were talking about the girls one day.

Tex said, "Ask Shirley if she wants to go to a drive-in on Saturday night after work. That way, we can double-date and go in his 1936 Ford sedan.

Tex had permission to go out with Nadine, and Shirley was just going to tag along. In other words, Shirley's parents didn't know I was going to the show too.

Dad said I could take the car and meet them in town, because we were just camped out in a wash south of town by an old wrecking yard. We didn't have a back seat in our car, so that's why we were taking Tex's car to the drive-in. I saw Tex's car pull up behind where I was parked in Hollister, so I got out of my car and climbed into the back seat with Shirley.

I put my arm around her, and she snuggled up tight as I said, "What movie are we going to see?"

Tex said, "Who cares? I just wanted to be with Nadine."

Well, who was I to argue, since I just wanted to be with Shirley! I had never snuggled up to a girl before, so I was feeling really flushed. The same way I had felt in the third grade sitting next to Georgia Powell.

Only this time it was really happening, and Shirley smelled so go too. I can't remember if it was Shirley or the perfume that had my head swirling around and making me dizzy. Maybe it was a little of both. I was seventeen, and this was my first real date. And the way she had been flirting, I knew she liked me too.

I honestly don't remember the movie that we saw because Tex and Nadine were making out in the front seat and only talked to us once in a while. I hadn't kissed a girl before so I guess I was clumsy and very inexperienced. But once I found Shirley's lips, it didn't take long to get passed my shyness, as I started devouring her one kiss at a time.

My hand must have found its way onto her knee because I remember feeling her hand lifting my hand and placing it back on my knee without saying anything. She gave my hand a pat as if to say, *Keep it there, kiddo.*

When the intermission came, Tex and I went to the snack bar for Cokes and popcorn. "Nadine said Shirley likes you a lot," Tex told me as we were walking back from the snack bar.

I said, "Well, I like her too, or I wouldn't be here."

The girls were laughing when we got back to the car, and we figured they had been talking about us too. All I can remember is the evening came to an end much too soon as I gave Shirley one last kiss good night. Monday we saw them at work, and I remember every time I looked over at Shirley, she was watching me, and I would grin at her as she smiled and waved at me.

I was hoping to get to go out with her the next weekend too, but something happened that put a stop to that idea. Shirley's younger brother started calling me names because he was friends with the boy Shirley had been going with before I entered the picture. I called him an asshole and gave him the finger.

One afternoon, he had come out to where Tex and I were laying the trays out in the sun to dry the apricots and was calling me names again, so I pushed him, and he fell down. Shirley was out talking to Tex and me when this happened. She wanted her brother to leave, but he just kept up the name-calling.

Shirley's stepmother saw me push her son and came out on the warpath and called me a no-good Arizona son of a bitch. I didn't know what to say, as no woman had cussed at me before. I had lived in Arizona for only a year and a half, and now I was an Arizona son of a bitch? What about all the years I'd lived in California?

I went back to putting the trays out in the sun with Tex, and Shirley's stepmother and her stepbrother went back to the cutting shed. Shirley hung around for a while and said she was sorry her brother had called me names. She told me he was a friend of the boy she had dumped to go out with me, and he didn't like it.

Shirley's stepmother watched her like a hawk after that, and we weren't able to go out to a movie again with Tex and Nadine. Shirley still flirted, and we talked when we could, but Shirley's stepmother was always glaring at me. So I tried not to look at her, but I still had to take her trays away when she had them full of cut apricots.

I could see that we were finishing up with the season on apricots because once the fruit was all picked and cut, they shut the shed down. We were going to be leaving Hollister and returning to Fresno. I asked Shirley for her address and told her I would write to her when we had a permanent address again, probably in Blythe.

It was sad for both of us because we liked each other a lot. I said goodbye to Tex and said, "Come out next summer, and we'll do it all again." He said he would like to do just that and was going to write to Nadine. I don't know if he did, because I never went back myself as I had a better paying job in Blythe.

Once we were in Blythe at the end of September, Dad rented a postal mailbox, and so with a return address, I was able to write to Shirley at her home in Hollister. I went back to using my real name when I wrote to her, but she didn't say anything about it being Paul instead of Frank.

I don't remember her writing right back, and when she did, she mostly was talking about school and some boy named Johnny Thompson that had a neat black Ford, all nosed and decked. She asked if I had seen it in Hollister when I was there. I told her no, I didn't remember seeing it.

She said Johnny had asked her out, but her stepmother still wouldn't let her date. I was wondering why she was telling me all this, as she knew I liked her. I was reluctant to answer her letter this time, because she seemed to have found someone she wanted to go out with, and I couldn't blame her because I was so far away. Eventually, I did write to her, but she didn't answer, but I never forgot her, or how pretty she was.

Dad, Everett, and I went down to Cibola, Arizona, and started trapping raccoon and muskrat. We were seeing a lot of cattle and dad talked about killing one of them, and butchering it and taking it to Buckeye to sell it to Queenie. The black lady who had the lunch wagon where we were picking cotton last fall.

So one day we went looking for a cow that Dad thought was right to kill.

Dad was looking for a cow two or three years old, which would be tender and a good piece of meat. Dad was leading the way as we walked quietly through the brush, following a cow trail that had really fresh tracks in the trail.

I tripped on a root that was growing across the trail and fell headfirst into my dad, startling him. I heard Dad whisper to me, "Goddamn it, son, will you pick up your feet. Hell, you'll run all the cattle out of the river bottom between here and Blythe."

I said, "I'm sorry, Dad. I was looking for cattle, and I didn't see that root."

"Well, for Christ's sake, son, watch where the hell you are stepping."

"Okay, Dad," I said. "I'll be careful."

"Well, see that you do. I don't want to walk clear out to the river before I shoot one." I was thinking he was making more noise than I did, complaining about me tripping over that dad gum root. We hadn't gone more than a couple hundred feet farther when we came up on three cows lying down in the brush just off the trail, and I saw Dad raise his gun to his shoulder. As the cows got to their feet, a big one turned to look at what has spooked them.

POW!

I heard the gun crack as Dad shot the cow right between the eyes. The other cows crashed through the brush as they scrambled to get away. But Dad wasn't concerned about them as he walked over to the cow he had shot and leaned his gun against a mesquite tree. He took out his pocketknife that he kept razor sharp and cut the cow's throat so the blood would drain out.

Dad then started skinning it, and I helped by pulling on the hide so he could get his knife deeper, cutting the hide loose. We had the cow skinned and cleaned. Then Dad said, "Son, you stay here, and I'll walk back to camp and get a rope so we can pull it up into this mesquite tree."

Dad took the heart and liver back to camp, for us to cook up to eat that night. And I sat down on a dead tree stump to wait for Dad to return. It must have been an hour before Dad returned, and I could see he had washed up because his hands were clean. And he had brought a handsaw to split the backbone with.

Dad tied the rope around the cow's legs at the knees where he had cut them off. Dad took the rope and threw it over a limb on the big mesquite tree and said, "Son, you'll have to help me pull on this rope. I doubt I can pull this heavy son of a bitch up by myself."

Once the critter was coming off the ground, Dad wrapped the rope around a limb and tied it off. Then he told me he would go to the cow and lift it and for me to untie the rope and pull the slack out of it and then tie it off again.

"Son, you'll have to work quick because I can't hold the son of a bitch forever. You think you can handle that, son?"

"I'll sure try, Dad," I told him.

Dad untied the rope, and with the rope over a coil so as not to let the dead cow down, I was able to hold the cow. Dad had his arms around the cow and asked if I was ready.

"I'm ready, Dad," I told him.

Soon the cow was off the ground, and we tied the rope to the tree.

Dad took his handsaw and sawed through the cow's backbone. Then he said, "We'll leave it hanging here in the shade to cool for now."

We dragged the hide out into the brush so it wouldn't be found and kicked dirt and brush over the blood that had run out on the ground.

"Okay, let's take the saw and we will head for camp," Dad said. "We'll cook the liver for supper. Then we can come back and carry the cow (which was cut into quarters) up closer to camp."

Everett had a big stack of wood chopped and stacked, so Dad cleaned his hands and started a fire to cook on. I peeled three potatoes, and Dad sliced them up and cooked them in one of his skillets as the liver was cooking in the other. I was hungry, and it had been real work getting that cow butchered.

We couldn't eat all. The liver made good sandwiches, even cold, so we planned to eat the rest tomorrow on the road to Buckeye. After supper, we took a couple of sheets out to the cow, and Dad wrapped it up so the flies wouldn't get to the meat. But we left it out in the brush. Dad didn't want it hanging in camp in case someone walked in on us. The cattle were wild, but it was still against the law to shoot one, and we didn't want to go to prison for shooting a wild cow that had no brand on it.

The next morning, just before daylight, we put the cow that Dad had cut into quarters into our car and placed our bedroll and cases with clothes on top of everything and started out of the river bottom over the rough road to the highway and turned east just as the sun's first rays were peeking over the mountains toward Quartzsite.

I wished we were going in the other direction since the sun was shining directly into my eyes this morning. I have blue eyes, and they have always been weak to the sunlight. So I was driving with my right hand on the steering wheel while shading my eyes with my left hand. Dad had his eyes shut as he sat in the passenger seat with his head resting against the car window as the morning sun made him drowsy. Everett had gone to sleep in the back of the car on top of our bedroll. It was about 8:30 a.m. when we came to the old dirt road that we were taking from Salome over to Buckeye.

STRANDED

I wasn't too crazy about driving this rough road again, but the highway went on east to Wickenburg, then southeast to Phoenix, then back west to Buckeye was the long way to go. I didn't like the dirt roads, but this was a shortcut, and it saved us time.

Hell, you couldn't drive it very fast without getting the wrath of God for driving too fast. Because all Dad was worried about was those stupid tires. Good grief, give me a break, would you? We have a good spare tire in the trunk, and I'm doing only fifty.

"Yeah, but, son, it don't take much to bust a tire on a rock, and the rock won't have to be very big, so if you're so goddamn hard headed and want to drive like a crazy man, you can get the hell out and change the flat all by yourself. And if we have to spend all our money from the sale of this meat on tires, we might as well stay in hell down at Cibola."

"Okay, Dad, I'll slow down, but I thought you were in a hurry because of the meat," I told him.

"No, if we get the meat to Queenie in the afternoon, she won't have to store it in her trunk for more than a couple of hours before she can go home and put it in the freezer," Dad explained.

In 1957, I drove across this same dirt road, but without Dad in the car. Orville and Everett were with me; we were going to trade a couple of skill saws we had found lying around somewhere, for an airplane ride with Caldwell Mothershed, Ershel's brother. I was driving my new 1957 Mercury Turnpike Cruiser. I was driving seventy miles an hour.

Mind you, this was still a dirt road, but without my dad to saying, "Goddamn it, son, slow down." Guess who busted a tire? Now remember, you only get one guess! That's right, it was I, the racecar driver, and these tires were new too.

A small, sharp rock had hit the tire just right, and it penetrated the tread, and the tubeless tire went flat. The car had started to fishtail on the rough gravel road, and by the time I got the car stopped, the tire was flat as a pancake. My brothers and I got the bumper jack out of the trunk and changed the tire. Dad had been right. I was just too dumb to listen. It cost me a new tire too, about forty bucks' worth! Anyway, back to the story.

I was driving, and we were about a half hour out of Salome, Arizona, when we came upon a car stopped in front of a signpost. But we were headed in the other direction. There was a big sign in the front windshield: STRANDED PLEASE HELP. As I was passing the car, Dad said, "Son, stop. Those people need help." I was past the car by the time I stopped our car. As I turned to look back, I also saw a sign in the rear window: STRANDED NEED HELP.

So I started backing up. I couldn't see into the car because there were things in the window to keep the sun out. I stopped even with the car, and I saw a woman peering out at us. I got out and walked over to the driver's side.

"Are you okay?" I asked.

She was either timid or afraid, probably a little of both. She had dark hair and looked to be of Mexican descent, but light skinned. She said something but I didn't understand her through the glass.

"Can you roll the window down a little?" I asked.

When she did, the towel in the window fell down, and that's when I saw she was holding a baby in her arms.

"What's wrong?" I asked again.

"The car won't start," she said.

"Are you out of gas?"

"No, I don't think so,"

Dad and Everett came up behind me, and Dad said, "What's wrong, son?"

"She told me the car won't start."

She was looking at Dad and Everett, probably thinking, *Should I trust them?*

I asked her through the small opening in the window, "What had happened?"

She told us they had taken the road at night thinking it was going to be a paved road. They soon found out it wasn't. The map didn't show it was a dirt road, or they failed to read it properly. After driving for about an hour, the lights of the car became dim. They saw the signpost and stopped to read it. The car lights were so dim her husband got out to read the sign with his cigarette lighter, and when he took his foot off the gas, the car died, and when her husband tried to restart it, the battery was dead.

She had rolled the window down some more by now, and she seemed more at ease.

"Don't worry, my dad's a good mechanic," I told her. "I think he can get you going."

"Why don't you get in the car and see if it turns over, son."

I asked her if I could try starting her car. She was still sitting in the passenger seat, but she reached over and opened the door for me. She said, "My husband tried before he left, but it won't start.

I sat down; the key was in the ignition. I turned it, but nothing happened. She explained to me that her husband had started walking last night because there hadn't been another car to come past them on the road all night. He didn't want to leave them, but he was going to come back with help as soon as he could walk out to the town of Salome.

Dad was in front of the car trying to get the hood open. He asked me if I saw a hood latch under the dashboard. "No, I don't see it in here," I said. "I think it's out there, Dad!" I got out and found the latch and opened the hood.

I heard Dad say, "Hell, the fan belt has come loose"!

He said it looked as though the bolt that held the generator in place had worked loose, and the generator had slipped down, and more or less, the generator wasn't ginning, so to speak, Dad explained to me.

Dad went on to explain that "with them driving last night with the lights on, it caused the battery to lose its charge, and when they stopped to look at the sign, there just wasn't enough juice to run the engine."

Dad walked over to our car and got the toolbox out of the trunk. He came back with a ratchet and a couple of sockets. He pulled the generator tight on the fan belt and tightened the bolt down. He told me it would work all right now. He walked over so he could see in the window and said, "It's an automatic. We'll have to push it nearly fifty miles an hour before it will start."

Dad said, "Let's take our battery out of our car and start their car. Then when it's running, we can take the battery cables off and reinstall their battery."

"You think that will work, Dad?"

"Hell, yes, 'course it'll work!"

"I was just wondering. Don't get mad," I said.

"Everett, you pull the hood latch, and I'll get some wrenches from the toolbox," Dad said to Everett. I also walked to the toolbox for a wrench, so I could start taking the dead battery out of their car.

The lady was just sitting there holding her baby and watching us, probably thinking, *I hope I'm doing the right thing*. I told her again, "Don't worry, my dad will get you going." I was hoping to put her at ease again.

Dad had our battery into her car and connected the battery cables. "Okay, son, try it. Let's see if it will start!"

I turned the key, and RRROOM. It started right up.

The woman asked me, "It's running?"

"Sounds like it to me," I said. "Now my dad wants to put your battery back into your car."

"But won't it die again?" she asked.

"My dad said it won't, and he knows what he's doing."

"Idle the engine a little faster, son," I heard Dad tell me while he switched her battery back into her car.

"Okay, Dad," I said out the side window. I was watching him through the windshield. He loosened the cables and removed both of them from our battery. Then he lifted our battery from her car and put hers back into the battery box and installed the two cables.

The car ran all the time. I thought it might die, but it didn't. It worked just like Dad said it would. I asked him how he did that. He said the generator was putting out enough juice to keep the motor running until he had the batteries switched.

He said, "Son, keep it a little fast so it will start charging the dead battery."

"Okay, Dad," I replied.

"Can you drive?" I asked her.

"No, I don't know how," she told me.

"That's okay," I said. "I can drive it for you."

"Dad, she can't drive!"

"Well, son, we'll have to drive her into Salome."

Neat, I thought. I wanted to drive this new car. By this time, Dad had our battery back into our car, and he said he would follow me. I dropped her car into drive, and it started moving. I had my left foot on the brake and was running the engine a little fast. I didn't want it to die.

I was watching my dad in the rearview mirror as he turned our car around.

I began to notice the car even smelled new. I was up to forty miles per hour in two shakes. No vibration at all, unlike our old Chevy. I was in heaven driving a new car. I was thinking, *This is what I want.* The only other new car I had driven was a 1951 Ford in driver's education at Riverside Polytechnic High School. Oh yeah, and my sister Rita let me drive her husband's 1950 Oldsmobile Rocket 88 fastback. Rita's husband, Truman, liked to take it to the drag races that were held in Bloomington and Santa Ana.

I can still remember that car: It was dark blue, and he had the hubcaps off of it for racing. The wheels were maroon. I was so thankful to her for letting me drive it.

"Paul, you be careful," she told me as I pulled out onto LaCadena, the main road from Riverside to Colton. "Truman will kill me if you get in an accident, for letting you drive his car. Truman thinks more of this car than he does of me, but enough of the past.

I looked down at the steering wheel, and I noticed that the horn emblem said, "1953 Fords Fiftieth Anniversary." What a nice car, and a nice color too. Kind of a seafoam green with a cream top. I was thinking, *This car is so neat.*

My thoughts were interrupted. "Did you see a man walking on the road when you were driving before you stopped to help me?" my passenger, whose car I was driving, asked me. "No, I didn't see anyone! Was he going to walk all the way on the road?" I asked.

"I think so," she said. "He wanted to find a tow truck."

"We'll find him," I said. *I wonder if she would care if I turned the radio on*, I thought. *Naw, I better not. I need the battery to get recharged so they won't have any more trouble. Still, it would be nice to hear some tunes.*

I bet the radio has a nice sound too, since it's brand new. Oh well, better to charge the battery. But still, it would be nice to just hear it, I was thinking as she said, "We are going to my parents' home in Los Angeles so they can see the baby," she explained.

I was still wondering why we didn't see her husband walking on the road. Maybe he got tired and sat down in the shade someplace and didn't hear us go by.

Finally, we came to the paved highway going from Blythe to Wickenburg. I turned left, and it was just a short distance to the service stations in Salome. I pulled into the only one I saw that said "Towing" on their sign. It was on the left side of the highway. I checked the mirror to make sure Dad was still behind me. As I pulled into the station, there were three men standing together talking as I pulled her car into the gas pumps.

She said, "That's my husband right there." He was trying to get a tow truck to go tow their car into the shop to have it fixed.

He was flabbergasted when he saw his car, his wife, and their baby right there in the station. They were so happy; he was thanking Dad and shaking his hand. He just couldn't thank us enough. He had only been there for about fifteen minutes, and they were going to call the tow truck operator to come down and go tow the car into the shop so it could be fixed.

The man's wife asked him if he had walked the road all the way. "No," he said when he saw the town in the distance. He had left the road and walked a straight line to the town. So that was why we didn't see him on the road that morning. The man was trying to put money into Dad's hand, but Dad said no. Again, the man was telling my Dad about how they were taking the baby to see the grandparents.

"Take the baby to see its grandparents. That will be payment enough," Dad told the man. "Come on, boys, let's flag Ol' Brownie. We still got a long way to go. What a good day. We helped someone who really needed it. I bet they told that story over and over, and we were the heroes—just Dad, Everett, and I. I was so proud that Dad refused payment. Now we had to get this beef on over to Buckeye.

―∞―

Well, we finally arrived in Buckeye. Then we had to drive up and down dirt roads around Buckeye, looking for the cotton pickers and their cars. Also, the cotton trailers had PORTER RANCH CO. painted on the side of each trailer.

Finally, Dad found the right group of pickers, and he told us, "You boys stay with the car, and I'll go see if I can make a deal to sell Queenie the beef." When Dad came back after talking to her, he said, "She wants it, all right, and when there aren't any pickers at the lunch wagon, she said for us to put it into the trunk of her car."

Dad said, "She has eighty dollars with her, and she said to come to her house in Phoenix tonight, and she'll give us the rest of the money." I asked, "How much more, Dad?"

"She's willing to pay one hundred dollars for the meat, so if we go to her place tonight, she'll give us another twenty dollars."

We saw our chance and put the meat into her car, which was parked in the back of the lunch wagon, and Dad got the eighty dollars from Queenie.

We drove over to Cold Water and filled our gas tank and got something to eat, but the more Dad thought about the situation, he said, "You know we'll have to stay here until Queenie gets done with the pickers tonight and then drives home to Phoenix. Then we'll have to drive clear into Phoenix to get the twenty dollars. It just isn't worth it."

"What do you want to do, Dad?" I asked. "Well, son, let's just write the twenty dollars off and get our ass back down to Cibola."

"If we leave now we can be back in camp shortly after dark. Besides, that meat is strong tasting anyway, because those cattle have been eating that salt cedar in the river bottom. If Queenie cooks up some of that meat, she just might want her money back.

"I'm afraid that beef will be tougher than a boiled owl," Dad continued.

So with that, we headed back to our camp over in the river bottom. Eighty dollars went a long way in the fall and winter of 1953, and besides, it was easy money for us to make. So we left Cold Water and returned to our camp in the river bottom below Cibola and went back to trapping.

One day I was up in the top of a huge mesquite tree looking for ducks on the slough. I could just sit down on the limbs of this tree, in the very top. I saw movement out of the corner of my eye and looked over to my right, and I saw the biggest buck deer I ever saw in my life. I motioned for Everett, who was on the ground under the tree to come up in the tree, as I wanted him to see how big this deer was.

Everett came up, and this deer was feeding off mesquite beans in a tree and with his head up his horns were clear back over his rump. This deer looked like an elk. I thought this was the biggest deer I had ever seen in all my years of hunting deer. I told Everett, "I'm climbing down and go see if I can shoot it. You let me know if he's still there when I get my gun."

I got my gun and looked up to see if Everett could still see the buck, and I saw him nod his head in the affirmative.

I started walking quietly in a line toward where I figured the buck to be. The brush was thick, but I found an old cow trail that I could walk in going in the direction I wanted to go. My heart was pumping in my chest as I was remembering how big this buck was and in anticipation of getting to shoot him and seeing how big he was up close.

Dad didn't want me shooting strong old bucks, but this was a really big deer. I kept stalking as quietly as I could and expecting to see the buck through the brush at any minute. I was almost out of breath, as I must have been holding it from the sheer excitement of the stalk.

But alas, it wasn't to be. I never found the buck, although I did come across some really big deer tracks. I tracked it for the better part of an hour, but I never saw it again. When I returned to our camp, Everett said he had lost sight of the buck just after I started stalking it. He said it had just walked under the tree, and that was last he saw of it.

Everett and I were just reminiscing about that big buck a few weeks ago.

BLAIR'S HOMESTEAD CIBOLA

One day we had come up from Cibola and were in Blythe picking up some groceries and supplies when Dad came back to the car and told Everett and me that he had run into Ralph Blair at the Safeway Market. He told us Ralph's father, Sam Blair, still had a section of land down the river from Blythe in Cibola. A section of land, Dad explained, was 640 acres. I guess they got to talking about cattle, and Dad explained that we had been down in Cibola, trapping, and had seen a few cattle roaming around on the old Blair place. Dad asked if Sam was still running cattle there on his ranch.

Ralph had said his dad had gotten too old and was living with him in Blythe.

He said that they had never completely rounded up all their cattle from the property. Ralph told Dad that they still had the bees and the extracting business at the ranch. Dad ask Ralph if he would be open to an arrangement where he and his two sons would go in and catch the cattle for half of what was caught.

Ralph said he would be open to such an arrangement, but he would have to speak to his father about it first. Ralph gave Dad his address (north of Blythe) and told him to come by in a few days.

Dad seemed happy about the prospects of going down there and catching cattle. He told me, "Son, there's a lot of cattle running loose in the river bottom below Cibola. He said it will be a good chance for us to make some easy money."

I told Dad, "I'm not a cowboy. I've never roped a cow."

"Son, with a little practice, anybody can rope a cow. You can ride already, so all you have to do is help to head it out straight, and I'll put the loop on it."

"Yeah, but we don't have any horses, Dad," I told him.

"Son, you just let me worry about that," Dad told me. "First, we need to find us a couple of good saddles. Let's go back down to Cibola and wind this trapping operation up."

We were camped below Blair's place way back in the brush on a slough. We had been trapping raccoon and some muskrat. Dad would skin them out and stretch the hide and then let them dry in the shade so it wouldn't turn black. The furriers wanted prime pelts, meaning the skin side of the pelt was white and the fur was set in the pelt.

You can only get prime hides in the winter when it's cold. If hides are taken in the summer when it's hot, the skin side will be black, and the fur will be shedding. Not good if you want to sell it.

Once the hides were dry, Dad wrapped them tight in a burlap sack. Then he took them to the post office and shipped them off to the furrier. He was paid about $2.50 to $3.50 for a muskrat hide and about $6.00 for raccoon hides. Sometimes he trapped beaver, and a large pelt stretched round would bring in $30.00 dollars. He would also cook the beaver meat, and we would eat it. It was a dark meat, but I can't remember what it tasted like. It must have tasted all right, or I would not have eaten it. He also pickled the beaver tail and then sliced it for sandwiches, and we ate that. I remember thinking it was pretty good.

We would trap muskrats by finding their hole in a bank just above the high watermark. We set the trap in the water below the hole so the muskrat coming in to his den would lower his hind legs to walk up the bank to his hole and would step into the trap. If you had it set just right, the next morning, there would be a muskrat in your trap.

Now raccoons were a different story. We would look along the slough for tracks that looked like a small hand, and that would be a raccoon's trail. They would walk along the shore at night looking for fish or something to eat. Once we found a lot of raccoon tracks, we set our traps. We put tin foil on the pan of the traps just below the water, being careful not to rile the water.

If you riled the water as the sediment settled, it would land on the pan of the trap, making it dull so it wouldn't shine in the moonlight. A raccoon walking along the shore at night would see the tin foil shining and think it was a fish and grab the pan of the trap, setting it off. There he would be the next morning, sitting there looking at you as you came to get him with his leg in the trap.

Dad would take a long stick and push the raccoon into deeper water so he would drown instead of shooting the critter. He wanted the pelt to be as perfect as possible, meaning no bullet holes. Because the furriers wanted good pelts with no holes, they would take hides that were damaged but didn't pay much for them. So it was all about getting top dollar for the pelts. Your trapper's license was only good during the winter months.

Dad always bought a hunting license and a trapping license. Anyway, that's what we were doing when Dad ran into Ralph Blair in Blythe. Several days later, we came back to Blythe to ship some hides, and while we were there, Dad drove out to talk to the Blairs. Sam said he would grubstake us for our undertaking if he could come along with us.

Dad told Sam he would be glad to have him come along with us. Sam was old and just sitting around waiting to die. "But first, Sam, I'll have to round up some horses. When I get things lined up, me and the boys will come back for you."

"All right, Dick," Sam said to Dad as we were leaving. "I'll throw some things together so I'll be ready when you come back for me, Dick."

"Okay Sam," dad said to him as we walked out to our car and climbed in. As Dad backed our car out onto the street, he said, "Now all we need is saddles, son, and a couple of good horses."

Dad wanted to head over toward Phoenix to try to find the saddles he spoke of a couple of days ago. So we lit out for Phoenix like the law was after us to see if we could borrow a couple of saddles. We pulled into the desert north of Buckeye and spent the night. The next day, we drove over around Glendale and hit some secondhand stores looking for saddles. We spent most of the day looking. Dad wanted a saddle with a high back and a high saddle horn.

Dad said, "Son, when you get old, your bones hurt. I need a saddle to fit me like a rocking chair. With a high back, if your horse jumps over something unexpectedly, you'll stay in the saddle. My old bones don't mend like they used to."

He didn't like a short saddle horn, either, because it was easy to get your fingers caught under the rope when you went to dally on it.

Sometimes with short saddle horns like they have on Mexican saddles, it's easy to miss the horn with your dally completely.

"If your fingers are under the rope when a cow comes to the end of it, you will get them broke just as sure as I'm sitting here," he said.

Also, Dad was looking for a saddle with a hardwood tree covered with rawhide. "Son, a well-built saddle when your cowboying is a must. You don't want some wild bull on the end of your rope and have your saddle break."

Every saddle he looked at he lifted the leathers and looked underneath to see how well it was made. Finally, he found the one he wanted hanging on a rail in an old barn. He carried it to the car, and we made off with it.

It took me another day of looking before I found one I could borrow. It didn't have a high back, but the saddle horn was as high as my fist. Dad's saddle was just plain leather, with wood stirrups. Nothing fancy. My saddle was tooled leather with a basket weave pattern. Someone had just thrown this saddle into a corner, where I was lucky to have found it since good saddles are hard to come by, as Dad said.

Dad picked up a couple of old wool blankets out of a secondhand store, and he cut them up and hand-stitched them into saddle blankets. Nothing fancy, but they would get the job done. It seemed that Dad could make anything he set his mind to.

The next morning, bright and early, we were on the way back to Blythe. I was driving and did not have a care in the world when one of our tires went flat. We pulled over and unloaded all the stuff in the trunk so we could get to the spare tire. Dad blocked the wheels with a rock and jacked up the car and changed the tire. Our spare wasn't that great so dad said, "When you get to Quartzsite, pull into that wrecking yard, and we'll buy another tire."

Once we were at the wrecking yard, Dad rummaged through the tires and found one he liked for $7.50. He said that when we made camp, he would mount the tire on the rim. He liked doing things himself. That afternoon, we were back in Blythe, and Dad told me to drive out west of town a couple miles. He said, "That's the place on the left there, son. Turn into the next driveway you come to." As I drove down the gravel driveway, Dad said, "This is Walter Scott's place."

Dad said he had ridden with Walt many times over across the river. They had been gathering up cattle out of the river bottom for Tom Wells.

We pulled up to the ranch house, and a man who looked to be about forty came out of the house, and Dad got out to talk to him. I watched them shake hands, so I got out and walked over to them.

"Walt, this is my oldest son, Paul," Dad said, looking toward me.

I said, "Hello," and shook the hand he extended to me.

"Dick, I can let you have a couple of horses. Where will you be keeping them?"

Dad told Walt he had entered into a contract with Sam Blair and his son Ralph to catch up the cattle they had still running loose on that section of land they still owned down in Cibola.

Walt said, "Hell, Dick, I didn't know Sam Blair was still alive. When do you want the horses, Dick?" Walt said as he shook a cigarette from a pack and offered some to Dad and me. Dad and I both shook our heads declining the cigarette. "When do you want them Dick?" Walt asked again as he lit his cigarette.

"Sometime in the next two or three days, Walt," Dad told him. "I'd like to get started as soon as possible, but first, I'll have to get some feed hauled down to Cibola for the horses," Dad said. "Sam wants to go down with us and oversee the operation. Then I have to check back with Sam to see when he will be ready to go. I'll take Sam and the hay down and then come back for the horses."

"Dick, if you don't have a trailer, you're welcome to borrow mine."

"Thanks, Walt. That was going to be my next question," Dad said. "As soon as I have a solid commitment from Sam, I'll get back to you, Walt," Dad was saying as we walked over to our car.

Dad got behind the steering wheel because he would be driving around Blythe since I still hadn't gotten my driver's license. No use taking a chance getting pulled over by the law.

Dad drove out of the driveway and turned right toward downtown. Dad looked over at me and said, "Well, son, looks like we're going to be catching some cattle."

I said, "Don't you mean you are, Dad?"

"Son if we can't catch them with a rope, we'll set some snares and catch them that way."

I remember, in 1948, when I was in sixth grade, Dad had a contract with the government to catch wild horses. He caught them by setting snares made from three-eighths-inch wire cable, which he set in a trail where horses were going to the river to water. So with the horses all arranged for, Dad went back to Ralph Blair's house to talk to Sam.

We drove up to Ralph's house, and Dad said, "You boys stay in the car while I go talk to Sam."

About a half hour later, Dad came back out with an old man with a walking cane who looked to be about seventy-five years old. He said, "Sam is coming down to Cibola with us."

"Howdy, boys," Sam said as he got into the car.

"Both these boys yours?" Sam said to Dad.

"Well, their mother said they are, Sam."

They both chuckled at the thought of it being iffy as to whether we were Dad's offspring. Dad said, "Sam is going to grubstake us on this venture, boys."

Dad backed the car out, and away we went to Safeway for groceries we would need for a week or two down at Cibola. They came back with thirty-five dollars' worth. In 1953, that was quite a few groceries. Dad pulled into the gas station at the side of the Safeway market, and the attendant filled our tank. Dad also bought four quarts of motor oil. The old Chevy we were driving used a little oil, so Dad liked to have extra. Especially since Sam was buying what we needed for this operation.

Dad figured we had everything we needed, so he headed east out of Blythe and crossed the Colorado River to Ehrenberg. He turned onto a dirt road just before the inspection station for fruit and vegetables that went south to Cibola. This road to Cibola was rough and washboardy, only semigraded. Meaning they only ran a grader on it once a year, if that.

Dad was talking to Sam about his brand, the hip O. The hip O was a six- inch ring of iron heated really hot in a fire and then placed over a cow's hipbone, burning an *O* into the animals hide. The result was a hip O branded critter. Dad asked Sam if the brand was current.

Sam said, "Dick, I renewed it in 1946, and it's good for ten years."

"That's all that's needed, then. Looks like we are in good shape."

Sam was muttering about how his mother had the bar brand and his daddy had the hip O, so how could they get back off it? To this day, Everett and I don't know what he was talking about. But he seemed like a nice old man, but just a little touched in the head, so to speak. Today he would be considered to have dementia.

Like I said before, Sam was a nice old man, but you couldn't carry on a conversation with him because his mind wandered so much. He talked about how his dad had homesteaded the section of land we were going down the river to. He said his dad had homesteaded it for twenty years and then proved up on it to get a clear title to the property. I guess that proving up meant showing proof you had lived there and made improvements, such as building a home and putting up fences. I'm just guessing, as I know nothing about homestead laws.

The Blair house was pretty big, about twenty feet by forty feet.

It was set back off the graded road that ran from Ehrenberg down past Cibola to Martinez Lake. It was about a hundred yards west of the road. There was a post office in Cibola that was run by the Bishop family, who were also homesteading a section of land. The Bishops were the only other people we saw in this neck of the woods, except for the Mexicans walking on the road. Most of the traffic, if any, was on the weekends, when fishermen drove down to Martinez Lake to go fishing.

A man whom Dad knew as Lopez had a section of land that bordered Blair's land on the south. Lopez ran some cattle on his section of land, but we never saw anyone working his ranch. Dad told me they probably worked it only once or twice a year. This river bottomland was mostly big mesquite trees, and in some places, it was like a forest.

There was a lot of land, though, that was alkali salts. Not much grew in the alkali except salt cedar bushes. Then there were a lot of dead mesquite trees scattered throughout the area. Mistletoe would grow on the mesquite trees, eventually killing them over the years. There was also a lot of brush that grew in spots with cattle trails and deer trails branching out in all directions. Dad knew the river bottom pretty well.

OUR OWN HAYSTACK

Dad told me, "We'll leave Sam and Everett to watch our belongings tomorrow, and we will drive back to Blythe to get some hay for the horses we will be bringing down later this week."

The next morning, after breakfast, Dad and I started up the road to Blythe. The road was rough and curved in and out of washes and canyons. I could drive only twenty-five miles an hour at top speed. But Dad was never in any hurry, unless he thought the law was after him.

Dad said, "Son, just take it easy. Let's don't bust a tire."

"That reminds me," I said, "did you ever fix that flat we had coming back from Phoenix the other day?"

"Son, did you see me fix it?" he asked me.

"No," I said.

"Well, I guess it's not fixed, then, son. I thought we would wait until we were in Blythe so we can take it to a filling station for air. I'm just getting too old to pump tires up by hand unless it's absolutely necessary."

"I could help you, Dad," I said. "We will have time when we reach Blythe," he told me. "We'll have all afternoon. That is if you don't bust a tire this morning."

Before we stopped at the inspection station coming back into California, Dad said, "Son, pull over and let me drive."

"How come?" I asked.

"Goddamn it, because you don't have a driver's license," he explained to me in no uncertain terms. I knew, but I wanted to hear him crab about it, because I knew he would get testy.

He pulled into Safeway again because he had forgotten to get some salt pork. He wanted more coffee since all Sam did was to sit around and drink coffee. Dad liked salt pork because it kept for a long time without refrigeration, which we didn't have.

Our manner of refrigeration was to set it out at night so it would be cold. Then in the morning, we would wrap it up good so it would stay cold in the daytime.

If Dad wanted bacon for something, he would slice the salt pork and then boil it in a pan of water to get the salt out. Then he would just fried it like bacon. He bought bacon too, but salt pork kept better. When Dad bought bacon, he always bought slab bacon and then he sliced his own. He liked the bacon rind so he could slice it to put into beans for flavor. I always liked to have a piece of the rind because it was chewy and tasted good. After he had gotten the things he wanted from Safeway, we filled our gas tank again, as Dad was always topping off our tank.

Dad said, "Let's go find a haystack, son. Then we'll see about fixing the spare tire."

I told Dad, "We won't get much hay in this car. We need a truck, Dad."

"Well, if you have one in your hip pocket, I'll be glad to use it, son."

"Maybe we could borrow one from Walt Scott."

"Son, lets don't push our luck. He's already offered horses and a trailer. You want him to go catch the goddamn cattle for us too?"

"I was just trying to figure out a way to haul more hay so we won't have to make so many trips," I told Dad.

"We can get four bales in the car, and that will last a week and a half, maybe more," Dad said. He told me he could get two bales of hay in the trunk on edge and two bales in behind the seat where we usually kept our bedroll. "If we break a bale, we can wedge flakes of hay anywhere we can wedge them in."

We found a haystack under some cottonwood trees that was back off the beaten path.

"Son, let's pull down alongside the river, and I'll tear the spare tire down and patch the tube and mount the new used tire on the rim. We don't want to be without a spare tire going back to Cibola tonight."

Dad had all the tools he needed to change tires behind the wheel well in the trunk. I still have those tire irons and have used them often over the years.

Dad went to work taking the tire off the rim. He vulcanized the inner tube and remounted the new used tire. We spent about two hours at the river just loafing. As the sun was going down, Dad said, "Let's go to the gas station and air up this tire."

With our tire all fixed, we drove back toward the haystack, where we were going to borrow the hay.

We got to the dirt road into the haystack, but Dad turned left instead of right.

"Dad, the haystack is the other way."

"That's right, son," Dad told me as he pulled to the side of the road and turned out our lights. He turned the car around in the road and drove back across the main road into the dirt road going back to the haystack. We were driving with our lights off because Dad didn't want anyone to know we were back at the haystack, borrowing a few bales of hay.

He stopped the car with the emergency brake so the brake lights didn't come on. We got out and loaded two bales in the trunk on end and then we put two into the front of our car. It was difficult getting the bales into the backseat area because of the back of the front seat. There was no room for flakes of hay in the car. It was loaded tight.

"Let's get the hell out of here, son," Dad said as he got in behind the wheel. We drove out to the paved road and turned left, heading back to Blythe. Dad turned on the lights, and in no time, we were turning right on the highway toward the river. After crossing the bridge, we turned onto the dirt road going back south to Cibola. It was about midnight when we got back to Blair's ranch house, and it had been a long day for us.

Dad said, "Son, let's turn in. This old man is tired. We can unload this hay in the morning."

"I am too, Dad, so let's hit the hay," I told him.

Dad laughed at me saying "hit the hay."

The next morning, I drove the car out beside the corral about a hundred yards north of the house. The corral was made from long poles stacked on each other in a circle so as to leave a space as wide as the log between each log. The way it was built, you could see between the logs into the corral. It had what Dad called a snubbing post set into the ground in the center of the corral.

The purpose of the snubbing post was so you could throw your rope around it and pull an animal up to the post. Then with the animal's head tight against the post, you could cut off the tips of the horns, or doctor them for screw worms if the animal had them in a wound or a cut. You could even castrate it if it was a bull and you wanted to make a steer out of him. Or you might want to brand the animal and earmark it so no one could dispute ownership.

Everett came out of the house and walked out to the corral and asked if I needed help getting the hay unloaded.

"I can always use help," I said. "I can pull it out of the trunk, but Dad and I had a hell of a time getting it into the car behind the seat last night." There was a kind of shed with only a roof made of palm tree branches, and that was where we wanted to stack the hay. It might keep the water off in a rainstorm, which were few and far between. But after all, this was winter, so anything could happen. Better to be safe than sorry.

There were tamarack trees scattered around the grounds of the house and corral area, so the place was shaded from the sun if it was a hot day. Over to the side of the big swinging gate, there were two poles set into the ground with a six-inch log on top about four feet above the ground. It was intended as a rail to tie up your horse, but we put our newly acquired saddles on it to keep them up off the ground. Dad had hung his bridle from his saddle horn and then looped the reins over the horn as well.

Dad had given me a hackamore instead of a bridle. He said it was easier on the horse's mouth because there's no bit through the horse's mouth. The hackamore had a chain that went behind the horses jaw. So when you pulled on the reins, it put pressure on the horse's jaw making him stop, or if you released it, you let him go on. I still prefer them over a bridle to this day. It's easy on the horse's mouth, as I said, and they aren't always fidgeting with the bit. I had my hackamore hanging over my saddle horn too; I wanted to be just like my dad.

We laid our saddle blankets on top of the saddles, giving them a little protection from the weather. I lifted my saddle blanket off so I could throw my leg over the saddle and sit down. It was the first time I had sat in it. It felt pretty good too, but the stirrups were a little bit long for my legs. Stirrups are adjustable. I didn't know how to do it, but I knew my dad would. Dad knew everything about horses except how to be kind to them. He would beat the hell out of them if they didn't behave.

Dad walked out on the porch of the house and hollered for us to come to breakfast, or he would throw the stuff out. He didn't have to call me twice. I jumped out of my new saddle and told Everett, "Let's go eat." I told him I was hungry, and he said, "Me too." He almost sounded like our brother Orville, who had run away last spring. *Me too, me too, me too.*

THE 1928 CHEVY TRUCK

The next morning, after we had eaten breakfast, Dad said, "Let's go see if we can get that old truck of Sam's started. Everett can clean up the dishes and look after Sam while he and I worked on the Chevy truck. The truck was parked along the right side of the corral, just beyond the shed where we put the four bales of hay the night before. The 1928 Chevy truck was a flatbed with an oak floor bed.

Dad had to clean all sorts of trash and limbs off the truck before he could open the hood on the motor. When he lifted the side of the hood, I could see it was an overhead valve engine. I didn't even know they made an overhead valve engine as far back as 1928.

Dad picked a long stick up off the ground, took the gas cap off, and stuck the stick into the tank. When he pulled it out it was dry as a bone. Dad turned to me and said, "Son, you and Everett go get the five-gallon gas can from the car and bring it here so we can put a little gas in the truck. Everett and I went to get the gas can from the bumper of our car parked beside Blair's old house.

Sam Blair was standing on the porch of the house, looking old and frail with his walking cane in his hand. He asked what Dick was doing this morning. I said, "Dad's out by the corral trying to get the old truck started."

Sam said, "That's a damn good truck, and it was running a few months ago when we parked it under those trees. We use it for hauling beehives into the shed to extract the honey."

Then he told us it might not have been run in over a year. Then he started telling us about all the bee apiaries they had, eight or ten of them around the river bottom with fifteen hives in each one. But we had worked the hives in a year or more. He kept going on.

If you don't work the hives the wax moths will get into a hive and destroy it. Or the bees will make a new queen, and the new queen will take half of the hive and swarm, leaving the hive weak. If we work the bees often, we can destroy the new queen cell before it has a chance to develop.

He was saying, "If you're there when they swarm, they will land nearby, and then they can be recaptured.

"Okay, Sam," I said. "But Dad's waiting for this gas."

I guess he didn't hear me because he kept talking about foul brood getting into a hive. "They can wipe you out."

"Okay, Sam," I said again, "we need to go. Dad is waiting."

Everett said. "He just told us it was running a few months ago. He don't remember anything anymore. He's old."

I said, "There would be gas still in it if it had only been parked a few months. Dad told me the tank was bone dry."

Everett and I finally were able to tear ourselves away from Sam and his ramblings about bees, and we were able to carry the gas to where Dad was still working on the old truck.

"Where you boys been?" Dad wanted to know. "I thought I was going to have to come get you," he said.

I told him, "Sam asked what you were doing out here, then started telling us about bees."

Dad had the fuel filter off the fuel pump, and he had cleaned out the glass jar that the little bronze fuel filter was in. He spilled a little fresh gas into the jar then screwed it back on the fuel pump. There was a funnel in the floor of the truck, and Dad got it and stuck it into the gas tank and told me to pour a couple of gallons into the tank. I asked if that would be enough.

"If it's not, we can put more in later. But first, let's see if the damn thing will start."

Dad sat down in the truck and pushed on the starter, but nothing happened. "Son, go drive the car back here so I can use the battery. This truck's battery is deader than a doornail."

"Okay, Dad, but why did you have us carry the five gallons of gas if you wanted the car driven back here?"

"I'm sorry, son. I just wasn't thinking this morning. Now run along and get the car for the old man, will you?"

When I returned with the car, Dad had the wooden floorboards out and was disconnecting the battery cables. Old cars and trucks usually had the batteries under the floor. I pulled the battery out of our car and carried it over and set it into the hole where Dad had taken the dead battery out of the battery box. Once Dad had it connected to the cables, he poured a little gas into the carburetor.

"Okay, son, get in and try it."

The starter was sticking through a hole in the floorboard, but under the dash a little.

"You ready?" I asked.

Dad said, "Go ahead and give it a spin, son."

I put my foot on the starter and pushed it in. *Ewe, ewe, ewe, POW.* It backfired through the carburetor.

Dad said, "Okay, try it again." *Ewe, ewe, ewe, VROOM.* It started up.

"Not too fast till it gets oil pressure up, son," I heard Dad say above the noise of the engine. "Just let it idle kind of slow. It's been sitting a long time."

So I let it idle as I climbed out of the cab to look at the engine. It ran pretty good after it stopped clacking from lack of oil. Dad climbed into the seat and pushed the clutch down and raced the engine a little. Then he shoved the gearshift forward into reverse and backed it up so he could turn it around.

I was watching, and it looked as though it took all his strength just to turn the steering wheel. Dad got out and went over to our car and started removing things from the trunk. Finally, he pulled out what he was looking for—his grease gun. He came back to the truck, and with the engine still running, he lay down behind the front wheel and stuck the grease gun on a grease fitting and gave the handle a pump.

After doing this to four fittings, he went to the other side, and lay down in the dirt and did the same thing again. He put the grease gun on the floorboard and climbed back into the cab and drove it around again, turning it first left, then right, trying to loosen up the steering. He came back to where Everett and I were standing and said, "That's as good as I can get it, son. It's still stiff, but we'll just have to live with it. It's old, I guess. Just like me."

"It will be all right, Dad," I said. He wouldn't be driving it that much anyway.

"I guess you're right, son," he told me as he wiped the dirt and grease off his hands. "Son, let's put the old battery back in and see if the damn thing will hold a charge."

This time I didn't have to ask if it would work because we had done the same thing for the couple stranded outside Salome, Arizona. Dad took the floorboard out again so he could get at the battery. Then with the engine still running, he removed the battery cables and lifted our battery out and put the dead battery back in and reconnected the cables. Once the floorboard was back in place, he said, "Let's let it run for a while and see if the battery will charge back up. While he was putting the battery in the truck, I had carried our battery over to our car and reinstalled it.

Dad said, "Come here, son. I want to show you something." He walked to the front of the truck and said, "See that crank handle hanging there under the radiator? Well, if we have to, we can crank the engine to start it. But let's hope the old battery will hold a charge. Now we need to look into getting some water for us and the horses when we bring them down."

There were several wells on the home site; there was a hand pump at the end of the stove inside the house.

Outside there were two other wells with motors on them. Dad put a little gas into the tank on the engine, and then he cranked it to see if it would start. They were odd-looking gasoline engines with only one cylinder. After cranking it two or three times, Dad pulled the spark plug and cleaned it, then dipped it in the gas can, gave it a shake, and then screwed it back into the engine.

When Dad cranked it this time, it started running, but no water came out of the pipe. "Go get me the water can so I can prime it," he said to no one in particular.

I said, "Hey, Everett, will you help me carry it over here?"

Everett didn't say anything, but he fell into line behind me as I headed to the car for the can of water. The army had thought of everything when they made the gas and water cans. There were three bars on the top for carrying the can. One person carried the can by the center handle, and two people would carry it by the two outside handles.

Dad had me pour a couple quarts of water into the pump to prime it and then set to cranking it again. After a few cranks and a few cusses, the stupid thing finally started, and after a minute or so, some dirty brown water came out of the discharge pipe.

"Let's let it run until the water clears up," Dad told us. "In the meantime, let's go check out the shed where they keep their bee equipment. We need a couple of cans of water to wash in and to do dishes in. We'll keep the water we brought from Blythe for our drinking water."

So with Everett and me following behind, Dad headed for the shed. The shed kept all their bee supplies out of the weather. There were new five-gallon cans that they used to put the extracted honey into. Also there were stacks of wooden beehive boxes that still needed to be assembled. There was a honey extractor sitting in the corner of the shed. Dad told us how it all worked. They would take a hot knife and decap the trays of honey.

Then they would set trays on end in the extractor in a frame made for this purpose. Once the motor started and the trays of honey started spinning, the honey would be spun out of the honeycomb and onto the sides of the extractor tank, where it ran to the bottom of the tank and was drawn off into the five-gallon cans through a spigot on the outside of the tank.

Once the extraction was finished, the cans of honey were loaded onto a truck and taken to the miller honey company and sold. Most of the honey that was collected here in the river bottom was from mesquite trees and desert wildflowers. It was a dark, strong-tasting honey—which was at the bottom of the price scale for honey. Miller Company paid more per gallon for light-colored honey, like clover or orange blossom, which has a milder taste.

"Son, now you know enough about the bee business to start your own bee business," Dad said as he picked up two of the shiny new cans and walked out of the shed.

I saw some woodpeckers flying around in the tamarack trees in the back of the corral. I went into the house and got my .22 rifle so I could shoot one. As I came out on the porch with my rifle, Dad was coming toward me with a honey can filled with water.

Dad asked, "What are you going to do with the gun?"

I told him, "I want to shoot a woodpecker."

"Aww, leave them be, son," Dad said. "Save your ammunition for something we can eat."

"Once you shoot up all the shells, you'll be shit out of luck until we go back to Blythe for supplies."

"I only wanted to shoot one, Dad," I said, hoping he would relent.

"I said leave 'em be, didn't I, son?"

"Yeah, but I just wanted to shoot one, Dad."

"If you want something to do, go carry that other can of water up here to the house for the old man."

"Okay, Dad," I told him as I turned to put my rifle away.

"While you're out getting the other can of water, go over to the truck and kill it. It's been running long enough. That will satisfy your need to kill something," Dad told me.

"Dad, you want me to bring the car back up to the house?" I asked, hoping to get to drive the car. Even a short distance was fun. "And I could load the can of water in the trunk and wouldn't have to carry it."

Dad said, "Suit yourself, son. If you want to drive it back, do it."

Then he said, "We'd head for Blythe in the morning to get the horses from Walter Scott."

The next morning, after breakfast, Dad told Sam we were going into Blythe to pick up the horses from Walt Scott. He told Everett to stay with Sam and to watch the house because Dad said some people used the road coming into the United States illegally. So away we went up the dirt road toward Blythe. We hadn't gone far from the house when we saw four deer crossing the road ahead of us.

"Shoot, Dad, we should have brought a gun with us," I said.

Dad said, "We don't have any time for killing deer today. We're after horses, and I want to get them and get back as soon as we can."

"I don't like to leave your brother and Sam by themselves for too long. I'd like to be back by sundown. Besides, those deer are probably using the same trail to go for water every day. We can come back here and watch the trail if we want fresh meat on another day. Son, we can't do everything at once," Dad told me. "Right now let's worry about getting the horses and getting them trailered down to Blair's property."

It took us about two hours to drive out to Blythe on this old dirt road. Finally, we were back across the river in Blythe, and Dad turned into Walt's driveway going back to his barn. We stopped at the ranch house, and Walt walk out to the car and said, "Good morning, Dick. You here for the horses?"

"That's what I'm hoping," Dad said.

"Well, pull your car around behind the barn there and we'll hook you up to the trailer."

Walt had several trailers parked at the end of the barn. One was a four-horse trailer. Then there was the one we were after—the two-horse trailer.

Dad got out of the car and said, "Son, you back it up, and I'll direct you onto the trailer hitch."

I sat in the car and turned in the seat so I could see Dad behind the car through the rear window. He had his arm high in the air, and I could see he was motioning me back. He waved his hand for me to stop and came up to my window.

"Son, pull ahead and get over. Look at your front end. You're jackknifing the car. Now pull up and keep it straight coming back."

Dad-gummed it, I wish he would do it. How am I supposed to keep it straight if he motions me over?

I tried again, turning the steering wheel as little as possible.

This time I got close enough, and Dad said, "That's good, son. We can scoot it over enough to make it. Kill the engine and come help me."

Walt walked over and helped us too. We didn't have a ball on our trailer hitch, but there was one in the tongue of Walt's trailer. Dad opened the trunk and got a crescent wrench out of the toolbox. I watched as he got the ball out of the hitch and pushed it into our hitch and put the nut on and then tightened it down.

Dad was sitting on the ground so he could pull on the crescent wrench with both hands. He told me he wanted it tight. He didn't want it to come off with the horses in the trailer going back on that rough road.

"Now, son, get in and ease it back." He was turning the crank handle to raise it a little. "Go easy," he told me. "Stop," he hollered. "Goddamn it, son. I told you to go easy. Now pull ahead a little."

I eased the clutch out and felt the hitch engage the ball. "Hold it," Dad said. "Come back here and give me a hand."

I got out and walked to the back of the car. Dad was cranking it all the way down on the ball.

"Son, crawl under the car and hook the safety chain."

There was an eye on the side of the hitch, and I stuck the chain through it and hooked the hook back on the chain."

Dad told me to pull the car and trailer over to the barn, where Walt had brought out the horses. One of them was a sorrel, and the other was a bay with a black mane and tail.

Walt said, "The sorrel mare is Nancy, and the bay gilding is Mike."

Dad let the tailgate down on the trailer, and Walt led the mare into it while Dad led Mike in and tied them off. Then Walt and Dad lifted the tailgate and stuck the pins into the locks.

Walt told Dad, "They're both good horses, Dick. The bay gilding is young and will need some training, but he's a good horse. He's smart too. Just give him a gentle hand, and he'll get the job done."

Dad thanked Walt for the horses and told him they would be at Blair's in Cibola.

"Okay, Dick. Tell Sam I said hello," Walt said.

"I'll do that, Walt," Dad said as he got behind the wheel of our car. He started the engine and pulled out of the driveway and turn right on the highway heading back into town.

In East Blythe, Dad pulled in to a Hancock station to top off our gas tank again. While the attendant filled the tank, Dad checked the trailer hitch and safety chain to make sure they were tight. When Dad was satisfied, we got back into the car and continued east again and crossed the river.

When Dad turned into the dirt road going south toward Cibola, he pulled over and said, "Okay, son, your turn to drive."

Well, it's about time, I thought. There were so many washes and ravines on this road that with the horse trailer and the horses, I was lucky to get out of second gear most of the time.

The horse trailer was either pushing me or pulling me back with a jerk. And every time I would shift, the trailer jerked on the trailer hitch.

But I was happy because I was driving.

I asked Dad if Walt Scott was any kin to Dave Scott who owned the Shell gas station and store over in Quartzsite.

"No, son, I don't believe there is any connection at all," Dad told me. "Why did you ask, son?"

"Oh, I was just wondering, Dad. Their last names are the same."

"I guess it's just a coincidence, son. There's no connection," Dad replied.

Sometimes I had to shift into low gear to climb out of a wash. A six-cylinder Chevy didn't have a whole lot of power. I had tried to talk Dad into a Ford V8.

"Son," Dad said, about those V8's, when they break down, it's like working on two engines. When you pull the head on a Chevrolet, the valves are in the head, and it's easy to work on. The damn Ford V8, you have to pull two heads. The valves are in the block. You have to buy two head gaskets, two water pump gaskets. The Chevrolet 6 is a good motor."

"Yeah but the V8 has more power," I said. "Well, when you buy yourself a car, you can get a V8, but don't ask me to work on the damn thing."

I was headed southwest as I came up out of the wash, and the sun was right in my eyes. I couldn't see shit. I was in second gear with the gas pedal all the way to the floor, trying to keep up my speed so I wouldn't have to downshift into low on a steep grade. I came flying up the road and broke over the top, and the sun was blinding me.

All of a sudden, the front end of the car came up off the ground as the car rolled over something. As whatever it was rolled under the car, it shook and reeled like crazy. I stepped on the brakes.

Dad was cussing like a son of a bitch. "Goddamn you, what the hell you doing? For Christ's sake, you knew the goddamn road turned right at the top of this ridge and went west! Goddamn, son of a bitchin'.

Goddamn luck to hell." He was still cussing a blue streak as we got out to see what had happened.

The road had turned west, and Dad could see it from the passenger's seat, but with the sun in my eyes, I didn't see the turn and ran the car up on some big rocks that had been graded up on the side of the road. Some of the rocks were at least a foot in diameter. With my speed and the weight of the horse trailer, it had pushed me right up on top of them. Dad was down on his knees, looking under the car.

"Goddamn, son of a bitchin', goddamn, son of a bitchin' luck to hell. How much god damn bad luck must a man endure in his lifetime?"

I wasn't saying anything, as I felt my life was in danger.

"Goddamn it to hell. All the goddamn oil has run out."

It tore a gash about seven inches long in the oil pan up about one and a half inches from the bottom of the pan.

"I'll be going to hell if this isn't a fine how do you do."

I was just hanging back and not saying anything. I knew I had really done it this time. I didn't know what we were going to do. We were still five miles from Blair's land. Dad opened the trunk and got the jack out. Then he carried it to the front of the car and threw it down.

Then he got down on his knees again. I was afraid to ask what we were going to do.

Dad had stopped cussing, and I didn't want to irritate him by asking questions. He had the car jacked up and was trying to roll some of the big rocks out from under the car.

I said, "Is there anything I can do, Dad?"

"For Christ's sake, haven't you done enough already?"

I felt so bad. I knew I had ruined things for us.

"Dad, I couldn't see the road. The sun was right in my eyes. I didn't know the road turned!"

"Aw, the hell you didn't!"

I shut up and just sat down on a rock. I would just have to let Dad figure out what to do. Lord knows I didn't know what to do, but we were in a fix. Dad was under the front end of the car with a pry bar he carried in the trunk. He rolled a couple more rocks out and then went to the back of the horse trailer and undid the tailgate. Then he took out the bay horse named, Mike.

Mike had a halter on and a rope tied to it.

"Here, get your ass on this horse and go on to Blair's and get that old Chevy truck and come back and tow the car home," Dad said. "You think you can do that without screwing it up?"

I told him, "I guess so."

"Well, get your ass up on this horse, then," Dad told me again. He gave me a leg up and said, "Look around the ranch for a chain or some kind of cable, anything we can make a tow rope out of."

"Okay, Dad," I said.

Then he said, "Son, if that battery won't start the truck, you have to crank it. Son, if you have to crank it to start it, don't push down on the crank handle. Hook the crank on the left side and give a quick jerk. If it doesn't start, set the crank again and give it another quick jerk. If you come up with the crank and go over the top and push down on the crank, it might kick back and break your arm. Bring Everett back with you, as we might need some help," he told me.

So I started for Blair's house, and I was feeling really bad. I didn't do it on purpose. I was blinded by the sun. I had really ruined our engine. Boy, Dad was really mad. I thought, *It's probably not a good time to ask if we could buy a Ford V8 if this engine is ruined. Shoot, it will be dark before I can go to the ranch and come back in that old truck.*

I guess I had gone about a mile when I heard a car coming from behind me. I turned on the horse to look and saw it was Dad in the car with the horse trailer.

He stopped beside me and said, "I took a stick and a piece of inner tube and stuck it in the hole in the oil pan. I started the engine, and it held oil pressure, so let's load that horse in and get the hell on down the road. As long as we take it easy and keep our oil pressure, we'll be okay."

So he opened the tailgate and put Mike back in, and away we went, with Dad driving, of course. *I never want to drive again*, I was thinking. I didn't say anything to Dad, especially about us getting a Ford with a V8 engine.

We were almost to the ranch now, and there was a bad spot in the road on a curve where there was a sand pocket just before we reached Blair's place.

The road was all torn to hell where fishermen had gotten stuck going down to Martinez Lake to fish. Well, Dad got the car stuck too. "Son, go get that truck while I dig the son of a bitch out, and don't dally around." There were pieces of plywood lying in the road where others had been stuck here in the same spot.

I started walking, and I could see the ranch house a short ways down the road, not even a quarter mile. Dad said, "If we had saddles and a rope, we could pull the goddamn thing out with the horses." It was late, and Dad didn't want to leave the car stuck there without lights on it.

I walked on to Blair's house, and the truck started up the first time I stepped on the starter. I was looking for a chain to tow our car out. Sam was standing on the porch and said there were some old chains in the bee-extracting house. I looked and found a rusty chain about ten feet long, thrown into a corner of the house. I threw it into the truck and told Everett to get in. He shut his door, and I took off up the road.

Dad had the car ready to pull out. He had dug out from under the front of the tires. He also had a couple pieces of wood lying in the ruts ahead of the rear tires. I thought he was going to try to drive the car out in case I couldn't get the truck started. I backed up to the front of our car, and Dad hooked the chain around the bumper. He climbed into the driver's seat and motioned for me to start.

So with me pulling and Dad driving the car, we were able to get it out of the sand holes in the road. Dad was waving out of the window for me to stop. I stopped, and he and Everett unhooked the chain, and I let him pass me, and I followed him on to Blair's house. We unloaded the horses and put them into the corral and called it a day.

Dad still had to fix supper as Sam and Everett hadn't eaten yet. They were waiting for us to come home. Everett asked what had taken so long, and I told him I had driven the car over some big rocks that had torn a big gash into the oil pan. After supper, I was tired, and I still felt bad about wrecking our car, so I went to bed. Let Dad tell how a numbskull had wrecked the car on purpose, but I didn't want to hear it all again as I had lived through it, although barely. If Dad's looks could kill, I'd be dead.

The next morning, we were up with the chickens. Dad made breakfast while Everett and I went out to give the two horses a flake of hay apiece. Dad had poured some water into a pump to prime it and had the hand pump working. So Everett and I pumped water into a couple of two-gallon galvanized buckets and carried water to the horses.

It was cold this morning, and we had our collars turned up on our coats. Our breath was like steam coming from our nose. You could see the horse's breath too. They nickered at us when we carried the flakes of hay to them. They were more interested in the hay than the water we were carrying to fill the water trough. Working the pump handle warmed us up, but I had my coat sleeves pulled over my hands because the iron handle was so cold. Most mornings, we found out there would be ice on top of the water trough. It was damn cold in that river bottom in the wintertime.

After breakfast, Dad told Sam, "We're going to ride out west toward the river and see what the situation looked like."

Everett was to do the dishes and stay with Sam.

So with our horses saddled with our newly acquired saddles, we rode out of the yard and down a fence line going west. The fence was barbed wire and was in pretty good shape. Once in a while, we would see a strand of wire hanging down where the staples had pulled out maybe a cow or a deer had run into the fence, knocking the staples out.

We rode up on a slough with brush growing almost as high as we were on the horses, and Dad turned his horse toward an opening in the brush and spurred his horse into the water, which was about four feet deep.

The water had a layer of ice on it about a quarter-inch thick. The ice broke as the horse's hooves stepped into the water. I saw Dad lift his legs high up on the saddle so he wouldn't get his boots wet, and I did the same. As cold as it was, if your boots got wet and your britches legs got wet, I'll bet they wouldn't dry all day.

In cowboy movies, I saw John Wayne and others ride into rivers and just let their boots and britches stay in the stirrups. Their boots just filled up with water. What a bunch of crap. Nobody would leave their boots in the stirrup and let them fill with water. I guess they wanted to look like men and show they were tough, but I'll tell you, it just wasn't so. No idiot would let their boots fill with water if they could just lift them up. I was sorry for our horses having to wade into the cold water, but they didn't seem to mind at all.

It wasn't very wide, just four or five steps, and we were going up the opposite bank. I saw Dad turn in his saddle to see if I had gotten wet. He smiled at me, and I could tell he was glad to be riding horseback again. I was excited about riding through the river bottom in search of wild cattle, but it would have been better if I weren't so cold. And just sitting in a saddle riding a horse wasn't' doing anything to get you warmed up.

Dad often pointed at some tracks and made a motion with his hand, which way the animal was traveling. Often, he would stop looking at a set of tracks, and he would say, "Deer tracks, and they look fresh," or maybe, "cattle tracks, and they are old." Tracks would look fresh a long time if the wind didn't blow or if there wasn't any rain, especially in this wet-looking alkali ground. Most of the trails where cattle tracks were predominant, they went into tules where the cattle would feed on young shoots growing from the main tule stalk.

The tules were so thick you couldn't see into them at all. Sometimes we would be riding on a trail into the tules, and we would hear cattle running out through the tules and never get to see them. We would just hear them run, breaking trails through the brush and tules. Dad had his loop made like he wanted it with the coils of the rope lying over the saddle horn and his loop lying on top of the coils. That way, he was always ready in a flicker of the eye.

That afternoon, we had been riding all day, and as yet, we hadn't seen a darned animal. We had ridden all over the place. We heard them running through the tules several times, but we hadn't seen them. There were a lot of tracks, though. We were still riding through heavy brush and mesquite, but we were heading in a direction that was taking us toward the homeplace. Dad was leading the way, as he always did, and as we came around some heavy brush and mesquite trees, he held his hand up and reined in his horse. He reached for his rope and lifted it from the saddle horn. Then with his loop in his right hand and the rope coils in his left hand, he motioned me forward as he pointed ahead and to the right.

That's when I saw four cows behind a mesquite thicket. Dad motioned for me to go to the right around the thicket as he turned his horse, Nancy, to the left. There was a big opening for about thirty yards on the left. I knew he wanted me to go slowly to the right, and as I did, the cows were watching me. I couldn't be quiet because it was brushy going this way. The four cows watched me for a minute or two. Then I could tell they were spooked. The biggest cow turned and started moving away from the mesquite trees, and I spurred my horse into a lope so I would come out on the right side of the cattle.

I don't think the cattle were watching my dad because they went almost straight away from him. I looked to see Dad with the loop of the rope on his shoulder, and he spurred his horse, and the chase was on. I knew he didn't want the cattle to break back to the right and into the brush. So I spurred Mike, the horse I was riding, into a full gallop. So there I was, riding full gallop through the mesquite trees. I had to lift my left elbow, trying to block the mesquite limbs with thorns about two inches long from striking me in the face. I would lean right, then left in the saddle, trying to stay clear of the mesquite branches. I also had to watch my horse to make sure that he didn't try going under a low limb and drag me off. YEEHAW, I was flying going after these cattle, and having fun doing it too.

As I came around the thicket, Dad was right on the biggest cow's tail with his loop swinging around his head. I saw his arm shoot forward, and the loop landed over the cow's head, as sweet as you please. Dad turned his horse left, away from the cow, and kept the rope tight as the cow hit the end of the rope. I reined my horse in, turning him to where Dad was fighting with the cow. "Son, see if you can get your loop under the back legs if you can, and we'll pull her down. I had my rope off and made a loop. I spurred Mike right up to the cow and laid the loop right on the cow's legs, and it stepped right into it, and I pulled it tight.

Mike was excited and fidgeting around, but I dallied the horn several times and pulled back on the reins, and Mike backed up, and the cow fell sideways into the alkali dirt.

My dad was telling me, "Keep it tight, son. Don't let it get up. Nancy had the rope around the cow's head and pulled tight on the other side. Dad took out his pocketknife, which he kept sharp as a razor, and cut an earmark into the cow's right ear. Then he took his knife and shaved the hair off the right hip, making a hip O. "That will do until we can do the real thing," Dad said. He told me to walk my horse up to give him some slack so he could get my rope off the cow. The cow didn't know it could get up, so it lay there with its ear bleeding where Dad cut the earmark.

Dad walked over to Nancy and stepped into the stirrup and swung his leg up and settled into the saddle. Dad nudged Nancy up close to the cow and dallied the rope, leaving about eight feet of slack. He turned Nancy toward the ranch house and started dragging the cow, and finally, she got to her feet and tried to pull away. I was right behind prodding her along with the end of my rope. It was a kind of drag, stumble, and fall for a while then the critter started to lead.

Every once in a while, it would balk or try to run to the side. But Dad would just jerk it back, and he was watching to make sure that the cow didn't hit Nancy with its horns. It took about an hour for us to get back to the corral. Dad threw a loop around the snubbing post and pulled the cow up with its head against the post. Dad left Nancy holding the rope around the post and went to our car and got a handsaw and came back and sawed about an inch off of both horns. Then he turned the cow loose.

Dad said, "The cow will stay in the corral with the horses. With the horns cut off, they can't hurt the horses." We gave the cow and horses each a flake of hay, and then we headed to the house so Dad could start our supper. I mean, I was starving. I was ready to eat the tips of the horns that Dad cut off that cow.

The next day, Dad and I rode all day and never saw a cow of any kind. We were seeing plenty of cattle tracks, but the river bottom was just too brushy. There are so many trails in and out of the tules, and we would hear animals but didn't see them. A cold wind was blowing out of the north, and I for one was glad to go home.

Dad said, "You boys still have time, so why don't you get the old truck and drive south into the mesquite trees and cut some mistletoe."

He wanted us to get as much as we could so we could feed it to the cow. Dad said he would see to fixing supper while we were gone. At least this old truck had glass in it so the wind didn't hit us.

Everett said, "You guys didn't catch any cows today?"

"No," I told him. "The river bottom is so brushy we couldn't see very far."

"What are you going to do?" he asked.

Dad said, "We might have to burn the river bottom so we can see."

"How you going to burn it?" Everett asked.

"Hell, I don't know." Dad was talking about touching a match to it.

"Won't we get into trouble if someone sees it burning?" Everett asked.

I said, "They can't see it all the way to Blythe. We'll probably just burn a little at a time." I got to where I was going and pulled the truck up under the old mesquite trees, which had a lot of mistletoe growing in them. Young trees didn't have any.

Everett and I drove out and we just pulled the truck up under a tree and took a hatchet to chop the mistletoe loose and let it fall into the back of the old truck. After three or four trees, we had the back of the truck full. We drove back and opened the corral gate and pulled the truck over against the backside of the corral and we kicked all the mistletoe off onto the ground.

The cow wouldn't come near us; she did lower her head and paw the dirt as if warning us to stay away. It was damn cold again today, and I had worn my peacoat all day trying to stay warm. Everett was wearing a warm coat as well, but at least he had been in the house most of the day. We drove out of the gate and put the truck away. Then we headed to the house.

BURNING THE RIVER BOTTOM

It was getting late when we came in. Dad was fixing supper on the wood stove. Sam Blair was sitting in a chair close to the stove, warming his hands. He asked me if I had found a lot of mistletoe, and I said I had. He said, "Sometimes when feed is scarce, by knocking mistletoe onto the ground, the cattle will come in to feed on it, and we could catch them that way and not have to ride all over hell and have half of Georgia looking for them."

Dad stopped stirring the beans he was cooking on the stove.

"No, Sam, I'm going to ride out into the tules tomorrow and set the goddamn things on fire." The brush and tules and goddamn salt cedar are too thick and high to see the cattle, let alone have room to chase the sons of bitches."

Sam said, "That will be all right, Dick, but you know it will burn for days, don't you?"

"I know that, Sam, but I have more time than money right now. And I'll have to repair that oil pan on the car before we can drive it much."

"Well, all right, Dick," Sam said, "but you better start the fire in a lot of places, or else the fire will burn up to a slough and burn itself out."

Dad told Sam he intended to do that very thing. He told Sam he would take me with him and ride all over the river bottom, setting fires by throwing matches into the tules. "That's the only way for us to clear an opening, Sam."

"You boys better get ready. I'll have supper ready in just a jiffy," Dad said as he wiped his hands on a dishtowel. After we had eaten our supper, Dad took out his violin and tuned it and then started to play a song I'd heard him play many times.

I am a roving gambler I've gambled all around.
Whenever I meet with a deck of cards, I lay my money down.
I had not been in Washington many more weeks than three,
When I fell in love with a pretty little girl, and she fell in love with me. She took me in her parlor; she cooled me with her fan.
She whispered low in her mother's ear,
I love this gambling man,
Love this gambling man.
Love this gambling man.
Daughter, oh dear daughter, why do you treat me so,
To leave your poor dear mother, and with a gambler go,
With a gambler go, with a gambler go.
Mother, oh dear mother, I'll tell you if I can,
If you ever see me coming back, I'll be with a gambling man.
With a gambling man, lord with a gambling man.

So the next morning, Everett and I went out to the corral and gave the horses each a flake of hay. Then after breakfast, we saddled them up. Dad had carried his single-barrel shotgun with him as he came from the house, and he shoved it into the scabbard on my horse and put two boxes of number 4 shotgun shells into my saddlebags.

"Just in case we see any ducks," Dad told me.

I was thinking, *Maybe he will let me shoot them.* At least I was hoping he would.

He then said, "Three or four ducks would be good for supper, wouldn't they, son?"

"You bet," I told him.

It was cold this morning, and Dad had his sheepskin-lined leather coat on. I wore an old navy peacoat that was good and warm. Dad climbed up on Nancy, and we rode west around the tamarack trees at the south end of the corral and down a fence line that went all the way to the river. The horses' breath was visible again this morning, so it was cold. Again we had to break the ice on the slough, holding our boots up high out of the water so they stayed dry. No cold, wet feet for us. We rode through mesquite trees until we reached the south end of Blair's property where it ended at the river.

There was a slight breeze blowing this morning out of the south. Dad took out his box of matches and struck one and threw it into the tules in one quick motion. Then he sat there looking at the match to see if it would start burning. It didn't, so Dad swung down from his horse and handed me his reins to hold while he struck another match and then held it under some of the cattails, or tules as Dad called them, until they caught fire. It didn't take them long to flare up into a pretty good blaze.

Dad stepped back aboard Nancy and said, "Come on, son, let's move out."

As we rode on, I looked back to see the fire and smoke were going really good. Dad was still trying to get the fires to start by striking the match and throwing it into the tules without getting off his horse. He told me, "We should have done this later in the day since the tules were damp from the morning dew."

He handed me the box of matches and said, "Son, let me see you start one."

"Okay," I said as I climbed down from Mike.

"Son, hold it to the underside of the tules where they are driest," Dad said from behind me.

I had to use a couple of matches, but they finally started to burn. I stood there watching them burn, and Dad said, "Come on, son, let's keep moving. We don't want this fire to catch up to us."

"I was just making sure it didn't go out," I told him as I handed the box of matches back to him.

The first fire Dad had started was really burning by now as the sky filled with black smoke.

We just kept riding and throwing matches, but if a fire didn't start, one of us would climb down and hold a match right under the tules until they did start. Sometimes if the fire flared up too fast, it would spook the horses, and they would fidget, wanting to be on the way.

After a half hour or so, it looked as though the whole river bottom was on fire. Flames and black smoke were billowing up all around us. Dad was looking back south from which we came and said, "Son, let's get the hell out of here before some son of a bitch comes snooping around. Hell, son, it looks like an oil well on fire. They might send an aeroplane down from Blythe to investigate," Dad said as he spurred his horse into a lope with me right behind him as we rode up through the mesquite trees, shittin' and gittin'.

Soon we were back at the slough, but the ice was already broken this time. We crossed it and the fence where it was lying on the ground and turned up the fence line for the homeplace. As we did, Dad kicked Nancy into a gallop, and I did the same with Mike. I loved to gallop the horses, but only for a short distance, maybe a quarter mile or so. Then we would go back to walking them. I still remember how much fun I had riding around Blair's ranch with my dad.

Sam and Everett were standing out in the yard looking at all the smoke as we rode back to the corral. Sam said, "Looks like you did a fine job, Dick. That fire will burn for days."

Then he asked if we had seen any cattle, and Dad said, "No, but they're in there, all right. I saw a lot of tracks coming and going in several washes down by Lopez old place."

The next day, we stayed around the ranch house because Dad wanted to get the oil pan off the car so he could fix the hole that had been sliced into it when I ran off the road.

"We can't go very far in the car until it's fixed," Dad told us. "Besides, the fire in the tules is still burning going north up the river." We could still see the black smoke from the house. Dad said, "We'll wait a day or two before going back into the river bottom to see if our fire did any good.

Dad told Everett and me to go take care of the horses, give them each a flake of hay. "When you're done, son, take that old truck and you and Everett go haul more mistletoe up to the corral. Be sure you check the gas in the tank before you go. I didn't put much in it until I knew it would run. That gas gauge doesn't work, so you'll have to put a stick into the tank, son," Dad said as he headed out to work on the car.

"Can I take my rifle in case I see a deer?" I asked.

"Yeah, go ahead, son, but don't shoot an old strong buck. Shoot a young doe."

"What if a buck is all I see, Dad?"

"Then shoot the son of a bitch," came Dad's reply.

"But you just said to shoot a doe."

"Never mind what I just said. Shoot whatever comes into sight. Now get the hell on out of here and leave me be."

"Okay, so it's okay to shoot a buck?" I wanted to make sure I had him right.

"Goddamn it, what did I just tell you? Now get the hell on out and get that mistletoe before I take that gun and shoot you with the son of a bitch." That was how Dad talked to us. But he was cool too. Remember, he grew up with the Indians.

So Everett and I checked the tank for gas and put five gallons into it from one of the gas cans. I flipped the ignition switch to On and stepped on the starter. It went *Eeew, eeew, eew,* and then nothing. The stupid battery was dead as a doornail.

"Everett, run tell Dad the truck won't start, will you?"

Everett said, "Want me to take the battery out of the car again?"

I said, "Just tell Dad and see what he wants to do."

When he left, I tried the starter once more, but nothing happened. I guess we didn't run the engine long enough to charge up the battery. I got out of the truck and lifted the floorboards up so we could get at the battery. I saw Dad and Everett approaching, but they didn't have the battery from the car. Dad said he wanted to try cranking the engine to start it. The crank was attached to the truck under the radiator so it wouldn't come out. Dad pushed it in with the crank handle on the left side of the engine. Then he gave the crank a quick jerk with his right hand. *Che, che.* It made a hissing sound, but it didn't start.

"Son, get up here where you can see me, so next time you'll know how to do this," Dad said. He put the crank back into the slot under the radiator on the right side, but this time the crank handle was at the top. He said, "Now, son, this is how not to do it." Then he put the crank back the right way and gave it another jerk. This time it started. "Son, you think you can do it now?" he asked.

I told him, "I think so."

Dad told me to never spin the crank, "Son, if it backfires, it can break your arm. Now, when you get over to the mistletoe, don't kill the engine. Just let it run."

"Okay, Dad," I said. "Everett, you ready? Let's go!"

We jumped into the truck and were off, with Everett holding my rifle between his legs. I told Everett to keep his eyes peeled for deer. I was driving again. What a good day, just bouncing along through the brush, making our road as we went with no one to tell me to slow down.

This old Chevy truck made a lot of racket and was rough to ride in, but I still liked to drive it. It sat up high off the ground, so if I came to brush or weeds that weren't too high, I just drove right over them instead of going around them. I pulled up under a mesquite tree with a lot of mistletoe in it, and Everett got out and stood on the truck bed. Then he swung up into the tree so he could knock the mistletoe loose.

We also had a shovel, so we could just reach up and knock some out. I would tromp on it with my feet so we could haul more. The mistletoe came out of the trees looking like tumbleweeds. Stomping on it flattened it out, and once we had all we could get on the truck, we went back to the ranch house. We never saw a deer. Oh well, maybe next time.

When we got back to the corral, we unloaded the mistletoe on the outside. We didn't want it all eaten up at once. We had a pretty big pile close to the corral, so all we had to do was throw it over. I left the truck sitting where I had stopped it and went on to see how Dad was doing working on the car.

Shoot, he already had the pan removed and the gash, about six inches long, pounded down flat, leaving just a seam in the metal to solder. He had his blowtorch fired up and was heating his soldering iron. I was watching him pour some soldering acid into a glass jar and then cut a big piece of zinc from a canning jar lid and dropped it into the acid.

"Why did you do that, Dad?" I asked?

"Son, you have to cut the acid with zinc, or it won't make the solder stick to the metal. Acid cleans the metal so the solder will adhere to the iron pan."

Dad's big soldering iron was made from copper. It had an iron handle and a wood end on it. He dipped the soldering tip into the acid when it was hot and brushed acid onto the pan. Then with his chunk of solder, he soldered the seam shut.

He said, "This is only a temporary fix. When we get back to Blythe, we will go to a wrecking yard and buy a new one off of a junker."

Once the oil pan was fixed, he scooted back under the car with a speed wrench and put the oil pan into place with two bolts. Then he asked me to put the remaining bolts into the pan and run them up tight. I always liked to work on cars, and I liked learning about engines.

"Get them tight, son, but don't twist them off."

Dad would be cussing because he couldn't see when he worked under a car. "Goddamn. A man ought to die when he can't see anymore. None of this horseshit about wearing glasses. You're either too close or too far away."

Dad never had a pair of prescription glasses. Most of the time, he would try on pair after pair in a secondhand store and buy what he thought would be a good pair.

I got the oil pan on and wiped off the excess Permatex gasket seal he had put on the old gasket to make it seal again.

Dad was putting oil back into the engine, and when I finished under the car, we took out the block and let the car down. Then I started the engine and checked for leaks.

"Good job, son," Dad told me. "There are no leaks."

We were done by two o'clock, so Dad said, "Son, why don't we saddle the horses and ride out into the river bottom and see if our fire has done us any good."

"Okay, Dad, but can we make a sandwich out of deviled ham before we go, because I'm hungry."

"Good idea. Let's go get something to eat!"

After lunch, we saddled our horses once again, but this time we rode south toward the Lopez ranch and Martinez Lake, formed by the water backed up behind the Imperial Dam in Yuma. The fire was still billowing up black and gray smoke as it burned north up the river on the Arizona side. We were following in the truck tracks Everett and I had made going out to gather mistletoe.

Dad, as always, was riding in the lead, because he knew every foot of this ranch. He looked up into the sky west of us and pointed at about twenty ducks that the fire had probably driven out. He said, "Son, see the way they have their wings set, like they are gliding?" I said yeah, and he said, "They are going to land on one of the sloughs up ahead. We'll see if we can get a couple for supper."

We were both watching for them to land as we rode through the brush and mesquite trees. Finally, they dropped out of sight behind some cottonwood trees a quarter mile ahead.

"Let's keep our eyes peeled and make sure that they don't take off again," Dad said as we headed the horses in the direction of the cottonwoods.

I saw Dad swing his arm, motioning me forward alongside of him, and he told me, "Pull that shotgun out of the scabbard and hand it to me, son. Now reach back there in those saddlebags and get me a box of shells."

I handed Dad the shells. He took six shells from the box and handed the box back to me. I watched as he broke the shotgun open and put a shell into the chamber and then closed the gun. Then he put the other shells into his coat pocket, but he kept two in his hand. He told me that when we got to where the ducks landed, he would get down and try to sneak up on them, and for me to stay back with the horses.

"Okay, Dad. I hope you get some," I told him.

"If they haven't swam off, or flown off, I'll do my best son," he said. "If they are still on the water, I'll have them dead to rights, and you can bet money on it."

When the horses were even with where we had last seen the ducks and figured they landed, Dad stepped down from his horse and handed me the reins without saying anything. He crouched down and started moving through the brush toward the slough. I didn't see or hear anything for twenty or thirty minutes. I was wondering if the ducks were still on the water, or if they had even landed at all.

We couldn't see them because the brush and salt cedar was so high. I was thinking they might have come down close to the water and kept flying a long ways. I've seen ducks do that many times. The horses had their ears pointed in the direction that Dad had gone. I felt that they knew right where he was, when all of a sudden, *BAM, BAM.*

I heard Dad shoot two shots really fast. And about fifty ducks rose up into the sky above the cottonwood trees. *QUACK, QUACK, QUACK.* They were all quacking as they flew off down the slough and out of sight. The horses had thrown their heads into the air as they looked toward the direction of the shots, which was a lot farther south than Dad had gone into the brush. I didn't know if Dad would come back the way he had gone in or if he would walk straight out from where he had shot.

I decided to stay put where Dad had left me until he came back into view. After about ten minutes, Dad walked out of the salt cedars a hundred yards south of me, and I started the horses toward him on my right. I didn't see him carrying anything but his shotgun, as far as I could see, so I guessed he must have missed the ducks. He walked up to the horses and told me he had shot two on the water, then another one in the air as they were flying away.

He told me two were mallard drakes and one was a hen.

He walked over and took my rope down off my saddle. "If the wind won't blow them to us or we can't splash them in by throwing chunks into the water, I may have to rope them and pull them to us," Dad told me. "Son, let's tie these horses up to this tree and go get them. It's getting late." Dad led his horse over to a mesquite tree. He tied his horse with a short rope, which he called a pigging string. Then he took another short rope from my saddle and tied my horse to the same tree.

With Dad leading the way, we pushed our way through the brush to the slough.

Dad said he had crawled on his hands and knees through the brush until he was close to the slough, trying to be quiet. The bank of the slough was mostly clear of brush ten feet from the edge of the water. There was a little breeze blowing from the south, and two of the ducks, a drake and a hen, had blown in fairly close to shore. Dad said the other drake was a little farther out because that was the one that he had shot when they lifted off the water.

Dad went along the bank of the slough and picked up sticks and rocks—anything he could find to throw that would make ripples so the duck would wash toward the shore. The wind was bringing it in toward the bank, but not fast enough. He was throwing big chunks of wood over the ducks so the ripple would carry it to him on the bank. I found a long branch lying back in the brush, and I was using it to pull the two ducks close to shore into the bank where I was standing.

Mallards are really pretty ducks—at least the drakes are. The hen didn't have much color, just brown.

"Hey, Dad, you want me to start plucking these ducks?" I hollered.

"Go ahead, son. I'll have this other one in a little bit."

I got back into the brush so the feathers wouldn't blow everywhere and got down on my knees and started picking. The duck was still warm, so the feathers came out easily, and it wasn't long before I had them both picked clean.

Dad came over with the other drake and said, "Son, you pick this one while I start cleaning the insides out."

Soon we were done, and we carried them over to the horses. Dad pulled an old leather shoelace from his coat pocket and tied the three ducks heads together and then hung them around my saddle horn.

"Okay, son, let's head for the house and cook these birds for supper." He took the shell out of the shotgun so it would be empty and then shoved it into the scabbard on my horse.

Dad climbed back in his saddle and took the loop and coils of rope from around his saddle horn so he would be ready in case he saw any cattle going home that he might be able to throw a noose onto.

Dad looked toward the northwest and said, "The wind is pushing the fire along pretty fast, son."

In all the excitement of shooting the ducks, I had forgotten about the fire. The smoke from the fire looked like it was pretty far away from us.

"The fire will clean out the river bottom pretty good, son," Dad told me. "We'll come back here in a few days, and we can really see what cattle there are in here, and give us an open place to run them down too. The cattle will move out of the river bottom and up on the mesa for a few days, but they'll be back after the new green shoots that will grow back on the tules. And they won't stay away from the water very long, either. It's going to make it a whole lot easier for us to catch them once this fire runs its course."

We arrived back at the ranch house late in the afternoon. Dad said, "Son, you and Everett take care of putting the horses away while I take these birds into the house and get them baking in the oven. Give the horses a couple of flakes of hay apiece tonight."

I told Everett, "I hope it won't take long to cook them because I'm hungry."

Everett said, "There's some bacon left from breakfast. We could eat piece so we don't starve until the ducks are cooked."

"Well, it can't be too soon for me. Let's get the horses fed," I told him.

Everett was a big help getting the saddles off the horses. We gave them both two flakes, like Dad had said, and one for the cow. Everett already had the horse trough full of water. That was a big help as he had to hand-pump the water into a bucket and then carry it out to the corral and dump it into the trough. Most of the time, if we came home across the slough, we let the horses water before crossing. But if we came north on the east side of the ranch, there was no water available for our horses, and they would be thirsty when we got home. Especially after eating hay.

When Everett and I finished with the horses, we headed for the house. Dad had a good fire going in the stove because I saw smoke coming from the stovepipe on the roof. I was cold coming into the house, but once inside, it was toasty warm. I washed up and went over to stand by the stove and watched Dad roll out some dough for making biscuits. He already had the ducks in the oven, and he took a canning jar lid and used it for a biscuit cutter. He cut the biscuits out and wiped them on his greased pan and then turned them over and laid them down in the pan. He had twelve in all when he was done.

Once in a while, he opened the oven door to check on the ducks to see how they were coming along. I was standing between the table and the stove while Dad was busy getting supper ready.

"Can I do anything to help, Dad?" I asked.

"You can stay the hell out of my way, that's what you can do," he told me in no uncertain terms. "I'll have this ready in just a bit," he said as he opened the oven and slipped the pan of biscuits in the rack above the pan with the ducks in it. "Were gonna have some good eats here, and it won't be long now. Sam, you better get washed up. These vittles will be ready directly," Dad said, wiping his hands on a dishcloth. "Don't let these boys beat you to it, Sam. Paul, you and Everett get those lamps lit so we'll have a little light on the subject. Then sit your ass down at the table."

All we had were two coal oil lamps, but they gave off plenty of light to eat by. As Sam came over to sit down, he asked if there were many ducks on the river and the sloughs behind the house this winter. Dad told him there were quite a few.

"Did you see any geese, Dick?" Sam asked.

"Only flying over, Sam. They have all been flying south. Probably landing on the lake behind Imperial Dam at Yuma," Dad said.

"Dick, if you get a chance, will you kill me a goose?" Sam asked. "I sure like them baked in the oven with a little rice stuffing."

"I'll do that, Sam," was dad's reply. "You hear that, son?" Dad said, looking at me. Sam wants us to kill a goose. I think we can oblige him, don't you?"

Dad winked at me, and I said, "We can sure give it a try, Dad."

We didn't stay up late after supper. Once the dishes were done, we just headed for bed. But sometimes Dad and Sam would sit up talking about the old days. And how things had changed since the war.

"Too damn many people going up and down the road nowadays," Sam told Dad. "Used to be you were lucky to see a car once a week. Now there's ten, twelve a day. Always raising a bunch of dust. Why the hell don't people stay home, Dick?"

Before Dad could answer, Sam continued, "Too much money, that's what it is, Dick. Just too goddamn much money. People didn't use to have this kind of money. If they did, they had to save it in case of a crop failure."

Dad said, "I guess you're right, Sam. It's not like it used to be, that's for sure. The world has seen a lot of changes, Sam, since we were kids. Well, Sam, I think I'll turn in. These old bones are getting tired," I heard Dad tell Sam as I was dozing off. "I'll see you in the morning, Sam."

"All right, Dick," was Sam's reply.

The next morning, I heard Dad cussing because some son of a bitch had stolen his bacon that he was going to make for breakfast. It must be some of those people we had seen walking out on the main road. They were coming from Mexico or Yuma to the south. They had slipped in during the night while we were sleeping and taken the slab of bacon. They were walking north on the road to Blythe, where they were finding work on farms and ranches.

Dad said, "By god, we're going to lock the door tonight and put something against it so we'll be awakened if they try it again. The thieving sons a bitches. Well, I just better not catch them in the act, is all I can say," Dad said. "They better stay the hell down in Mexico where they belong," Dad kept grumbling, mostly to himself.

"How do you know it was them, Dad?" I finally asked Dad.

"Hell, son, you seen anybody else poking around here that would be looking to steal food?" Dad asked.

"I haven't seen anybody, Dad. Just you guys," I told him.

"Well, mark my word, it was Mexicans," Dad said again as he walked to the door and looked out. I guess he expected to see them on the porch or taking a siesta under the trees.

Sam told Dad when he was here working the bees that Mexicans would sometimes stop to ask for *trabajo* ("work"). "No *trabajo*," Sam would tell them. But he said he always gave them water if they were thirsty. Sam said he didn't know of them stealing anything; they just wanted work.

"Well, if I catch them in here taking food, I'll give them a load of number 7's in the behind from this shotgun," Dad told Sam. "But right now, I have to get this breakfast cooked and these boys fed."

As Dad went about fixing breakfast, he was kicking his own ass for not putting the bacon where it wouldn't be found. I was just glad they didn't take my rifle that was standing in the corner by the stove. Boy, I would really be upset if they had. Dad said they didn't want to be seen carrying a gun because somebody would call the law if they saw them with a gun.

We had finished eating breakfast (without bacon, of course) when Dad told me, "Son, lets saddle the horses and see if our handiwork did any good."

With the horses saddled, we rode west down the fence line again.

We came to the end of the fence close to the river's edge and then turned south around the end of the fence through the blackened ground where the fire had gone through the tules. The horses' hooves kicked up ashes as we rode along. I could see sloughs winding inland from the river, with black mesquite stumps left from the fire several days before.

I said, "Dad, I didn't know there were so many sloughs in the river bottom." We saw fresh cow tracks in the ashes, so the cattle were back in here. Dad figured they were in here last evening. Probably as soon as the fire burned on upriver, they had come back looking for food.

We were riding along, and I was looking down for more cow tracks in the ashes when Dad stopped his horse. He was pointing over to his left. I looked to see what he was pointing at and saw a couple of cows back in the brush and mesquite. They were watching us ride past them.

Dad already had his rope out and whipped a loop into it. The cows were just watching us, unconcerned. I reached for my rope, but Dad had already spurred his horse forward. He wasn't waiting for me at all. The cows turned away from us and started to run through the brush and away from the burned tules.

They didn't come out into the open where we could get a good run at them. They were trying to get back through the brush, but Dad was on them in two shakes of a lamb's tail. The cows were in a line in the thick brush, and the lead cow didn't know dad was on their ass. The last one knew, but with the brush being so thick, it couldn't get past the lead cows. Dad's loop circled his head about three times and then shot through the air and settled over the last cow's head.

Dad turned his horse and dragged the cow back out of the brush. The cow looked to be about two years old and was tan colored and skinny as a rail. Most of what the cow had to eat was salt cedar and tules (cattails), or, when the mesquite beans were ripe, they ate them. Dad's throw was right on the money, but he had the cow by the head and not the horns. A cow roped by the horns is easier to handle. I was distracted watching Dad I forgot about the other cattle, and they just disappeared into the brush. Anyway, we had all we could handle with this one. This skinny old cow was full of fight and charged Dad's horse a couple of times. The second time it ran at Nancy, Dad flipped his rope over the cow's rump as it came past him. Then he spurred his horse forward and jerked the cow down when it came to the end of the rope.

Dad motioned me over and said, "Son, get down and put your rope around her horns. Then give me your rope and you take mine."

So I put my loop over the cow's horns and gave the end of the rope to Dad. Then Dad said, "Son, put both your knees on her neck and hold her down while I switch ropes with you." He rode up to the cow while I was holding it down and told me to take his rope from around the neck. So now I had Dad's rope, and he had mine.

I let the cow up and then coiled up Dad's rope and climbed back onto Mike and hung dad's rope around my saddle horn. The cow tried to run past Dad, but Dad just spurred his horse out of the way and jerked the critter down when she hit the end of the rope. The cow was tiring out, so Dad started for the corral, with me slapping the cow on the rump with my rope to make her move along.

Everett was outside and saw us coming and ran to open the gate when we got close.

"Careful, son. Don't let the other cow out," Dad hollered as we came leading another cow into the corral. The first cow we had caught was at the far side of the corral and was watching as we brought in a roommate, or corral mate, whichever you prefer. Either way, we now had two cows in our corral.

Dad pulled this one up to the snubbing post, as he had done with the first one, and earmarked it and cut the tips off the horns. But this one he didn't shave a brand onto the hip like he did the first one.

"Aren't you going to shave a brand on it, Dad?" I asked?

"No, son, I'm going to brand it in the morning with a hot branding iron."

We took the horses over by the fence and unsaddled them and put our saddles on the hitching rail.

Everett gave the horses a flake of hay apiece while dad and I headed for the house to wash up.

Dad had put a pot of beans on the stove that morning before we rode out.

Sam had kept them stirred and had the fire going on them all day. Dad had the cornmeal and flour out and was making cornbread to go with the beans. As always, I was hungry, and Dad set out a can of peach halves for dessert. I even drank part of the juice.

After supper, Sam wanted to see the new addition, so we all walked out to the corral. Sam said, "They're not in very good shape, Dick."

"If we can get more hay, they'll fatten up, all right," Dad replied. "They just need some good feed, Sam. All I can afford to feed them is this mistletoe. I have to save the hay for the horses."

"When you figured on branding them, Dick?" Sam asked. "I figure I'd lay the iron in the stove when I'm cooking in the morning. The coals will get it hot while I rope the one I caught today and tie her down. Once the iron is hot, it will be good as done, Sam."

Sometimes Dad would talk Everett and me into playing poker with him, with matchsticks as chips. I wasn't very good at playing poker, and after four or five hands, I would be sleepy and call it a day. I landed in bed in two shakes; I knew it wouldn't be long before everybody joined me. It wasn't long before I was out like a light, and visions of sugarplums danced in my head. Or was that some other story.

Dad was shaking my shoulder and whispering, "Keep quiet. Take the flashlight."

He had a pistol that he kept under the pillow in his hand.

"Someone is in the kitchen," he whispered again. "A Mexican, or I miss my guess. I'll jerk open the door, and you shine the light and keep it in anybody's eyes you see. I'll have the gun and keep them covered."

I was kind of scared. "What if they have a gun and shoot at us?"

"Just keep the light in their eyes like I told you to do," Dad said.

He turned the doorknob and quickly pulled the door open. I kept my body behind the wall and shined the flashlight around the room.

Nothing doing. There was nobody in there. Dad took the light from my hand and shined it all around slowly. He had the pistol next to the flashlight with his right hand.

"By God, I know someone was in here because I heard them."

He shined the light on the kitchen table and said, "Look there, the last slab of bacon is gone," he said. "I'll be go to hell if they didn't take our last piece of bacon." He was still shining the light around and picked up two big eyes peering down at us from the top of a cabinet in the far corner of the kitchen.

"There the thieving son of a bitch is," Dad said.

"It's a ringtail cat!" It had a cute little face with big round eyes. "Oh, Dad, let's catch him," I said.

Dad had the flashlight shining straight into his eyes as he walked as quietly as he could toward the critter.

He must have heard us because all of a sudden, he disappeared behind the cabinet, which was six or seven feet high. Dad shoved the cabinet back against the wall in one quick move. He was shining the light into the small space behind the cabinet and the wall.

"We got him pinned, son. Get those leather gloves on and see if you can catch him."

I put the gloves on and went to the side of the cabinet where Dad was shining the light into his eyes to blind him.

"Son, there's a hole in the wall here where he came into the house, so you'll have to be quick, or he'll get back out that hole."

My arm was pretty skinny, so I got my arm into the crack and felt the critter. I worked my hand up to his neck. He was biting the glove, but his teeth didn't go through. I could feel the pressure from his teeth, though.

"I think I got him, Dad," I said.

"Well, hang on tight, or you'll lose him," Dad told me.

I told Dad to pull the cabinet away quick so I could grab him with both hands. As Dad pulled the cabinet back, I quickly reached with my other gloved hand and held on tight.

The ringtail cat was kicking with his hind legs and squirming like crazy. I hung on to him, but I had to squeeze him pretty good to keep him from getting away.

"Hang on to him, son," Dad told me. I could tell he was excited too.

"What can we put him in, Dad?"

"I don't know, son. I hadn't thought that far ahead yet. You sure can't hold it in your hands all night," he told me. "Unless you've a mind to sleep with it."

There was an old broken bridle in a box in the corner of our bedroom, and Dad got it and cut the chinstrap off with the buckle attached. He cut the chinstrap so it would buckle around the critters neck. Dad got his leather punch out and made several holes in the strap so it could be adjusted around the cat's neck. I had the cat by the head with one hand so he couldn't bite Dad.

Once the collar was on tight, Dad took a piece of copper wire maybe four feet long and wired it into the new collar he had made. The other end he wrapped around the leg of the kitchen stove.

"Turn him loose, son. Let's see him get out of that collar."

We'd just put the criminal into lockup. The ringtail cat sat there for a moment before trying to get loose, but Dad's homemade leash worked, although the critter was rolling around the floor just to test the leash.

Dad said, "I don't think this guy will be going anywhere tonight."

Dad pulled a chair over to the cabinet where we had first seen the critter peering down at us. He stepped up on the chair and felt around and came away with our slab of bacon that the ringtail cat was trying to carry off. I think the bacon weighed more than the darn cat. It must have jumped from the floor to the top of the cabinet with the bacon in its mouth. The thievin' little bastard! I guess we taught him a lesson.

Dad wiped the bacon off with a brown paper bag that he kept between his cast iron skillets. Then he wrapped it back up in the white butcher paper the cat had taken it from. Then he turned his biggest skillet upside down over the bacon "Now let's see if you can get at it this time," Dad said, looking toward the cat.

"Well, boys, I'm heading back to bed. Morning gets here awful quick, and I still have some sleeping to do. You boys going with me, or you want to sit up all night looking at that damn cat."

Reluctantly, we headed back to bed. Sam Blair had slept through the whole thing. I was having a hard time getting back to sleep as I lay there thinking about my ringtail cat. I was thinking if I could catch one of the opposite sex, I could breed them and raise tame ones. They were so pretty.

I wanted a bunch of them. This was the first one I had ever seen, but I remember Dad had spoken of them when I was trapping on the gunnery range over at Quartzsite. But swift foxes were what I was trapping there. I didn't have the least idea what a ringtail cat looked like. Dad told me that in the early fifties, it was against the law to trap the ringtail cats. He told me they were nocturnal, that you never saw one in the daylight. I was going to raise a bunch of them, I was thinking as I went back to sleep.

The next morning, when I woke up, my dreams of raising ringtail cats was shattered. There on the floor by the stove was my new leash, but it was empty. We guessed the critter had used its hind legs to push the collar over its head. Boy, to say I was disappointed wasn't enough. I looked over at the hole in the wall behind the cabinets where my ringtail cat had escaped. If only I had shoved the cabinet back against the wall, he would still be in the house somewhere. I was so excited last night that I didn't think he could escape.

I went into the bedroom and told Dad the ringtail cat got away. Dad got up, but he didn't say much because he thought the cat was secured good and tight. Dad knew I was disappointed. He said, "Son, maybe we can catch another one. We'll set a trap tonight in case he comes back for more bacon."

I said, "Dad, if we trap one, it will break its leg like it did on the foxes. I don't want one with a broken leg," I told him.

"Well, I don't know what you're going to do, then, son. The chance of your catching another one in the house with your hands is slim and none because I'm not leaving the bacon out on the table anymore."

Dad lifted his skillet to make sure the bacon was still there. He seemed happy that the critter hadn't taken the bacon with him.

"You can bet I'm going to take care of the bacon this time," he told me as he was slicing the bacon for breakfast.

I said, "Maybe I could make a box trap like the one Mr. Waller made in Hemet to catch rabbits."

Dad said, "Well, if you think you can, go ahead and build yourself one, son. But right now, we need to go to work and catch some more cattle. That's what we came down here for, wasn't it? You boys go out to the corral and feed the cows and horses while I get breakfast."

Everett and I put our coats on and went out to the corral. The horses saw us coming and nickered at us. They were always happy to see us coming to feed them. The cows were staying far back in the corral. They still didn't trust us. When we threw the mistletoe over the fence, they would wait until we were gone before coming to eat it.

We returned to the house, and Dad said, "Get washed up. These pancakes are getting cold."

Boy, it sure smelled good—pancakes with bacon and honey.

I was hungry too. Dad sat down in a chair with his plate and said he had the branding iron in the stove getting hot. He looked over at me and said, "We'll leave Everett to do the dishes while you and I go brand that cow. Sound good, son?" he asked me.

I said, "Okay, Dad, I'll help, but I've never branded a cow before."

"That's why I want you to help, so you'll learn, son."

"Then we're going to have to see about putting the cattle in a pen by themselves. That fenced-in area back of the corral made from mesquite limbs and barbed wire should work out for a pen to hold these cattle. And the well is close by also," he continued. "Everett won't have to carry water so far in his bucket. The cows right now are eating the horses' hay, and we don't want that. We have to keep the hay solely for the horses. If we have to keep running up to Blythe for more hay, we'll run out of money in short order," Dad said.

"Sam is grubstaking us but there is a limit to what he will do. The more cattle we catch, the harder you and Everett will have to work gathering mistletoe. And as we get more cattle in the pen, Sam won't mind coming up with a little more cash for groceries as he sees us working hard. As he sees the pen filling with cattle, he'll know his investment is safe."

BRANDED

So after breakfast, Dad and I put our coats on, and we went to the corral, where Dad got a rope and caught the cow we had caught the night before and tied it to the snubbing post.

"Son, get your rope from your saddle and bring it to me so I can put this old cow down on the ground."

He took the rope and made a loop and laid it on the ground by the cow's hooves. Then he put his shoulder in the cow's flank and pushed her so she would step into the loop. Then he pulled the rope tight. He told me to take the end of the rope and pull it tight. I had the rope pulled over my hip so I could really lean back and hold the cow tight. Dad pushed the cow again with his shoulder, and this time she went down on the ground because I had her legs held tight.

"Son, get down on your knees, on this cows neck, and hold her while I go get that branding iron from the stove."

I saw Everett coming from the house, and as he came up to me, he said, "Dad told me to come hold the rope on the cow's legs so it will be harder for it to get up."

"Okay, just grab the end of the rope and hang on," I told him.

Dad was coming from the house with a bucket in his hand. The bucket contained hot coals with the iron-branding ring in them to keep it hot. He also had a big pair of pliers in his other hand.

He took the pliers and lifted the hot iron ring out and carefully placed it over the cow's right hipbone just so.

MOO, MOO!

The cow was bawling from the hot branding iron and was struggling to get to her feet. I could see the frantic look in the right eye of the cow as it kept struggling, with Everett holding the rope real tight.

This all happened fast, maybe five or six seconds. Then Dad lifted the ring with his pliers and said, "Son, let her up."

He went to the snubbing post and untied the cow and told Everett to give him some slack. The wild-eyed cow didn't take long getting up and running to the back of the corral with the other cow we had caught several days ago.

The cow kind of jackknifed itself so it could lick the new brand where it was burned into her hip. Dad was coiling his rope up and told us, "We'll catch her up again tomorrow and put grease on the hip so the flies will leave it alone until it heals."

Sam Blair was standing outside on the porch when we returned from branding the cow. I was in the lead, and as I came to the porch steps, Sam asked, "What's Dick doing?"

"We were branding the cow we caught yesterday," I told him.

"With the hip O?" he asked me. Then he told me his mother had the bar brand and his daddy had the hip O.

"Yeah, Sam, I know, you told me already," I said, kind of irritated.

Dad and Everett were coming up on the porch, and as I looked at Dad, he took his finger and made circles around his ear, letting me know Sam was a little touched in the head.

"Son, don't pay any attention to him. He's old and can't think straight anymore," Dad said. He put his pliers away in his toolbox and said, "Son, it's still early. Let's saddle up and take a ride down through the burn area this morning."

So we saddled the horses and came out around the tamarack trees and rode down the fence line toward the river. We always rode west in the morning so we could go around the end of the fence at the river's edge. Riding along the riverbank made the cattle have to run into the burned-out tules, giving us a good chance of catching them before they could enter the brush and mesquite trees along the mesa.

In the afternoon, it was different, because we would just head home from wherever we happened to be at the time we decided to call it quits. Once, we were riding back late in the afternoon. We were coming in from the north of Blair's place going southeast. We rode out of the brush into a clearing where the mesquite trees had all been cut down. There were four Mexicans chopping down mesquite trees and chopping off the limbs.

They had piles of mesquite wood all chopped into lengths that they had stacked together in piles that looked like huts or the Indian hogans I had seen in western New Mexico.

Some of the piles had mud covering them, which really made them look like hogans.

Six or seven of the mud-covered piles of wood had smoke coming from the top of the pile. Dad knew what they were doing. "They're making charcoal," he told me.

I asked what they were going to use charcoal for. Dad said, "They use it to barbecue meat, son. Once they get the wood stacked and the mud applied, they set fire to it and let it burn for a few days. They stacked the wood so there is a draft hole from the bottom of the pile to the top. That way, the wood burns but doesn't burn up. After it's burned for a few days, they can seal the air hole so the fire will go out. Then after a few more days, they break the pile open and start breaking the burned mesquite into chunks and bag it up.

Over at the north end of the open field were stacks of white paper sacks of the charcoal in rows. Dad just waved at the men and said, "Buenos dias, muchachos," as we rode right through the middle of their operation. We saw the men every few days when we rode in this area, and Dad always waved to them. They were always hard at work.

At the south end of the clearing, they had a green army surplus tent set up where they ate and slept. Once, when we came riding into the clearing on horseback, there was a man in a green Dodge truck that had brought them supplies. He was checking on how they were coming along making charcoal. Dad stopped to talk to the man in the truck. The man said he hired the men to make the charcoal and was paying them by the bag.

He said, "I'm also buying their food so I want to make sure they are really working."

"Well, you have a good day," Dad told the man as we rode on across the clearing towards Blair's.

"Did he say how much he was paying them, Dad?" I asked.

"No, and it isn't any of our business, son. The less you know, the better off you are," Dad told me.

We didn't know how long they had been there making charcoal before we came up on them. But we saw them every three or four days as we rode through the clearing just north of Blair's fence looking for cattle. Dad figured it was State land since nobody ran them off. We always waved to them, and Dad would holler, "Buenos dias!"

They had been there working about a month when we came riding through the area once again and saw a Border Patrol van that had stopped to talk to the men. We didn't get back in there for a few days, but the next time we did come through the clearing, the Mexicans were gone.

Dad and I rode over to the tent to just check it out. Their axes and shovels and a set of scales were still there beside the tent, but no one was around. We got down from our horses and looked into the tent. There were pots and pans and dishes and blankets inside the tent.

Dad said, "I'll bet the man who had checked on them when we came through last time had called immigration on them."

"Why would that guy call the immigration for?" I asked Dad.

"So the son of a bitch wouldn't have to pay them for their work, son," Dad replied.

"Yeah, but now he doesn't have anybody to make the charcoal."

"Son, they will just bring in more Mexicans. And probably do the same thing to them. The dirty ol' son of a bitch was too cheap to pay them for their labor." Dad seemed pissed the men were cheated after all their work.

Several days later, Dad wanted to check out the clearing again and make sure all the sacks of charcoal had been loaded onto a truck with dual rear wheels. We saw the tracks of the truck where it had been backed in beside the stacks of charcoal so they could be loaded onto the truck. We rode our horses over to the tent, and Dad got down and lifted the set of scales up into my lap where I was sitting in the saddle. Then he handed me four shovels, which I also laid across my lap with the scales. Dad put the four axes over his shoulder and climbed back onto his horse. "The sons a bitches come back, they won't have tools to work with," he told me.

We rode on over to Blair's house, where we put the shovels and axes out by the corral fence. Dad took the scales from me and set them down by the shovels and axes. We unsaddled the horses and put them into the corral. Dad took one of the shovels and dug a hole in the corral big enough for the shovels and axes and scales. Then he placed them into the hole and covered them up.

The horses still had their bridles on, so Dad said, "Let's walk the horses over the ground where he had dug the hole." When we were done, you couldn't tell there had been a hole dug there. We took the bridles off the two horses and turned them loose with the two cows we had caught.

"Son, let's go put the feed bag on," Dad said. "I'll send Everett to feed the animals."

As usual, I was hungry. We had been riding most of the day and hadn't gotten any more cows, and it was cloudy and cold.

I was ready to be in the warm house by the stove. Everett had chopped a lot of wood for the cookstove. The mesquite wood made good coals that kept the room warm all night.

There was also a potbellied stove over in the corner where Sam Blair sat in his rocking chair so he could open the door on the stove and spit snuff into the fire. I guess that was the only enjoyment he got out of life anymore.

After three weeks, Sam was feeling sick, so we had to take him to his son's house in Blythe. We went by our haystack and borrowed four more bales of hay. Then we drove back down to Cibola. Everett stayed there to feed and water the animals.

When we got back that night, Everett was already in bed, but he woke up as we came in.

I told him we had gotten four more bales of hay. He said he would help me unload it in the morning and that he had taken the horses to the river for water. I told him Sam didn't feel good all the way home. I said he was old and Dad didn't think he would be around much longer.

Everett said, "Well, all he does is tell the same thing over and over."

So I said, "Well, how they going to get back off it?" And we both laughed.

KILLING MY SECOND BUCK DEER

One morning it was raining and had been raining hard for most of the night. Dad had breakfast made, and while we ate, Dad said, "Son, there's no use to ride the river bottom with it muddy and slick". I asked Dad if I could take my rifle and go look for a deer to shoot.

Dad said, "Hell, son, I don't care. If you want to go shoot a deer, then have at it. A steak off a deer's ass would go good right about now, wouldn't it, son," Dad said, looking over at Everett.

Everett just smiled and said, "I guess so."

"Well it would, wouldn't it, son?" Dad asked again.

Everett said, "Yeah, but let's wait and see if he gets a deer before we start eating it, Dad."

Then Dad said, "I guess you're right, son, but just thinking of how that venison steak would taste made my mouth water."

I pulled my warm coat on and took my hat down from the nail and slipped my hat onto my head. I went out to the corral to saddle Mike, who was all wet from standing in the rain. The horses were still eating hay that Everett had gone out to feed them while Dad was making breakfast.

I put my bridle on Mike and then took an old piece of blanket and wiped him down a little so he wasn't so wet. I led him out of the corral and saddled him and led him to the house to get my rifle. I slipped my rifle into the scabbard and then climbed aboard and rode out around the bee-extracting shed heading east toward the mountains.

The rain had slowed to a drizzle as I crossed the gravel road that ran south to Lake Martinez. On the east side of the road was where I entered the bushes and trees. I loved the smell of the rain on the wet bushes, and so I took a deep breath to inhale the fragrance of the plants. Riding horseback, it was easy to ride up on a deer, because all they smelled was another animal. I kept watching ahead for some sign or movement. I was glancing down at the ground for any sign of fresh deer tracks.

I guess I had been gone a half hour or more when I saw deer tracks going up toward the mountains. They were fresh because old ones would have been rained out, or at least made to look old. These were really sharp and made within the last couple of hours. I was following the tracks, and they went through a pool of water that had formed on a depression in a rock.

I pulled my horse to a stop and stepped down for a closer look.

I had my rifle in my hand and was looking where the deer had walked through the water. It took a minute for it to sink in that the track was riled up (cloudy looking). When I realized the fact that the sediment hadn't settled yet, I knew the track had just been made.

I looked up and to my left a little, and I'll be go to hell if a buck wasn't standing out about seventy-five yards, looking at me. Up came my rifle, and I shot him in the chest. I jacked in another round and put the gun to my shoulder again as the buck turned away from me. As soon as my gun came to my shoulder, Mike was jerking his head and pulling on the reins and running backward. I couldn't get a shot off. "Goddamn you," I said half out loud. I stepped back toward Mike to get some slack in the reins and threw my gun to my shoulder again.

I was on the buck with my front sight, but I couldn't get off a shot because Mike was jerking his head and throwing off my aim. I just jerked the trigger as the front sight of my gun crossed the chest of the buck because I wanted to get off another shot before it was too late as the buck had started to run. I have no idea what part of the buck I shot at because my damn horse was jerking his head, and if I dropped the reins, the stupid horse would run off for home and the corral, leaving me high but not dry.

When I fired the second shot, he really became excited and was running back over brush like he was crazy. I guess no one had fired a gun this close to him before. I was used to my dad's horses, Tony and Suzie, that you could shoot beside them and they wouldn't get excited. When I looked toward the buck again, he was nowhere to be seen. I tried to climb back onto Mike, but he was backing up and turning in a circle away from me. I was excited, which didn't do either of us any good because I jerked him around, making him even more excited, if that was possible.

Finally, I stood my rifle against a large rock and started rubbing Mike's head and talking calmly to him. "You son of a bitch, if you don't stand still, I'm going to shoot you, you dirty son of a bitch!"

He seemed to be at ease, as my voice must have had a calming effect on him since I didn't have the rifle in my hands. So with the reins in my hand, I reached for the saddle horn, and with my boot in the stirrup, I quickly swung up into the saddle.

Mike immediately turned and started back toward Blair's and his corral. I lifted the reins to stop him and rein him around and kicked him in the sides with my boots, as I didn't put spurs on to go hunting. He reluctantly started up the trail again, and as he passed the rock my rifle was leaning against, I reached down and picked it up. Mike saw me pick up the gun and turned a little sideways and was tossing his head. I could see in his eye, and I could tell he was still excited and spooked. I kicked him in the sides again, trying to straighten him out as we went forward toward where I had last shot at the buck.

The dirty bastard reared up and scared the shit out of me because I thought he was going to fall over backward. When he finally came down, I felt like hitting him over the damn head with my rifle stock. He finally settled down, and I got him under control, and I was able to go back to finding the buck that had disappeared by now.

I kept looking everywhere, hoping the buck had gone down, but no such luck.

His tracks were plainly visible in the wet ground, and he was running. The tracks were deep and about twelve feet apart. I knew he wasn't wasting any time in getting the hell out of there.

"Mike, you son of a bitch," I said, mostly to myself. I didn't care if he knew what I thought of him. "Shit, I should have rode Nancy." She was older and calmer. Hell, Dad wasn't going anywhere today anyway, I said to myself.

I didn't know this stupid horse had never been shot around. When Dad shot those ducks, he was farther away and out of sight. I kept following the tracks that were going up the wash toward the mountains. After about two hundred yards, the buck was still running, and he turned left around a small ridge where the wash separated and went in two directions, like an island in the wash.

I thought I saw blood for the first time, so I pulled Mike to a stop and stuck my rifle back in the scabbard. I didn't want Mike to get excited again. It was blood, all right, so I walked to the next set of tracks, and there I saw more blood. *He's hit*, I thought, but I didn't know how badly. I looked ahead for the buck, but I didn't see him.

I pulled Mike to me and caught the saddle horn, and at the same time, I lifted my boot into the stirrup and swung back into the saddle. I gave him another kick in the sides and pulled my rifle back out of the scabbard just in case I had to do business with it again.

The buck had started walking, and he was dripping blood with every step. *A good sign*, I thought. I rode about three hundred yards, and as I came over a little rise, there he lay, all in a pile. A nice buck too. I could tell I had shot him in the lungs as the blood was foamy. The buck had three points on both sides and looked like he was in good shape too. His hips and sides looked filled out pretty good.

Mike didn't like being around the dead deer. He was fidgeting and turning sideways, blowing out of his nostrils. "It's okay, it's okay," I kept telling him. I saw a palo verde tree nearby in the wash, and I took Mike over and tied him with the short rope that Dad had tied to the back of both our saddles, the one Dad called a pigging string. I made a Bolin knot on Mike's neck and then tied him to the palo verde tree.

Then I went over and cleaned the buck and cut off its head, making him lighter. I dragged him to the tree where Mike was tied, because I was going to try lifting the deer onto Mike's back. I put the headless buck in a sitting position. Then I put my arms around it just under the front legs. I tried lifting it but the only thing that moved was the skin on its body.

I knew I would pay hell lifting the buck up high enough to put it into the saddle. And getting Mike to stand still was a problem too, because he kept moving sideways as he watched the dead deer I was trying to put on his back. He wasn't having any part of it. I figured I was a mile or more from the house.

What to do? I thought.

Finally, I decided to use my rope and drag the buck home. Once a deer is dead, it won't bruise, but the hair will drag off. I hadn't cut the legs off yet, so I proceeded to cut the front legs to the knees and then removed the bone just as I had done on the buck I had shot over in Quartzsite the year before. I tied the front legs together with the skin that I removed the bone from.

I took my rope off the saddle and went around the front legs with a double half hitch. Then I went under the half hitch and back over it through the center of the legs. That way, the harder I pulled, the tighter it would become. I climbed back on Mike and walked him fairly close to the deer, which he didn't like. When he started to balk, I turned him away and I dallied the saddle horn and started dragging the buck. Hey this worked pretty well. I wished I had a horse when I shot the Quartzsite buck. It would have made getting that buck out a lot easier.

Best not to remember that day. I think I still have aches and pains from that day. When I came dragging the buck into Blair's, I just threw the rope on the ground as I went past the house and took Mike out to the corral and unsaddled him and gave him another flake of hay because he didn't get to eat this morning, and Nancy had cleaned his hay all up.

I went to the house, walked in, and one look at my bloody hands told Dad that I had killed something. He asked, "You get a deer?"

I said, "Yeah, but it's a buck, Dad. I didn't see any does."

"Hell, that's all right, son. Did you pack it out?"

I said, "I had to drag him, Dad, because I couldn't lift him up on the horse's back."

"Well, let me get a skinning knife, and I'll be right with you."

Everett was already outside looking at the deer. I told him it was a big three point. When Dad came out of the house, he had his knife in his hand and was sharpening it on a whetstone. Everett and I grabbed the buck by the hind legs and dragged it over to a tree by the bee equipment house.

Dad threw my rope over a limb, and with Everett and me lifting the deer, Dad pulled it up into the tree so the front legs would clear the ground and tied it off. Then Dad and Everett skinned it out. Dad took a handsaw and sawed through the backbone. He had to wipe some gravel out of the chest cavity as dragging the deer had gotten gravel into it. Dad didn't put water on any fresh meat because he said it would make the meat sour. He just took a cloth and wiped it out. He would wash it before he cooked it. I was cold and damp, but it hadn't rained hard, so I wasn't wet. I told Dad about Mike going crazy when I shot.

"Well, son, we'll have to take him out and do a little target practice, and he'll settle down. "Maybe it hurt his ears," Dad said. "He'll get used to it, just takes time."

We left the deer hanging because the night temperature was down to freezing. Dad got the heart and liver and then headed for the house to cook it. The deer was hanging at least three feet above the ground so no animals could get more than a bite if they came snooping around looking for a meal.

Dad was already slicing the liver when Everett and I came in. I watched him salt and pepper the meat and then roll it in flour, and then into the skillet of hot grease it went. He sautéed the onions in another skillet, so we were having liver and onions. When the heart and liver was done, he made gravy in the drippings after he poured the grease off. Dad's gravy was always great made with canned milk. Sometimes I try making it his way, but it never tastes the same as Dad's.

My sister Rita tells me the same thing. Sometimes we would shoot a mess of doves, and Dad would cook them up in lard. He would make gravy from the giblets (the heart, liver, and gizzard), and it was really a good meal for hungry boys, especially if Dad made biscuits to put the gravy on. Sometimes we would catch a mess of catfish that were plentiful in the sloughs, and he would roll the fish fillets in cornmeal and fry them up, and they were hard to beat for a meal.

But tonight we were having liver and onions. Boy, the meal was really good, and with the liver that was left over, we could make sandwiches to carry on horseback when we rode out into the river bottom looking for cattle. Sometimes I would make sandwiches from canned deviled ham, but mostly I went without until we returned home, but Dad always carried a canteen.

If we were close to the river and it was running clean, we would get down and drink from the river. The horses were always grateful for a drink also. There were high steep riverbanks straight off in most places, so we would look for a cattle trail where they had been going down for a drink. Often, there would be green grass growing along the river, and the horses always wanted to stop and eat a bite, just to top off their tank, so to speak, because at the ranch, all they were eating was the dry baled hay. So the moist grass was a nice change of diet for the horses.

BUCKED OFF

One morning, Dad and I rode into the burned tules, which had grown back at least a foot high by now. We saw four cows out feeding on the tule shoots, quite far from any brush or cover. We both had our ropes out with our loops all ready. Dad motioned me back so I was behind him and was walking his horse straight at the cows that were not aware of us as they had their backs to us.

One of the cows must have finally heard us and threw up its head and turned toward us. Dad kicked his horse with his spurs, and I did the same, but I went left to keep the cattle from reaching the brush that I knew they would head for. Dad's horse was running full out and slipped in some wet alkali ground and damn near went down.

Dad jerked the reins up trying to help his horse recover. As I was riding wide to the left, I didn't go through the wet alkali. The cows had reached the high brush and mesquite trees, with me right on their ass. I guess the lead cow didn't realize I was so close because it had slowed as it entered the heavy brush. The other three cows were locked in behind the lead cow and couldn't get past.

I knew I couldn't rope the one in the rear, as the brush wouldn't let my loop come down on the rear cow's head. I swung down to the ground and dropped my reins with my rope in my hand and ran into the brushy trail. The last cow, which turned out to be a bull, was only about ten feet ahead of me. I ran right up to it and threw my loop around its horns since it couldn't get past the other three cows.

Letting the rope slip through my hands, I ran back out of the brush and into the clearing. Dad, who was riding Nancy, who had recovered from her fall in the alkali, said, "Quick, son, hand me the end of the rope."

So with Nancy's chest and neck right in my face, I handed Dad the loose end of my rope.

Dad quickly dallied the saddle horn and stopped the bull. He pulled back on his reins, and Nancy started backing up, pulling the young bull back out of the heavy brush. I caught my horse, which was standing nearby, with the reins dragging, and I stepped up into the saddle. I didn't have a rope because it was around the bull's horns. The bull made a run at Nancy, and Dad turned her aside as he quickly pulled the slack from the rope and re-dallied the saddle horn. The bull was still fighting the rope around its horns and made a few more charges at Nancy. Dad was wise to what the bull was trying to do and turned Nancy out of the way. Nancy was quick to respond, as she was a smart horse with a lot of experience in dealing with cattle.

I rode Mike up behind the bull and prodded it along. The only rope I had was my pigging string. Dad's rope was under my rope, which he had dallied around his saddle horn. So he couldn't give me his rope unless he loosened his rope on the bull—which he didn't want to do just yet. I had my pigging string rope doubled in my hand, and on occasion, I gave the bull a slap on the behind, just to let him know we meant business about him moving along.

Once in a while, the bull would balk, just like the other cattle we had caught. But a rap on his behind with my rope made him move right along.

"Nice bull, huh, Dad?" I said.

"Damn sure is, son. I didn't know what you had in mind when you jumped down from your horse. When you ran in behind him, I thought maybe you were going to climb on the son of a bitch and ride him out. That was some quick thinking, son," Dad told me.

"Well, Dad, I could tell he couldn't get past the other three cows in that thick brush, so I knew he couldn't get away from me, if I could just get my loop around his horns.0"

I was almost up beside Dad now, and I wanted to keep talking about how I had caught my first cow, even if I was on foot. "Hell, I caught it, didn't I?" That was good enough for me. But I did need Dad's help to hold the bull.

I thought, *Boy, won't Everett be surprised I caught one, and it's a bull too.*

MOOO! The bull jumped ahead against Nancy's side, and having slack in the rope, he was able to sling his head in my direction, hitting Mike right behind his front leg. Mike jumped forward, bucking like a son of a bitch, and after two or three jumps, I was launched skyward. I saw the ground coming up fast as I landed on my face in the alkali dirt. I rolled to the side, groaning and spitting dirt from my mouth. I was dazed from hitting the ground so hard. I got up cussing at my horse, which was still bucking and heading for home. My reins were tied in a knot on his neck. Otherwise, he might have stepped on the reins and stopped. But he lit out for home and never looked back.

"You all right, son?" I heard my dad ask me from behind. "You should have stayed back, son. Now you'll have to walk home to get your horse, 'cause he won't stop till he gets to the house. I'm just glad he didn't ask me if I wanted to ride the bull home, because I was pissed. I'll come along with this bull, son. You go take care of your horse," Dad said to me as I started after Mike. I was still spiting dirt and a little blood from my mouth. My lips were bruised and sore from my teeth pushing my lips into the ground.

That son of a bitchin' horse! I was going to kill the son of a bitch when I caught him. *That dirty bastard*, I was thinking as I walked toward home. These stupid spurs were slowing me down. I sat down on a stump where a mesquite tree had fallen over and removed them and put them in my coat pocket. I got back up thinking about how that dirty bastard had thrown me off. I had a lot of time to think about how I was going to kill the son of a bitch because it was a long walk home.

I turned around and saw Dad coming along behind me, and the bull was leading pretty good because dad wasn't that far back. I looked back at the trail, thinking, *I'll beat the son of a bitch to death.* "Boy, he's going to get it, that's all I can say." *That sorry son of a bitch will be sorry he bucked me to hell off,* I was thinking. I couldn't even remember putting my arms out to break my fall. It all just happened so fast. That dirty bastard was all I could think of as I walked home.

When I came to the clearing around the homeplace with the corrals out back, I saw the dirty bastard looking through the fence at the back of the corral.

I started talking calmly to him as I approached the front of the corral and reached down and picked up a flake of hay so he would see it and think he would be fed. Once I had the reins in my hand, I could put him in the corral where he couldn't get away and kill the son of a bitch.

"Here, Mike, you want some hay?" I said calmly to him as I shook it so he could smell it and not be afraid.

I could tell he was ready to turn and run if I made a wrong move. The bastard knew he had done a bad thing. Just a little more, and I would have the reins in my hand. He put his muzzle forward and took a nibble at the hay. He could eat it because he had my hackamore on with no bit in his mouth.

He stepped forward for another bite, and when he did, I grabbed him by the reins with one hand and his bridle with the other, letting the hay fall to the ground.

"You son of a bitch," I called out to him, and he went to backing up and looking wild-eyed like he was when I shot the buck and was trying to shoot it again.

I guess I better get him into the corral before I start killing him, I said to myself. I was going to lead him around to the gate, and that was when I saw Dad coming, leading the bull. I put Mike in the corral and shut the gate so the other cows didn't get out. I heard Dad say, "Son, stay there and open the gate for me so I can put this bull in the corral."

"Okay, Dad. Then I'm going to get my rope and beat the shit out of this stupid horse."

"Son, it wasn't that horse's fault. You let him get too close to the bull, and he horned him. He was just reacting the only way he knew how. Now open that gate and help me get the bull up to the snubbing post so I can saw the tips of the horns off."

I opened the gate, but I didn't like the idea that I couldn't beat the shit out of my horse. My lips and my mouth were sore as hell. Dad rode Nancy past the snubbing post, and I took my hat off and shooed the bull around the post, and as I did, Dad flipped the rope over the post and pulled the bull's head tight to the post.

Everett came out of the house so he could see our new addition. Dad looked and saw Everett coming and said, "Son, go back and get that little handsaw so I can cut these horns before I turn this bull loose in the corral."

Everett turned around and went back into the house. Dad told me to hold the rope tight while he undid the rope from his saddle horn. Dad stepped down from his horse as I put a half hitch on the post. Everett walked into the corral and handed Dad the saw. Then he and I held the rope tight as Dad sawed off the tips of the horns.

"Untie it, son. I'm done. Enough cowboying for today."

"We'll brand it and earmark it tomorrow," Dad told us. "You boys let the bull go, we can catch it up again tomorrow. You boys feed these animals while I go start supper."

I was ready to wash up and get a mirror to look at my lip, which felt really swollen by now. I was really tired from walking home. It had been a good day until I was thrown from my horse. I didn't even feel like bragging to Everett about how I caught the bull.

Everett put hay into the corral while I unsaddled the two horses and put the saddle on the hitch rail. For once, I wasn't hungry because my lips were swollen.

Everett could tell I was sore and tired, so he said, "Go on, and I'll give the cows some mistletoe. I didn't argue. I just wanted to wash up. When my face was clean, I looked at it in the mirror and saw my lips were puffy.

Dad said, "Let me look at it, son. It will be all right in a couple of days. Son, you have to watch yourself around these wild cattle. These cattle aren't like the tame cattle you were milking over at the Carters in that foster home."

"Okay, Dad, but can we eat and talk about it tomorrow?"

"Sure, son, I'll have it ready before you know it. We're having deer steaks and fried potatoes and gravy. Sound good?"

"Yeah, Dad, that sounds good," I said through my puffy lips. It took several days before I didn't think about killing my horse, because the first few days, that was all that was on my mind.

One morning, Everett and I were at the corral feeding mistletoe and hay to the animals. As we were walking back to the house, I saw a ringtail cat stick his head out of the well casing we were approaching. It quickly disappeared back down the well casing. It happened so quickly I wondered if I imagined it.

"Did you see that?" I asked Everett.

"Yeah, it looked like a ringtail cat," was Everett's reply.

We quickly ran forward to take a look down the well casing, which was about eight inches in diameter. The casing had an inch and a half of galvanized pipe going down the middle of it. The cat was about ten feet down and looking up at us.

I told Everett, "Stay here and keep him from getting out, and I'll run get my leather gloves and a long stick so we can poke him out of the well."

"Go ahead," Everett told me. "I won't let him out."

I had left my gloves on my saddle the night before after unsaddling the horses. So I ran to the corral to get them. There were some limbs lying alongside the corral that someone had cut off the tamarack trees. I found a pretty straight one about ten to twelve feet long. I grabbed it and ran back to the well.

"Is he still there?" I asked Everett.

"Yeah, he hasn't moved at all."

I put my gloves on and started lowering the limb down into the casing.

When it touched the ringtail cat, he climbed up the galvanized pipe like it was a tree limb. I was surprised it could climb like that, and fast too. When it would stop, I would move the limb so it touched the cat and made it climb higher up the pipe.

"Everett, you take the limb and keep him climbing the pipe, and when he gets close enough, I'll grab him," I said.

So Everett took the limb and moved it up and down, making the cat come close to the top. I figured I could reach him, and so I grabbed him by the back of his neck before he could jump out and run away. I lifted him clear of the well casing squirming and kicking.

"Where we going to put it?" Everett asked me.

"We sure as hell don't want to put the leash on it," I said.

Everett said we could make a cage out of an empty beehive.

"Okay, go get one and we'll try it. Get one with a bottom on it so we only have to nail some wire on one side," I told Everett as he left to go to the shed where they kept the bee supplies. He came back carrying a bee super, or hive, but no bottom.

He said, "None of them have bottoms."

"Okay, can you get some chicken wire, hammer, and nails?"

"Okay, I'll look and see what I can find," Everett said.

The cat squirmed once in a while, but I couldn't put him down. I hollered to Everett, "See if you can find a big bucket we can put him in until we build a cage."

Everett came back carrying an old rusty five-gallon paint can that was empty. He also had a piece of chicken wire about a two-foot square. He said, "We can put him in the can and put the wire on top, then set a rock on top so he won't get away."

"Okay," I said and stuck the cat into the bucket.

Everett had the wire ready, and as I released the cat, he pushed the wire tight on my arm, and I slid my arm out, leaving the cat inside. He stuck his nose up against the wire a couple of times and then kind of cowered in the bottom. Everett said, "Want me to find a big rock?"

"No, just get some bailing wire and I'll bend the chicken wire down and twist some of this bailing wire around it."

I held the wire in place while Everett went to the corral, where we had the hay for the horses, and came back with a long piece of bailing wire. I put it around the chicken wire over the bucket and pulled it real tight and twisted it. This little critter wasn't going anywhere this time. I was determined he would stay put.

I told Everett, "If he gets out of here, I'm going to call him Houdini."

"What are we going to feed it?" Everett asked as I picked up the bucket and started for the house.

"I don't know. Maybe Dad will let us have a piece of bacon. We know they like that."

As I came through the door, I called out, "Hey, Dad, we caught the ringtail cat again."

"The hell you did!" And Dad went out to see it. When he saw our cage, he said, "He has to have more room than that, son."

"I know, Dad. I just put him in the bucket until I can build a cage for him. I'm going to get one of the beehive boxes and nail chicken wire on the sides."

"Well, you'll need to make a door so you can give it food and water, son," Dad suggested.

"I know, Dad. I can take your keyhole saw and saw a round hole in the top of the bee box. Then I'll make a gate or a door to slide over the holes.

I went to the car and got Dad's brace and bit, a primitive hand-cranked type of drilling device that was hand operated. No electricity needed. A good thing too, because we were far from any electrical lines. I drilled a small hole into the side of the bee box, then took a gallon paint can and set it on the box so the edge of the can just covered the hole I had drilled. Then with my pencil, I drew a line around the can. I started the keyhole saw into the hole I had drilled. Then following the line I had drawn around the can, I finished sawing the hole out of the box.

I cut a piece of leather from an old boot I found in the honey-extracting shed and made a leather hinge. This I tacked to the wooden hole piece I had cut from the box. Then I put the round piece back into the hole. The other side of the hinge I tacked to the box. I nailed a short board across the new door on the opposite side of the hinge. That way, the door wouldn't fall through the opening.

Now all I needed was a latch so it couldn't come open. I made the latch from a small piece of metal I found in Dad's big can of nuts and bolts that he carried in the trunk of our car. It was about two inches long with a small hole at each end. I found a wood screw in my Dad's can, and I put it into the hole in the end of the metal piece and screwed it down just snug enough that I could still turn it. Now it would overlap the door piece, keeping it from being pushed open from the inside by the critter wanting out. Who was soon to call this place home.

Everett was very careful untying the baling wire from the bucket so my cat wouldn't escape. I put my leather gloves on and lifted the chicken wire a little and slipped my hand down and got the cat around the neck. When he quit kicking and squirming around, I lifted him out of the bucket and caught his hind legs and pushed him head first through the hole I had sawn into the box.

I let go of his neck and let his legs hold him as I pushed him all the way inside and turned him loose. He started searching both sides of the box, looking for an escape hole in the wire sides. But this guy wasn't going anywhere. I filled a tin can with water and placed it into the cage. I started for the house to get a piece of deer meat in case he was hungry. He didn't pay any attention to the meat when I dropped it in. He lay down in one corner of the cage, and that's where he stayed for most of the day.

I knew the critter liked bacon because either he or one just like him had tried to steal the slab of bacon the week before. I went into the house where Dad was making us dinner.

"Dad, can I have a little piece of bacon for the ringtail cat?" I asked.

"Son, you can cut off a small piece, but if you think you're going to feed that son of a bitch all our bacon, you have another think a coming. You get your rifle and go shoot him a bird and get the hell out and leave me to my cooking now, do you hear me?"

"Okay, Dad, just one little piece ain't much. I won't eat any next time you make it to make up for your loss."

"No need to do that. Now get the hell on out there and shoot him a bird." Then Dad asked, "Did you boys water the livestock this morning." He was looking out the door toward the corral?

"Yeah, we did that first thing, Dad," I told him.

"What's your brother doing?"

"I don't know. He was out by the corral a while ago," I said. Well, send him in here if you see him. I need some dishes done up so we have something to eat off of."

I took my rifle from over by the stove and headed outside to look for birds. As I came down off the porch, I looked over at the tamarack trees to see if I could spot any birds. I was walking toward the trees, and I saw a couple of woodpeckers flying from tree to tree.

I saw Everett out by the corral, and I shouted, "Hey, Everett, Dad wants you in the house to do the dishes!"

I was easing myself into a place by the trunk of the tree and started watching out for a bird to shoot. Everett was going past and asked me, "Why didn't you wash the dishes?"

"Because Dad told me to kill a bird for the ringtail cat, and besides, he told me to go get you to do it so we can eat."

I went back to watching out for birds, and soon one of the woodpeckers came flying back into the tree I was under. I pulled on the wooden forend and jacked a .22 shell into the chamber as I was putting the rifle to my shoulder. I took a rest on the side of the limb as I looked for the woodpecker high in the tree.

The woodpecker kept bobbing around the limb as he was pecking. His head was moving in and out as he pecked holes in the tree. I took a deep breath and put my sights right on him. I let out a little air as I squeezed the trigger. *POW!* Down he came. He went to jumping around the ground and running, trying to get away as I tried to run him down. I caught him, and I had barely broken his wing.

I carried it over to my newly made cage and turned the piece of metal that secured the door. I just lifted the door and dropped the woodpecker inside. It bounced around the cage trying to escape. It was even sitting on top of the cat's head. The ringtail cat didn't pay it any attention; he just acted as though it wasn't there. I thought he would pounce on the bird, but he was oblivious to the woodpecker.

Soon I left, thinking he didn't want to eat the bird with me watching. I came back later, but they just acted as though they were friends. I couldn't figure out why the critter didn't want the deer meat, bacon, or even the woodpecker. Every time I walked past the cage, he was still lying in the corner with his eyes shut. Once or twice, the woodpecker was sitting on the cat's head. That evening, I carried the cat cage over and set it on the porch and put a small piece of canvas over it. Just in case it might rain, since it was wintertime. It had rained the week before. The morning I rode into the mountains and I had shot the big buck.

The next morning, when I came out to check on my critter, the woodpecker had been devoured, there were just a few feathers lying in one corner of the cage. He had eaten it during the night, and the deer meat and the bacon had been eaten too.

"Good boy," I told him. At least he ate a variety of food. I could tell we were going to do just fine.

I found out that the ringtail cat liked honey. I had a spoonful of honey that had turned to sugar, and I was eating it like candy. I still had some on the spoon and stuck it into the cage right under the critter's nose, and it started licking the honey off the spoon. I went back inside the house and wiped my spoon on a piece of paper. Then I dipped it into the honey and got a spoonful for the cat. He ate the whole thing except for a bite I took walking from the house. I mean, I didn't want to make a pig out of him. Half a spoonful was enough for a little ringtail cat. I could get him more later.

Once, after Dad and I came back from Blythe and getting groceries, I had bought a sack of candy and orange slices. I was eating one as I came out to feed the critter in the cage. I was thinking: He liked honey. Maybe he would like a piece of the candy. I mean, who wouldn't like candy? I bit off half and gave the cat critter the other half. He quickly bit into the candy, and it being a solid jell, it stuck to the roof of his mouth.

He tried to dislodge the candy as he rolled around in his cage. Flipping first one way and then the other, wanting to get the candy to come loose from the roof of its mouth. He was acting as though I had poisoned him. The little guy would probably never trust me again. He continued to twist and roll around in his cage. I knew there was no use taking him out of the cage to get it out of his mouth. I couldn't dig the candy loose with my gloved finger, and I wasn't about to put my bare finger into its mouth and get it bit. *He will just have to work it loose himself*, I thought. I left him to his ordeal because I had other things to do.

Later that day, I came past his cage, and everything was back to normal, and he was sleeping in the corner of the cage. I guess he had worked it loose with his tongue and had swallowed it. In the afternoon, I got my .22 rifle from the house and shot the critter another bird that was sitting high up in the tree chirping. I stuck the dead bird into the cage, but the ringtail cat paid it no mind.

I knew it would be gone the next morning. This critter liked to eat at night. I had the ringtail cat for more than a week. When I came out one morning, I found he had somehow worked the latch loose and was gone.

That was the last I saw of him, and I never was able to catch another one. Needless to say, I was very disappointed. They were just so pretty with the biggest eyes. And that is the sad ending to my ringtail cat story.

We caught four more cows in the next couple of weeks. We branded and earmarked them the same as the others. One morning, Dad and I saddled the horses and rode west down the fence line in the cold morning air. The horses' breath looked like steam coming from their nostrils.

I was riding alongside Dad one morning, when he said, "Son, you think you could put all of this down on paper?"

I said, "What do you mean put it down on paper?"

"Hell, you know, tell the story about going over to Quartzsite and picking up shells and coming down here and catching these cattle. The trapping we've done, and selling the hides, even rescuing that woman with the baby over by Salome when her car broke down. Could you put it down on paper?"

"You mean, like, write a book?" I asked.

"Yeah, I guess that's what I do mean, son."

"Shoot, nobody would want to read about this kind of stuff, Dad. Besides, I'm not very good at writing, I don't know anything about it. Why do you want to know, Dad?" I asked him.

"I don't know, son. Just studying"—Dad called thinking studying—"as we rode along and thought you could write a book about all this."

"Dad, we better stick to catching cattle if we want to make some money."

"Yeah, I guess you're right, son."

Everett and I were kept pretty busy gathering mistletoe to feed to the cattle. Everett even remarked that he thought they were putting on weight. I said they ought to, given how much mistletoe they were eating. Then I added, "Yeah, they do look healthy."

For some reason I can't remember now, Everett was taking the horses to the river to drink nearly every day. But we had water for the cattle, and we had put the cattle in a fenced-in area separate from the horses. Seven heads of cattle eat a lot of feed, so it had become a full-time job just keeping them fed.

SUPERCHARGING OUR CHEVY

We rode along the Lopez fence line one day when Dad pulled his horse to a stop and was looking to his left. He didn't say anything as he spurred his horse toward whatever had caught his eye. I turned my horse to follow him, and that was when I saw a big yellow Caterpillar tractor parked in the brush and mesquite trees.

The Caterpillar tracks were all over as they had cleared some ground with the Cat. There were two fifty-five-gallon drums setting on the front right side of the tractor. Dad rode his horse up real close and leaned out and touched the tractor to see if it was hot or cold. The motor of the big Cat was cold, so they hadn't brought it in here today. "Why do you think they brought this Caterpillar in here dad" I asked? "Well son I don't know, but it looks like they're going to start to clear the river bottom."

"But I thought this was Blair's land."

"It is, son. I'll have to contact Ralph Blair and see what's taking place. Somebody may be setting up to try to claim this land." I was looking at the barrels: One said "Diesel Fuel" and the other one said "Starting Fluid." We knew we couldn't burn diesel fuel in the Chevy, but we might be able to burn the starting fluid in it.

Since we were horseback, Dad said, "We'll get the car and come back later and borrow five gallons of the starting fluid and see if it will burn in the car."

After returning to the house that day and after putting the horses away and feeding them and the cattle, we got in the car with our gas can and siphoning hose and drove off down the graded road toward Martinez Lake to the south.

Dad was in the passenger seat watching out of his window for the tracks of the truck that had brought the Caterpillar tractor and drums of fuel.

"I was driving along slowly when Dad said, "Here they are, son."

"Want me to stop?" I asked.

"No. Drive down the road a little farther," came Dad's reply. "We don't want to leave any tracks that can be traced back to us."

Down the road about a hundred yards was a patch of weeds with a turnout.

Dad said, "Pull off the road into those weeds, son."

So I quickly turned the car into the weeds on the shoulder of the road and stopped. We were off the road, so if a vehicle came along, there was plenty of room to get past.

Dad said, "We'll leave the car here and take our gas can and siphoning hose and walk back to the drums of fuel."

I saw him put some things in his pocket from our toolbox in the trunk. As I got out of the car, I heard dad tell me, "Son, watch where you step. Try to step on weeds and grass whenever you can, son. We don't want to leave any tracks."

We started walking, and in a short time, we came to a cow trail heading in the direction we wanted to go. We started following the trail, but on the side of it in the weeds that were on both sides.

I kept looking back to make sure I wasn't leaving any boot prints on the ground. I was careful putting my feet down, and I couldn't see my tracks at all. *Anyone would play hell tracking us in these weeds and brush*, I thought.

We came upon the truck tracks and stayed off to one side as we continued on until we saw the tractor and drums of fuel.

It was impossible to walk through the cleared ground without leaving tracks on the graded ground. Dad broke off brush and laid it out ahead of us so we had something to step onto without leaving tracks in the smooth dirt. Dad pulled the pliers and screwdriver from his hip pocket and used them to unscrew the bung from the fifty-five-gallon drum containing the starting fluid. Once the bung was removed, he pushed one end of the siphoning hose into the drum and kissed the end of the hose and quickly put the hose down into our gas can sitting on the ground. The starting fluid started running into the gas can, and I stood watching back the way we had come in case someone came in behind us.

Dad said, "Son, you listen for a car engine. We don't want anyone driving in here on to us."

"Yeah, I'm listening, Dad," I told him. My dad couldn't hear very good anymore because of his age.

"Son, you listen close. You have young ears." He repeated things too.

"Okay, Dad, I'm listening," I quickly replied.

After the can had filled, Dad carried it back out of the clearing and told me to reach back behind me and pick up the pieces of brush we had used to walk on without leaving tracks. Once we reached the weeds and bushes where we could walk without leaving tracks, I reached down and caught one side of the gas can so I could give Dad a hand carrying it back to the car.

It was late in the day as we put the gas can onto the back bumper and climbed into the car. Dad said, "Son, drive on down the road a bit before you turn around."

"How come?" I asked him.

"Well, son, we don't want to leave tracks on the road right where we walked back in there. They'd be too easy to spot."

I drove on down the road a quarter mile and then turned around and headed for home. I was tired and hungry; it had been a long day.

I don't know what was in the starting engine fluid, but it sure gave our old Chevy a kick in the ass. With the five gallons we had siphoned from the big drum added to our gas in the tank, this Chevy six-cylinder engine came to life and started pulling like a V8. The trip upriver to Blythe turned into a piece of cake.

On grades where I had to shift into low gear before, I could now drive them in second gear. And on grades where I had to downshift to second, I could now pull them in high gear. I loved the extra power the old Chevy had. I remember reading on the fuel drum that the starting engine fluid contained ether. So that probably explains the increase in power.

After our trip into Blythe, I was checking the oil level in the engine one day when I noticed our exhaust manifold was completely white from the heat of the hot-burning fuel. I would hate to think what would have happened if we had tried to burn the starting fluid straight out of the drum. It would have probably ruined our engine.

Shucks. Then we could have bought a Ford V8. I was thinking how much power a V8 would have on this souped-up mixture of ours. I'll bet I could have torn the roads up between here and Blythe. It would be like the movie with Robert Mitchum, I think it was called *Thunder Road*. He was running moonshine in it during Prohibition; he was driving a souped-up Ford in it just like the one I wanted. He could outrun the law with his souped-up Ford, and that's what I wanted to do. Robert Mitchum sang a song in the movie:

> *Thunder, thunder over thunder road,*
> *Thunder was his engine,*
> *And white lightning was his load*
> *There was moonshine,*
> *Moonshine to quench the devil's thirst*
> *The law they swore they'd get him*
> *But the devil got him first.*

The law would be eating my dust if I only had a Ford V8. They couldn't even come close to me because of all the dust I would leave them in. I'm going to tell dad the next time we buy a car, let's get a Ford. If we have to work on it, I'll pull both heads off. He can just set and watch me. He's getting kind of old anyway; I'll have to turn him out to pasture one of these days. But I best keep him around to cook though because I haven't done much cooking. But who knew, I might be getting married soon. All I have to do is find the right girl.

At breakfast one morning, Dad was telling Everett and me that we were going to have to do something about more feed for the cattle and horses. We now had two horses and seven heads of cattle. Everett and I were kept busy gathering mistletoe and feeding and watering the animals. Once we were done with that in the morning, Dad and I rode the river bottom looking for more cattle. The cattle were getting spooky because we had chased some of them before when we roped the ones we had caught. Dad rode through different areas of the ranch each day to let the cattle settle down before jumping them again.

The cattle that had been chased by our horses had begun taking flight as soon as they saw or smelled our horses. So Dad and I had been separated by a hundred yards or more. That way, if one of us startled some cattle, we were hoping they might run into one or other of us. That way, we stood a better chance of catching a cow.

But we didn't stay out of sight of each other for long. If either of us didn't see the other for more than about fifteen minutes, we would turn our horses in the direction of the other. This morning, I saw a couple of deer (both Doe's) going toward the river for water. They were just stopped under a mesquite tree with their ears spread wide, looking at the horse I was riding.

I heard a donkey braying up ahead of me. I had seen a couple of wild burros once when I had ridden out looking for deer. Dad said there were a lot of wild burros running loose in the desert. He said he had killed one once and butchered it and ate it. He claimed it tasted just like venison.

He said, "Son, if I cooked you a steak from a burro and one from a deer, you wouldn't be able to tell the difference."

I guess Dad had tried eating just about anything and everything. I wasn't so sure I wanted to do the taste test. I was willing to take Dad at his word.

I saw Dad over on my left, and he waved at me. Then I saw him point to the ground and wave his hand in the air. I took it to mean he was following tracks and was showing me the direction they were going. When you're riding with someone for weeks at a time, you get to know what his hand signs mean. Our ride this morning wasn't turning up very much.

I was wondering what Everett was doing back at the house besides feeding the cattle in the pen. Dad and I were the only ones with a horse, so Everett had to stay at home. I don't know if it was all that bad staying home because it was so cold when we rode out in the mornings. Everett was in a warm house, but he didn't have anyone to talk to until we returned in the afternoon.

Dad rode over to me and said, "Son, let's take the horses to the river and let them drink before we head back to the house. Nancy has been favoring her right front leg. I got down and checked it, and she has a loose horseshoe on that hoof. I need to get my tools and reset that shoe. So after they drink, we'll mosey on home. But keep watching for cattle just the same, son. We don't want to pass up any opportunity to catch some cattle just because we're heading to the barn.

WE FINALLY MADE THE BIG TIME

"Cattle Rustlers"

We got up one morning, and while Dad made breakfast, Everett and I went out and were feeding the animals. I heard the noise of a vehicle and looked over to the driveway coming into Blair's place off the main road and saw several trucks pulling up by our car. There were a couple of men in khaki uniforms that climbed out of one of the trucks. My dad must have heard them drive into the place because he came out of the house and went over to talk to the men.

Everett and I continued to feed the animals and also had to pump them water by hand and carry it to them. These animals drank a lot of water. When we were finished with them, Everett and I walked over to the vehicles. Dad was still talking with the men. One of them stood out because I knew him. It was Tom Wells, the man my dad had worked for.

I had ridden with Tom Wells at his lower ranch one Christmas vacation, about six miles upriver from where we were right now. He also owned the McCormick place north of Ehrenberg, Arizona. The same place I had picked up beer bottles, ridden on horseback with my dad, and sold to Tom for two cents apiece at Tom's Saloon a little north of the McCormick place.

I was wondering what they were doing down here at Blair's place?

Dad said, "Boys, these men say they are taking our cattle."

I looked at Dad to see what he thought of that. He shrugged as though he wasn't sure what to do.

He looked at me and said, "It seems Sam's brand is no good, son. Sam's brand expired in 1951. It wasn't good for ten years like he told us."

Tom Wells said, "Dick, they asked me to come down with them because they had been told Dick Huff was kind of an outlaw. The men were worried that if they tried to take the cattle, there might be a shootout. The men didn't know what to expect, Dick. I told them you were a good hand with cattle and had worked for me for many years," Tom said. They figured the face of a man Dad knew would defuse the situation. They came to take the cattle and had brought a big truck to haul them in.

I saw Walt Scott in one of the pickups with a horse trailer hitched up behind it. So Walt Scott was there to get his horses. Maybe he thought we would be arrested, leaving nobody to care for his horses. Or maybe he thought there would be a shootout and we would all be dead, leaving no one to care for the horses.

The men in khaki uniforms said they were from the Phoenix Livestock Sanitary Board. They explained that the fences on the Blair property were not all up and in good repair. In fact, the fences were lying on the ground in some places. The fences had to be up for Blair to lay claim to the cattle on his section of land. Since the fences were down, this was considered open range, and these cattle could belong to anyone with cattle in the river bottom. The Phoenix Livestock Sanitary Board claimed any cattle over a year old that hadn't been earmarked or branded for the State of Arizona.

They were talking, trying to figure out what to do since two of the cattle had an old hip O brand on them. And they were on Sam Blair's property. The other five cattle had new hip O brands and a new earmark. So there was no question about them being anyone's cattle. Another problem that had them confused, though, was why the two cows with the old brands had new earmarks that hadn't healed. They knew something wasn't according to Hoyle, but they couldn't figure it out. (The two they thought had old brands weren't branded at all because Dad had shaved the brands on the two cows with his pocketknife.)

The men went about loading the seven heads of cattle into the big truck. They said they were taking the cattle to Tom Well's place east of Ehrenberg and would be held there until a judge in Phoenix ruled on it. In the meantime, we could file a claim against the cattle with the sanitary board in Phoenix if we wanted to.

"What do you think, Dad?" I asked as the men and trucks were leaving. Dad told Everett and me, "Hell, son, we don't have a leg to stand on ourselves. If a claim is to be filed, it will have be Sam Blair or his son Ralph," Dad explained to us.

I told Dad, "I don't see how they could take them since we caught them.

"Son, Sam thought his brand was good. His brand was supposed to be registered in 1941, but Sam waited until 1946. If Sam had registered it in 1941 like he was supposed to do, the brand would have been good for ten years. But since Sam waited until 1946, the brand was only good for five years. Sam's brand should have been renewed in 1951, and it would have been good until 1961 or ten years."

"Sam thinking it was good for ten years in 1946 when he renewed it. Thought he didn't have to renew it until 1956?"

"So, son, Sam's brand expired in 1951, and we were branding his cattle with a brand that was no good, or had expired like the license plate on a car. Sam didn't stay on top of things, son, and we're just shit out of luck any way you look at it. It's 1954, son, so if Sam renews his brand now, it will only be good until 1961," Dad explained to us. "That's when all brands renew in Arizona."

Dad said, "We'd have to go see Ralph Blair because technically, the cattle are his. Son, it don't look good for us. I think we've lost our cattle. Those men from the Livestock Sanitary Board said we were lucky not to have cattle rustling charges brought against us. We will run up to Blythe tomorrow and see if Ralph and Sam want to fight for the cattle. They'll have to get a lawyer and prove the fences are all up and in good repair. And, son, we know the fences are down in a lot of places. I don't think Ralph will go to the expense of hiring a lawyer. I just don't think he'll do it, not for seven skinny cows. But we'll make the trip tomorrow and tell them what came about down here. Then it will all be up to them."

"I'd just like to know who in hell told the sons a bitches we were down here in the first place. You think it was Tom Wells, Dad?" I asked.

"No, son. Tom Wells didn't even know we were down here in the first place. I hate to think it, son, but the only one of those men who came down here that knew we were here was Walt Scott."

"The man we borrowed the horses from?" I asked.

"None other, and it wasn't any coincidence that he came with them, and pulling a trailer to pick up his horses. Yes, sir. Son I think ol' Walt Scott was the villain in this picture. I don't know why he threw a monkey wrench into the machinery, but I do believe it was him."

We still had a big pile of mistletoe and three bales of hay and no livestock to feed it to. Dad said, "Let's get our shit gathered up, and tomorrow we'll load our plunder into the car and drive up to Blythe and talk to Ralph Blair. Sound good to you, boys?" Dad asked.

"I guess we might as well, Dad. There' nothing left for us here," I said.

The next morning, we loaded our bedroll and chuck boxes in our old Chevy and lit out for Blythe. We pulled up to Ralph Blair's house, and Dad went in to talk to Ralph. Dad was in there about a half hour when he came out and said, "Boys, we're out of luck."

Ralph said, "It would cost too much to get the cattle back. He wasn't going to do any more. Just let them have them. I guess we better start looking for work."

We drove down intake Boulevard to where we had been staying before we ran away and quit school. The place was still there, so we moved back into the old lean-to shed Dad had built years before—the one Orville had stayed at when he ran away from the Carters' foster home.

Dad said, "Son, one of us has to get out and find a job, and I mean PRONTO."

The next day, we drove into Blythe to inquire about work. We were sitting in front of the Blythe Drug Store on the curb, talking with Jim Bell, a man Dad had known for forty-five years. Jim Bell was about eighty years old. He had been a Texas Ranger when he was younger. These days, he just walked into town from his daughter's place and sat on the curb talking to other old cronies like himself. They would bring sticks to whittle on and sit there whittling, the chips falling into the gutter. Sometimes Jim Bell would just sit on the curb and take his walking cane and reach out for a piece of gum wrapper and pull it to him with the cane. Then he would just sit there tearing it into little pieces and dropping them into the gutter. I was sitting there listening to Dad and Jim talking.

Jim said, "You know, Dick, the television store a block down on Hobsonway needed a man to install TV antennas. You might go apply," he said, looking over at me.

I said, "Really! The one just around the corner on the other side of the street?"

He said, "That's the one. I'll go talk to him." And he left for the TV store.

Somebody had to go to work, and it looked like it was going to be me. Our bankroll had gotten pretty thin because Sam Blair's money hadn't paid for everything. Dad had kicked in a little too. Our money from the brass .50 caliber shells was long gone.

I opened the door of the store and walked in. A man in a wheelchair came rolling out of the backroom and asked if he could help me. I said, "My name is Paul Huff, and I have been talking to Jim Bell, and he said you needed someone to install TV antennas."

He told me his name was John and then asked if I had ever installed television antennas. I told him that I had helped put an antenna up in Riverside a year ago. I lied. I had really just watched some men installing one on a roof one day.

"Well, no matter, you would be helping my installer, Russ. Are you reliable? I need a man I can count on. It won't be every day, but work is picking up as more people buy televisions."

I said I would like to do the work if he was interested in having me work for him.

"Okay, come in tomorrow, and I'll send you out with my installer."

Dad had gone to the post office, and when I came back, he handed me a letter. I looked and saw Shirley Gibbs's return address on it. She said she had gotten pregnant, and she and this Johnny Thompson were going to be married. She also told me that she was so sorry, because she said she had liked me. I wrote and told her I was happy for her. What else could I say? But I was very sad and disappointed, because I liked Shirley a lot. But she was so far away in Hollister, California. And I didn't even have a job, so I needed a girlfriend like I needed a hole in the head. I must have moped around for a week before I could forget about her my every waking minute. But getting hired for a job that I would be starting the next day helped a little. Working, I didn't have so much time to sit and think about Shirley and the fact that she was getting married.

I came in to work the next day, and Russ and I loaded a couple of boxes with T V antennas inside, onto a truck with toolboxes down each side. We drove three or four miles southwest of Blythe to a ranch house down a dusty road with big cottonwood trees surrounding it. Russ told me to get the ladder off the truck and place it against the house while he got one of the antennas and started to remove it from the box. He also unloaded the mast that the antenna was to be mounted onto.

Russ put on his tool belt with all the tools he would need to install the antenna. He had a big bucket with wire cable in it, and we started carrying everything up the ladder to the roof. Once on the roof, he showed me how to screw an eyebolt into the eave of the roof in all four corners.

Then at the ridge of the roof, Russ nailed a metal shoe into the center of the ridge where he attached the mast to the shoe with a bolt. The mast was ten feet long and came in four sections, one inside the other.

Russ had me wire the cables into a ring in four places that was attached to each section. The four cables ran from the mast to the four eyebolts in the corners of the roof. Now we could stand the mast up and secure it with the cables so it was standing plumb. I carried another ladder to the roof and placed it next to the mast. Russ carried the TV antennas up the ladder and began attaching it to the innermost section of the mast, which he had extended out and clamped with vise grips.

Once the antenna was clamped to the mast. Russ raised the mast high enough to clamp the second antenna to the mast and then ran a TV lead from the top antenna to the bottom antenna. Then he attached a coiled TV lead to the bottom antenna with the coil lying on the roof. Russ attached a standoff to the mast so the TV lead ran through it, keeping the lead away from the metal mast. Now we were ready to attach the cables to the mast just below the antenna for guy wires.

The guy wires were coils of wire cable that attached to each section of the mast as Russ extended it up higher into the sky. Each section got a standoff to hold the TV lead away from the mast. We couldn't anchor the guy wires until the four sections were extended all the way out, making it forty feet high. Then we took the four guy wires from each section and ran them through the eyebolts and wired them tight, making sure the mast stayed straight. I screwed four or five standoffs into the roof to support the TV lead as it ran over to the edge of the roof. The TV lead went to a window close to the television set in the house, and we attached it to the back of the television.

Once the television was turned on, we adjusted the antenna for the best reception, and the job was finished.

We put the ladders onto the truck and returned to the TV store in Blythe to see what was on the agenda for the next day. Sometimes there would be work the next day, and sometimes not. We never knew if there was going to be work until we returned to the store in the afternoon. I was being paid seventy-five cents an hour for this work, which lasted about four months. The work wasn't steady enough, so I looked for another job and found one with a surveyor.

It paid one dollar an hour, so I quit the television store and became a rod man for the surveyor.

FINALLY, A FORD V8

Mr. Steadman was an old man about seventy-five years old, but he was a good surveyor. He was happy to have me work for him because he had a lot of work as they were leveling the river bottom from Ripley to Palo Verde for a farmland.

I quit the TV store, telling John I needed steady work, part time wasn't any good, I told him, because I had my dad and my brother to support. At this time, I was the only one working.

Mr. Steadman had a 1938 Buick when I started to work for him. He told me he had just put a new 1950 Buick motor in it. The Buick ran really well for an old car. This was 1954, so the car was old but had a new motor. The Colorado River bottom was mostly fine silt from years of the river flooding.

We were stuck all the time in that old Buick, so Mr. Steadman bought an old four-wheel drive army truck someplace. It had a windshield but no top. It had all the traction in the world, and we were never stuck again. Day after day, we surveyed in the river bottom to make it into farmland. This was wintertime, and it was cold as all get out. Driving to work with no top, only a windshield and no heater. Mr. Steadman would just laugh and puff on the old pipe that he smoked constantly. Maybe it helped to keep him warm, but for me, I froze.

I gave Dad part of my money each week, but I was saving some too so I could finally buy me a Ford V8. I found a faded-out light-blue '47 Ford Tudor sedan out in East Blythe with no engine for seventy-five dollars. I bought it, and Dad towed it home for me while I steered it. At least the brakes were working. I went to wrecking yards looking for an engine. I bought a '49 Mercury flathead engine for another seventy-five dollars, and Dad helped me haul it home in the trunk of our Chevy. "Ah, life is good."

Dad was grumbling all the way home with the engine. "I don't know why you have your mind set on a damned old V8 for? You better start listening to the old man," he told me.

When we got back home, he got his tools out and helped me tear the engine down so it could be rebuilt. Of course, he was still griping about the damn V8 engine.

He took the valves out and started grinding them, and the next time I was in town, I took the heads to a machine shop to have them milled 20 thousandths. Hot Rod books I was reading said that would increase the compression and give it more horsepower. I wanted it to go fast.

While my heads were being resurfaced, Dad and I tore the rest of the motor down and cleaned everything. Then put in new rod bearings and rings. The pistons and wrist pins were in good shape, so we left them as they were. I bought a new three-quarter racing cam from the auto parts store, and Dad put it into the engine with new cam bearings. When I came in from work a few days later, Dad had the engine reassembled, and he had picked up the heads from the machine shop and had them installed as well. Now all that was left to do was paint the engine and we would be ready to put the engine into the car.

I bought a dual carburetor manifold with two Stromberg 97's on it and put that on the engine. This was just like Hambone's motor in the roadster at the Carters' foster home. I had everything I had dreamed of in this car, and I could hardly wait to get it into the car and start it. Dad told me to go by the auto parts store and buy a new clutch and pressure plate. "You don't want the clutch slipping with all that horsepower."

Dad borrowed a chain hoist from the Richfield station where he used to work, and we tied three logs together and hoisted the engine up and pushed the car forward so the engine would come down in the right place.

Dad lay down under the car so he could guide the engine clutch onto the transmission jackshaft. "Son, let the engine down slow now so I can get this to line up on the transmission."

"Okay, Dad," I said. Finally, the engine was in and bolted down on the motor mounts. The radiator had been in the trunk of the car when I bought it, so I installed it and put new hoses on the radiator and connected them to the water pumps.

Two water pumps on the Ford engine, not one like on the Chevy. Dad was quick to point that out to me too. Once everything was in place, we put the hood back on the car and siphoned five gallons of gas into the tank, and I filled the radiator with water. I was ready for Dad to tow it so I could start the engine. I was anxious to hear it run because this was my first Ford V8. I had the Ford Model A, but it was just a four- cylinder engine and didn't move fast enough to get out of the way of other cars.

Dad backed the Chevy up to my Ford, and I hooked the chain to both cars. We were ready to give it a tow. Dad said, "Son, put the transmission in second gear, but don't turn the ignition on. I'll tow you down the street a ways with the engine turning over so the oil pump will fill the oil passageways with oil before we try starting it."

"Okay, Dad," I told him. "When you want me to turn the ignition on, just wave your hand out the window and I'll flip the switch and start the engine."

My brother Everett jumped into the front passenger seat beside me. He wanted to be with me when the new engine fired up.

I told Everett, "Can you believe we're going to start it?"

Everett said he hoped it would run good.

"It should," I told him, "as everything in it is brand new."

Dad had towed me about half a mile down the road when I saw his arm wave to me to start the engine.

Finally, the big moment had arrived, and I reached down and gave the switch a flip. Right away, the engine caught and came to life. *AROOM*. It was running really good, but there was a lot of smoke coming from the exhaust as the oil we had put on the rings burned off. The engine was running a little fast, and I could tell the two carburetors needed adjusting because the engine coughed once in a while.

I waved to Dad to stop, and I pulled to the side of the road so I could get out and adjust the carburetors. There were two needle valves on each carburetor, and I could screw them in and out with my fingers. Dad unhooked the chain and put it in the trunk of his car.

"Don't run it too fast yet, son. It needs to break in. Everything in that engine is tight," he was saying as he walked back to his car. He told me to turn the car around and he would follow me back to the house. "We might have to adjust the timing a little bit, but the engine sounds like it's running good, son."

Going back to the house, I kept looking at the temperature and oil gauge. I didn't want the oil pressure to drop or the temperature to get hot. The oil pressure was holding steady at about thirty pounds on the oil gauge. At idle, the pressure dropped to about fifteen pounds. Everett asked me if it felt like it had a lot of power.

I said, "Yes, way more than that old six-cylinder Chevy, but Dad doesn't want me to race the engine until it gets broken in."

Everett asked if I was going to drive it to work in the morning, and I said, "I want to if it runs all right after Dad adjusts the timing."

After Dad was done tuning on the engine, it loped a little, but he said it was because of the three-quarter racing camshaft I had put into the engine to make it run faster. That evening, I drove it to town to fill the tank with gas, and Dad and Everett went with me. It took about twelve gallons, as it was a sixteen-gallon tank, and I had put five gallons into it before starting it earlier.

I wanted to push the gas pedal down in second gear to see how much power it had, but Dad said, "Son, don't do it because this engine is tight. You wait until it breaks in before you go to goosing the damn thing. If you burn out a bearing, all our work will have been for nothing, not to mention the money you've spent."

"Okay, Dad," I said. "I'll treat it easy for a while."

"Well, just see that you do! You blow the son of a bitch up, I won't help you again."

"Okay, Dad, I hear you."

Next morning, it started right up, so I drove it to Mr. Steadman's house, where I left it while we went on in the old army truck to work in Palo Verde. It seemed like the day was a week long as I thought about my car all the while I was working. I knew I wanted to have the car painted.

I was in town a week later, and I saw a 50 Ford go by that was painted pink. Wow, it sure looked sharp as it passed by and turned into a parking spot next to the Blythe drugstore. Everett and I walked over to the car to look it over while the boy driving it went into the drugstore.

We were still admiring the car when the boy came back out to the car.

"Nice car," I told him. "What color do you call this?"

He opened the door to get in, and as he did, he said, "Passionate Pink."

I told Everett, "Boy, I like that color." Then I said, "I might paint my car that color because it is such a striking color." This was the first car I had ever seen painted pink. I knew I had to save up some money before I could get my car painted, because buying the car and rebuilding the engine had left me broke. And I was giving Dad money for groceries too. We didn't pay any rent because we were just camping out on the five acres on south Intake Boulevard. Dad had permission to stay there and look after the place.

I was lucky to be working steady for Mr. Steadman, because it wasn't long (maybe a month) before I figured I'd stop at an auto body shop in east Blythe and see what a paint job was going to cost me. Everett and I pulled into H and E Auto Body, and I went inside to talk to the shop foreman. I told the man I wanted to get my car painted.

The foreman walked out and looked at my car to see what condition it was in. "What color you thinking of painting it," he asked.

"Pink. Passionate Pink."

The man started laughing.

I said, "I saw a car, and the boy said the color was Passionate Pink."

"Hell, son," the man said, "that boy was pulling your leg. There's no color named Passionate Pink. Or Titty Pink, either, for that matter." Then he said, "That's like sending a kid out to get a bucket of steam. All he will come back with is an empty bucket."

I felt embarrassed that I had been conned by the boy in the pink car.

The man said, "It's okay, son. You're just naïve. Let's walk over to the counter and look at a book with paint chips in them."

I followed him to the counter and leafed through the books, but I didn't see any pink colors. So after much thinking and looking, I picked out Polar White, which was a Cadillac color.

"Okay, son," the man said, "I can paint your car that color for eighty bucks, and I'll need the car for four or five days."

So Dad followed me down to the shop to drop the car off. It was a long five days before I got it back, but my car really looked good with a new coat of paint. I was glad I hadn't painted it pink, because the boy would have known I had copied him. If I lived in another town, it would have been different.

This was a Friday, and I had picked the car up after work, so I spent the afternoon just driving it around town. Showing it off more or less, since I didn't have many friends in Blythe. One boy I was acquainted with was John Elam. He had graduated from high school and was working for the Southern California Gas Company east of Blythe.

His folks had bought a U Finish Home up on the Mesa west of Blythe. The builder framed the house on the foundation and put all the piping in and the roof on, and stuccoed the house. Then the purchaser moved in and did their own drywall and baseboards and cabinets themselves. They were able to save money this way, as the house sold for six thousand dollars in 1954.

I was mostly listening to western music on the radio: Hank Williams, Lefty Frizzel, Hank Snow, Carl Smith, and Kitty Wells were just some of my favorite singers. One day John asked me if I liked rock 'n' roll music. I said I didn't know, and I asked who sang it. He said that Bill Halley and the Comets had a real rocking song out that he liked. I think the name of that first Bill Halley song was "Rock Around the Clock."

So we tuned the radio in to a station he liked, and that was my introduction to rock 'n' roll. After that, my radio was always on a rock 'n' roll station, as I would snap my fingers to the beat. "Sh-Boom" was another song that was getting a lot of airplay about this time.

In the fall of 1954, my sister Rita and a new husband, Brian Rhodes, located us in Blythe. They had been to visit our brother Orville in Phoenix, where he was living with Ersel and Viola Mothershed, the couple with three daughters, who had kind of adopted Orville after he ran away from Dad in the spring of 1953.

Rita told us our mother had remarried and was living with her husband, Lloyd Merritt, in Long Beach, California. Since I now had my mother's address, I decided to write to her, as we had not been in contact in two years.

I received an answer saying she wanted Everett and me to come to Long Beach and spend Christmas with her and her new husband. My sister Alice was living with them, and she also wrote and asked us to come. She told us Orville had said he would drive over from Phoenix.

Everett and I drove to Long Beach in my '47 Ford, three days before Christmas, leaving Dad in Blythe. Orville showed up driving a dark blue '41 Ford coupe. It was a nice-looking car, and we were busy talking about all the things that had happened since he ran away. He said he was happy living with Ersel and Viola, and he was working for the Waddell Ranch Company.

I remember going to see a movie that had just been released called *Young at Heart*, starring Frank Sinatra. It was a very good movie. Also, it was good to see Alice again, as it had been more than two years since we had seen her at the Carters' foster home.

I had to be back to work for Mr. Steadman, so we left for Blythe the day after Christmas, and Orville was also leaving and agreed to follow Everett and me as far as Blythe. The motor on my car started to knock down around Indio. I was very concerned about my engine, and I dropped my speed to seventy miles per hour, to around forty-five.

Orville dropped his speed to stay with me in case I needed help. Once in Blythe, Orville said goodbye to Dad and us and headed out to Phoenix. I told him I would come see him once my car was running good again. Then I told Dad about the rod bearing knocking in my car, and that I would have to pull the head and drop the pan on the engine.

So Dad told me to drive the Chevy so I could go to work, because he didn't want me to lose my job. The next day, when I came in from working for Mr. Steadman Dad already had the head off on the side of the engine that had the bearing knocking on. He said he had talked with Shorty Cornelius, and he would turn the crankshaft bearing 20 thousandths under size for us. So once the crankshaft had been turned, Dad reinstalled the rod bearing and piston and put the engine back together.

Cool. Now I had my car back, and Dad had his as well. Shortly after that, Everett and I were coming from town going south on Intake

Boulevard. I was opening it up and had the gas pedal hard to the floor again to see what my car would do.

I was at ninety miles an hour when all of a sudden, the hood blew open, and I couldn't see anything except the back of the hood. I was able to duck down and look through a gap at the bottom of the hood and was able to drive in a straight line.

Lucky for me, I was able to stop the car without any damage, I hoped. It had scared the hell out of me. I got out to shut the hood, and the corners of the hood had split where it had come against the body of the car. I had screwed up my paint job. Evidently, the hood latch was weak, and with the wind blasting though the grill at ninety miles an hour, it had made the hood come open.

I closed the hood, and we drove on home, but I don't remember mentioning it to Dad. He would have had a stroke because he had warned me not to drive fast because we had just put that new bearing into the engine. He said, "Son, you'll have to take it easy again until the new bearing wears in."

"Okay, Dad, I will," I told him. Then he said, "You'll have to break that engine in all over again. Now will you listen to me this time?"

"Yeah, I got it, Dad, I won't drive fast," I told him. Next morning, I backed my car up so I could turn around in the driveway, and as I stopped to go forward, the steering wheel just spun around in my hands. I got out and looked under the car and saw a tie-rod end had broken off, leaving me with no steering control whatsoever. If that tie-rod end had broken the day before when I was driving ninety miles per hour, I would have probably rolled my car. Another day that God was looking out for a dumb kid.

Thank you, God.

ORVILLE'S 1955 FORD

One day my brother Orville came into the place we were living in on south Intake Boulevard. He was driving a brand-new 1955 Ford Tudor Customline. It was a soft mint color, and it was so pretty compared to my '47 Ford. The hood on the '55 Ford was big and wide compared to the Ford I was driving. When Orville stepped out of the car, I saw he had his foot in a cast.

Hey, what happened to you?" I asked, not really waiting for him to answer me, as I had stuck my head through the window, checking out the interior on this new car. "Who's car?" I asked.

Orville grinned and said, "Mine."

"Are you kidding me?" I asked.

Then I said, "In your wildest dreams. Is it Ershel's?" I asked again.

"No, but he cosigned for me to buy it."

"Where are you going?" I asked.

"Oh, I was going to see Mom again in Long Beach," he said. "I stopped by to see if you want to go with me because it's hard to drive a stick shift with this broken foot."

"How did you break it?" I asked.

"Well, I was driving a hay mower, and the cycle bar jammed. And while I was working on it, it fell on my foot and broke it," Orville told me. I had been off work for a few days with Mr. Steadman, and I still had three more days before I could return to work.

Orville said, "You can drive." That was the magic word.

I could drive his new Ford; I was in hog heaven. What a nice car.

My '47 Ford had a narrow hood in front of me while Orville's car had a wide flat hood with narrow fenders that when I stepped on the gas, both of them came up in the front, and the windshield was a wraparound, the latest thing from Detroit this year. I never wanted to stop driving that car.

We drove over to Long Beach and saw our mother again and visited with Alice our younger sister. We stopped to visit another sister, Loreda, who was living in Colton. She had a house rented from a Mr. Moore on H Street and was working for the phone company as an operator.

I told Rita as we called her now, about how much I liked Orville's new car.

She quickly told me. "Well, you could have one too." She asked why I didn't leave Blythe and then said to come stay with her and look for a job in San Bernardino. I told her all I knew how to do was farm work. Rita told me there were higher-paying jobs in the city.

I guess I told her I would think about it because she told me it wouldn't cost anything because I could stay with her. Orville and I left Colton and drove back to Blythe, where Orville dropped me off at our dad's place on South Intake Boulevard. I stood watching his taillights disappear in the dust as he drove out of sight around the corner of our driveway, and he went on to his home in Phoenix.

I was wondering what my life would have in store for me as I dream of finding a job that will pay me enough to afford a snazzy new car like the one Orville just drove off in. I know I must have been green with envy as I wondered if I would ever be able to fulfill my dream. One never knows what tomorrow might bring.

LEAVING BLYTHE AND DAD BEHIND

When Orville left us in Blythe and returned to the Mothersheds' in Phoenix, I couldn't get it out of my head that he had a new Ford. I knew I had to get a better job so I could buy me a new car also. My sister Rita, had invited me to come stay with her in Colton, where I could look for a better-paying job. I began to think along those lines because Blythe was just a small town and not many jobs were available except for farm work which didn't pay much in wages. I had quit school halfway through the tenth grade, so manual labor was all I had to offer.

I told Dad I wanted to leave and try finding a job in Colton. Dad said, "Well, do what you want." But I could tell he wasn't happy because he became solemn. He started moving things around and doing things he generally didn't do, trying not to face the fact that I wanted to leave for greener pastures. It had been two and a half years since Dad had picked us up at Mrs. Carter's in 1952. So we had been together constantly all this time. We had done so much together, and he had taught me how to find a job and to be on my own and take care of myself.

One morning, after we had eaten our breakfast, I told Dad, "I'm going to go to Rita's and look for a job."

Dad said, "Well, go on, then, if that's what you want." He looked over at Everett standing by his car and said, "What are you going to do? You going to stay with me, or are you going with your brother?"

Everett said, "I want to go with Paul."

"Well, that settles it, then. Get your ass out of here. Just get your goddamn ass out of here, the both of you."

I knew Everett wanted to go with me because Dad wasn't treating him very good. And with me gone, I think Everett thought his life would be miserable, with no one to hold Dad accountable for the things he did. Everett and I set about packing our few clothes and loading them into my '47 Ford. I don't remember taking any of my guns with me, and I told Dad we would be back to visit him as soon as I found work and had some money.

I remember him standing there by the door of the old shack we had been living in for seven or eight months. Dad looked so sad as I backed my car up so I could turn around. I had never seen my dad look so devastated and forlorn because he was now alone for the first time in two and a half years. It would have been easy for me to turn around right there and stay because of how sad he was. I was later to know just how Dad felt that day so long ago as I went through two divorces and my daughters getting married and me facing life in a big empty house. It was like life wasn't worth living anymore because everything important had gone.

For Everett and me, though, we were looking forward to a life in a city with four movie theaters instead of one.

Once as my dad and I rode along on horseback in the river bottom, he looked over at me and said, "Son, you think you could put all this down on paper?"

"What do you mean, write a book?" I asked.

"Yeah that's it, tell about all the things we've done," he said.

"Dad, nobody would read it."

I never thought I'd do it. But at long last, "I did it Dad, just for you" and my girls!

Dick Owen Huff (1887-1959)

www.ingramcontent.com/pod-product-compliance
Lightning Source LLC
Chambersburg PA
CBHW031939080426
42735CB00007B/186